CASEBOOK

Succession:
THE LAW OF WILLS AND ESTATES

CONSULTANT EDITOR: LORD TEMPLEMAN
EDITOR: LINDA S SPEDDING
LLM, PhD, Solicitor

OLD BAILEY PRESS

OLD BAILEY PRESS
200 Greyhound Road, London W14 9RY

1st edition 1997
Reprinted 2000
Reprinted 2002

Previous editions published under The HLT Group Ltd.

ISBN 1 85836 263 6

British Library Cataloguing-in-Publication.
A CIP Catalogue record for this book is available from the British Library.

Printed and bound in Great Britain

Acknowledgement
The publishers and author would like to thank the Incorporated Council of Law Reporting for England and Wales for kind permission to reproduce extracts from the Weekly Law Reports, and Butterworths for their kind permission to reproduce extracts from the All England Law Reports.

Contents

Preface

Old Bailey Press casebooks are intended as companion volumes to the textbooks but they also comprise invaluable reference tools in themselves. Their aim is to supplement and enhance a student's understanding and interpretation of a particular area of law and provide essential background reading. Companion Revision WorkBooks and Statutes are also published.

While the *Succession* casebook is divided into chapters and sections which often reflect the headings in the textbook, the selection of topics is essentially governed by the significance of the case law. In the interests of clarity relevant legislation is fully cited and case summaries provided. In some instances extracts from judgments have been added to case summaries in order to clarify the issues involved.

The most topical recent case which illustrates the modern trends of the courts is the appeal decision in *White* v *Jones* concerning professional negligence. In *White* v *Jones* the House of Lords, by a majority of three to two, confirmed the Court of Appeal's previous decision and applied the decision in *Hedley Byrne & Co* v *Heller & Partners*, dismissing the solicitors' appeal so that they remained liable in negligence to potential third party beneficiaries.

The developments in this edition represent the law as at 31 January 1996.

Table of Cases

1 Introduction

Attorney-General v *Jones and Bartlett* (1817) 3 Price 368 Court of Chancery (Wood B, Graham B, Thomson CB)

Indenture – whether a valid will – legacy duly payable

Facts

In 1813 William Franklin executed an indenture with Jones and Bartlett for nominal consideration by which he conveyed to them specified leaseholds, all his stocks and shares and all his personal estate. The indenture directed Jones and Bartlett to hold these for William Franklin for life and on his death for his daughter, Helena, when she attained twenty-one or married. The indenture contained a proviso which allowed William Franklin to alter or change the respective trusts. One month after executing the indenture he executed a will confirming the indenture and bequeathing a number of legacies. On William Franklin's death the Crown claimed that the indenture was in fact a will and that legacy duty was payable in respect of the gifts which passed under it.

Held

(Wood B dissenting) The document amounted to a will and legacy duty was payable on it.

Thomson CB:

> 'Now here is first an instrument which purports, by the form of it to be a deed; it bears the name of an indenture, and is made by a person who may be called testator or grantor. For the present, we will call him grantor, while we talk of this instrument. He conveys, for a nominal consideration, to two trustees, who are parties to the deed, in general terms, first, a leasehold estate, of which he is possessed; and, after that, he assigns to them his government stock, which he specifies, and all the dividends which shall be due from it at the time of his death, and in short all his property, whatsoever, emunerating specifically certain things, as plate, linen, furniture, glass and pictures, and all the movable property, which in its nature was fluctuating during his lifetime, and must be so.
>
> He assigns to these two persons all that sort of property which would belong to him at the time of his death, to hold to them upon certain trusts; and those trusts are, that they should be possessed of it 'for the use, benefit and advantage of William Franklin, for and during the term of his natural life': leaving him in the possession of the corpus of the gift, or legacy, during his life, with full power of disposing of it, at his will, and pleasure; for it is not till after his death, that any other of the trusts are to arise. It is not in trust for during his life, to receive the dividends merely, but the whole property is his, as long as he lives, implying a power in him to dispose of it, and spend it as he shall think proper; then on his death only, are the other trusts to arise, and then the trustees are to act only on such property as is found 'all the property he is possessed of at the time of his death': and then it is to be applied to this lady, in the way mentioned. And he has reserved a power by any deed or writing, to revoke or alter all or any of the trusts limited to the indenture of all that has been assigned. He then makes a will, and I think it is not immaterial, as has been observed, that that will expressly refers to the deed. By that he confirms the deed; he incorporates therefore the deed into the will, or I should rather say, he makes it a part of the testamentary act which he is then executing, and therefore they ought to be taken and construed together, as being of the same effect. The

deed has no operation during his life; he remains master of the property till after his death, and then the deed can only take effect in the nature of a will, to be proved by the executors.

It would be very strange to suppose that that should be thought a gift, which leaves it in the power of the donor, whether shall be 50001 or 51 at his death; he may dispose of it or squander it, or do what he pleases. It seems to me, then, that there is no way of dealing with this instrument, but by giving it the effect of a testamentary paper and I should have no difficulty in supposing the Ecclesiastical Court would grant probate of it, and I think they would in granting probate of it, designate the trustees as exeucutors. In fact, the testator has made these very persons his executors, and they have obtained probate of the will; which will does refer in terms, and does confirm, excepting in the gift of a few legacies, the general provisions of the former instrument, which I call testamentary, in favour of this lady. The consequences of this is, as two of my learned brothers concur with me in thinking, that this is to be taken to be a testamentary act, and that the property in question is therefore subject to the legacy duty, and that there ought to be judgment for the Crown.'

Baird* v *Baird [1990] 2 WLR 1412; [1990] 2 All ER 300

Validity of nomination – execution of a will distinguished

Facts

A Trinidad oil company provided a contributory pension scheme whereby an employee was entitled to nominate a beneficiary to receive the death benefit payable on the employee's death before retirement. Nominations and revocations or alterations thereto were subject to the consent of the management committee of the scheme. In the absence of a nomination, the benefit was payable to the employee's widow or widower or to his or her estate. In this instance, an employee nominated his brother as beneficiary. Five years later he married, without revoking or varying the nomination. Two years afterwards he died while still in the company's employment. Both the brother and the widow claimed the death benefit. The High Court and Court of Appeal of Trinidad held that the brother was entitled. The widow appealed to the Privy Council contending that the nomination was a testamentary disposition which was only valid if executed with the formalities required for a will.

Held

The Judicial Committee (Lords Bridge of Harwich, Roskill, Brandon of Oakbrook and Oliver of Aylmerton and Sir Roger Ormrod) dismissed that appeal. It was held that the nomination was in essence no different from any other power of appointment, since it disposed of no property of the employee, who retained no proprietary interest in his contributions under the pension scheme. The nomination did not have to be executed as if it were a will. (*Re Danish Bacon Co Ltd Staff Pension Fund, Christensen* v *Arnett* [1971] 1 WLR 248 applied.)

Lord Oliver, delivering the Privy Council's judgment, distinguished such cases as *In the Goods of Baxter* [1903] P 12, *Re MacInnes* (1935) 1 DLR 401, *Re Shirley* (1965) 49 DLR (2d) 474 and *Norris* v *Norris* (1977) 29 WIR 22, but found that *Re Danish Bacon Co Ltd* was more applicable when upholding the validity of the nomination.

In the latter case the rules of the fund provided that a member might, and must if required by the trustees, appoint a beneficiary to receive the amount of his contributions, which would otherwise become due to his personal representatives on his death in service. The rules enabled the member to cancel the nomination, but only for the purpose of appointing a new nominee. One of the matters raised in this case was whether a nomination which was signed in the presence of one witness was effective, or whether it was a testamentary disposition which required to be attested in the same way as a will. Megarry J held that the nomination was effective on the ground that:

> '... although a nomination had certain testamentary characteristics, and not least that of being ambulatory, it took effect as a contractual arrangement and not as a disposition by the deceased. The contributions and interest did not come to the deceased and then pass on from him by force of his will or the nomination: they went directly from the fund to the nominee, and formed no part of the estate of the deceased ... Despite certain testamentary characteristics, the nomination takes effect under the trust deed and rules, and the nominee in no way claims through the deceased.'

Similarly, in this case it was decided that the member's nomination of the beneficiary to receive his 'death-in-employment benefit' was not a testamentary disposition by the member and the Wills and Probate Ordinance had no application. Lord Oliver emphasised that it depended upon the provisions of the pension scheme in each case as to whether the Wills legislation applied. He concluded that:

> 'In what is now the normal case of non-assignable interests such as that in the present case and, a fortiori, where the power of nomination and revocation requires the prior approval of the trustees or of a management committee [there was] no reason to doubt the correctness of Megarry J's decision in the *Danish Bacon Co* case.'

Baker* v *Baker and Another (1993) The Times 19 February Court of Appeal (Dillon, Beldam and Roche LJJ)

Resulting trust distinguished from equitable estoppel – nature of relief

Facts

The plaintiff was a tenant of a council house in Finchley in 1987. He lived on his own and enjoyed security of tenure. Evidently he had built up some savings and he had indicated to his son and daughter-in-law, the defendants, that the son was likely to receive about £20,000 under his will. The son and daughter-in-law purchased a house with the assistance of a mortgage and the plaintiff contributed £33,950 representing the balance of the purchase price. The intention was that the plaintiff would live there rent free for the rest of his life. However, as a result of a family dispute, this arrangement broke up and the plaintiff commenced proceedings claiming a beneficial interest in the property by way of resulting trust.

Although the action claiming a beneficial interest did not succeed, the plaintiff did succeed in an alternative way of putting the case in reliance on equitable estoppel. The deputy Judge gave judgment to the plaintiff in the sum of £33,950 with interest as of 13 June 1988.

The defendants appealed.

Held

Dillon LJ stated that the course taken by the court in some cases of equitable estoppel in order to satisfy the equity was to order the defendant to repay the plaintiff's expenditure. The judge had concluded that the plaintiff had lost the gift that he had made to the defendants in reliance on the understanding that he would be able to live in the property for the rest of his life. However, in his Lordship's judgment the gift in the present case was directed to achieve two goals, that is the provision of a family home for the defendants and their children and the rent free occupation by the plaintiff for life.

In his Lordship's view the correct application was that what the plaintiff had lost was not the whole £33,950 but merely the right to rent free occupation in the house for the rest of his life.

Accordingly, the Appeal was allowed and the case was remitted for hearing into the assessment of the compensation payable.

Beldam and Roche LJJ delivered concurring judgments.

Berger, Re [1989] 2 WLR 147 Court of Appeal (Mustill, Mann LJJ and Sir Denys Buckley)

Will – zavah in Hebrew language

Facts

The deceased was a devout orthodox Jew and it was assumed that he had died domiciled in England. Over the years he had executed parallel series of wills and zavah, handwritten documents in Hebrew. The judge found that the deceased had intended that his wishes expressed in the zavah should be obeyed and, if necessary, enforced by the rabbinical tribunal. The last zavah was executed on 6 August 1977, in accordance with the Wills Act 1837; the last will three days later, but its execution did not satisfy the requirements of the 1837 Act. Should the last zavah (with or without the incorporation of the invalid will) or the last valid will (executed on 15 July 1975) be admitted to probate? The judge decided in favour of the zavah, incorporating the invalid will: the beneficiaries under the 1975 will appealed.

Held

The appeal would be dismissed.

Sir Denys Buckley:

> '*Jarman on Wills* ... stated that "in a general and comprehensive sense, a will consists of the aggregate of all the papers through which it is dispersed". Sir JP Wilde said in Lemage v Goodban (1865) LR 1 P & D 57 at 62 that a will is the aggregate of a man's testamentary intentions so far as they are manifested in writing duly executed according to the Wills Act 1837. So, to discover what the deceased's testamentary intentions were when he died, we must identify whatever duly executed testamentary documents were made by him and were in operation at his death ...
>
> *Jarman* describes a document qualified to be recognised as a will or testamentary instrument in this way:
>
> > "A will is an instrument by which a person makes a disposition of his property to take effect after his decease, and which is in its own nature ambulatory and revocable during his life."
>
> It must be manifest that the instrument is not to operate until the testator dies and is to be revocable meanwhile.
>
> It is, to my mind, perfectly clear that the deceased intended to make certain dispositions of his property by the 1977 zavah ...
>
> ... in my judgment, the 1977 zavah has, in at least some respects, the characteristics of a testamentary instrument. No special ground for excluding the document from probate, such as lack of testamentary capacity, fraud or undue influence is alleged. Consequently, in my judgment, the 1977 zavah should be admitted to probate as part of the deceased's will, unless it can be established either that it was not executed in accordance with the 1837 Act or that it was written without any intention that it should have any operation and effect as a testamentary disposition, that is without animus testandi.
>
> The 1977 zavah consists of two sheets, each of which the deceased signed, and each signature was attested by two witnesses. The trial judge found as a fact that the 1977 zavah was duly executed in accordance with the Act. There is no appeal against that finding. He also found as a fact that the deceased had no positive intention that the zavah should not take effect in English law. The appellant contends that that finding was against the weight of the evidence and inconsistent with another finding of the judge that the deceased saw his English and Hebrew wills as being in separate and parallel streams, one to be enforced in the English courts and one in the rabbinical courts. The appellant contends that the judge ought to have held that the deceased did not intend that the 1977 zavah should have any effect *in English law*. I emphasise the last three words ...
>
> English law does not require a document which is intended to have testamentary effect to assume any particular form or to be couched in language technically appropriate to its testamentary character. It is,

says *Jarman*, sufficient that the instrument, however irregular in form or artificial in expression, discloses the intention of the maker respecting the posthumous destination of his property. It may be made in any language. If it is made in a foreign language, the court must be furnished with an authenticated translation made by a qualified translator. It is that translation, not the text in the foreign language, which is admitted to probate. It is from the document so admitted to probate together with any other relevant testamentary instruments that an English court will ascertain the testator's testamentary intentions and determine their effect and validity.

The 1977 zavah as translated contains the following passage:

> "Each of my sons … should know that what I have written in this will is binding on you and additional to what was written in the English language will, and should any clarification be needed, the present will (in the Holy Tongue) [Hebrew] is the definitive one."

This seems to me to be irreconcilable with any suggestion that that zavah was not intended to have any testamentary force. On the contrary, the deceased's signature on it was attested by two witnesses which, according to the evidence, would render its provisions judicially enforceable in a rabbinical court.

I would therefore reject any argument to the effect that the 1977 zavah was intended only to have exhortatory or advisory effect but no legal effect under any system of law.

The function in English law of a probate court is to ascertain and determine what testamentary paper or papers is or are to be regarded as constituting the last will of the testator and who is entitled to be constituted his legal personal representative. However many testamentary documents a testator may leave:

> "It is the aggregate or the net result that constitutes his will, or, in other words, the expression of his testamentary wishes … In this sense it is inaccurate to speak of a man leaving two wills; he does leave, and can leave, but one will."

(See *Douglas-Menzies* v *Umphelby* [1908] AC 224 at 233.) …

The 1977 zavah and the 1977 English will (had it been duly executed) should, in my opinion, have been regarded as mutually incorporated in one testamentary exercise, that is to say as together constituting the deceased's last will. If that had been the case, the presence in the English will of a revocation clause would not, in my judgment, have occasioned, as has been suggested, a revocation of the 1977 zavah.

For reasons which I hope I have sufficiently explained, I am of the opinion that the 1977 zavah, which unquestionably contains some provisions which seem to relate to matters over which the deceased had no testamentary powers of control, nevertheless equally unquestionably contains provisions which have all the indicia of being testamentary dispositions of property over which he had power to dispose by will. Consequently, in my judgment, the judge was right in holding that the 1977 zavah should be admitted to probate. The operation and effect of such provisions of the 1977 zavah as are capable of having testamentary effect and what that effect should be are matters for the court charged with the duty of controlling the administration of the deceased's estate.

The judge's order pronounced in favour of the force and validity of the 1977 zavah incorporating therein the defectively executed English will dated 9 August 1977. In my opinion he was justified on the facts in treating the English will as incorporated in the zavah by virtue of the reference to the English will contained in the zavah. It is clear on the facts and from the language used in the zavah that the English will was a document which was in existence when the zavah was signed and so was capable of incorporation in the zavah.'

Burton* v *Collingwood (1832) 4 Hagg 176

Conditional will distinguished from Reasons for making a will

Facts

The will began 'All men are mortal, and no one knows how soon his life may be required of him. Lest I should die before the next sun, I make this my last will and testament.'

Held

The will was not conditional; the testator had merely given reasons for making a will.

Cleaver (deceased), Re [1981] 1 WLR 939 Chancery Division (Nourse J)

Mutual wills – need to show mutual agreement and intention

Facts

Testator and testatrix were married to each other and were aged 78 and 74 respectively in 1967. Testator had three children by previous marriage; testatrix had none, but she had two nieces. In December 1967 and on 7 February 1974 they made wills in almost identical terms. Testator gave each of his three children a legacy of £500 and his residuary estate to his wife absolutely, subject to her surviving him for one month. If she did not so survive then the residue was divided into three equal parts, one third each to his two younger children; the remaining third to go to his eldest daughter for life, remainder to his two younger children absolutely in equal shares with gift over if those two younger children should predecease the life tenant. The wife's will was in identical terms save that in lieu of the legacies of £500 to her husband's children, there were two legacies of £500 to each of her two nieces. Testator died in 1975. His widow duly received the residue. On 23 June 1977 she made her last will leaving her residuary estate to the testator's eldest daughter and her husband (or the survivor of them), in equal shares absolutely. No provision was made for either the younger children, or her two nieces. She died on 20 May 1978.

The two younger children sued for a declaration that her estate was held on trust to give effect to the terms of her 1974 will.

Held

For two wills to be enforceable as mutual wills it must be established by satisfactory evidence that the makers of the wills had agreed amongst themselves and intended that they should be bound by the agreement. The mere fact that wills are made simultaneously is relevant but not sufficient proof of such an agreement. In the present case there was extrinsic evidence to show that the 1974 wills were executed in pursuance of such an agreement which imposed on them mutual legal obligations as to the disposal of their property, and that since the testatrix had the benefit of the agreement a constructive trust was created binding the executors of her estate to administer it in accordance with the terms of the 1974 will and not that of 1977.

Nourse J:

> 'The foundation of the plaintiffs' claim is the well-known case of *Dufour* v *Pereira* (1769) 1 Dick 419 which was decided by Lord Camden LC in 1769. That case is fully discussed in *Hargrave's Judicial Arguments* (1799) vol 2, pp304 et seq. That was a case where Lord Camden LC relying as it appears only on the terms of a joint will executed by a husband and wife concluded that there had been a prior agreement. There have not been so very many cases on the subject since, but in one of them, *Gray* v *Perpetual Trustee Co Ltd* [1928] AC 391 the Privy Council decided in clear terms that the mere simultaneity of the wills and the similarity of their terms are not enough taken by themselves to establish the necessary agreement. I will read what appears to me to be the material passages in the judgment of the Board, which was delivered by Viscount Haldane. The first passage reads, at p399:
>
> > "In *Dufour* v *Pereira* the conclusion reached was that if there was in point of fact an agreement come to, that the wills should not be revoked after the death of one of the parties without mutual consent, they are binding. That they were mutual wills to the same effect was at least treated as a relevant circumstance, to be taken into account in determining whether there was such an agreement. But the mere simultaneity of the wills and the similarity of their terms do not appear, taken by themselves, to have been looked on as

> more than some evidence of an agreement not to revoke. The agreement, which does not restrain the legal right to revoke, was the foundation of the right in equity which might emerge, although it was a fact which had in itself to be established by evidence, and in such cases the whole of the evidence must be looked at."

Their Lordships then proceeded to mention two authorities, the second of which was the decision of Astbury J in *Re Oldham* [1925] Ch 75. The judgment of the Privy Council continues, at p400:

> "Their Lordships agree with the view taken by Astbury J. The case before them is one in which the evidence of an agreement, apart from that of making the wills in question, is so lacking that they are unable to come to the conclusion that an agreement to contstitute equitable interests has been shown to have been made. As they have already said, the mere fact of making wills mutually is not, at least by the law of England, evidence of such an agreement having been come to. And without such a definite agreement there can no more be a trust in equity than a right to damages at law."

As to the penultimate sentence of that passage it must, in the light of the earlier passage, to be read as meaning that the mere fact of making mutual wills is not by itself sufficient evidence of such an agreement having been come to.

It is therefore clear that there must be a definite agreement between the makers of the two wills; that this must be established by evidence, that the fact that there are mutual wills to the same effect is a relevant circumstance to be taken into account, although not enough of itself; and that the whole of the evidence must be looked at.

I do not find it necessary to refer to any other English case, but I have derived great assistance from the decision of the High Court of Australia in *Birmingham* v *Renfrew* (1937) 57 CLR 666. That was a case where the available extrinsic evidence was held to be sufficient to establish the necessary agreement between two spouses. It is chiefly of interest because both Sir John Latham CJ and more especially Dixon J examined with some care the whole nature of the legal theory on which these and other similar cases proceed. I would like to read three passages from the judgment of Dixon J which state, with all the clarity and learning for which the judgments of that most eminent judge are renowned, what I believe to be a correct analysis of the principles on which a case of enforceable mutual wills depends. The first passage reads, at pp682-683:

> "I think the legal result was a contract between husband and wife. The contract bound him, I think, during her lifetime not to revoke his will without notice to her. If she died without altering her will, then he was bound after her death not to revoke his will at all. She was on her part afforded the consideration for his promise by making her will. His obligation not to revoke his will during her life without notice to her is to be implied. For I think the express promise should be understood as meaning that if she died leaving her will unrevoked then he would not revoke his. But the agreement really assumes that neither party will alter his or her will without the knowledge of the other. It has long been established that a contract between persons to make corresponding wills gives rise to equitable obligations when one acts on the faith of such an agreement and dies leaving his will unrevoked so that the other takes property under its dispositions. It operates to impose upon the survivor an obligation regarded as specifically enforceable. It is true that he cannot be compelled to make and leave unrevoked a testamentary document and if he dies leaving a last will containing provisions inconsistent with his agreement it is neverthe-less valid as a testamentary act. But the doctrines of equity attach the obligation to the property. The effect is, I think, that the survivor becomes a constructive trustee and the terms of the trust are those of the will he undertook would be his last will."

Next, at p689:

> "There is a third element which appears to me to be inherent in the nature of such a contract or agreement, although I do not think it has been expressly considered. The purpose of an arrangement for corresponding wills must often be, as in this case, to enable the survivor during his life to deal as absolute owner with the property passing under the will of the party first dying. That is to say, the object of the transaction is to put the survivor in a position to enjoy for his own benefit the full ownership so that, for instance, he may convert it and expand the proceeds if he chooses. But when he dies he is to bequeath what is left in the manner agreed upon. It is only by the special doctrines of equity that such a floating obligation,

> suspended, so to speak, during the lifetime of the survivor can descend upon the assets at his death and crystallise into a trust. No doubt gifts and settlements, inter vivos, if calculated to defeat the intention of the compact, could not be made by the survivor and his right of disposition, inter vivos, is therefore, not unqualified.
>
> But, substantially, the purpose of the arrangement will often be to allow full enjoyment for the survivor's own benefit and advantage upon condition that at his death the residue shall pass as arranged."

Finally, at p690:

> "In the *Re Oldham* Astbury J pointed out, in dealing with the question whether an agreement should be inferred, that in *Dufour* v *Pereira* the compact was that the survivor should take a life estate only in the combined property. It was, therefore, easy to fix the corpus with a trust as from the death of the survivor. But I do not see any difficulty in modern equity in attaching to the assets a constructive trust which allowed the survivor to enjoy the property subject to a fiduciary duty which, so to speak, crystallised on his death and disabled him only from voluntary dispositions inter vivos."

I interject to say that Dixon J was there clearly referring only to voluntary dispositions inter vivos, which are calculated to defeat the intention of the compact. No objection could normally be taken to ordinary gifts of small value. He went on:

> "On the contrary, as I have said, it seems rather to provide a reason for the intervention of equity. The objection that the intended beneficiaries could not enforce a contract is met by the fact that a constructive trust arises from the contract and the fact that testamenary dispositions made upon the faith of it have taken effect. It is the constructive trust and not the contract that they are entitled to enforce."

It is also clear from *Birmingham* v *Renfrew* that these cases of mutual wills are only one example of a wider category of cases, for example secret trusts, in which a court of equity will intervene to impose a constructive trust. A helpful and interesting summary of that wider category of cases will be found in the argument of Mr Nugee in *Ottaway* v *Norman* [1972] Ch 698. The principle of all these cases is that a court of equity will not permit a person to whom property is transferred by way of gift, but on the faith of an agreement or clear understanding that it is to be dealt with in a particular way for the benefit of a third person, to deal with that property inconsistently with that agreement or understanding. If he attempts to do so after having received the benefit of the gift equity will intervene by imposing a constructive trust on the property which is the subject matter of the agreement or understanding. I take that statement of principle, and much else which is of assistance in this case, from the judgment of Slade J *In Re Pearson Fund Trusts* (1977) (unreported). The statement of principle is at p52 of the official transcript. The judgment of Brightman J in *Ottaway* v *Norman* is to much the same effect.

I would emphasise that the agreement or understanding would be such as to impose on the donee a legally binding obligation to deal with the property in the particular way and that the other two certainties, namely, those as to the subject matter of the trust and the persons intended to benefit under it, are as essential to this species of trust as they are to any other. In spite of an argument by Mr Keenan, who appears for Mr and Mrs Oble, to the contrary, I find it hard to see how there could be any difficulties about the second or third certainties in a case of mutual will unless it was in the terms of the wills themselves. There, as in this case, the principal difficulty is always whether there was a legally binding obligation or merely what Lord Loughborough LC in *Lord Walpole* v *Lord Oxford* (1797) 3 Ves Jun 402 described as an honourable engagement.

Before turning in detail to the evidence which relates to the question whether there was a legally binding obligation on the testatrix in the present case or not, I must return once more to *Birmingham* v *Renfrew*. It is clear from that case, if from nowhere else, that an enforceable agreement to dispose of property in pursuance of mutual wills can be established only by clear and satisfactory evidence. That seems to me to be no more than a particular appliction of the general rules that all claims to the property of deceased persons must be scrutinised with very great care. However, that does not mean that there has to be a departure from the ordinary standard of proof required in civil proceedings. I have to be satisfied on the balance of probabilities that the alleged agreement was made, but before I can be satisfied of that I must find clear and satisfactory evidence to that effect.'

Dale (Monica) (deceased), In re Estate of, Proctor v *Dale* (1993) The Times 11 February Chancery Division (Morritt J)

Mutual wills – trust distinguished from specific performance

Facts

A mother and father made identical wills, in accordance with a purported agreement, in favour of their plaintiff daughter and defendant son, bequeathing to them all their real and personal property in equal shares or the survivor of them. The father died without having altered or revoked his will and probate was granted to the plaintiff and defendant as executors.

After two years approximately the mother made a new will revoking all her former wills and appointed the defendant as executor, and bequeathed to the plaintiff £300 and to the defendant the remainder of her property.

The plaintiff commenced proceedings against the defendant, claiming that the defendant held the real and personal estate of the mother as trustee for them both in equal shares. A preliminary question arose as to whether it was necessary for the second testator to die to have obtained a personal and financial benefit under the will of the first to die in order for the doctrine of mutual wills to apply.

Held

The judge stated that the principles to be acted upon in imposing a trust to give effect to an agreement to make and not to revoke mutual wills would be found in the cases dealing with that topic and not those dealing with the availability of the remedy of specific performance. Accordingly, it was not necessary for the second testator to die to have obtained such a benefit under the will of the first to die for the doctrine of mutual wills to apply. The judge considered the case of *Dufour* v *Pereira* (1769) 1 Dick 419. In that case it had been held that there had to be a legally binding contract to make and not to make mutual wills and that the first testator had died having performed his part of the agreement. The aim of the principle was to prevent him from being defrauded. A fraud would include cases where the second testator benefited, but there was no reason to confine the principle to just these cases. This was consistent with all authorities supported by some of them and was in furtherance of equity's original jurisdiction to intervene in cases of fraud.

It was ordered accordingly.

Duddell, Re [1932] 1 Ch 585 Chancery Division (Farwell J)

Joint will and joint power of appointment

Facts

By his will a testator left his residuary estate to his wife for life and after her death to his son and daughter for their sole and separate use for their natural lives and after their deaths to such ends and purposes as they should by will appoint and in default of appointment to his right heirs for ever. The brother and sister executed a joint will. When the brother died in 1917 he had by a separate will confirmed the joint will and the joint will, the separate will and a codicil thereto were admitted to probate. The mother died in 1931 and the question arose whether the appointment by the joint will was a good exercise of the power of appointment by the brother and sister.

Held

A joint will could be made by two persons and if the sister did not revoke the joint will then on her death it would be admitted to probate as part of her testamentary wishes as an effective exercise of the power of appointment in accordance with her father's will.

Farwell J:

> 'That a power may be given to two or more persons to appoint by deed jointly is of course, unquestionable, and equally a power to appoint by will given to one person creates no difficulty for in such a case, if the power is exercised by will, then on the death of the appointer the will operates as an execution of the power and the property passes accordingly. But in the case of a joint will, on the death of the first of the two joint appointers, the property which is subject to the power does not pass at all, it may be (though I do not decide this) that, if the survivor of the two were to revoke or seek to revoke the joint appointment, the result would be that there would be no effective appointment at all. Moreover, in any case the joint will on the death of the first of the two appointers cannot operate as an exercise of the power so as to pass any property or interest in the property at all. That I think is clear. There would be no divesting of the estate in default of appointment and revesting, as for example would be the case where an appointment is made to take effect at the termination of a life interest, which is still subsisting. In a case of that kind the appointment, although it does not entitle the appointee to immediate possession of the property by reason of the existing life interest, does operate there and then to divest the vested interest in default of appointment, and give the person in whose favour the appointment is made a vested interest. The joint will on the death of the first of the two appointers cannot have any such operation, but nonetheless the document is, in my judgment, rightly admitted to probate as being part of the dispositions which the testator, the first appointer has made of his own property and of the property over which he has a power of appointment. On the death of the second of the appointers, assuming that no attempt has been made by the survivor to revoke the joint will, the joint will will again be admitted to probate, together with any other will that the second appointer has made, as being together the dispositions of that person's property and of the power of appointment given to that person.'

Eccles Provident Industrial Co-operative Society Ltd* v *Griffiths [1912] AC 483
House of Lords (Lord Loreburn LC, Lords Atkinson, Shaw and Mersey)

Nomination – 'poor man's will'

Facts

The Eccles etc Society Ltd was registered under the Industrial and Provident Societies Act 1893 and under s25 of that Act a member of the society was empowered to make a nomination of his property in the society 'provided the amount credited to him in the books of the society does not then exceed £100 sterling'. A nomination had been made in favour of Griffiths in April 1909 by one James Parry who at that date had £98 13s 0d (now £98.65p) in his account. At the date of his death in February 1910 the amount standing to Parry's credit in the account was £103 6s 7d (about £103.33p today). The Society refused to pay the money to Griffiths contending that the nomination was invalid as there was now more than £100 standing to Parry's credit in the Society.

Held

The nomination was good; the word 'then' in s25 referred to the nominator not having more than £100 in the Society at the date of the nomination rather than the date of decease.

Lord Mersey:

> 'The object of s25 is, in my view, to give the poorer members of a society, that is to say those who have not more than £100 to their credit, the power to make provision for the disposal, at their death, of this small sum without the expense being incurred of the making of a will or administering this part of their estate. The nomination can only be made by the members who are within this poorer class, and it is the duty of the secretary of the Society, before he enters the name of the nominee in the Society's books, to see that there is not more than £100 to the member's credit. If the exercise of the right to nominate is delayed

until the amount of credit is more than £100 the right itself is lost. Once made the nomination takes effect, not by creating any charge or trust in favour of the nominee as against the nominator as was suggested during the argument (for the nominator can at any moment revoke the nomination) but by giving to the nominee a right as against the Society, in the event of the death of the member without having revoked the nomination, to require the Society to transfer the property in accordance with the nomination. Until death the property is the property of the member, and all benefits accruing in respect of it during his lifetime are his also."

Law Debenture Trust Corporation v *Ural Caspian Oil Corporation Ltd and Others* (1992) The Independent 12 March (Hoffmann J)

Equitable rights – whether a contractual covenant can be binding on predecessor

Facts

The plaintiff was the trustee for shareholders in four English registered companies. These companies carried on business in Russia and expected compensation for the Soviet confiscation of their assets. The plaintiff entered into agreements with the companies regarding the paying over to the corporation of this money when it should be received.

L Limited bought the Russian companies' shares and covenanted with the plaintiff as trustee that it would procure that the Russian companies would perform their agreements or covenants. Further covenants by L Limited were to the effect that the company would not part with its control of the Russian companies without ensuring that any transferee company entered into similar covenants. In the event L Limited disposed of its shares to H Limited without imposing any requirement that H Limited should covenant with the plaintiff. Later, H Limited sold the shares to C Limited.

The plaintiff issued proceedings on the basis of the right as trustee to the compensation money. The proceedings were against the Russian companies and H Limited and C Limited. H Limited applied to strike out the plaintiff's statement of claim in part, while C Limited applied to strike out the whole of the statement of claim.

Held

The plaintiff had based the claim on the allegations that H Limited came under an implied collateral obligation to the plaintiff to observe and perform the covenants and that C Limited in turn had come under a similar obligation by accepting the transfer of the shares in the Russian companies with knowledge of the agreements. The plaintiff's argument was that this obligation arose either in equity under the principle of *De Mattos* v *Gibson* (1858) 4 De G & J 276 or in law under a developing principle relating to benefits and burdens. However, the equitable principle under the *De Mattos* case permitted no more than the grant of an injunction restraining a third party from doing acts inconsistent with performance by the original contracting party. There was no case in which the *De Mattos* principle had been used to impose on a purchaser a positive duty to perform the covenants of their predecessor. The right and the burden did not arise under the same instrument, nor were the obligations clearly reciprocal.

There was nothing in any transfer of the shares from the Russian companies to which H Limited and C Limited became successors in title linking them to the agreements about the payment over of the compensation money.

As against H Limited the plaintiff's statement of claim would be struck out in part and as against C Limited the whole of the plaintiff's statement of claim would be struck out, with leave to serve an amended statement of claim against all parties.

It was ordered accordingly.

Nichols v *Nichols* (1814) 2 Phil Ecc 180 Prerogative Court (Sir John Nicholl)

Will – testamentary intention

Facts

The deceased asked for a pen and ink and then took some paper and wrote on it. When he had finished writing he threw it at a friend saying, very carelessly, 'There, that is as good a will as I shall probably ever make.' The deceased had only written out the will after being shown a specimen copy of a will by the friend who gave evidence that he believed that the deceased had only written the instrument in imitation of the specimen because the deceased had done the same when shown specimen leases on other occasions.

Held

The document, although properly executed as a will, was not made with testamentary intention and could not be admitted to probate.

Sir John Nicholl:

> '... if this evidence is to be received, and is to be credited, this is not the will of the deceased, for it wants the great requisite, the animus testandi; it was not written with the mind and intention to make a will.'

Parsons v *Lanoe* (1748) 1 Ves Sen 189 (Lord Hardwicke)

Conditional will

Facts

The testator intended to go to Ireland and to remain there for some time. Before departing he made a will in the following manner: 'If I die before my return from my journey to Ireland, that my house and land at Farly Hill ... be sold as soon as possible after my death.'

Held

The instrument as a whole was conditional; the contingency was death during the testator's stay in Ireland.

Porter, In the Goods of (1869) LR 2 P & M 22 (Lord Penzance)

Conditional will

Facts

The testator, who was about to join his regiment in China, used the following language in his will:

> 'Being obliged to leave England to join my regiment in China and not having time to make a will, I leave this paper containing my wishes and desires. Should anything unfortunately happen to me while abroad I wish everything that I may be in possession of at that time or anything appertaining to me hereafter to be equally divided.'

Held

The will was conditional because of the nature of the disposition it contained, but the period during which it was expressed to operate would not have made it contingent.

***Sen* v *Headley* (1991) The Times 6 March Court of Appeal**

Donatio mortis cause – death-bed donation of house by delivery of title deeds

Facts

During his final illness the evidence stated that the deceased said to the plaintiff: 'The house is yours, Margaret. You have the keys. They are in your bag. The deeds are in the steel box.' After the deceased's death, the plaintiff found that she held the only keys to the steel box. She therefore claimed that the deceased had given the house to her by way of donatio mortis causa so that the gift was made in anticipation of death giving her title to the property. The defendant, who was administrator of the estate, counterclaimed for return of the deeds.

Held

The plaintiff's claim failed, according to Mummery J.

Despite being taken by counsel on 'an instructive world tour' examining the law of various jurisdictions which have developed the doctrine of donatio mortis causa, Mummery J could find no authority to persuade him to depart from a dictum of Lord Eldon that there could not be a valid donatio mortis causa of real property (*Duffield* v *Elwes* (1827) 1 Bli (NS) 497). On the contrary, there was authority cautioning judges against extending the doctrine of donatio mortis causa beyond the limits decided in earlier cases. Further, the policy of the law had long been to require *additional formalities* in connection with dispositions of land and interests in land. The doctrine had no application to informal gifts of land that did not comply with either the Law of Property Act 1925 or the Wills Act 1837. The judge also found difficulty in seeing how the requirement for a donatio mortis causa that the donor should have parted with dominion over the subject matter of the gift could ever be satisfied by delivery of title deeds. Accordingly the plaintiff's action was dismissed and judgment was given for the defendant on the counterclaim.

On an appeal against the decision that the gift failed, the appeal was allowed.

Nourse LJ, delivering the Court's judgment, stated that the question whether the doctrine applied to a gift of land by delivery of the title deeds had not been directly decided in England. In *Duffield* v *Elwes* (1827) 1 Bli (NS) 497, at 538, Lord Eldon considered that it did not. Since then this view had generally been assumed to be correct. While the doctrine was agreed to be anomalous, this did not justify anomalous exceptions. If due account were taken of the present state of the law regarding mortgages and choses in action it was apparent that to make a distinction in the case of land would be anomalous. A donatio mortis causa was neither more nor less anomalous than any other. Every such gift was a circumvention of the requirements of the Wills Act 1837. Accordingly, subject to the general requirements in all such cases, land was capable of passing by donatio mortis causa.

There was no reason why the additional statutory formalities for the creation and transfer of interests in land should be regarded as some greater obstacle. The only necessary step was the extension of the application of the implied or constructive trust arising on the death of the donor from the conditional to the absolute estate. While it was true that the House of Lords would not have taken this step in *Duffield*, the point was not decided in the 1827 case: had it been so they would have followed it. However, they could not in 1991 decide a case as the House of Lords would have decided it in 1827. They had to decide according to the law of the day. Accordingly, they held that land was capable of passing by way of donatio mortis causa and that the three general requirements for such a gift had been satisfied.

Spratt, In the Goods of [1897] P 28 (Sir Francis Jeune P)

Conditional will – need to show nature of condition

Facts

The testator, a military officer on active service, wrote a letter to his sister in the following language:

> 'If we remain here taking pahs for some time to come the chances are in favour of more of us being killed, and I may not have another opportunity of saying what I wish to be done with any little money I may possess in case of an accident, I wish to make everything I possess over to you. In the first place there is money at ... keep this until I ask you for it.'

Held

The document was not a conditional will as it was not dependent on the deceased's death while on active service.

Sir Francis Jeune P:

> '... if the will is clearly expressed to take effect only on the happening, or not happening, of any event, cadit quaestio, it is conditional. If the testator says, in effect, that he is led to make his will by reason of the uncertainty of life in general, or for some special reasons, cadit quaestio, it is not conditional. But, if it be not clear whether the words used import a reason for making the will or impress a conditional character on it, the whole language of the document, and also the surrounding circumstances must be considered. In such cases there are two criteria which are especially useful for determining the problem: first whether the nature of disposition made appears to have relation to the time or circumstances of the contingency; and, secondly, where the contingency is connected with a period of danger to the testator, whether it is coincident with that period, because if it is, there is ground to suppose that the danger was regarded by the testator as only a reason for making a will but, if it is not it is difficult to see the object of referring to a particular period unless it be to limit the operation of the will ...'

Synge v *Synge* [1894] 1 QB 466 Court of Appeal (Kay LJ)

Contract to make a will – breach – measure of damages

Facts

The defendant, in order to induce the plaintiff to marry him, promised in writing to leave a house and land to her for life. The plaintiff consented to marry the defendant on those terms and the marriage took place. Later the defendant conveyed the property promised to the plaintiff to a third party. The plaintiff sued for damages for breach of contract.

Held

Since the defendant had put it out of his power to perform the contract there was a breach in respect of which the plaintiff could recover damages and the measure of damages was the value of the life estate to which she would have become entitled.

Kay LJ:

> 'The questions which arise in this case are these:
>
> 1 Was there a binding contract?
> 2 Was it such a contract as could be enforced in equity, or was there a remedy in damages for breach of it?
> 3 Has the time arrived at which such a remedy can be asserted?
> 4 If the remedy be by way of damages, what amount of damages should be given? ...'
>
> [His Lordship considered the first two questions and held marriage was valuable consideration enabling the plaintiff to enforce the contract, and that the contract could be enforced in equity if it was a definite proposal in writing so as to satisfy the Statute of Frauds (now s40 LPA 1925), and continued]:

Then, what is the remedy where the proposal relates to a defined piece of property? We have no doubt of the power of the Court to decree a conveyance of that property after the death of the person making the proposal against all who claim under him as volunteers. It is argued that the Courts of Equity cannot compel a man to make a will. But neither can they compel him to make a deed. They, however, can decree the heir or devisee in such a case to convey the land to the widow for life, and under the Trustees Acts can make a vesting order, or direct that someone shall convey for him if he refuses. And under like circumstances, the Court has power to make a declaration of the lady's right.

But counsel do not press for such relief, or ask for a declaration to bind the house and land. The relief they ask is damages for breach of contract. It seems to be proved that the grantee of the property under the deeds executed by Sir R Synge took without notice of the letter; they acquired, as we understand, the legal estate by the grant. If there was any valuable consideration moving from them, no relief in the nature of specific performance could be given against them; and it is suggested that the property being partly leasehold, according to the decision in *Price* v *Jenkins* (1877) 5 Ch D 619 there was such valuable consideration. It is not necessary to examine this argument, as counsel elect to ask for damages only.

Sir R Synge had all his lifetime to perform this contract; but, in order to perform it, he must in his lifetime make a disposition in favour of Lady Synge. If he died without having done so, he would have broken his contract. The breach would be omitting in his lifetime to make such a disposition. True, it would only take effect at his death; but the breach must take place in his lifetime, and as by the conveyance to his daughters he put it absolutely out of his power to perform this contract, Lady Synge, according to the well-known decisions (*Hochester* v *De La Tour* (1885) 2 ECB 678, *Frost* v *Knight* (1872) LR Ex 111), had a right to treat that conveyance as an absolute breach of contract, and to sue at once for damages; and as this Court has both legal and equitable jurisdiction, we are of opinion that such relief should be granted ...'

T, Re [1992] 3 WLR 782

Living will – refusal of life-saving medical treatment

Facts

The case concerned a young woman who signed a Form of Refusal to a blood transfusion. Afterwards she became seriously ill, and her father made an application to the court. The question for the court was whether or not such a form of refusal was valid. Consideration had to be given to the long established English legal principle that a person who is mentally competent has the absolute right to grant or withhold consent to medical treatment. Adults are presumed to be competent unless evidence is adduced to the contrary.

Held

T had not validly withheld consent to the administration of a blood transfusion in the circumstances because at the time of the signature of the form she was under the influence of drugs. T had also been subject to the undue influence of her mother, who was a practising Jehovah's Witness.

Lord Donaldson:

> 'This right of choice is not limited to decisions which others might regard as sensible. It exists notwithstanding that the reasons for making the choice are rational, irrational, unknown or even non-existent.'

The court held that four criteria must be fulfilled in order to grant legal validity to any refusal to consent to life saving treatment. These were:

a) the patient must have the capacity to make the decision, ie they must not be influenced by drugs or be suffering from mental illness;

b) the patient should not be under the influence of a third party;
c) the nature and effect of the treatment which is being refused or consented to must be broadly understood by the patient;
d) the refusal by the patient must concern the actual circumstances in which the treatment is required.

In such a situation, therefore, these would amount to the test of mental competency.

Thorne, In the Goods of (1865) 4 Sw & Tr 36 (Lord Penzance)

Conditional will distinguished from Need to make a will

Facts
The testamentary document was in the form of a letter which contained the following expression:

> 'I request that in the event of my death while serving in this horrid climate or any accident happening to me I leave and bequeath ... I consider that every person should be prepared for the worst, and particularly in such a treacherous climate as this, which is considered one of the worst in the world, which has compelled me to write this letter.'

The testator wrote the letter in the Gold Coast, Africa, in November 1863, returned to London in July 1864 and died there in September of the same year.

Held
The language of the will pointed to the testator feeling the necessity to make a will rather than desiring to limit the operation of it to his death happening in Africa. The will was not conditional.

Woodard* v *Woodard (1991) The Times 15 March Court of Appeal

Donatio mortis cause – deathbed gift of a car

Facts
The question arose whether a deathbed gift of a car by a father to his son was a donation mortis causa (gift by reason of death). In the circumstances of this case the logbook and a second set of keys were not handed over to the donee.

Held
Sufficient dominion over the car had been given to the donee to establish a donatio mortis causa.

Wordingham* v *Royal Exchange Trust Co Ltd and Another [1992] 2 WLR 496 Chancery Division (Edward Evans-Lombe QC sitting as a deputy High Court Judge)

Rectification – s20(1)(A) Administration of Justice Act 1982

Facts
In 1979 the testatrix made her will. Under clause 4 of the will she exercised the Power of Appointment in order to appoint her interest in the income from her share of the residue under her father's will to the plaintiff for life if he should survive her. The plaintiff indeed outlived the testatrix. In 1989 the testatrix, wishing to make a new will, explained to her solicitor that she intended to alter the 1979 will instead of re-drafting a brand new will, leaving the earlier provisions to stand where it was not necessary to alter them.

A new will was drafted and executed. However the new will did not contain the clause that corresponded to clause 4 of the 1979 will.

The plaintiff's application was for an order by the court that the will should be rectified pursuant to s20(1)(A) of the Administration of Justice Act 1982 in order to include such a clause on the basis that the omission of the clause was the result of a clerical error.

Held

The words 'clerical error' used in s20 were to be construed as meaning an error made in the process of recording the intended words of the testator in the drafting or transcription of his will. This meaning was to be distinguished from an error made in carrying out his intentions through the choice of words of the draftsman, and contrasted with the mistaken choice of words because of a failure to understand the testator's intention. These cases were covered by sub-clause (b) of the Administration of Justice Act s20.

Having regard to the circumstances of this case and the evidence, the testatrix intended that a clause exactly along the lines of clause 4 of her 1979 will should appear in her new will. It was clear that her instructions to her solicitor were to alter the 1979 will in certain defined respects, but in no other respects. Further, the alterations did not include the exclusion of that provision.

As a result, the error in failing to include in the draft new will a paragraph following the provisions of clause 4 of the 1979 will was an error made in the process of recording the intended words of the testatrix which constituted a clerical error within s20(1)(A). It was therefore found that the order rectifying the 1989 will was justified.

An order was made accordingly.

2 The Formal Requirements for Making a Will

Adams, In b (1872) LR 2 P & D 367 Probate Division (Lord Penzance)

Wills Act 1837 s9 – formalities – writing in ink and in pencil

Facts

The deceased executed a printed form will. The blanks were filled up by the deceased in her own handwriting, partly with ink and partly with pencil. Some of the writing in ink extended over that in pencil and some words in pencil had been rubbed out and obliterated. The words in ink were sensible as read with the printed part of the will.

Held

The words in pencil were deliberative only and probate would be granted without them.

Lord Penzance:

> '... it is clear, therefore, that some of the dispositions are intended to be superseded by others, and, that being so, the presumption is, that the writing in ink is the will, and not the pencil writing, especially as the former is of such character as to work in with the printed matter.'

Anderson, In the Estate of [1916] P 49 Probate Division (Bargrave Deane J)

Privileged will – seaman never at sea – loss of privilege

Facts

The deceased, a member of the local corps of the St John's Ambulance Association, was ordered to join HMS *Pembroke* which was permanently stationed at Chatham. On the morning of his departure he wrote out a document at his home which purported to dispose of his property. On arrival at Chatham he was billeted in barracks and did not go on board a ship for several weeks until he was ordered to join HMS *Rohilla* instead. He was lost at sea.

Held

The deceased was not within s11; he was not a seaman at sea when he wrote out the document which purported to be his will. This was because at the time he wrote it he had never been at sea and could not be described as a 'sailor at sea' until he had been at sea.

Bargrave Deane J:

> 'This would be a perfectly good will if made when this man was at sea. The language of section 11 of the Wills Act is peculiar; the words are not identical with regard to soldiers and mariners. To come within the exceptions in that section, a soldier must be in actual military service, and if this deceased man had been a soldier, or if those words had applied to sailors or mariners, it might have been argued

successfully that he came within the exceptions. But when the deceased wrote out his document he was not at sea: he was in fact at his father's house.'

Arthur, In b (1871) LR 2 P & D 273 Probate Division (Lord Penzance)

Wills Act 1837 s9 – position of signature – need to acknowledge all clauses

Facts
A testator signed his will in the presence of two witnesses who duly attested. Afterwards he added a clause to the will and squeezed it into the space above and beside the signature. Immediately afterwards the witnesses signed their names.

Held
The testator did not sign or acknowledge his signature to the will as containing such a clause; probate should be granted without it.

Lord Penzance:

> 'The object of the signature is to affirm what was before written. In this case the signature was written first and the clause afterwards, so the signature affirms nothing as to that clause. If after having written the clause the deceased had acknowledged the paper to be his will, that might have been an affirmation of the clause; but according to the evidence, he neither signed nor acknowledged the will inclusive of the final clause ...'

Barnard v *Birch* [1912] 2 IR 404 Probate Division (Dodd J)

Privileged will – employees on ferry boats and other short voyages

Facts
Captain Birch was the captain of the cross-channel steamship *Leinster* during its voyages from Kingstown to Holyhead. He was actually at sea for the time each day he spent in transit but was at home on shore for the remainder of each day at his house in Holyhead where he resided with his wife and family. When his boat was laid up he remained on shore with his wife and family. He had been so living for some weeks, and his time for resumed daily sailings was approaching when he made his will in the form of an unattested document. The question arose whether the document was made on a privileged occasion.

Held
Captain Birch was 'a seaman' but he was not a 'seaman being at sea' within s11 when he made out the unattested document because at that time his boat was laid up and another voyage was not contemplated for a very considerable time. He was therefore a seaman on shore at home.

Beadle, Re [1974] 1 WLR 417 Chancery Division (Goff J)

Wills Acts 1837 and 1852 – signatures on several pieces of paper or on envelope containing a will

Facts
A testatrix dictated her will to an old friend who wrote it down on a single sheet of paper. The testatrix signed the will in the top right-hand corner and one of the witnesses signed below. There were no other

signatures on the paper. The testatrix then placed the paper in an envelope and wrote on the front 'My last will and testament, E A Beadle to Charlie and Maysie' (the executors). On the back of the envelope was written 'we certify that the contents of this letter was written in the presence of ourselves' and both the executors signed. The question arose whether the will on the single sheet alone or on the sheet with the envelope was duly executed under the Wills Act 1837 and the Wills Act Amendment Act 1852.

Held

The sheet of paper was insufficient as a will since the signature of the testatrix was not at 'the foot or end', within s9, and it was not properly attested. The envelope together with the sheet of paper was not a will either because when the testatrix signed the envelope she only intended that her signature should be a label identifying the document when she placed it with her other papers. In any case the signature on the front of the envelope was not properly attested since the executors' signatures were not signatures to witness it but only to record that both were present when the will was signed, even though only one of them had attested it.

Goff J:

> 'I now have to determine whether the will propounded by the plaintiffs, either the single sheet alone or that sheet with the envelope, is a will duly executed in accordance with the statutory requirements. There is no other question. I approach this problem in the way which Willmer LJ approved as proper in *In the Estate of Bercovitz, decd* [1962] 1 WLR 321 at 326 when (quoting from the judgment of Phillimore J below) he said:
>
> > "'I approach this question from the point of view that this man' – in my case "this woman" – "'clearly wanted to make this disposition, and that any court should give effect to his wishes, if it is at all possible to do so'."
>
> Even so I have regretfully come to a clear conclusion that I cannot uphold this will on either basis without drawing distinctions where none exist or flying in the face of authority; and I must therefore pronounce against the will.
>
> I will deal first with the case for the paper alone. Counsel argued – albeit, very understandably, with little confidence and rather as a tabula in naufragio – that since the testatrix meant by her signature at the top of this paper to authenticate the whole, that is good enough; and he cited *In the Goods of Hornby, decd* [1946] P 171, *In the Estate of Roberts, decd* [1934] P 102 and *In the Goods of Usbourne, decd* (1909) 25 TLR 519 referred to in *In the Goods of Harris, decd* [1952] P 319 at 323. In my judgment, however, such an argument is wholly untenable in the face of the express terms of section of the Wills Act Amendment Act 1852 and *In re Stalman, decd* (1931) 145 LT 339 …
>
> Turning to the paper with the envelope, it is clear on authority that they are sufficiently connected to be admitted to probate together if otherwise duly executed, and that was not disputed. In my judgment, however, the plaintiffs must satisfy the court that, in writing her name on the front of the envelope, the testatrix meant that to be a signature to her will, and that they cannot do so in the light of *In the Estate of Bean* [1944] P 83. The words there, and also in *In the Goods of Mann, decd* [1942] P 146, were 'the last will and testament of' and then follows the relevant name, whereas in this case they are 'My last will and testament' and then follows the name 'E A Beadle'. But, in my judgment, that is a distinction without a difference. I am satisfied that, on the facts of this case, the testatrix did not intend her name on the envelope to be a signature to her will, but merely a label. In *In the Goods of Mann, decd* the testatrix said that the documents – that is, paper and envelope – were her will and asked the witnesses to sign. They signed the contents. She did not; but she did sign the envelope. That was distinguished in *In the Estate of Bean* where there was no calling attention to the combined documents as the will. In distinguishing *In the Goods of Mann, decd* Hodson J said at p84:
>
> > "It is, therefore, necessary to determine, first, whether the name 'George Bean', written on the envelope, is a signature at all. If this question is answered in the affirmative, then it is necessary to determine whether or not it makes any difference that the signature was written on a separate piece of paper."

Thereafter referring to *In the Goods of Mann, decd* Hodson J continued:

> "Langton J found that the signature on the envelope was the signature to the will, and then dealt at some length with the second question, namely, to whether or not there was any difficulty in admitting both documents to probate as to together constituting the last will of the deceased. On the facts of the case which I have to consider I find it impossible to answer the first question in the affirmative. The executrix has sworn that she did not know that the deceased had not signed the will form, and it appears to me to be plain that this omission on the part of the deceased was purely accidental in that he failed to sign his name in the space provided for the purpose. The writing on the envelope was equally clearly, I think, put there for the purpose of identifying the contents of the envelope and not as a signature at all. The deceased never indicated that the testamentary document and the enveloppe together constituted his will. He had written his name not only on the envelope, but also on the indorsement which appers on the back sheet. It is true that the indorsement was not visible to the attesting witnesses whereas the writing on the envelope was seen. Nevertheless, in my opinion, it is possible to be satisfied that the deceased intended to give effect to the will by writing on the envelope since in all probability, he, like the executrix, was under the impression that he had already signed the will on the form itself."

It will be observed that Hodson J there used these words "the deceased never indicated that the testamentary document and the envelope together constituted his will"; and again, "in all probability, he, like the executrix, was under the impression that he had already signed the will on the form itself".

The present case, therefore, in my judgment, falls within *In the Estate of Bean* and not *In the Goods of Mann, decd* and indeed it is an *a fortiori* one, since in *Bean's* case the judge was not satisfied because he thought the testator had forgotten he had not signed the paper. Here, Mr Mayes said she wrote out the envelope because he said he would put it with her papers. The inference is clearly that she signed the envelope not to sign her will, which she had already done, but to identify the document which was going to be put away ...

... That is sufficient to dispose of the case. But lest I be wrong on that, I should also deal with another difficulty in the plaintiffs' way, which I find fatal to their case, and that is that neither of the witnesses attested her signature on the envelope. Mr Mayes wrote what he did on the back of the envelope and he and Mrs Mayes both signed, not to attest what was on the front, but to place on record that although the paper inside was signed by only one of them, both were present when it was written and signed. Mr Mayes' evidence was:

> "It was certifying that the document inside was written in our presence." [Counsel]: "So the purpose was to recognise the fact that when she had signed at the top, you were both there?" [Answer] "Yes".

In Mrs Mayes' evidence, counsel asked:

> "When you signed the envelope, is it right you were certifying the contents of the letter that had been written in the presence of yourselves?" (Answer): "That is what we meant."

This, in my judgment, brings the matter precisely within *In the Estate of Bercovitz, decd*, where Ormrod LJ quoted the finding of Phillimore J in the court below:

> "I am quite satisfied that when she signed she intended to witness his signature at the top of the paper and had no knowledge whatever of any signature at the foot or any intention of attesting any such signature."

Plaintiffs' counsel argued that attestation is not a matter of intention, and that case, he submits, turned entirely on knowledge. But in my judgment that is not so. Of course, where a witness subscribes one signature on a will (or, indeed, any document) and does not know that there is another signature, it is ordinarily difficult, if not impossible, to reach the conclusion that he meant also to attest that other signature of which he was unaware. The same principle, however, in my judgment, applies where a witness, knowing that there are two signatures, signs the document but says 'I am only dealing with part of the document', being the part containing one only of the signatures. That, in my view, is the effect of what Mr Mayes wrote on the back of the envelope, and is confirmed by what he and Mrs Mayes both said in the witness-box ...'

Brown* v *Skirrow [1902] P 3 Probate Division (Gorell Barnes J)

Wills Act 1837 s9 – attestation in the presence of witnesses

Facts

The testatrix signed her will in a grocer's shop near where she lived. One of the witnesses to the will saw the testatrix sign the will on a counter and she attested it. The testatrix then went over to another counter on the other side of the shop and had the other witness sign the will. At the time the testatrix and the first witness signed the second witness had been serving a customer and did not see them sign or know what they were doing until he was asked to be a witness.

Held

The will was not properly attested, it had not been signed 'in the presence of' the second witness because he had no idea what was going on at the time and saw nothing; moreover, he had no opportunity of seeing, there being a customer between him and the testatrix at the time she signed the will.

Casson* v *Dade (1781) 1 Bro CC 99

Attestation – need for witnesses to subscribe the will in testator's presence

Facts

The testatrix signed her will in her solicitor's office and then left it to sit in her carriage outside. The carriage was at the door of the solicitor's office. When the witnesses were subscribing the will there was a line of sight from the carriage through a window in the solicitor's office which enabled the testatrix to see this, had she wished.

Held

The attestation was valid as it had been in the testatrix's presence.

Chalcraft, In b [1948] P 222 Court of Probate Willmer J

Wills Act 1837 s9 – formalities – partial signature

Facts

The deceased was on her death-bed and had been given a large dose of drugs. Her draft will had not been prepared in time so another document was hurridly drafted and read to her and given to her to sign. However, the deceased only managed to sign 'E Chal' instead of 'E Chalcraft'. The witnesses signed without delay in her presence and shortly afterwards she became unconscious.

Held

The document was a testamentary document and in the circumstances the partial signature should be accepted; although the deceased was losing her faculties at the time of the attestation she was still mentally present to a sufficient degree to bring the will within the Wills Act 1837.

Willmer J:

> 'I come now to the next point, whether what the deceased wrote can be accepted as her signature within the provisions of section 9 of the Wills Act 1837. As I have said there is no question of it being acknowledged as her mark. Reliance was placed by counsel for the defendants on three cases in relation to

this point. He referred, first, to *In the Goods of Maddock* (1874) LR 3 P & D 169. That was a case where the signature in question was that of a witness, not of a testator, the particular witness being old and infirm. As a result he was unable to complete his signature legibly, and desisted having only written a part of his Christian name, and no surname at all. It was held that, in those circumstances, that was not a proper attestation of the will. The next case relied on by the defendants was *In the Goods of Blewitt* (1880) 5 PD 116. The question there was whether initials placed alongside certain interlineations in a will were acceptable as a signature.

It was held that they were. In the course of the learned President's judgment in that case he cited the language of members of the House of Lords in the earlier case of *Hindmarsh* v *Charlton* (1861) 8 HLC 160, which, he said 5 PD 116, 117, seems "equally applicable to the testator's signature as to the witnesses' subscription". Then, quoting from the Lord Chancellor in *Hindmarsh* v *Charlton*, he goes on 8 HLC 160, 170: "I will lay down this as to my notion of the law: that to make a valid subscription of a witness there must either be the name or some mark which is intended to represent the name". In the same case Lord Chelmsford says Ibid 171:

> "The subscription must mean such a signature as is descriptive of the witness, whether by a mark or by initials, or by writing a name in full."

What is said on behalf of the defendants in this case is that here you have not any of those three things – this is not a case of a mark, it is not a case of initials, and it is not a case of writing the name in full. Instead of that it is the initials followed by half the surname.

The third case to which I was referred was an Irish case. *In the Goods of Kieran, dec'd* [1933] IR 222. That was a case in which the facts are much more similar to those of the present case. It was a case of a testator who was in bed very ill, and who tried to write his name but did not succeed in doing more than write two more or less indecipherable initials. The similarity with this case ceases after that, because in that case a solicitor was present and he then asked the testator whether what the testator had written could be accepted as his mark, and the testator accepted what he had writen as his mark; it was so endorsed on the will by the solicitor, and was so attested by the witnesses. In that case it was decided that although the mark did not take the usual form of a cross, nevertheless it was a mark acknowledged by the testator as his own in the presence of witnesses and, therefore, sufficient to amount to a signature under the Act. But the learned judge in that case does, I think, go a little wider than was necessary for the decision of the case in giving his reasons. I think it valuable to read the last few sentences of his judgment [1933] IR 222, 229. He says this:

> "What is the test that I am to apply? It is, in my opinion, whether I am satisfied that the two scrawls were placed there by the testator as a personal act or acknowledged as such by him, *animo testandi*, to verify the making of the will as his own act. If a testator cannot, or does not, sign his name, or place legible initials on the will, but, on the other hand, places on it or acknowledges something upon it as his mark, in my opinion the court should not be concerned as to the particular character or shape of the mark. It may be the time-honoured cross, that has been referred to, or it may be some other character. I am satisfied on the evidence here that not only did the testator commence to make his signature *animo testandi* but continued in the same state of mind until the termination of the execution of his will, and accordingly I admit this will to probate."

I find this a very difficult point to decide. What is said for the defendants is that if a testator sets out with the intention of signing his name, but never succeeds in completing a signature, and never develops any intention to execute the document in any other way, then it is not a signature. He can if he chooses, and if he forms the intention of doing so, execute the document by putting his initials on it; and he can, if he wishes to do so, and forms the intention of doing so, execute a document by making his mark and acknowledging his mark in the presence of witnesses. But what is said is that if he starts out with the intention of doing any one of these things, and never departs from that intention, but yet never completes that which he sets out to do, then there can in law be no execution of document. In *In the Goods of Maddock*, if what was said about witnesses is to apply to testators, it certainly seems to go a long way towards establishing that proposition. The Irish case to which I have referred does not help very much, partly because it did ultimately turn on the testator's acknowledgement of his mark, and partly because of the rather wider grounds on which the learned judge put his judgment in the last few sentences, which I have read. Indeed, if one took those last few sentences, by themselves, it could be read as an authority to the contrary of what has been contended on behalf of the defendants. It seems to me that there must necessarily be some question of degree involved in this. I put in argument the case of the man who signs his name (a practice which we all know very well) by making the first few letters of his signature fairly distinct, and the last few letters of his signature completely indecipherable. Supposing, for the sake of argument, in this case the deceased instead of stopping at the 'l' in 'Chalcraft' had followed it by a few, or even one, indecipherable line. What would be the effect then? Would that be a completed signature? It seems to me that one ought to give a broad interpretation to the words used by the Lord Chancellor in the case of *Hindmarsh* v *Charlton* in the passage which I have read. There must either be the name or some mark which is intended to represent the name. It seems to me that I must have regard to all the facts of this case: the fact that this lady was in an extremely weak condition; that she was lying, if not on her back, very nearly on her back, in a position in which it must have been very difficult to write at all. I must ask myself the question whether on all the facts I can draw the inference that what she wrote was intended by her to be the best that she could do by way of writing her name. It seems to me that if I come to that conclusion, then I ought to accept this writing of "E Chal" as being in law the signature of the deceased. Bearing in mind all the circumstances of the case – the weaknesses of the deceased, the difficulty of writing in that position – I come to the conclusion that this mark "E Chal" on this document does amount, in all the circumstances, to a signature on the part of the deceased. I think *In the Goods of Maddock* (1) is distinguishable, because in that case there was no question of writing any surname at all; the writing stopped short at a part only of the Christian name. Hence we have something a good deal better than that and, in all the circumstances, I am satisfied that I ought to accept it as the signature of the deceased.'

Corby, In b (1854) 1 Spink Ecc & Adm 292 (Dr Lushington)

Privileged will – absence of evidence that will was written on board ship

Facts
The deceased was resident in Melbourne, Australia; he joined a ship there 15 days before she sailed and made an unattested will before she sailed to England. Prior to the ship sailing the deceased was both on the ship and ashore many times. The question arose whether he was entitled to the privilege.

Held
Probate would be refused under s11 because it was impossible to conclude whether the testator had made the will on the ship or ashore because he had been on both during the time, and it was also a fact that he was in his home town so he could not be at sea.

Garnett, In b [1894] P 90 Probate Division (Gorell Barnes J)

Incorporation by reference – need for will to identify document clearly

Facts
A testator made a will, which was duly executed and attested, which appointed no executors and contained no bequest but referred to 'the enclosed papers, numbered 1, 2, 3, 4, 5 and 6' as containing his testamentary wishes and recited that those papers had been signed by himself in the presence of the witnesses. The witnesses said they had never seen any of the papers and said that the testator had called

them into his study to attest alterations to his will, saying 'The will is in the drawer'. The papers 1 to 6 had various dates antecedent to the will.

Held

The papers 1 to 6 were not clearly identified with the description given of them in the attested paper, so as to exclude the possibility of mistake. They could not, in these circumstances, be incorporated into the will.

Gibson, Re [1949] P 434 Court of Probate (Pearce J)

Attestation – capacity to act as a witness – blindness

Facts

The testator executed a codicil to his will in the presence of two witnesses, one of whom was a man who had gone blind some 18 months previously. Both witnesses had attested the codicil.

Held

The codicil was invalid; it had not been signed 'in the presence of' the blind man and he was not a 'witness' for the purposes of s9.

Pearce J:

> 'There is no direct authority on the capacity of a blind man to witness a will. The normal meaning of "attesting" is testifying or bearing witness to something, and the normal meaning of "witness" is one who is a spectator of an incident or who is present at an incident. Is mere presence, without the faculty of sight, enough to constitute a person a "witness" for the purpose of s9? And is an act which he cannot see done "in his presence"? The object of the Act is clear. One witness is not enough. The presence of two witnesses is made necessary to give certainty and avoid fraud. In the light of commonsense and without any authority I should be inclined to hold that for the purposes of the Act a "witness" means one who, in regard to things audible, has the faculty of hearing, and, in regard to things visible, has the faculty of seeing. The signing of a will is a visible matter, and, therefore, I think a will is not signed "in the presence of" a blind person, nor is a blind person a witness for the purposes of the section ...'

Gossage, In the Estate of [1921] P 194 Court of Appeal (Lord Sterndale MR, Warrington and Younger LJJ)

Privileged will – absence of formalities for making a revocation

Facts

The testator, a soldier, was called up for active service in South Africa in 1915. Whilst under orders to proceed to South Africa he made a will in accordance with the Wills Act 1837 by which he made certain legacies and gave the residue of his estate to his fiancée, the plaintiff. Before leaving he gave the plaintiff a sealed envelope containing the will and directed her not to open it unless anything happened to him. Whilst in South Africa the testator received letters about the plaintiff's conduct and accordingly he wrote to her directing her to hand his will over to his sister, Kate. The plaintiff did so and in 1918 the testator wrote to Kate from Cape Town requesting her to burn his will as he had already cancelled it. Kate obliged. Subsequently the testator died in South Africa and amongst his belongings was found a copy of his original will. The plaintiff brought an action to establish that will.

Held

The formal requirements set out in s20 of the Wills Act 1837 for the revocation of wills did not apply to soldiers' wills and therefore the will had been effectively revoked by the letter he wrote in 1918.

Younger LJ:

> '... as Sir Francis Jeune P in *In the Goods of Hiscock* [1909] P 78, 80, referring to s11 of the Wills Act, said: "I am inclined to the view that the reason and principle underlying those words are the same as prevailed under the Roman Law, namely, that a soldier in the circumstances mentioned, or a sailor who is actually at sea, is, possibly, not altogether, but certainly to a great extent, *inops concilii,* and therefore not in a position to make his will in the form required of persons in ordinary circumstances." That statement remains, I think, correct. That s11 of the Act must now be recognised to have a further effect results from the declaratory enactment contained in s1 of the Wills (Soldiers and Sailors) Act 1918, that s11 of the Wills Act authorises and always has authorised any soldier being on active military service to dispose of his personal estate as he might have done before the passing of the Act, though under the age of twenty-one years. The result follows that, for example, s7 which enacts that "no will made by any person under the age of twenty-one years shall be valid", general as are its terms, has, on the now declared construction, no application to a soldier's or a sailor's will. Similarly, in my judgment, s20 has no relation to such a will. Its language is no more general than the language of s9 and if it were held so far as its prescribed formalities are concerned, to extend to dispositions of soldiers and sailors referred to in s11, it would, in my judgment, go far to deprive these testators of the privileges reserved to them in the matter of formalities by that section. For the power which a soldier has to revoke his soldier's disposition follows, as I think, from the power reserved to him by the statute to make one. It is, in my judgment, true to say that the power of revoction is merely another aspect of the power of disposition, and that power which he had before the statute remained, I think, unaffected by the statute ...'

Groffman, Re [1969] 1 WLR 733 Court of Probate (Sir Jocelyn Simon P)

Wills Act 1837 s9 – need to acknowledge his signature in the presence of witnesses

Facts

The testator had a will prepared for him by solicitors. One evening while out visiting friends with his wife, he asked two friends to witness his will. He made a gesture towards his coat pocket where the will was. As the lounge was congested the testator and one of the witnesses went to an adjoining room; the testator pulled the will from his pocket revealing his signature thereon and the witness signed it. The witness left the room and the other witness came in and signed beneath the first witness's signature. The testator's widow claimed the will was not properly executed.

Held

There was no proper acknowledgement by the testator of his signature within s9; he had failed to acknowledge it in front of both witnesses at the same time.

Sir Jocelyn Simon P:

> 'The question, as I have indicated, is whether the testator acknowledged his signature in the presence of Mr Block and Mr Leigh those two witnesses being present at the same time. The matter has been considered by a number of eminent judges, starting with Dr Lushington, and followed by the members of the Court of Appeal in *Blake* v *Blake* (1882) 7 PD 102 and *Daintree* v *Butcher and Fasulo* (1888) 13 PD 102. It seems presumptuous to say that I agree with their construction of the statute; but it appears to me to be clear. In any event, I am bound by what was decided by the Court of Appeal, even if authorities establish that the signature of the testator must be on the document at the time of acknowledgment (as I think it

was), and that the witnesses saw or had an opportunity of seeing the signature at that time, in other words, at the time of acknowledgment.

In *Blake* v *Blake*, Sir George Jessel MR gave a judgment in which he said "The question then arises whether the testatrix acknowledged her signature before the witnesses". This was a case where the testatrix had signed and had asked two attesting witnesses to add their signature, but had covered her own signature with blotting paper, so they could not see it. Sir George Jessel in those circumstances posed the question:

> "What is in law a sufficient acknowledgement under the statute?"

He answers:

> "What I take to be the law is correctly laid down in *Jarman on Wills* 4th Ed p108, in the following terms: 'There is no sufficient acknowledgement unless the witnesses either saw or might have seen the signature, not even though the testator should expressly declare that the paper to be attested by them is his will'."

He quotes Dr Lushington in *Hudson* v *Parker* (1844) 1 Rob Ecc 14:

> "What do the words import but this? 'Here is my name written, I acknowledged that name so written to have been written by me; bear witness'."

Then Sir George Jessel MR said that "if the witnesses would not be able to see his signature, that is not a sufficient acknowledgement". Then discussing *Hudson* v *Parker* again, he said, at p100:

> "The witnesses were taken to have seen the signature and the testator having then asked them to witness his will, he was held to have acknowledged his signature."

Brett LJ is even more strongly to the same effect; and, although this differed in one respect from Jessel MR he like Holker LJ the third member of the court, agreed that the witnesses at the moment of acknowledgement must either see or have the opportunity of seeing that the signature is on the will.

Mr Craig, who has argued this case vigorously for the plaintiffs, had propounded that the decision in *Daintree* v *Butcher and Fasulo* in the Court of Appeal is in his favour. I cannot read it as such. Whilst Cotton LJ with whom Fry and Lopes LJJ concurred, was dealing with what amounts to acknowledgement, he adverted to the case of *Ilott* v *Genge* (1842) 4 Moo PC 265 and said: "The paper there was so folded that the witnesses could not see the signature". That was, therefore, held to be insufficient acknowledgement. Then he said

> "No doubt, if they cannot see the signature, the mere calling on them to sign as witness is not enough. But here there was a signature on the paper which they could have seen, and which the testatrix would suppose that they did see."

At the end of the judgment he gave his view as to what was decided in *Blake* v *Blake*, saying, "The court only affirmed the proposition laid down in Jarman on Wills." (which I read when citing from *Blake* v *Blake*). In my view, *Daintree* v *Butcher and Fasulo* bears out what I have described from *Blake* v *Blake*, namely that if there is to be an acknowledgement within the statute the attesting witnesses must either see or be capable of seeing the signature; or at the very least must see or be capable of seeing a will on which there is a signature. In the present case, none of those conditions was satisfied.

In defence, however, to the interest and vigour of Mr Craig's argument, I must deal with various alternative ways in which he puts his case. He says, first, that *Blake* is to be distinguished in that there was a deliberate concealment by the testatrix of her signature, which, he says, is the very negation of acknowledgement. But there is nothing at all in the judgments of *Blake* v *Blake* to indicate that that was the *ratio decidendi,* which was indeed afterwards explained in *Daintree* v *Butcher and Fasulo.*

Secondly, he says, there is sufficient acknowledgement if the attesting witnesses had an opportunity to see the will or the signature or both if they had wished to do so. Opportunity to see, says Mr Craig, does not mean physical opportunity: it means that they could have seen if they expressed a desire to see. If that were so, it seems to me that *Blake* v *Blake* could not have been decided in the way it was. The attesting witnesses could have asked the testatrix to remove the blotting paper, just as in the present case

Mr Block or Mr Leigh could have asked the testator to remove the paper from his pocket and show it to them, or at least show them his signature.

There is however, one final argument. Having submitted originally that there was a sufficient acknowledgement to satisfy the statute in what happened in the lounge, when admittedly both attesting witnesses were present, Mr Craig puts his argument alternatively in this way. He says that what happened was all part of one *res gestae* – there was no break in the continuity of the transaction. Both attesting witnesses had an opportunity of seeing the signature at the time they signed the will, which was within a matter of seconds of each other and within a matter of seconds of being asked to witness it. On that argument the acknowledgement started in the lounge but ended in the dining room. Now, it seems to me that there is one fatal flaw in that argument; namely, that if the acknowledgement was not completed until the dining room then there was no completed acknowledgement in the presence of both attesting witnesses being present at the same time.

In the end, therefore, although I would gladly accede to the arguments for the plaintiffs if I could consistently with my judicial duty, in my view there was no acknowledgement or signature by the testator in the presence of two or more witnesses present at the same time; and I am bound to pronounce against this will.'

Hale, Sarah, In b [1915] 2 IR 362 (Madden J)

Privileged will – effect of order to sail

Fact

The deceased was employed by a steamship company as a typist on board the *Lusitania*. She travelled from Liverpool to New York and between voyages worked in the company's officers in Liverpool. The deceased's testamentary wishes were contained in three unattested letters written from her lodgings in Liverpool when she was in contemplation of sailing. She was afterwards lost in the sinking of the *Lusitania*.

Held

Every person employed in any branch of the Royal Navy or Merchant Service, from the highest to the lowest, is included, when at sea, and the deceased was 'at sea' within the meaning of the section when she wrote the letters, so she was within the provisions of s11.

Madden J decided three things in this case: (1) That s11 of the Wills Act was not confined to actual seamen but extended to all persons employed in the Royal Navy or Merchant Navy. On this it appears that a yachtsman on a race on the high seas would be entitled to the privilege. (2) That the section extends to women. (3) That a person who is not actually at sea may be a seaman.

In coming to his decision Madden J applied the cases concerning actual military service by analogy. Applying the words of Sir F H Jeune in *In b Hiscock* [1901] P 78 who held a volunteer who went into a barracks for a medical test and made his will there was entitled to the privilege because he satisfied the test 'Had he taken some step at the time when he made the will to bring himself within the words of the section?' Madden J said in the same sense Sarah Hale had taken steps towards being 'at sea'.

Hornby, In b [1946] P 171 Probate Division (Wallington J)

Wills (Amendment) Act 1852 – position of signature

Facts

The deceased ruled an oblong box on the right hand side of the sheet on which his will was written out. Some of the dispositive words appeared above and some below the box. The will was written in the same ink the whole way down the sheet, but the signature of the testator in the box and the signatures of the attesting witnesses were in a different ink but themselves in the same ink. It was found as a fact that the oblong space was deliberately ruled out at the time of writing out the will with the intention that the testator's signature could be placed in it.

Held

The intention shown in advance to sign the will in the box reserved for it indicated that the signature was to apply to the whole will and not just those words above the signature. The signature therefore 'made it apparent on the face of the will that the testator intended to give effect' by it 'to the writing signed as his will' within s1 of the Wills Act (Amendment Act) 1852. The words 'and the enumeration of the above circumstances shall not restrict the generality of the above enactment' gave the court power to consider the signature, whatever its position, and to decide if the testator's intention was to give effect to the document by it.

Wallington J:

> '... what was the object of the deceased in apparently reserving the oblong space on the right-hand side of the sheet and higher up on it than some of the words of the document. As was said in argument, it is possible to enter into a bewildering variety of speculations as to how this came about, and I do not think that it would serve any useful purpose to do so. The outstanding facts are that the deceased has written the whole of the words of the will in his own handwriting, quite plainly, and in an ink nearer to green than to any other colour, for it is not a very good green and that inside the oblong space he has written, in the same ink and apparently at the same time, the word "Signed". It is plain to my mind that he must have had some serious motive in drawing the oblong space. The words written on the left-hand side of it are "equally between my sister Sarah Goulden her two daughters Lillain and Connie Gouldon and to my sister". There follow on, at a level lower than the lower line of the oblong space, "Annie this latter request being" and so on. Thus the words of the document run straight on, as if they had been prepared at the same time, written at the same time and intended to be signed at the same time. It cannot have been, therefore, that the testator thought, after writing out the whole document, that that would be a convenient and prominent place at which to append his signature: it looks to me as if it must have been thought of by him before he had finished writing the document, and that he intended to sign it as his will in that oblong space which he had prepared beforehand.
>
> The next facts of importance are that in a different ink, either at a different time or in a different room, the deceased has written his name as his signature in that oblong space, and that the two witnesses, in the same ink, at the foot of the paper, have written their names as witnesses, one of them specifying the branch of the bank at which presumably he worked. If intention to sign the will in that place has any significance for the purposes of s1 of the amending Act of 1852, I find that there is no doubt that Henry Hornby intended that signature sufficiently to authenticate the whole of the document written on that side of the sheet of paper ...
>
> It is for the these reasons that I must regard this signature as being, in the intention of the testator, at the end of the will. I have no doubt that when he made this document he prepared that space because he thought that it would be more convenient to have his signature in that position or that the end of the will might very likely be must there or that the sheet would be full so that at the end of the will would come in the space where the signatures would be. In my opinion, he so signed it with the intention of making it apparent on the face of the will that he intended to give effect by the signature to the writing signed as his will. For these reasons I come to the conclusion that the whole of this document is valid and properly executed testamentary document, and I admit it to probate.'

Jones (deceased), Re [1981] 1 Fam 7 Family Division (Arnold P)

Privileged will – soldier in actual military service

Facts

The deceased was killed by a terrorist gunman whilst on patrol in Northern Ireland in March 1978. Before he died he made a declaration to an officer and a warrant officer of his battalion in the following words: 'If I don't make it, make sure that Anne gets all my stuff'. Anne was his fiancée. The question arose whether the deceased was entitled to make a privileged will and this depended on whether he was in service at the time the will was made and whether this service was active and military in character. In nearly all the previous cases the privilege accorded by s11 had been exercised where there were hostilities between two sovereign governments.

Held

In order to decide whether the deceased was in actual military service it was necessary to look at the nature of the activities in which the deceased was involved rather than the nature of those against whom those activities were directed and in the circumstances engagement against a terrorist force could, and on the present facts did, amount to actual military service.

Arnold P:

> '... there have been other cases in which either there has been an absence of what could ordinarily be referred to as a war, or the state of the facts has not been spelled out sufficiently to enable one to form any real conclusion on that matter and it is really to those cases which one must look for guidance in the circumstances of the present case.
>
> ... there is the nearest of all cases to the present in an Australian decision, In the Will of Anderson (1958) 75 NW (NSW) 334. That concerned the death in action of a soldier in the Australian contingent made available for the assistance of the government of the Federation of Malaya to suppress what is described in the report as "armed and organised aggression and violence against the Government and the people of Malaya designed to overthrow the Government by force". This was the terrorist activity which prevailed in or about the year 1956, when the deceased was killed; and the very question which arises in this case, how far what is conventionally called and regarded as a state of war is necessary to the exercise of the jurisdiction, was considered by the judge, albeit on an unopposed application supporting the nuncupative will. Myers J said (at 335):
>
>> "In the present case there was no state of war and it is difficult to see how there could have been, for there was no nation or state with which a state of war could have been proclaimed to exist, but in all other respects there was no difference between the situation of a member of this force and that of a member of any military force in time of war. In my opinion the deceased was in actual military service and it would be unreasonable to hold otherwise."
>
> That decision is valuable persuasive authority which in my judgment is not distinguishable in any material particular from that which I have to decide.
>
> When the deceased in the present case was ordered to out on patrol, the fatal patrol, he was obliged by the conditions of his service in accordance with the discipline which prevailed in his military unit, so to do. That the service was military, that the service was active, seems to me to be beyond contest. The fact that the enemy was not a uniformed force engaged in regular warfare, or even an insurgent force organised on conventional military lines, but rather a conjuration of clandestine assassins and arsonists, cannot in my judgment affect any of those questions and I have no hesitation in pronouncing for this will. It is not the state of the opponent, or the character of the opponent's operations, in my judgment, which affect the answers to the questions which arise. They must be answered by reference to the activities of the deceased and those with whom he is associated; and it is nihil ad rem in relation to the answers to the questions whether there is a service, whether it is active and whether it is military that the context in which it occurs is that of foreign expenditure, foreign invasion, or local insurrection.'

Kecskemeti* v *Rubens Rabin & Co (1992) The Times 31 December Queen's Bench Division (Macpherson of Cluny J)

Duty of care owed by solicitor – to beneficiary named in will – in respect of advice given to testator

Facts

Mr Stanley Rubens of Rubens Rabin & Co, together with another solicitor from another firm, the latter never being the testator's legal adviser, were executors of the deceased's 1981 will. The beneficiaries were the testator's second wife Eva and his son by his first wife, the plaintiff. The argument centred around two properties and their proceeds of sale in relation to the estate.

Evidently it had been the intention of the testator that when the disputed properties were sold the plaintiff should receive half of the proceeds of the sale. Despite this intention, when the will was made these properties were held as joint tenancies by the testator and his second wife. Accordingly when the testator died the whole interest in both of the properties passed on to the second wife Eva by way of survivorship. The 1981 will had been made revoking an earlier will made in 1974.

The question was whether the law firm of Rubens Rabin & Co owed a duty of care to the plaintiff in respect of advice given to the testator when he made his new will.

Held

The judge, Mr Justice Macpherson, said that the question was whether the defendants owed a duty of care to the plaintiff which could give rise to liability in negligence without there being any reliance by him upon the solicitor or his advice.

In the absence of any overruling or overtaking by other authorities, the law was that set out in the case of *Ross* v *Caunters* [1980] Chancery 207. This decision had been criticised. The issue was whether the decision of the House of Lords in *Murphy* v *Brentwood District Council* [1991] AC 398 had affected *Ross* v *Caunters*. The defendants argued that the decision of Mr Justice Turner in *White and Another* v *Jones and Another* (unreported 18 October 1990) should be followed insofar as this decision, together with that of *Murphy*, had overtaken that of *Ross* v *Caunters*. In effect they argued that *Ross* v *Caunters* was not good law and that his Lordship should depart from it.

Mr Justice Macpherson did not accept these arguments. He noted that *Murphy* had overruled *Dutton* v *Bognor Regis Urban District Council* [1972] 1 QB 373 and had departed from *Anns* v *Merton London Borough Council* [1978] AC 728. His Lordship also referred to *Punjab National Bank* v *De Boinville and Others* [1992] 1 Lloyd's Rep 7 and *Caparo Industries plc* v *Dickman* [1990] AC 605. He stated that the law of negligence was incremental as was clear from *Dorset Yacht Company Ltd* v *The Home Office* [1970] AC 1004. Mr Justice Macpherson did not consider that the House of Lords intended in *Murphy* to do more than stamp out the type of case illustrated by *Dutton* of which there had been several. Otherwise, he noted, why did Lord Oliver refer to *Ross* v *Caunters* without any evident disapproval? The same was true in *Punjab National Bank* v *De Boinville*.

In the present circumstances there was a classic example of a situation where the relationship was proximate and where it was fair, just and reasonable that the law should impose a duty of a given scope upon the one party for the benefit of the other.

His Lordship was referred to a passage in Rupert M Jackson and John L Powell's *Professional Negligence* (3rd ed (1992) pp317-326). When examining the relevant jurisprudence, including the decision of Mr Justice Turner in *White* v *Jones* (above), in spite of recent developments the authors concluded that '*Ross* v *Caunters* is probably good law'. His Lordship agreed with this expression of opinion which was referred to by the plaintiffs.

While the decision of Mr Justice Turner in *White* was currently subject to appeal, in the view of his

Lordship there were important factual differences between that case and this one. The great factual differences between the position of the plaintiff in *Ross* v *Caunters* from that of the plaintiffs in *White* was the reason for Mr Justice Turner's decision and not, in his Lordship's judgment, a wholesale rejection of the decision in *Ross* v *Caunters*.

His Lordship did not accept the broad assertion by the defendant that if there was a duty in this case, then such a duty must be owed generally to beneficiaries whatever the circumstances and however far in the future they may be identifiable. *Ross* v *Caunters* defined a limited area within which a solicitor might be liable to persons who were not his clients. Indeterminate classes of potential beneficiaries had to be individually considered.

Accordingly, in the circumstances of this case the defendants did owe a duty of care to the plaintiff when advising the testator in 1981.

Knibbs, In the Estate of [1962] 1 WLR 852 Court of Probate (Wrangham J)

Privileged will – need for deliberate intention

Facts

The deceased, a barman in an ocean liner, and therefore a mariner at sea within s11 of the Wills Act 1837, had given to his employers the name of his sister, Iris, as his next-of-kin. One evening in a discussion with the head barman concerning family affairs, the deceased said: 'If anything ever happens to me, Iris will get anything I have got.' The deceased died in hospital in March 1961. Iris brought an action in which she propounded these words as a privileged will within s11 of the Wills Act 1837.

Held

The deceased was entitled to the privilege under s11 of the Wills Act at the time he spoke the words since he was then a mariner at sea. However, the words did not amount to a privileged will because there must be a statement by the deceased of his wishes for the disposition of his property after his death which is not imparted to his audience as a matter of information or interest, but is intended by him to convey a request, explicit or implicit, to see that his wishes are acted upon.

Wrangham J:

> '... there is no question that words just as informal as the words used in this case are capable of being admitted to probate; no special formality is required. The question is whether these words, which I find to have been used substantially as Wills (the head barman) told me, constituted a testamentary act on the part of the deceased. The fundamental principle applicable to this question is contained in a speech of Lord Selborne LC in *Whyte* v *Pollock* (1882) 7 App Cas 400, 405 HL, in which he said:
>
> > "In the first place, I lay it down that it is, in my judgment, a proposition universally true that nothing can receive probate which is not intended to be a testamentary act by the testator".
>
> A testamentary act does not have to be a document or act of any sort attended by any particular formalities. Indeed, an act may be testamentary in this sense even though the speaker did not know that he was making a will, or even that he was capable of making a will at the time when he uttered the words in issue. That has been the law ever since *Re Stable decd* [1919] P 7 and it is further laid down by Lord Sterndale MR in *In the Estate of Beech, decd* [1923] P 46, 57, 60. Although, however, a testamentary act may be one not recognised by the testator to be an actual will, it must be an act which is intended to operate so far as possible as a disposition of his property after his death. As Salter J said in *Beech's* case:
>
> > "I think that, in order to constitute a will the words used by a testator must be intended by him, at or after the time he uses them, to be preserved or remembered so as to form the guide to those who survive in carrying out his wishes."

In other words, in order to be a testamentary act there must be a statement of the deceased's wishes for the disposition of his property after his death which is not merely imparted to his audience as a matter of information or interest, but is intended by him to convey to that audience a request, explicit or implicit, to see that his wishes are acted upon.

I take two extreme cases to illustrate my meaning. A man telephoned to his solicitor (under the conditions under which the privilege would be applicable) telling him what dispositions of property he intended to operate after his death, and asking him to do what was required, would clearly be performing a testamentary act because he would not only be stating what his intentions were, but stating them in circumstances which showed that he wished his intentions to be carried out as a result of what he was then saying. On the other hand, if a man said to a friend of his:

> "Well my intention is to cut out my wife and family altogether from my will and leave everything to my mistress but don't you say a word to anybody about what I have told you."

such a conversation could not possibly be a testamentary act, because although it reveals clearly the intentions of the deceased, it does so in such circumstances that the person hearing them could not be expected, and was indeed, forbidden, to take any step to see they were put into effect. So also where a person has indicated what his intentions for the disposition of his property were, but only by way of summarising an existing will, as in *Beech's* case, or by way of explanation why he was not making a will at all, and in *In the Estate of Donner* (1917) 34 TLR 138 it has been held that the expression of his intentions did not constitute a testamentary act.'

Lay, In b (1840) 2 Curt 375

Privileged will – seaman ashore at a port in the middle of a voyage

Facts

The deceased belonged to a Royal Navy ship. While the ship was in harbour in Buenos Aires he obtained leave to go on shore and there he met with a severe fall from which he died five days later. Immediately after the accident the deceased wrote out his will on a watch-bill and it was certified by officers on board the ship but unattested.

Held

The will was privileged; the deceased was a seaman at sea although he had leave to go ashore and was not actually on board the ship at the time.

Layzell v *Smith Morton & Long* [1992] 13 EG 118 Queen's Bench Division (Schiemann J)

Negligent advice of solicitors – succession rights to agricultural holdings

Facts

The plaintiff's father had held an agricultural yearly tenancy of a farm with some 164 acres in Essex until the date of his death. The plaintiff and the deceased had managed the farm through a partnership but, because the farm required drainage, it was not a very profitable concern. In the absence of sufficient capital the plaintiff entered into an agreement with an uncle and a neighbour whereby contractual services were provided for the farm in return for certain financial payments. The deceased died on 17 August 1986, and on 26 September 1986 the landlord gave notice to quit the holding. The plaintiff's solicitors, the defendants, had failed to claim a right of succession for the plaintiff pursuant to s39 of the Agricultural Holdings Act 1986.

In this case the defendants acknowledged that this failure to claim rights of succession was negligent and constituted a breach of contract. The court therefore considered the following questions:

1. What were the prospects for the plaintiff succeeding his father as a tenant of the farm?
2. What compensation should he receive for the loss of those prospects?

The defendants argued that the plaintiff did not satisfy condition (a) in s36(3) of the 1986 Act. This provides for the eligible period throughout which an applicant must show that his only or principal source of livelihood was derived from agricultural work on the holding. In addition the plaintiff was not a suitable person.

Held

Although the contractual services provided under the agreement with his uncle were at below market value, condition (a) in s36(3) of the Act was satisfied because the plaintiff's only or principal source of livelihood came from the farm during the material time.

There was no reason to suppose that there was a significant chance that the Agricultural Land Tribunal would have concluded that the plaintiff was not eligible to succeed. The evidence of unsuitability would have been regarded as trivial by the Agricultural Land Tribunal and there was no reason to suppose that there would have been a significant chance that the Tribunal would have concluded that the plaintiff was not suitable.

The fairest way to compensate the plaintiff for his loss and to put him in a position to retrieve his loss was through a sale and lease back approach to the assessment of damages. A calculation based on the initial capital required to acquire the freehold of a similar farm and the value to sell the freehold and then to enter a tenancy agreement similar to the one that he had lost were used as a measure of damages.

Little, In the Estate of [1960] 1 WLR 495 Court of Probate (Sachs J)

Wills Acts 1837 and 1852 – effect of unattached papers

Facts

The testator in the course of signing and attesting his will placed a number of unattached sheets of paper on the table with the reverse of the back sheet on the top. He wrote his own name some eight inches down the page and had the attesting witnesses sign beneath. On the testator's death the will was found stapled together in the order in which he had sent the draft will to his solicitor, prior to attestation, for approval.

Held

Even if there were no mechanical attachment of the separate sheets of the will at the time of execution the pressing of the sheets together by the testator constituted a sufficient nexus to make all the sheets a single testamentary document.

Sachs J:

> 'Next I mention that there was clear evidence, wholly undisputed, that, during the period of signing, the five sheets were pressed together on the table by the deceased. In my view, even though there was no mechanical attachment between those sheets, such a pressing provides a sufficient nexus between all five of them for the purpose of establishing that there was a single testamentary document. In that belief I follow the lead given in *Lewis* v *Lewis* [1908] P 1, where it was stated that two pieces of paper being held together for the moment by the testator's finger and thumb was a sufficient nexus.
>
> I should also mention, of course, that Mr Elphinstone in his helpful argument referred to the careful judgment of Hanna J in *In the Goods of Tiernan, decd* [1942] IR 572. There, at the end of a close consideration of the English authorities, Hanna J stated that, in his opinion, they established

> "that if a will be written on several separate and disconnected sheets of paper and the last only be attested, although no part of the will may have been seen by the witnesses, it should be admitted to probate on the presumption that the whole will was in the room and under the control of the testator at the time of execution".

All I need say is that on the facts of the case before me there is no need for the plaintiff to rely on the wider presumption stated by Hanna J and I do not need to have to consider it here ...'

Lynne* v *Gordon Doctors and Walton (1991) 135 SJ 29 Queen's Bench Division (Phillips J)

Alleged negligence of solicitor – deceased mortgagee – failure to obtain appropriate life assurance

Facts
The circumstances involved a straightforward transaction of a mortgage loan supported by life assurance. A Mr Dryan raised a loan of £155,000 on the security of his home in November 1987. It was a term of the mortgage offer that there should be in place a policy of assurance on Mr Dryan's life for a term of 13 years and for a sum of at least equal to the amount of the loan. When Mr Dryan died in October 1988 it was discovered that no such policy had been taken out. It was argued that the defendant's solicitors, who had acted for both Mr Dryan and the lending bank in respect of the mortgage, were at fault. When proceedings were commenced on behalf of Mr Dryan's estate, alleging breach of contract or tortious negligence, the defendants argued that the estate could enforce only such claims as it had inherited from Mr Dryan. Since he would have had no claim during his lifetime he had suffered no loss. As a preliminary issue the point was taken before Judge Phillips.

Held
The failure by a professional adviser to ensure that a term policy is taken out on a client's life in fact means that the client is richer rather than poorer since he has no life assurance premium to pay. Further, the client could not be said to be deprived of the value which the policy would have had it been taken out; while the client still lives he can remedy the position by himself taking out a policy and, even if the premiums were then higher, this amount would be offset by those which had not been paid. As a result the deceased client could not be regarded as having suffered any loss as a result of the solicitor's negligence.

McMurdo, In b (1868) LR 1 P & D 540 (Sir James Wilde P)

Privileged will – mariner or sailor 'being at sea' – harbour mooring

Facts
The deceased, a mariner, on board a gunboat permanently stationed in Portsmouth Harbour executed an unattested will at the time he was on board the ship.

Held
Even though he had no present intention of sailing he was within the description of sailor or mariner 'being at sea'.

Sir James Wilde said he could find no distinction between a case such as *In b Lay* where a ship was lying in harbour in Buenos Aires and the present where the ship was lying in harbour in Portsmouth. Further, in both cases the seamen were subject to the restraints of the service, ie the Royal Navy, and might have no opportunity of making a will with the usual formalities if taken ill on board when no lawyer was available.

Newland, In the Goods of [1952] P 71 Court of Probate (Havers J)

Privileged will – mariner or seaman being at sea

Facts

The deceased was an apprentice in the merchant navy. On 25 July 1944, while on leave in England from his ship, he wrote out a testamentary document, and shortly afterwards he joined his ship, which sailed on 1 August 1944. The document was properly executed under s9 but at the time the deceased was only 16 years old. The question therefore arose whether the document could be regarded as a privileged will and if at the time it was executed he was a 'seaman being at sea' within the meaning of s11.

Held

The document was executed in contemplation of a fresh voyage and as the deceased was under orders to join his ship he was a 'seaman being at sea' when he made his will.

Havers J stated the facts and, after reading ss7 and 11 of the Wills Act 1837, continued:

> 'It will be observed that the language of section 11 differs according to whether it is referring to a soldier or to a mariner or seaman. As regards the soldier, the condition is that he must be in actual military service. As regards a mariner or seaman, the requirement is being at sea.
>
> It was always recognised by the courts that if a person came within the definition of section 11 and was therefore entitled to make a privileged will, he was entitled to do it although he was not of the age of 21 years. That was recognised and approved by section 1 of the Wills (Soldiers and Sailors) Act 1918.'

His Lordship read the section and continued:

> 'The applicant, therefore, had to satisfy me that at the date when the deceased made his will he was a seaman at sea within the meaning of section 11 of the Wills Act 1837.'

His Lordship then read s2 of the Act of 1918.

> 'It is to be observed, however, that that section only applies to any member of His Majesty's naval or marine forces and in my view does not apply to persons who are seamen in the merchant navy.
>
> In considering the true construction of these words "at sea", it will be observed that the words contained in section 11 are "seaman being at sea" not "on the sea". It is clear from the authorities which have been cited to me that the court has put a liberal interpretation on these words. For instance, it seems to me to be clearly established by authority that a seaman who is ashore on leave at a port during the course of a voyage and, while ashore on such leave, makes a will is a seaman "at sea".
>
> I have examined the various authorities which have been cited to me to see whether I could extract from them some general principle which was of universal application, but I have been unable to find any such principle. Perhaps that is not suprising in view of the variety of circumstances which may arise and, of course, the court, certainly a court of first instance, is not concerned so much to lay down any general principle; its function is to determine the true position on the particular facts of the case with which it has to deal. Accordingly, on examination of the authorities, it appears that at times the court has stressed a particular factor or a number of factors and at other times emphasis has been laid upon a different factor, or series of factors. In one case the fact that the voyage had begun appeared to have been the decisive factor, and the voyage was deemed to have begun although the ship was in the river preparatory to sailing. In another case a mate on board a ship that was stationed permanently in Portsmouth Harbour was held to be a seaman "at sea". In yet another case a man who was attached to a ship but did not go on

board that ship or any other ship, but remained ashore when he wrote out the document, was held not to be "at sea". It appears from the judgment that the court might possibly have decided the case the other way if he had been at sea at any period before he wrote out the document. In another case the decision appears to have been based on these facts, namely, that the deceased, though on shore at the time of the writing of the document, was under orders to sail and the documents were written in contemplation of sailing; or, putting it in other words, that the particular person was preparing for a voyage. Consequently one finds, on examining the authorities, that some cases have been held to fall on one side of the line and others on the other side of the line.'

Paterson, In b (1898) 79 LT 123 (Gorell Barnes J)

Privileged will – sailor waiting to sail

Facts
The deceased, on a gunboat in the Thames which was waiting to sail, wrote a letter containing testamentary dispositions. The letter was unattested.

Held
The voyage had begun for the purpose of constituting the document the will of a seaman at sea though in fact the ship was actually lying in a river preparatory to sailing.

Rapley's Estate, Re [1983] 1 WLR 1069 Chancery Division (Judge Finlay QC)

Privileged will – mariner or seaman being at sea

Facts
In 1960 the deceased executed a document, witnessed by one witness, which purported to dispose of all his property to his mother in the event of his death. At the time the document was executed the deceased was aged 19, and, therefore, a minor in law and had recently been apprenticed to a shipping company. The document was executed in England while the deceased was on leave and awaiting orders to join the crew of a ship for a voyage. The deceased died in 1980 because a ship on which he was serving was lost in a typhoon in the Pacific Ocean. The issue was whether the document made in 1960 was a valid privileged will.

Held
Judge Finlay reviewed the earlier authorities and concluded that it was not because it had been made on land at a time when the deceased had no orders to go to sea but was merely awaiting such orders. In conclusion he said:

> 'I find that none of the authorities which have been cited to me goes so far as to decide that when one who is a mariner or seaman by calling and employment makes a will when on shore on leave and is not at that time a member of the complement of a particular ship and has not at that time been posted to a ship, he is yet to be treated as being at sea. To extend the meaning of s11 to such a case would appear to me to result in according no significance to the words "at sea" in the section, because it would make the section applicable to anyone who at the relevant time was a mariner or seaman, since any mariner or seaman must always be in contemplation of another voyage until in fact he gives up the sea, retires from the marine service and so ceases at that point to be a mariner or seaman.
>
> The cases have gone very far to extend the meaning of "at sea" to include those who are in a state of preparation for going to sea, being under orders to do so, but to go beyond that and to extend the ambit

> of the section to cover the case where a mariner or seaman is on furlough or leave, knows well that he may at any time be instructed to join another ship but has not at the moment received such instructions is, I think, to extend the operation of the section beyond the circumstances which were no doubt in the contemplation of the legislature when this provision was originally enacted and when it was re-enacted in 1837. The ground and justification for this privilege is no doubt the circumstance that those who are at sea are both without the advantage of legal assistance and also the justification for the privilege is no doubt the danger of the calling and the fact that to those who follow the danger of the calling and the fact that to those who follow the sea death is an always present likelihood and not the remote certainty which it is for others.'

Singleton* v *Tomlinson (1878) 1 App Cas 404 House of Lords (Lord Cairns LC, Lord Hatherley, Lord Blackburn and Lord Gordon)

Incorporation by reference – need for document to be in existence

Facts

A testator's will began 'I direct my executors to pay the expenses of my funeral and all my lawful debts, out of the proceeds of my property'. It then went on 'whereas I am possessed of landed and chattel property, as stated in the annexed schedule, I direct my executors to sell my landed property ... for its full value' (four pieces of landed property were named). A fifth landed property was specifically devised. The will was written on three sides of a sheet of paper, with the signature and attestation at the bottom of the third side and the schedule was on the fourth side. The schedule was in the testator's handwriting and signed by him and bore the same date as the will. It referred to the four pieces of landed estate named in the will in detail. A question arose as to the precise identification of the landed estate in the will itself and whether the descriptions in the schedule should be admitted to probate to aid in construction of the will. The witnesses to the will had not seen the schedule when they attested it.

Held

As the schedule had not been proved to have been written at the time of the execution of the will, it could not be incorporated into the will and therefore it could not be referred to for the purpose of assisting in construction.

Lord Cairns LC:

> 'The question which arose in the court below was whether in construing the will and in determining what the meaning of the testator was this schedule could be looked at, and, my Lords, on that point it will be sufficient if I refer to two propositions which were laid down, and which indeed were not challenged by any of the counsel at your Lordship's Bar. It was said that there are certain cases in which, although a document is not admitted to probate, still it may be referred to in a will in such a way as that you are entitled to look at the document, because it is virtually incorporated in that which is admitted to probate; and the two propositions which were laid down as the tests of the case in which a document under those circumstances could be looked at were these: first, that it must be clearly indentified by the description given of it in the will; and, secondly, that it must be shown to have been in existence at the time when the will was executed.
>
> With regard to the first of these propositions, no controversy I think was raised, but the schedule to which I have referred was taken as identified with the schedule spoken of in the will, but with regard to the second, those who object to the schedule being looked at say the is no sufficient evidence to prove that this schedule was in existence at the time when the will was executed ... My Lords, it appears to me that this is one of the cases in which the onus is clearly thrown on those who contend for the incorporation of the particular document to prove, by parol extrinsic evidence, that the document was in existence at the date

of the will. Here they prove nothing of the kind, for the witnesses who were present at, and attested, the execution of the will, have no recollection of seeing the schedule and cannot given any explanation in regard to it. The words used in the will would, as I have said, be as well satisfied by a schedule annexed to the will after it was executed as by a schedule in existence at the time the will was executed. Therefore I feel myself obliged to come to the conclusion that there is not here that evidence, that the schedule was in existence at the time the will was executed, which is necessary in order to entitle us to look at it.'

Smith v *Claremont Haynes & Co* (1991) The Times 3 September Queen's Bench Division (Deputy Judge Barnett)

Alleged negligence of solicitor – failure to take instructions

Facts
In this case a client wished to alter her will in favour of two specific relatives. She made her solicitor aware of her wishes. Despite knowing that the client was seriously ill the solicitor delayed several weeks before making an appointment to visit her, by which time the client was too ill to give instructions. The two intended beneficiaries commenced proceedings in a claim for negligence against the solicitor's firm.

Held
Deputy Judge Barnett followed, and indeed extended, the controversial case of *Ross* v *Caunters* [1980] Ch 297 whereby solicitors were held liable for positive negligence in the execution of a will which rendered a bequest invalid.

Smith v *Smith* (1866) LR 1 P & D 239 Probate Division (Sir J P Wilde)

Wills Act 1837 s9 – attestation in the presence of witnesses

Facts
The attesting witness of a will saw the testatrix writing something on her will before they signed, but they did not see what she wrote, and they did not know that it was a will. When they subscribed their names they did not see the attestation clause, which contained the testatrix's signature, or any writing on the will, as the testatrix concealed it from them by holding a piece of blotting-paper over it. There was a full attestation clause in the testatrix's handwriting.

Held
As the witnesses had seen the testatrix write what was presumed to be her signature, although they did not see the signature, and she did not acknowledge it to them, the attestation was sufficient.

Sir J P Wilde:

> 'The presumption omnia rite esse acta is strong in a case like the present, and the Court ought to be very careful not to defeat the intention of the testatrix by setting aside the will, unless the evidence clearly rebuts that presumption.
>
> The conclusion of fact which I draw is, that what she then wrote was her name. The next question is, what did the witnesses see and attest? They both saw her write that which I am now satisfied was her name, but they did not see the name, and did not know that it was her name. The question is, whether that is a sufficient attestation? If the Court were to hold that it is not, it would invalidate a great many wills, because it must often happen that when a testator calls witnesses into a room to attest his will they stand at some distance from him, perhaps at the opposite side of a large table, and see his pen going but do not see what he is writing, and that they then write their names without seeing his signature in consequence

> of a piece of blotting paper being placed over it, or of their not being asked to look at it, and nothing occuring to direct their attention to it. I am, therefore, unwilling to hold that it is not sufficient for the attesting witnesses to have seen the fact of writing, which I am satisfied was the signature, take place, unless they also saw what that writing was; nor does the statute, in my opinion, require such a decision.'

Stanley, In the Estate of [1916] P 192 Probate Division (Bargrave Deane J)

Privileged will – person employed on a ship – nurse on hospital ship

Facts

The deceased, a nurse, employed under a contract by the War Office on hospital ships, wrote a letter giving the addressee full liberty to deal with her affairs and giving directions as to the disposal of her property. The letter was written during leave on shore in England but after the writer had received orders to re-embark.

Held

The letter, which was unattested, was privileged as a soldier's will within s11, and the person to whom it was addressed was executor according to tenor and entitled to probate of the document.

Streatley, In b [1891] P 172 Probate Division (Butt J)

Attestation – position of witnesses' signatures

Facts

The attesting witnesses to a will signed their names in the margin of the first and second pages of the will. On the first page one executor was named half-way down the margin and the witnesses had attested this as it was an alteration. The name occurred on the second page where the name of another executor had been altered. There was a full attestation clause at the end of the will and the testator had signed his name opposite it but the attesting witness had not signed there.

Held

Following *Roberts* v *Phillips* (1855) 4 E & B 450 the will was valid and the witnesses had subscribed it sufficiently. In that case Lord Campbell CJ considered this point in detail and said:

> 'Unassisted by authority, we are therefore called upon to put a construction for the first time on the words of the statute; and the question is one of the utmost importance, the new Wills Act, 7 W4 & 1 Vict c26 s9, enacting that the signature of the testator shall be made or acknowledged by him "in the presence of two or more witnesses present at the same time, and such witnesses shall attest and shall *subscribe* the will in the presence of the testator", without any further direction as to the place where the witnesses shall sign their names, although minute directions are given as to the locality of the signature of the testator by this Act, and by the amending Act, 15 & 16 Vict c24.
>
> On the part of the defendants it is powerfully urged that the primary meaning of the word "subscribe" is *written under;* that it must here mean *written under the concluding words of the will,* and the signature of the testator; that this meaning is emphatically to be given to the word "subscribed" in this section of the Statute of Frauds, from the words which require only *signing* by the testator; and that the signature of the names of the witnesses ought to be so affixed to the instrument as effectually to prevent any spurious addition to it after it had been executed. But we are bound to consider whether the Legislature did here use the word exclusively in its primary and strict sense, and whether this construction would not in many cases defeat the real object of the enactment, by nullifying wills which the Legislature intended to be valid ...

Many familiar instances might be given in which "subscribe" is used merely to denote a signing of the name without any reference to the part of the paper on which the name is written.

After satisfactory proof that witnesesses were called in by the testator to see him execute his will and to attest it, that they saw him execute it, and that they then signed the will with the intention of attesting it, ought we to hold that the will is void, on the ground that their signatures are not under his? If *subscribe* is taken in its strict primary sense, such a will is a nullity. But suppose that a will is written on a sheet of paper of four pages; that the will and the testator's signature entirely fill up the first three pages; and that the witnesses write their names at the top of the fourth page: is the will properly attested? The signatures of the witnesses are not under the testator's; and, literally speaking, they cannot be said to have *subscribed* the will. But was it meant by the legislature that a will so attested should be void? ...

If the Legislature in its wisdom should think that the signatures of the witnesses should be put upon the same footing with the signature of the testator, they ought to use express language to indicate this intention. The mere requisition that the will shall be *subscribed* by the witnesses, we think, is complied with, by the witnesses who saw it executed by the testator immediately signing their names on any part of it at his request, with the intention of attesting it. If the proposed change is to be introduced, we may be allowed respectfully to express a hope that it will be accomplished more felicitously than was the change as to the signature of the testator by stat 7 W 4 & 1 Vict c26, the decisions upon which nullified many sincere and seemingly well executed wills ...'

Sweetland* v *Sweetland (1865) 4 Sw & Tr 6 Court of Probate (Sir J P Wilde)

Wills Acts 1837 and 1852 – signature on several pages.

Facts

The deceased wrote out dispositions of his entire property on five sheets of paper each sheet being signed by the deceased and two witnesses. A sixth sheet contained an attestation clause and the signatures of two witnesses as well as the deceased's initials in pencil. The witnesses gave evidence that the deceased's signature was not on the sixth sheet when they signed it. The question arose whether the signature at the end of the fifth page could be treated as the execution thereof.

Held

The signatures on the other pages were merely for the purpose of authentication and not valid under s9.

Sir J P Wilde:

> 'The first difficulty is, quo animo, did the testator sign the fifth sheet? Ordinarily such a signature would be, I think, "intended to guard against other sheets being interpolated". So said Sir John Dodson in *Ewen* v *Franklin* (1855) Deane's Eccl Rep 7. Certainly no one would, on the face of the will, conclude that it was intended as the final signature by which the testator's affirmation of the will was to be signified ...'

University College of North Wales* v *Taylor [1908] P 140 Court of Appeal (Cozens-Hardy MR, Fletcher-Moulton and Farwell LJJ)

Incorporation by reference – need for will to acknowledge existence of document

Facts

A will contained a gift of £10,000 to the trustees for the time being of the University of Wales, and a trust to invest and apply the income of such investments

> 'in founding in it (the University) new scholarships and prizes in my name to be held upon such terms

> and conditions and subject to such rules and regulations as are contained and specified in any memorandum amongst my papers written or signed by me relating thereto'.

The question arose whether the document had been validly incorporated.

Held

The words in the will did not purport to refer to an existing document but seemed to have been chosen to express the intention of the testator at some future time or times to draw up one or more memoranda. It was necessary that the document should be referred to as in existence in order to be admitted to probate.

Weatherhill* v *Pearce (1994) The Times 7 November; (1994) The Independent 5 December Chancery Division (Judge Kolbert sitting as Deputy Judge)

Will – attestation – name of testator written by hand by testator – whether sufficient signature

Facts

The testatrix, Mrs Doris Weatherhill, carrying her will, called at the home of two elderly ladies who were retired civil servants in Truro. The will was headed 'The Will of ...' in Gothic printing and underneath in handwriting 'Mrs Doris Weatherhill' in capital letters. The word 'Dated' then appeared in printing and '10 June 1985'. The date was assumed to be correct and was not challenged in any event. The will was written in the testatrix's own handwriting and the attestation clause read 'signed by the said testator, Doris Weatherhill, in the presence of us present at the same time who ... having subscribed our names as witnesses'. Counsel for the plaintiff argued that the appearance of Doris Weatherhill's name in her own handwriting in the attestation clause was a signature for the purposes of s9 of the Wills Act 1837, as amended by s17 of the Administration of Justice Act 1982 and that this was clearly intended to give effect to the will.

Held

The presence of the testatrix's name did constitute a sufficient signature and all the evidence pointed to the fact that the testatrix intended to make the document her will. It was certain that the ladies had been asked to witness the will and there was no evidence to suggest that the three ladies were not all present together at some stage in order to do so. The court was satisfied that, in the light of the Court of Appeal's judgment in *Wood* v *Smith* [1993] Ch 90, it should endeavour to give effect to the testatrix's intentions which were perfectly clear in this case. It was sufficient acknowledgment of the testatrix's signature for her to proffer the document for the witnesses to sign. The will was validly executed. The presumption omne rite esse acte praesumuntur was applied. Also, the fact that the ladies were former civil servants '... and plainly conscientious and careful ladies with an eye for detail in the best tradition of the civil service ...' seemed significant in the finding.

Comment

Although this decision appears logical and unsurprising, it is helpful and enlightening in terms of understanding the formal requirements for making a will.

Webb, In b (1855) Dea & Sw 1

Attestation – timing of witnesses' signatures

Facts
The testatrix made and signed her will on 18 March. On the following 13 May she executed it by acknowledging her signature in the presence of A and B, both present at the same time; immediately after B left the room and during her absence but in the presence of the testatrix A subscribed the will as a witness, B returned to the room and then subscribed in the presence of the testatrix and A.

Held
Where the witnesses attesting subscribe the will in the presence of the testator but not in the presence of each other, the execution is good.

Welby and Another* v *Casswell (1994) The Times 1 April Queen's Bench Division (Mr Justice Popplewell)

Succession rights to agricultural holdings – income qualification for inheriting tenancy

Facts
An appeal was made by Sir Richard Bruno, Gregory Welby and D & S Farms Ltd by way of case stated of a decision of the Agricultural Land Tribunal (Eastern Area) on 21 March 1992 that Thomas Andrew Casswell had satisfied the principal source of livelihood test. This test is found in s36(3)(a) of the Agricultural Holdings Act 1986.

Held
The section under consideration related to the right of an eligible person to apply for a new tenancy on the death of a tenant. It was for the court to decide whether the tenant qualified by deriving his principal source of livelihood from his agricultural work on the holding.

To exercise the right to apply for a new tenancy on the death of the tenant of an agricultural holding, an otherwise eligible applicant had to derive his only and principal source of livelihood from his work on the holding and from no other source. It was immaterial that money from elsewhere might come into the farm account and be used for farming purposes.

Comment
The various elements required to fulfil this form of succession must be properly fulfilled by the applicant and/or their adviser. In view of the frequency of cases in this area, the case is noteworthy.

White* v *Jones [1995] 2 WLR 187 House of Lords (Lords Keith, Goff, Browne Wilkinson, Mustill and Nolan); [1993] 3 WLR 730 Court of Appeal (Sir Donald Nicholls VC, Farquharson and Steyn LJJ)

Duty of care – delay in carrying out instructions – whether the duty owed to beneficiary of will

Facts
Following a family argument a testator executed a will disinheriting the plaintiffs. The parties were then reconciled and the testator gave fresh instructions to the defendant solicitors to prepare wills bequeathing £9,000 to each of the plaintiffs. However, the solicitors delayed carrying out these new instructions and the testator died before an amended will was executed. The intended beneficiaries claimed in negligence against the solicitors. At first instance the plaintiffs' claim was dismissed on the basis that the defendants owed no duty of care to them, and that in any event the damage was too speculative and too uncertain in extent to be recoverable. The plaintiffs appealed.

Held

1. The solicitors were guilty of professional negligence by not preparing the new will.
2. It was reasonably foreseeable that the defendants' failure to prepare a will as instructed by their client would cause the intended beneficiaries financial loss which could not be recompensed by the payment of damages to the client's estate.
3. Although the defendants' paramount duty of care was to the testator, their client, and normally excluded any duties to third parties, the acceptance of instructions to prepare a will created a special relationship between the defendants and the plaintiffs in respect of which it was fair, just and reasonable that the defendants should be under a duty of care to the plaintiffs. Otherwise, there would be no sanction for the defendants' breach of duty.
4. The judge at first instance was entitled on the evidence to find that the defendants were clearly in breach of their professional duty and the damages claimed were not too speculative or uncertain in extent to be irrecoverable.
5. The judge's order would be set aside and judgment entered for the plaintiffs, with the damages awarded to them equal to the loss of potential benefit.

This case was dismissed on appeal to the House of Lords.

Wingham, Re [1949] P 187 Court of Appeal (Bucknill, Cohen and Denning LJJ)

Privileged will – soldier in actual military service

Facts

The deceased joined the RAF in February 1942 and was sent to train as a pilot at a camp in Canada in March 1943. While in Canada he wrote out a document which was described as his will but which was not attested. He died in an accident while training in 1943. The question arose whether the will was privileged and therefore exempt from the requirements of attestation.

Held

He was in actual military service when the document was made and therefore it was a privileged will, because he was liable at any time to be ordered to proceed to some area in order to take part in active warfare.

Denning LJ:

> 'The first case in which the scope of the privilege came under close review was the case of General Drummond in *Drummond* v *Parish* (1843) 3 Curt 522. General Drummond made a will in peacetime whilst serving in Woolwich Barracks but it was not witnessed. He was held not to be in "actual military service". This is the case which has given rise to all the trouble; for in it Sir Herbert Jenner Fust fell into an error. He thought that, because the idea of a soldier's privilege was taken from the Roman Law, therefore "in order to ascertain the extent and meaning of the exception, the civil law may fairly be resorted to". Successive courts of first instance have consequently felt themselves bound to ignore the words of the statute and to substitute for them this test: "Can the soldier be considered as having been so circumstanced that he would under Roman Law have been regarded as 'in expeditione'?" Sitting in this court I am free to say that the test should no longer be applied. The words of our statute are in plain English: "in actual military service". I find them easier to understand and to apply than the Latin: "in expeditione". If I were to inquire into the Roman law, I could perhaps after some research say how Roman Law would have dealt with its soldiers on Hadrian's Wall or in the camp at Chester, but I cannot say how it would have dealt with an airman in Saskatchewan, who is only a day's flying from the enemy. Nor can anyone else. This supposed throw-back to Roman Law has confused this branch of the law too

long. It is time to get back to the statute. I find myself in full agreement with what Lord Merrivale P said in the case of *In re Booth* [1926] P 118:

> "The proposition that the English law as to the solider's military testamentary privilege is identical with the privilege of the Roman legionary is an entirely erroneous proposition."

Rid of this Roman test, this court has to decide what is the proper test. It must be both simple and certain: simple, because it is to be understood by all ranks; certain, because every soldier must be able to apply it without difficulty in the situation in which he finds himself. It is quite beside the mark to enquire what are the reasons for the privilege. The privilege is one thing. The reasons for it are another. The reasons are, no doubt, that a soldier "in actual military service" is likely to be in danger and to be bereft of legal advice. It would be a great mistake, however, to argue therefrom that a soldier, who is not in danger, or who has legal advice at his elbow, cannot make a soldier's will. That would be to confound the reasons for the rule with the rule itself. The rule is that a soldier "in actual military service" is privileged to make a will without any formalities. The plain meaning of the statutes is that any soldier, sailor or airman is entitled to the privilege, if he is actually serving with the Armed Forces in connection with military operations which are of have been taking place or are believed to be imminent. It does not, of course, include officers on half-pay or men on the reserve, or the territorials, when not called up for service. They are not actually serving. Nor does it include members of the Forces serving in this country, or on routine garrison duty overseas, in time of peace, when millitary operations are not imminent. They are actually serving, but are not in actual "military" service, because no military operations are afoot. It does, however, include all our men serving – or called up for service – in the wars; and women too, for that matter. It includes not only those actively engaged with the enemy but all who are training to fight him. It also includes those members of the Forces who, under stress of war, both work at their jobs and man the defences, such as the Home Guard. It includes not only the fighting men but also those who serve in the Forces, doctors, nurses, chaplains, WRNS, ATS, and so forth. It includes them all, whether they are in the field or in barracks, in billets or sleeping at home. In includes them although they may be captured by the enemy or interned by neutrals. It includes them not only in time of war but also when war is imminent. After hostilities are ended, it may still include them, as, for instance, when they garrison the countries which we occupy, or when they are engaged in military operations overseas. In all these cases they are plainly "in actual military service". Doubtful cases may arise in peacetime when a soldier is in, or is about to be sent to, a disturbed area or an isolated post, where he may be involved in military operations. As to these cases, all I say is that, in case of doubt, the serving soldier should be given the benefit of the privilege. I do not stop to discuss all the cases in detail. I need only say that *In Re the Estate of Hill* (1845) 1 Rob Ecc 276 and *Bowles* v *Jackson* (1854) 1 Spinks Ecc & Ad 294 are inconsistent with many later cases: that *In the Estate of Gibson* [1942] P 118 is inconsistent with a later decision of Hodson J: and that *In the Estate of Anderson* [1944] P 1 must be read in the light of the House of Lords decision on the Home Guard. In my opinion, those four cases should no longer be regarded as of authority.

Applying the test I have mentioned, this airman was in "actual military service" and, therefore, I agree that this appeal should be allowed.'

Yates, In the Estate of [1919] P 93 Probate Division (Lord Coleridge J)

Privileged will – member of HM naval or marine forces

Facts

The deceased, a lieutenant in the Royal Navy, had served since the start of World War I. On 22 June 1916, while he was at home in Southsea, he was appointed to a ship stationed at the Cape and left home a few days later to join his ship. On that day, when leaving the railway station, he said to his son: 'Remember that if anything happens to me everything I possess, or am likely to possess, is to go to your mother.' He died in August 1918 in Cape Town. The question arose whether this was a privileged will under s2 of the Wills (Soldiers and Sailors) Act 1918 which came into effect in February 1918.

Held

The will was entitled to probate as a privileged will; s2 enlarged the qualification of a seaman under s11 of the Wills Act 1837. Further, s2 applied to a will made before the Wills (Soldiers and Sailors) Act 1918 was passed but where the testator died after the Act was passed.

3 Testamentary Capacity

Allen* v *McPherson (1847) 1 HLC 191 House of Lords (Lord Cottenham LC, Lords Lyndhurst, Brougham, Langdal and Campbell)

Wills – effect of fraudulent representation as to character

Facts

By his will and codicils the testator gave large bequests to the appellant but by a final codicil he revoked these and left him only a small weekly allowance during his life. The appellant alleged that the last codicil had been executed under the undue influence of the residuary legatee, Mrs Evans, and false representations as to the appellant's character and manner of life made by her to the testator so as to prejudice the testator against him. The Ecclesiastical Court granted probate to the will and the codicils and the appellant claimed that he had not been permitted to take objection to the final codicil in that court.

Held

On the question as to whether the Court of Chancery had any jurisdiction on the matter the House of Lords held that it had not (Lord Cottenham LC and Lord Langdale MR dissenting). However, on the matter of fraud affecting a will Lord Lyndhurst said:

> 'Would such a case (ie fraud), if established by evidence to the satisfaction of that tribunal, be a sufficient ground for refusing probate? Upon this point no doubt can, I think, be entertained. "If a testator be circumvented by fraud, the testament loseth its force" Swimb. part 1 sec 3 pla 32. There cannot be a stronger instance of fraud than a false representation respecting the character of an individual to a weak old man, for the purpose of inducing him to revoke a bequest made in favour of a person so caluminated. The case of *Grindhall* v *Grindhall* (1831) 4 Hagg 10, before Sir J Nicholl, was founded upon a charge of this description, and though the Court decided against the plaintiff, that decision proceeded on the failure of the plaintiff's proof, and not upon any doubt of the authority and duty of the Court, if the charge had been established, to refuse the probate. In the course of his judgment, Sir J Nicholl observed, that:
>
> > "The argument was that the testator's intention of excluding John Grindhall, and giving the property to Captain Sturt, was produced in the mind of the deceased by fraud and contrivance practised upon him ... I cannot",
>
> he said,
>
> > "for one moment, hesitate, after reading the evidence, in holding that the fraud is not proved (and where fraud is charged it must be proved); but on the contrary, I think the probability is most decidely and infinitely more strong on the other side, viz that the alteration in the deceased's intention was not produced by any fraudulent practice on the part of Captain Sturt; because it is quite clearly proved that the deceased did intend to exclude John Grindhall as early as the 7th November."
>
> We were furnished, by the kindness of Dr Lushington, during the argument with a reference to a similar case, *Butterfield* v *Scawen* decided in 1775. The question there was whether a will had been revoked in consequence of fraud and imposition practised on the testator. The fraud consisted of a false representation made to the testator, that the woman, who was the principle legatee, had attempted to poison him, and that in consequence of this representaion he had revoked the bequest in her favour. That learned judge

entertained no doubt as to the jurisdiction of the Ecclesiastical Court to refuse probate, and upon sufficient proof of the facts charged, that it would be its duty to do so. Sir H J Fust, who was also consulted, expressed himself thus:

> "If it should appear, as in the case stated by your Lordship, that an old and infirm testator who had bequeathed a legacy to AB, had been induced by false and fraudulent representations with reference to the conduct of AB, made to him for the purpose by CD to make a subsequent codicil revoking that bequest, and substituting for it a much smaller legacy, the effect of which would be to give a larger share of the residue to CD, than he otherwise would take, I conceive that the Ecclesiastical Court would not, under such circumstances, grant probate of such revoking codicil, providing it should be clearly established in point of evidence that such an act and intention were produced by such false and fraudulent representations."

I think therefore your Lordships will be of opinion that this is a case coming distinctly within the jurisdiction of the Ecclesiastical Court, and in which, if the charge were established, it would be the duty of that Court to refuse the probate. It did, in fact, come before that tribunal; the parties were heard, and probate was granted.

It is stated in the bill, "that the appellant was confined in the Prerogative Court to grounds of objection which affected the codicil as an entire instrument, and was not permitted to go into the case stated in the bill, or into any other case solely relating to the parts of the codicil which affected only the appellant." The grounds of this alleged decision of the Court are not stated; it may have proceeded from the manner in which the plaintiff shaped his case, from the form of the allegations, or from the nature of the evidence.

It is perfectly clear that the Ecclesiastical Court may admit a part of an instrument to probate, and refuse it as to the rest. There are numerous cases to this effect, as *Billinghurst* v *Vickers* (1810) 1 Phill 187, *Barton* v *Robins* (1769) 3 Phill 455.

It is in fact, the constant practice of the Court; but if an error has been committed in this or any other respect, which I am very far from supposing, that would not be a ground for coming to a Court of Equity. The matter should have been set right upon appeal. But the present is an attempt to review the decision of the Court of Probate, not by the Judicial Committee of the Privy Council, the proper tribunal for that purpose, but by the Court of Chancery.'

Banks* v *Goodfellow (1870) LR 5 QB 549 Court of Appeal (Cockburn CJ, Blackburn, Mellor and Hannen LJJ)

Testamentary capacity – the three conditions for capacity

Facts

A testator had made a will in 1863. In 1841 the testator had been confined as a lunatic as he had delusions that he was being molested by a man who was long since dead and was being pursued by evil spirits which he believed were visibly present. These delusions affected the testator both before and after the date of his will and up until his death in 1865. The evidence as to whether the testator was capable of making a will was long and contradictory. That being so the trial judge (Brett J) directed the jury to consider whether, at the time of making the will,

> 'the testator was capable of having such a knowledge and appreciation of the facts, and was so far master of his intentions, free from delusions, as would enable him to have a will of his own in the disposition of his property, and act upon it. The mere fact of his being able to recollect things, or to converse rationally on some subjects, or to manage some business is not sufficient to show that he was sane. On the other hands, slowness, feebleness and eccentricities, are not sufficient to show that he was insane.'

Held

1. The direction was for all practical purposes correct. Where a testator was suffering from delusions it was immaterial whether the delusions remained latent or not at the time he made the will provided

that he was competent, in all other respects, to make a will, for the delusions could not have any influence on his disposing of his property. The will was therefore valid and the appeal would be dismissed.

2. The requirements as to mental capacity to make a will were:
   (a) The testator's mind must be sound so as to be capable of forming testamentary intentions embodied in the will
   (b) The testator's memory must be sound to recall the several persons who ought to be considered as beneficiaries.
   (c) The testator's understanding must be sound to comprehend the various ties by blood or friendship and their claims on these or other grounds upon his testamentary conditions.

In the circumstances the testator satisfied all three conditions.

Cockburn CJ:

> 'The question whether partial unsoundness, not affecting the general faculties, and not operating on the mind of a testator in regard to the particular testamentary disposition, will be sufficient to deprive a person of the power of disposing of his property, presents itself here for judicial decision, so far as we are aware, for the first time. It is true that, in the case of *Waring* v *Waring* (1848) 6 Moo PC 341, the Judicial Committee of the Privy Council, and in the more recent case of *Smith* v *Tebbitt* (1867) Law Rep 1 P & M 398, Lord Penzance in the Court of Probate, have laid down a doctrine, according to which any degree of mental unsoundness, however slight, and however unconnected with the testamentary disposition in question, must be held fatal to the capacity of a testator. But in both these cases, as we shall presently show, the wide doctrine embraced in the judgment was wholly unnecessary to the decision, and we therefore feel outselves warranted, and indeed bound, to consider the question as one not concluded by authority, and on which we are called upon to form our own judgment. The question is one of equal importance and difficulty, and we have given it our best consideration.
>
> The textwriters throw no light upon the point. They content themselves with stating in general terms that to be capable of making a will a man must be of sound disposing mind and memory, and that person *non compotes* cannot make a will; but they are silent as to the degree of mental disturbance which will amount to a want of disposing mind and memory. The cases prior to *Waring* v *Waring*, in which the law on the subject of mental unsoundness, as affecting the capability to make a will, has come into question, are by no means numerous. It may be as well to pass them in review.
>
> In *Combe's Case* (1512) Moore 759 it is said to have been agreed by the judges,
>
> > "that sane memory for the making of a will is not always where the party can in some things answer with sense, but he ought to have judgment to discern and to be of perfect memory, otherwise the will is void".
>
> So again, in the *Marquis of Winchester's Case* 6 Rep 23,
>
> > "By the law, it is not sufficient that the testator be of memory, when he makes the will, to answer familiar and usual questions, but he ought to have a disposing memory, so as to be able to make a disposition of his estate with understanding and reason".
>
> In the case of *Greenwood* v *Greenwood* (1840) 3 Curt App XXX, an action brought to recover estates under a will, the validity of which was disputed, the principal indication of insanity relied on being a strange aversion on the part of the testator towards his only brother, his heir at law, and a groundless suspicion of the latter having attempted to poison him. Lord Kenyon, in charging his jury, said:
>
> > "I take it a mind and memory competent to dispose of property, when it is a little explained, perhaps may stand thus:– having that degree of recollection about him that would enable him to look about the property he had to dispose of, and the persons to whom he wished to dispose of it. If he had a power of summoning up his mind, so as to know what his property was, and who those persons were that then were the objects of his bounty, then he was competent to make his will."
>
> In other cases, such as the well-known case of *Dew* v *Clark* (1826) 3 Add 79, the insane delusion had a

direct bearing on the provisions of the will. In such cases, the delusion being once proved, and its connection with the will being manifest, there could be no difficulty in setting aside the will. Cases of this description afford little or no assistance towards the solution of the question before us. Again, other cases occurring prior to the case of *Waring* v *Waring* , such as *The Attorney-General* v *Parnther* 3 Bro CC 441, and *Cartwright* v *Cartwright* (1793) 1 Phill 90, 100, had reference to the effect to be given to a lucid interval at the time of making the will, rather than to the degree of mental unsoundness which would constitute testamentary incapacity. The judgment in the latter case, is however, not unworthy of attention. The case was a remarkable one, from the fact that the will had been made by a person actually confined in a lunatic asylum, and who was undoubtedly insane both before and after the making of the will; nevertheless, it was upheld. Sir William Wynne, the then Judge of the Prerogative Court of Canterbury, in giving judgment, used language tending strongly to show that, in his opinion, the rationality of the act done affords an effectual test of the mental capacity of the party doing it ...

Without going to the length of adopting to its full extent what is here said as to the effect of the rational character of the will, or at all saying that effect can be given to the rationality of the disposition beyond that which is due to it as evidence of the sanity of the testator, we advert to this case and the judgment of Sir William Wynne as showing that a more indulgent view of the effect of insanity, as affecting testamentary incapacity, was then taken than has latterly prevailed.

We come now to the case of *Waring* v *Waring*, (since followed by that of *Smith* v *Tebbitt*) in which the doctrine now contended for on behalf of the plaintiff was for the first time laid down. It may be shortly stated thus:

> "To constitute testamentary capacity, soundness of mind is indispenably necessary. But the mind, though it has various faculties, is one and indivisible. If it is disordered in any one of these faculties, if it labours under any delusion arising from such disorder, though its other faculties and functions remain undisturbed it cannot be said to be sound. Such a mind is unsound, and testamentary incapacity is the necessary consequence."

As has already been observed, neither in *Waring* v *Waring* nor in *Smith* v *Tebbitt*, was the doctrine thus laid down in any degree necessary to the decision. Both these were cases of general, not of partial, insanity; in both the delusions were multifarious, and of the wildest and most irrational character, abundantly indicating that the mind was diseased throughout. In both there was an insane suspicion or dislike of persons who should have been objects of affection; and, what is still more important, in both it was palpable that the delusions must have influenced the testamentary disposition impugned. In both these cases, therefore, there existed ample grounds for setting aside the will without resorting to the doctrine in question. Unable to concur in it, we have felt at liberty to consider for ourselves the principle properly applicable to such a case as the present. We do not think it necessary to consider the position assumed in *Waring* v *Waring*, that the mind is one and indivisible, or to discuss the subject as matter of metaphysical or psychological inquiry. It is not given to man to fathom the mystery of the human intelligence, or to ascertain the constitution of our sentient and intellectual being. But whatever may be its essence, every one must be conscious that the faculties and functions of the mind are various and distinct, as are the powers and functions of our physical organisation. The senses, the instincts, the affections, the passions, the moral qualities, the will, perception, thought, reason, imagination, memory, are so many distinct faculties or functions of the mind. The pathology of mental disease and the experience of insanity in its various forms teach us that while, on one hand, all the faculties, moral and intellectual, may be involved in one common ruin, as in the case of the raving maniac, in other instances one or more only of these faculties or functions may be disordered, while the rest are left impaired and undisturbed – that while the mind may be overpowered by delusions which utterly demoralize it and unfit it for the perception of the true nature of surrounding things, or for the discharge of the common obligations of life, there often are, on the other hand, delusions, which, though the offspring of mental disease and so far constituting insanity, yet leave the individual in all other respects rational, and capable of transacting the ordinary affairs and fulfilling the duties and obligations incidental to the various relations of life. No doubt when delusions exist which have no foundation in reality, and spring only from a diseased and morbid condition of the mind, to that extent the mind must necessarily be taken to be unsound; just as the body, if any of its parts or functions is affected by local disease, may be said to be unsound, though all its other members may be healthy, and their powers or functions unimpaired. But the question still remains, whether such partial unsoundness of the mind, if it leaves the affections, the moral sense, and the general power of the understanding unaffected, and is wholly unconnected with the testamentary disposition, should have the effect of taking away the testamentary capacity.

We readily concede that where a delusion has had, as in the case of *Dew* v *Clark*, or is calculated to have had, an influence on the testamentary disposition, it must be held to be fatal to its validity. Thus, if, as occurs in a common form of monomania, a man is under a delusion that he is the object of persecution or attack, and makes a will in which he excludes a child for whom he ought to have provided; though he may not have adverted to that child as one of his supposed enemies, it would be but reasonable to infer that the insane condition had influenced him in the disposal of his property. But, in the case we are dealing with, the delusion must be taken neither to have had any influence on the provisions of the will, or to have been capable of having any, and the question is, whether a delusion, thus wholly innocuous in its results as regards the disposition of the will, is to be held to have the effect of destroying the capacity to make one.

The state of our authorities being such as we have shown, we have turned to the jurisprudence of other countries, as on a matter of common judicial interest, to see whether we could there find any assistance towards the solution of the question. We have, however, derived but little advantage from the inquiry. The Roman Law, the great storehouse of judicial science, is as vague and general on the subject as our own. The madman (furiosus), and the person of defective intelligence (mente captus), are declared incapable of making a testament; but as to what shall constitute madness or defectiveness of intelligence, sufficient to prevent the exercise of the testamentary right, the authorities are silent. The continental codes are equally general in their terms, simply providing, either that persons must be of sound mind to make a will, or that persons of unsound mind shall be disabled from doing so. The older writers appear not to have been alive to the distinction between total and partial unsoundness as affecting testamentary capacity. In recent times, however,the question has been mooted by eminent and distinguished jurists, but unfortunately with a marked discordance of opinion …

In the case of *Harwood* v *Baker* (1870) 3 Moo PC 282 before the Judicial Committee of the Privy Council, in which case a will had been executed by a testator on his death-bed, in favour of a second wife, to the exclusion of the other members of his family, he being in a state of weakened and impaired capacity from disease producing torpor of the brain, and rendering his mind incapable of exertion unless roused, Erskine J delivered the judgment of the Court in these terms:

> "Their Lordships are of opinion that, in order to constitute a sound disposing mind, a testator must not only be able to understand that he is by his will givng the whole of his property to one object of his regard, and the nature of the claims of others, whom by his will he is excluding from all participation in that property; and that the protection of the law is in no cases more needed that it is in those where the mind has been too much enfeebled to comprehend more objects than one; and more especially, when that one object may be so forced upon the attention of the invalid, as to shut out all others that might require consideration. And, therefore, the question which their Lordships propose to decide in this case is, not whether Mr Baker knew, when he executed his will, that he was giving all his property to his wife, and excluding all his other relations from any share in it, but whether he was at that time capable of recollecting who those relations were, of understanding their respective claims upon his regard and bounty, and of deliberately forming an intelligent purpose of excluding them from any share of his property. If he had not the capacity required, the propriety of the disposition made by the will is a matter of no importance. If he had it, the injustice of the exclusion would not affect the validity of the disposition, though the justice or injustice of the disposition might cast down some light upon the question as to his capacity."

From this language it is to be inferred that the standard of capacity in cases of impaired mental power is, to use the words of the judgments, the capacity on the part of the testator to comprehend the extent of the property to be disposed of, and the nature of the claims of those he is excluding. Why should not this standard be also applicable to mental unsoundness produced by mental disease?

It may be said that the analogy between the two cases is imperfect; that there is an essential difference between unsoundness of mind arising from congential defect, or supervening infirmity, and the perversion of thought and feeling produced by mental disease, the latter being far more likely to give rise to an inofficious will than the mere deficiency of mental power. This is, no doubt, true, but it becomes immaterial on the hypothesis that the disorder of the mind has left the faculties, on which the proper exercise of the testamentary power depends, unaffected, and that a rational will, uninfluenced by a mental disorder, has been the result.

It is said, indeed, by those who insist that any degree of unsoundness should suffice to take away testamentary capacity, that where insane delusion has shown itself, it is always possible, and indeed may be assumed to be probable, that a greater degree of mental unsoundness exists than has actually become manifest. But this view, which is by no means universally admitted, is unsupported by proof, and must be looked upon as matter of speculative opinion. It seems unreasonable to deny testamentary capacity on the speculative possibility of unsoundness which has failed to display itself, and which, if existing in a latent and undiscovered form, would be little likely to have any influence on the disposition of the will. No doubt, where the fact that the testator has been subject to any insane delusion is established, a will should be regarded with great distrust, and every presumption should in the first instance be made against it. Where insane delusion has once been shown to have existed, it may be difficult to say whether the mental disorder may not possibly have extended beyond the particular form or instance in which it has manifested itself. It may be equally difficult to say how far the delusion may not have influenced the testator in the particular disposal of his property. And the presumption against a will made under such circumstances becomes additionally strong where the will is, to use the term of the civilians, an inofficious one, that is to say, one in which natural affection and the claims of near relationships have been disregarded. But where in the result a jury are satisfied that the delusion has not affected the general faculties of the mind, and can have no effect upon the will, we will see no sufficient reason why the testator should be held to have lost his right to make a will, or why a will made under such circumstances should not be upheld. Such an inquiry may involve, it is true, considerable difficulty, and require much nicety of discrimination, but we see no reason to think that it is beyond the power of judicial investigation and decision, or may not be disposed of by a jury, directed and guided by a judge. In the case before us two delusions disturbed the mind of the testator, the one that he was pursued by spirits, the other that a man long since dead came personally to molest him. Neither of these delusions – the dead man not having been in any way connected with him – had, or could have had any influence upon him in disposing of his property. The will, though in one sense an idle one, inasmuch as the object of his bounty was his heir at law, and therefore would have taken the property without its being devised to her, was yet rational in this, that it was made in favour of a niece, who lived with him, and who was the object of his affection and regard. And we must take it on the finding of the jury that irrespective of the question of these dormant delusions, the testator was in possession of his faculties when the will was executed.

In these circumstances, we see no ground for holding the will to be invalid. If, indeed, it had been possible to connect the dispositions of the will with the delusions of the testator, the form in which the case was left to the jury might have been open to exception. It may be, as was contended on the part of the plaintiff, that in a case of unsoundness, founded on delusion, but which delusion was not manifested at the time of making the will, it is a question for the jury whether the delusion was not latent in the mind of the testator. But, then, for the reasons we have given in the course of this judgment, we are of opinion that a jury should be told, in such a case, that the existence of a delusion, compatible with the retention of the general powers and faculties of the mind, will not be sufficient to overthrow the will, unless it were such as was calculated to influence the testator in making it.'

Barry* v *Butlin (1838) 2 Moo PC 480 Privy Council (Lord Broughton, Parke B, Bosanquet and Erskine JJ)

Wills – effect of suspicious circumstances – party preparing a will taking a benefit under it

Facts

The testator died in 1833 leaving one son as his only next of kin. In 1827 the testator made a will at the house of his attorney, one Percy, in the presence of two independent and respectable witnesses. At the time he made the will the testator was estranged from his son because he had been charged with violent conduct and absconded to avoid being taken on a bench warrant. The testator from that time forth refused to speak to his son and so on one occasion excluded him from his presence. By his will the testator left Percy a legacy of £3,000, Butlin, the respondent, a legacy of £2,000 and one Whithead, his old servant in whom he reposed great confidence and trust, a legacy of £33,000. The testator's son alleged that the will was procured by the fraud and conspiracy of the three legatees, and suspicious circumstances, at the time when the testator was of unsound mind and incapable of making a will. There was evidence that the testator was addicted to drinking but no satsifactory evidence that he did not have the necessary mental capacity to make a will.

Held

The fact of a party preparing a will, with a legacy to himself, is at most only one of suspicion, of more or less weight according to the circumstances, demanding however, the vigilant care of the court in investigating the case before granting probate. In the present case the circumstances showed good reason for the testator excluding his son from his will and it would therefore be pronounced for.

Parke B:

> 'The rules of law according to which cases of this nature are to be decided, do not admit to any dispute, so far as they are necessary to the determination of the present Appeal: and they have been acquiesced in on both sides. These rules are two: the first that the *onus probandi* is in every case upon the party propounding the will; and he must satisfy the conscience of the court that the instrument so propounded is the last will of a free and capable testator.
>
> The second is that if a party writes or prepares a will, under which he takes a benefit, that is a circumstance that ought generally to excite the suspicion of the court, and calls upon it to be vigilant and jealous in examining the evidence in support of the instrument, in favour of which it ought not to pronounce unless the suspicion is removed, and it is judicially satisfied that the paper propounded does express the true will of the deceased.
>
> These principles to the extent that I have stated, are well established. The former is undisputed. The latter is laid down by Sir John Nicholl in substance, in *Paske* v *Ollatt* (1815) 2 Phill 323; *Ingram* v *Wyatt* (1827) 1 Hagg Ecc Rep 388; and *Billinghurst* v *Vickers* (1841) 1 Phill 187 and is stated by that very learned and experienced judge to have been handed down to him by his predeccesors, and this tribunal have sanctioned and acted upon it, in a recent case; that of *Barker* v *Batt* (1838) 2 Moo PC 317.
>
> Their Lordships are fully sensible to the wisdom of this rule, and the importance of its practical application on all occasions. At the same time their Lordships think it fit to observe, especially as there has been some discussion upon these points, towards the close of this inquiry, that some of the expressions reported to have been used by Sir John Nicholl in laying down the doctrine, appear to them to be somewhat equivocal, and capable of leading into error in the investigation and decision of questions of this nature. It is said that where the party benefited prepared the will, "the presumption and *onus probandi* is against the instrument, and the proof must go not merely to the act of signing, but the knowledge of the contents of the paper: [*Paske*]" and that "where the capacity is doubtful, there must be proof of instructions or reading over [*Billingshurst*]". If by these expressions, the learned judge meant merely to say, that there are cases of wills prepared by a Legatee, so pregnant with suspicion, that they ought to be pronounced against in the absence of evidence in support of them, and that extending to clear proof of the actual knowledge of the contents, by the supposed Testator, and that instructions proceedings from him, or the reading over the instrument by or to him, are the most satisfactory evidence of such knowledge; we fully concur in the proposition so understood; in all probability the learned judge intended no more than this. But if the words are to be construed *strictly*: if it is intended to be stated as a rule of law, that in every

case in which the party preparing a will derives a benefit under it, the *onus probandi* is shifted, and that not only a certain measure but a particular species of proof is thereupon required from the party propounding the will, we feel bound to say that we assume the doctrine to be incorrect.

The strict meaning of the term *onus probandi* is this, that if no evidence is given by the party on whom the burden is cast, the issue must be found against him. In all cases the *onus* is imposed on the party propounding a will, it is in general discharged by proof of capacity, and the fact of execution, from which the knowledge of and assent to the contents of the instrument are assumed, and it cannot be that the simple fact of the party who prepared the will being himself a Legatee, is in every case, and under all circumstances, to create a contrary presumption, and to call upon the Court to pronounce against the will, unless additional evidence is produced to prove the knowledge of its contents by the deceased. A single instance, of not unfrequent occurrence, will test the truth of this proposition. A man of acknowledged competence and habits of business, worth £100,000, leaves the bulk of his property to his family, and a Legacy of £50 to his confidential attorney, who prepared the will: would this fact throw the burden of proof of actual cognizance by the Testator, of the contents of the will, on the party propounding it, so that if such proof were not supplied, the will would be propounded against? the answer is obvious, it would not. All that can be truly said is, that if a person, whether attorney or not, prepared a will with a legacy to himself, it is, at most, a suspicious circumstance, of more or less weight, according to the facts of each particular case; in some of no circumstances; for instance, the *quantum* of the legacy, and the contingencies; but in no case amounting to more than a circumstance of suspicion, demanding the vigilant care and circumspection of the Court in investigating the case, and calling upon it not to grant probate without full and entire satisfaction that the instrument did express the real intention of the deceased.

Nor can it be necessary, that *in all such cases*, even if the Testator's capacity is doubtful, the precise species of evidence of the deceased's knowledge of the will is to be in the shape of instructions for, or reading over the instrument. They form, no doubt, the *most* satisfactory, but they are not the *only* satisfactory description of proof, by which the cognizance of the contents of the will may be brought home to the deceased. The Court would naturally look for such evidence; in some cases it might be impossible to establish a will without it, but it has no right in every case to require it ...'

***Battan Singh* v *Amirchand* [1948] AC 161 Privy Council (Lords Roche and Normand and Mr James Stratford)**

Testamentary capacity – effect of physical disease

Facts

A testator, who was in the last stages of pulmonary tuberculosis and reduced to extreme weaknesses by the disease made a will the day before he died leaving all his property to the respondents, who were not related to him. In the same will the testator declared that he had no relations anywhere, but he must have known, if he had been of sound mind, that this statement was untrue, since he had four nephews. The nephews claimed the will was invalid on the principles in *Banks* v *Goodfellow* since it was made by a man whose mind was so enfeebled by disease as to be no longer of sound mind or memory and who had a delusion as to his nephews' existence.

Held

If a testator was at the time he made a will, through infirmity or disease, so deficient in memory that he could not remember the claims of his relations and disposed of his property to strangers instead, he was incapable of making a will. The will was therefore invalid.

Beaney, Re [1978] 1 WLR 770 Ch D (Martin Nourse QC)

Testamentary capacity – effect of senile dementia

Facts

The deceased, a widow, had three grown-up children, V, P, and G, all of whom were on good terms with her. V was unmarried; in 1971 she went to live with the deceased, who was then suffering from senile dementia and whose condition was deteriorating rapidly. Both P and G were married and lived away from home. On 7 May 1973 the deceased was admitted to hospital; at this time her memory was nil and she kept imagining things. V was anxious that the deceased's house should be transferred into her name at this time so that, if necessary, it could be sold, or otherwise dealt with, to make provision for the deceased. This the deceased assented to and on 16 May a deed of transfer was executed. P and G knew nothing of the deed until the death of the deceased, intestate, a year later. As administrators of her estate they brought an action against V claiming, inter alia, a declaration that the deed was void and of no effect because the deceased was of unsound mind when she executed it and was therefore incapable of understanding the effect.

Held

Nourse QC:

> 'The degree or extent of understanding required in respect of any instrument is relative to the particular transaction which it is to effect. In the case of a will the degree required is always high. In the case of a contract, a deed made for consideration or a gift *inter vivos,* whether by deed or otherwise, the degree required varies with the circumstances of the transaction. Thus, at one extreme, if the subject matter and the value of the gift are trivial in relation to the donor's other assets a low degree of understanding will suffice. But, at the other, if its effect is to dispose of the donor's only asset of value and thus for practical purposes to pre-empt the devolution of his estate under his will or on his intestacy, then the degree of understanding required is as high as that required for a will, and the donor must understand the claim of all potential donees and the extent of the property to be disposed of.'

The deed would therefore be set aside since the deceased did not understand that its effect was to make an absolute gift of the house to V.

Bohrmann, In the Estate of [1938] 1 All ER 271 Probate Division (Langton J)

Testamentary capacity – effect of paranoid psychosis

Facts

The testator made his will on 26 November 1926 and executed four codicils thereto, the last of these in 1932. The codicil of 1932 altered certain gifts to charities in England by declaring that 'England' should be read as 'United States of America'. Prior to the execution of this codicil the testator came under the delusion that London County Council was trying to dispossess him of his house. In fact the council wished to acquire it for hospital purposes. It was found as a fact that, at the time he made the 1932 codicil, the testator was a paranoid psychopath who believed London County Council was persecuting him.

Held

The 1926 will and all the codicils were valid, but the clause in the 1932 codicil altering the word 'England' to 'United States of America' should be deleted therefrom, as it was made under a delusion.

C (a patient), Re [1991] 3 All ER 866 Ch D (Court of Protection) (Hoffmann J)

Statutory wills – court's power to make a will for a person mentally handicapped from a young age

Facts

A mental patient, Miss C, had been born on 16 February 1916 suffering from severe mental problems. She lived at a hospital near London where she had been from the age of ten; she was now 75 years old. Miss C's mother died in 1918, and her father died in 1953, leaving her property consisting of cash and investments valued at £1,600,000. Miss C had little memory, understanding or capacity to communicate; she was completely blind and could not dress or undress herself, or bath herself. She enjoyed, however, the sound of birds, the smell of flowers and outings or coach expeditions provided by the hospital. Miss C was evidently incapable – and had always been incapable – of understanding the meaning or effect of a disposition of her property.

Apart from the staff and other hospital patients, the only person to take an interest in Miss C had been a member of a voluntary organisation called Citizen Advocacy Alliance, which befriended mental patients. The current gross annual income of the fund was £57,000: from this sum £13,000 in income tax and £3,500 costs of administration had to be deducted. Under an earlier order of the Court of Protection Miss C made a covenanted payment of £3,000 to the hospital, leaving about £36,000 a year disposable income.

An application was made to the Court of Protection for an order making a will for her and for immediate gifts to be made out of her property.

Held

Where a person who has been mentally handicapped since birth has inherited a substantial sum and would otherwise die intestate the court will make inter vivos dispositions and direct the execution of a will for the patient on the assumption that he or she would have been a normal decent person who would have acted in accordance with contemporary standards of morality. In doing so the court exercises its powers under s95(1)(c) of the Mental Health Act 1983 to make provision for other persons or purposes for whom or which the patient would might be expected to provide if he or she were not mentally disordered.

It is helpful to quote from the judgment of Hoffmann J in this case in order to understand the scope of the court's powers under ss95 and 96 of the Mental Health Act 1983.

Hoffmann J:

> 'This is an application to the Court of Protection under ss95 and 96 of the Mental Health Act 1983 for an order making a will for a mental patient and for immediate gifts out of her property.
>
> Section 95 provides:
>
> > "(1) The judge may, with respect to the property and affairs of a patient, do or secure the doing of all such things as appear necessary or expedient – (a) for the maintenance or other benefit of the patient; (b) for the maintenance or other benefit of the patient's family; (c) for making provision for other persons or purposes for whom or which the patient might be expected to provide if he were not mentally disordered or (d) otherwise for administering the patient's affairs. (2) In the exercise of the powers conferred by this section regard shall be had first of all to the requirements of the patient ..."
>
> Section 96 confers a number of specific powers prefaced by the words:
>
> > "(1) Without prejudice to the generality of s95 above, the judge shall have power to make such orders and give such directions and authorities as he thinks fit for the purposes of that section and in particular may for those purposes make orders to give directions or authorities for ..."
>
> There follows a list of specific acts or transactions, including in para (d):

> "the gift of any property of the patient to any such persons or for any such purposes as are mentioned in paragraphs (v) and (c) of s95(10) above [and in paragraph (e)] the execution for the patient of a will".

It is clear from the words I have emphasised that s96 does not extend the powers conferred by s95 but enumerates a number of the ways in which those powers may be exercised. Any act or transaction mentioned in s96 must still be justified under one or other of the sub-paragraphs of s95(1) and satisfy the order of priorities laid down by s95(2) ... The only paragraph of s95(1) upon which the gifts to charity, legatees or next of kin can be authorised is para (c). They are not for the benefit of the patient or the patient's "family" within the meaning of para (b) (see *Re DML* [1965] 2 All ER 129 and *Re WJGL* [1965] 3 All ER 865). I must therefore be satisfied that they constitute provision which "the patient might be expected to provide if she were not mentally disordered". It was decided by Cross J in *Re WJGL* that "if she were not mentally disordered" means that the only statutory counter-factual assumption is that the patient has full mental capacity and awareness of her situation for the sole purpose of making a gift or will. It does not mean that the patient's mental capacity and circumstances must be assumed to be in any other respect or for any other purposes different from what they are. Further guidance was given by Megarry VC in *Re JD* [1982] 2 All ER 37. The will or gift must reflect the court's view of what the actual patient "might be expected to provide" and not (if different) what some reasonable person in the patient's position would have done:

> "The court must take the patient as he or she was before losing testamentary capacity. No doubt allowance may be made for the passage of the years ... Furthermore, I do not think that the court should give effect to antipathies or affection of the patient which are beyond reason. But subject to all due allowances, I think that the court must seek to make the will which the actual patient, acting reasonably, would have made if notionally restored to full mental capacity, memory and foresight."

In this case, the patient has lacked capacity since birth. In all relevant respects, the record of her individual preference and personality is a blank on which nothing has been written. Accordingly, there is no material on which to construct a subjective assessment of what the patient would have wanted to do ... I recognise the difficulty in forming a view of what might have been expected from a person who has never enjoyed a rational mind. But I think that in those circumstances the court must assume that she would have been a normal decent person, acting in accordance with contemporary standards of morality. In the absence of actual evidence to the contrary, no less should be assumed of any person and in this case there is nothing to displace such an assumption. A person in the position of Miss C, looking back over her life, would in my view have been influenced by two principal considerations. First, that she had spent the whole of her life in the care of the community, as embodied in the National Health Service, the hospital and voluntary mental health charities like the Friends of the Hospital and the Citizen Advocacy Alliance. Secondly, that she had derived from her fortune from being a child of a family. She would therefore in my view have felt moral obligations to show recognition to the community and to her family. Once one has arrived at the conclusion that the disposition of her property would have been guided by these principles, I do not think it is necessary for the court to be satisfied that the patient would definitely have chosen a particular way of giving effect to them rather than another. A distribution which can be rationally justified as a way of giving effect to these principles would in my view be a provision which the patient "might be expected to provide", even though a somewhat different distribution could also be so described. The court cannot of course indulge its own whims in these matters. The gifts and will it makes for the patient must be capable of being explained as something which the patient "might be expected to provide" ...

The proportions in which a person in the position of Miss C would wish to give effect to these two principles must depend upon all the circumstances, including her relations with her family, the services which have been rendered to her by strangers and the size of the fortune ... Taking her family as a whole, therefore, I think that she would have wished to distribute her estate equally between them and the community. The recognition of the claims of the community would in my view have taken the form of gifts to mental health charities ... I am less confident about the particular choice which she would have made, but on the principle that people tend to prefer local and familiar causes to those which are more general and remote, I think that she would have wished primarily to benefit mentally handicapped people at the hospital or within the area which the hospital serves …

I accept Mr Crampin's submission that the court should be cautious in disposing of the patient's estate while she is alive. But I think that there is still ample scope for a substantial distribution which would give the family a chance of saving inheritance tax and an immediate benefit from the estate. I would therefore propose to order an immediate gift of £100,000 to the Friends of the Hospital and £400,000 to the family. I will then direct that a will be executed for the patient which, subject to the legacies I shall mention, will divide the residuary estate between charity and the family in equal shares, subject to bringing into account the sums distributed by way of immediate gift.

As between members of the family, counsel were agreed that special reasons would be required for departing from the rules for distribution on intestacy … I therefore propose that distribution of both the inter vivos gift and the residuary estate be in accordance with the rules of intestacy.'

Chambers & Yatman* v *The Queen's Proctor (1840) 2 Curt 415 (Sir Herbert Jenner)

Testamentary capacity – mental illness and effect of lucid intervals

Facts

The deceased, a barrister, was for some years a man of strange and eccentric habits, very irritable and hasty in his temper, violent in his language, and jealous and sensitive towards personal slights. About two or three years before his death he had a delusion that he had become an object of scorn and contempt not only amongst his friends and acquaintances but to strangers also. His friends and acquaintances tried to remove this delusion. In November 1839 the deceased had a delusion that the Benchers of the Inner Temple were going to disbar him for giving false information on his admission to the Inn. There was no foundation whatever for this but the deceased decided to flee the country and on 12 November 1839 implored Yatman to get him out of the country. On 13 November 1839 the deceased came under the delusion that he was the victim of a conspiracy. On 15 November the deceased made his will in a rational manner, devising and bequeathing his estate to various friends and acquaintances as he had no relatives. On 16 November the deceased was found dead in bed, having killed himself with his own hand. The Queen's Proctor claimed that the will should be refused probate.

Held

Since it had been proved that the delusion that he was an object of scorn and contempt had been effaced from his mind before he made his will, and considering that the will was in a rational form, it should be admitted to probate. None of the delusions operating on the deceased's mind at the date of the will could have had any effect on the will.

Christian* v *Instiful [1954] 1 WLR 253 Privy Council (Lords Porter and Oaksey, Mr L M D de Silva)

Wills – knowledge and approval of contents from handicapped testator

Facts

In 1944 the testator, aged 86 and with eyesight so defective that he was almost blind, handed a document to someone who had been a solicitor's clerk and asked him to type it. He did so, and then gave it back to the testator who afterwards signed it and had it duly attested by two witnesses. The will was then placed in an envelope which was sealed and put into the custody of the court. The testator died in 1950, aged 93. The executors sought to propound the will which was an elaborate one, leaving to a large number of parties, relations and friends of the deceased, various sums of money. It was not suggested to the solicitor's clerk that he had any such knowledge of the testator's relationships and friendships. The appellant alleged that the testator did not know and approve of the contents of the will since he was at the relevant date blind. However, the evidence did not establish that the testator was incapable of reading the document.

Held

Assuming that the testator was blind and could not have read the will, the court, in determining if in the circumstances the testator knew and approved of the contents of the will was entitled to take into consideration the elaborate nature of the will, being one which someone such as the solicitor's clerk, who was not acquainted with the testator's life could not possibly have devised. Taking both of the above matters into consideration, viz eyesight and the nature of the document, it appeared that the testator knew and approved of what he was doing. The will was therefore valid.

Corbert* v *Newey and Others [1994] 3 WLR 548 Chancery Division (Mr Eben Hamilton QC sitting as a Deputy High Court Judge)

Will – conditional will – extrinsic evidence – will to take effect as satisfaction of condition – whether will valid as conditional will

Facts

A will which was made on the condition that deeds of gift were completed was a valid conditional will despite the absence of any reference to the condition on the face of the will.

Having executed a will in February 1989 leaving one farm to A her niece, and one farm to B her nephew, with the residuary estate left equally between them, the testatrix asked her solicitor to draw up deeds of gift in order to gift the farms inter vivos to A and B respectively, hoping to complete the gifts in September 1989. A new will was drawn up by her solicitor to reflect the fact that the farms no longer formed part of her estate. No mention of the farms was made in the will which bequeathed various gifts to B and A and the residue to the joint third defendants. The will was executed by the testatrix but not dated in the mistaken belief that this would postpone its entry into force until the completion of the deeds of gift. When the deeds were completed on 25 December 1989 the date of the following day, ie 26 December 1989, was inserted in the will. The testatrix later died. B claimed that the second will was invalid. A counterclaimed for its pronouncement in solemn form.

Held

Dismissing the claim, it was held that the second will was valid as the testatrix had the necessary animus testandi. However it was valid as a conditional will and came into effect on the completion of the deeds of gift, whereupon the old will was revoked. Extrinsic evidence was admissible to establish the existence of the conditions and its fulfilment. The second will was admitted to probate in solemn form.

Mr Eben Hamilton QC:

> 'In my judgment Miss Tresawna did have the necessary animus testandi when she executed the September will, and the question therefore arises whether, in the absence of any condition or contingency expressed on the face of that will the court is entitled to consider extraneous evidence to establish the existence of any contingency or condition and its fulfilment ...
>
> For my part I fail to see the logic in the suggestion that the court is entitled to consider extrinsic evidence to decide whether a document was executed animo testandi, but must stop short of considering whether the bequests made in the document were subject to a condition, albeit that such condition is not expressed in the document itself, and whether such condition has been satisfied. In the present case it is

quite clear that Miss Tresawna in executing the September will intended that it should govern the distribution of her estate on her death, subject only to the completion of the inter vivos gifts to William and Sarah. I agree with Mr Barlow's submission that the imposition of such a condition is entirely consistent with Miss Tresawna having the requisite testamentary intention. In my judgment the court is entitled to consider extrinsic evidence and, where the evidence is as clear as it is in the present case, to hold that there is a valid conditional will and that the condition has been satisfied. I should add that I consider the dating of the will by Mr Nicholson to be irrelevant as, in my judgment, the September will was executed as a valid conditional will and would have been admitted to probate on proof of the condition having been fulfilled even if it had not been dated by Mr. Nicholson, albeit that Miss Tresawna may have misguidedly thought it could only come into effect once dated.

Accordingly, I dismiss the plaintiff's claim and order that the September will be admitted to probate in solemn form.'

Comment

This case makes clear that, provided the animus testandi is clear at the time of the execution of the will, a will can be a valid conditional will even though extrinsic evidence has to be admitted.

Craig v *Lamoureux* [1920] AC 349 Privy Council (Viscount Haldane, Lord Buckmaster and Lord Dunedin)

Wills – undue influence – burden of proof

Facts

The appellant, the husband to the testatrix, was the sole beneficiary under her will, which was made after the testatrix had become seriously ill. The will was drafted by the husband's brother who was a lawyer and given to the testatrix to sign. The testatrix's sister alleged undue influence. The Supreme Court of Canada held that the onus of proof lay on the husband to show that he had not procured the execution of the will by undue influence. This onus he had failed to discharge.

Held

Once it has been proved that a will has been executed with due solemnities by a person of competent understanding, and apparently a free agent, the burden of proving that it was executed under undue influencee rests on the person who so alleges. That burden is not discharged by showing merely that a beneficiary had the power to unduly influence the will of the testator; it must be shown that in the particular case the power has been exercised and that the execution of the will was obtained thereby.

D (J), Re [1982] Ch 237 Chancery Division (Megarry V-C)

Statutory wills – court's power to make a will for mentally ill person

Facts

The patient had five children, and after the death of her husband in 1956 a daughter, A, lived with the patient in the patient's house. In 1962 A met a man whom she proposed to marry and in the light of this the patient then made a will by which she devised and bequeathed her house and its contents to A and left the residue of her estate to her five children in equal shares. A married in 1972 and went to live with her husband. At this time the patient was showing signs of senile dementia and she insisted on coming to live with A and her husband. In 1973 the patient sold her house, thereby adeeming the gift of it to A, and she bought a smaller house so that she could live nearer A, but she never really occupied the house as she preferred to live with A. In 1978 the patient's affairs were placed in the hands of a receiver appointed by the Court of Protection. In 1979 a summons was issued by A and the receiver so that the adeemed gift in the patient's will could be dealt with by executing a codicil to the 1962 will devising and bequeathing the patient's new house to A. The deputy master of the Court of Protection ordered that a legacy of £10,000 be substituted instead. The receiver and A appealed.

Held

On the facts of the case it would be appropriate to award A a legacy of £15,000 because of the burden she incurred in looking after the patient.

Megarry V-C (after reading the relevant statutory provisions set out the following factors as governing the execution of a statutory will on behalf of a patient):

> 'The first of the principles or factors which I think it is possible to discern is that it is to be assumed that the patient is having a brief lucid interval at the time when the will is made. The second is that during the lucid interval the patient has a full knowledge of the past, and a full realisation that as soon as the will is executed he or she will relapse into the actual mental state that previously existed, with the prognosis as it actually is. These propositions emerge, I think, from the judgment of Cross J in *Re WJGL* [1966] Ch 135. In that case the judge was dealing with the making of a settlement for the patient, not a will: but I cannot see that the distinction matters. Paragraph (dd), dealing with wills, has been inserted immediately after para (d), dealing with settlements and gifts, and both are governed by the same general statutory provisions.
>
> The third proposition is that it is the actual patient who has to be considered and not a hypothetical patient. One is not concerned with the patient on the Clapham omnibus. I say that because the will is being made by the court, and so by an impartial entity skilled in the law, rather than the actual patient, whose views whilst still of a sound disposing mind might be idosyncratic and far from impartial. In *Re Davey (decd)* [1981] 1 WLR 164 Fox J is reported as saying, in relation to a will made by the Court of Protection, that the essential question was "what if anything would be reasonable provision in all the circumstances for the various contestants", and could it be said that this indicates an objective approach made with the wisdom of the court rather than the approach likely to be made by the patient if restored to full testamentary capacity; I very much doubt if the judge meant to indicate this and in any case I do not think it is right. The whole approach of Cross J in *Re WJGL* was that of considering the particular patient, momentarily restored to full mental capacity, as being the settlor. Further, in s102(1)(c) the question is one of making provision for persons or purposes "for whom or which the patient might be expected to provide if he were not mentally disordered"; and I think that this provision governs the making of a will for the patient, and contemplates the particular patient: and see *Re CMG* [1970] Ch 574. Before losing testamentary capacity the patient was then able to give effect to those views when making a will. I think that the court must take the patient as he or she was before losing testamentary capacity. No doubt allowance may be made for the passage of years since the patient was last of full capacity, for sometimes strong feelings mellow into indifference, and even family feuds evaporate. Furthermore, I do not think that the court should give effect to antipathies or affections of the patient which are beyond reason. But subject to all due allowances, I think that the court must seek to make the will which the actual patient acting reasonably would have made if notionally restored to full mental capacity, memory and foresight. If I may adapt Dr Johnson's words, used for another purpose, the court is to do for the patient what the patient would fairly do for himself, if he could.
>
> Fourth, I think that during the hypothetical lucid interval the patient is to be envisaged as being advised by competent solicitors. The court will in fact be making the will, of course, and the court should not make a will on the assumption that the terms of the will are to be framed by someone who, for instance, knows nothing about lapse and ademption. Furthermore, as the court will be surveying the past and the future, the hypothetically lucid patient should be assumed to have a skilled solicitor, to draw his or her attention to matters which a testator should bear in mind. In *Re DML* [1965] 1 Ch 1133, a case on a proposed purchase of an annuity in order to save estate duty, Cross J put a lucid explanation of the proposal into the mouth

of a hypothetical legal adviser to the hypothetically lucid patient. In any case, I cannot imagine that Parliament intended the court to match the sort of home-made will that some testator's make. I do not, of course, say that one must treat the patient as being bound to accept the imaginary legal advice that is being given to him; but the patient is to be treated as doing what he does either because of the advice or in spite of it, and not without having had it.

Fifth, in all normal cases the patient is to be envisaged as taking a broad brush to the claims on his bounty, rather than an accountant's pen. There will be nothing like a balance sheet or profit and loss account. There may be many to whom the patient feels morally indebted; and some of that moral indebtedness may be readily expressible in terms of money, and some of it may not. But, when giving legacies or shares of residue few testators are likely to reckon up in terms of cash the value of the hospitality and gifts that he has received from his friends and relations, and then seek to make some form of testamentary repayment, even if his estate is large enough for this. Instead, there is likely to be some general recognition of outstanding kindness by some gift which in quantum may bear a little relation to the cost or value of those kindnesses.'

Davey, Re [1981] 1 WLR 164 Chancery Division (Fox J)

Statutory wills – extent of discretion of Court of Protection

Facts

In June 1979 Miss Olive St Barbe 'the patient', aged 92, moved into a private nursing home in London. On 10 September 1979 the patient made a will by which she bequeathed two small legacies and gave the residue of her estate worth about £100,000 to be divided equally among 17 named people who should survive her, all but one of whom were related to her. On 15 October 1979 the patient was examined at the nursing home by a consultant psychiatrist and found to be suffering from senile deterioration and therefore incapable of managing her affairs. Another consultant psychiatrist examined the patient on 15 November 1979 and came to the same conclusion. Both psychiatrists recommended that the patient's affairs be placed under the control of the Court of Protection. The patient's affairs were placed in the hands of the Court of Protection on 18 December 1979 and the Official Solicitor was appointed receiver. On 14 December 1979 it had come to the notice of the Official Solicitor that the patient had married Mr Davey (the appellant) at the Fulham Register Office. He was 48 years of age and an employee of the nursing home. None of the patient's relatives was informed of the marriage until it came to the notice of the Official Solicitor. Because the will of 10 September 1979 would have been revoked by the marriage, the Official Solicitor made an application to the Court of Protection for a order for the execution of a statutory will for the patient in the same terms as the will of 10 September 1979. This application was made on and granted on 20 December 1979. It was ordered that the Assistant Official Solicitor should execute the will in the name and on behalf of the patient. This was done on 21 December 1979. The patient died six days later, on 27 December. The appellant was informed of the order for the execution of a statutory will on 21 December 1979. He appealed against that order, asking that it be discharged and the will set aside because he had not been notified of the application.

Held

The appeal would be dismissed since the Court of Protection had a discretion as to what persons were to be made respondents or given notice of an application under s103(1)(dd).

Fox J:

'The deputy master's reasons for ordering the execution of a will without notice to Mr Davey were, in effect, as follows:

(i) If Mr Davey was joined as a party there would inevitably be delay before the matter could be

determined. The patient was 93 years old and in poor health. The matter was, accordingly, one of considerable urgency.
(ii) If the patient died before the court could give directions for the execution of a will, it would no longer be possible to challenge the validity of the marriage and the estate would devolve under an intestacy. The basis of that view is the decision of the Court of Appeal in *Re Roberts (deceased)* [1978] 1 WLR 653 where it was held that a voidable marriage, whether subsequently annulled or not, is a marriage for the purposes of s18 of the Wills Act 1837 and therefore automatically revokes an existing will of a party to the marriage. On an intestacy Mr Davey would take, if the estate was sufficient, the statutory legacy of £55,000 plus half the residuary estate.
(iii) The marriage was apparently clandestine, embarked on at short notice and without notification to the patient's relatives.
(iv) If a statutory will was executed as proposed (that is to say in effect restoring the will of Septemmber 1979) Mr Davey could, if he wished, make application for a further statutory will in his favour. If the patient died before that could be dealt with, Mr Davey could make an application under the Inheritance (Provision for Family and Dependants) Act 1975 ...

... the patient is now dead. It seems to me, therefore, that the effect of s103A(3) is that the statutory will must be treated as if it were a will duly made by her and as if she were of testamentary capacity when she made it. It was her last will. One cannot, I think, in this case get rid of the will simply by attacking the order. The order had no dispositive effect at all. If the patient had died after the order but before the assistant official solicitor executed the will, the patient would have died intestate just as a person of full capacity who gave instructions for a will had died before executing it would die intestate, assuming he left no other will. But the statutory will having been executed, s103A(3) makes it the patient's will for all purposes. Suppose the deputy master was wrong and that I took the view that the proper order would have been to direct a will under which the estate was divided in some way between Mr Davey and the beneficiaries, or some of them, under the September will. It does not seem to me that the Court of Protection now has any jurisdiction to procure such a distribution. It could not be achieved by order alone. It could only be achieved by revoking the statutory will and making a new will in its place. But that, I think, is impossible. First, it seems to me that the powers of the Court of Protection under s102 of the 1959 Act came to an end on the patient's death; see, for example, *Re Wheater* [1928] Ch 223 and *Re Bennett* [1913] 2 Ch 318. Second, it is not possible to make a will for, or to revoke the will of, a deceased person, and it cannot, I think, be right to say that in such a case even though it was not possible to achieve the disposition contemplated by the appellate tribunal, nevertheless, the order of that tribunal would in some way, by itself invalidate the existing will; that seems to me to be wrong in principle and quite likely, in many cases, to produce an unintended, and unfair, intestacy ...'

Fulton* v *Andrew (1875) LR 7 HL 448 House of Lords (Lord Cairns LC Lords Chelmsford, Hatherley and O'Hagan)

Wills – effect of suspicious circumstances – partial invalidity

Facts

The testator made his will in 1870 and by it he appointed Messrs Andrew and Wilson his executors. The will was executed in the handwriting of Wilson and it contained a long list of bequests of about £1000 each to various nephews and nieces and servants and legacies of £1000 to Andrew and £100 to Wilson. The testator then devised and bequeathed the residue of his estate equally to Andrew and Wilson. The testator's nephew, Fulton, challenged the will on the grounds that at the time of execution of the will the testator lacked the necessary mental capacity through drunkenness and disease of the brain; that the execution of the will was obtained by the undue influence of Andrew and Wilson and that the testator did not know and approve of the contents of the will. It was alleged by Andrew and Wilson that the will was read over to the testator and left with him for a few days. Other evidence showed discrepancies between the instructions given for the will and the executed will in Wilson's handwriting. A jury found in favour of the will except that they found that the testator did not know and approve of the residuary gift. Probate was nevertheless granted of the whole will but the nephew Fulton appealed on the ground that probate should not have been granted of the whole will.

Held

The jury's verdict ought to stand; probate should only have been given to those parts of the will which the jury's verdict found for, and the gift of residue ought to have been excluded from probate in accordance with their verdict.

Lord Hatherley:

> '... there is one rule which has always been laid down by the Courts having to deal with wills, and that is that a person who is instrumental in framing the will as these two persons undoubtedly were, and who obtains a bounty by that will, is placed in a different position from other ordinary legatees who are not called upon to substantiate the truth and honesty of the transaction as regards their legacies. It is enough in their case that the will was read over to the testator and that he was of sound mind and memory, and capable of comprehending it. But there is a further onus upon those who take for their own benefit, after having been instrumental in preparing or obtaining a will. They have thrown upon them the onus of showing the righteousness of the transaction. Now, how did these persons discharge the onus in the present case? They only discharged it by themselves giving evidence before the jury of the reading over of the will, and they were the only persons who did give that evidence. It would not have been difficult for them to have had other persons present when the reading over of the will took place; but that does not appear to have been done ...'

Guardhouse* v *Blackburn (1866) LR 1 P & D 109 Probate Division (Lord Penzance)

Wills – knowledge and approval of contents – standard of proof

Facts

The testatrix made a will in 1851 by which she disposed of three different estates called Folds, Scales and Stainton and charged the estate of Scales with various legacies of £500 and £100. In 1852 the testatrix executed a codicil to her will which was drawn up for her by her attorney and which revoked certain legacies in the will, increased the amount of others and added new ones. The testatrix's instructions to her attorney were that the legacies in the codicil were to be paid out of her personal estate but the attorney drafted the codicil, which referred to the will, in the following terms: 'I direct all the legacies, *therein and* herein given (and not revoked) to be paid out of my personal estate.' The codicil had been read over to the testatrix and duly attested by her in this form.

Held

The court would not exclude these words from probate since they were read over to and approved by her.

Lord Penzance:

> 'The ground on which the Court is asked to expunge them (the words "therein and") is that they were inserted by the attorney who drew the codicil by mistake, and without instructions. This is proved to be the fact (if the evidence is admissible, and can be relied upon) by the oath of the attorney, and by a paper which he swears to have been the rough draft of the codicil made by him in the presence of the testatrix, and from her verbal directions ... Supposing then, parol evidence to be admissible in such a case as the

present, the question recurs to what extent is it still open to the Court since the statute, to act upon such evidence, for the purpose of rejecting the whole or expunging any portion of the written testament to which the testator has duly affixed his name? A more important inquiry could hardly arise. For you may as effectually incline the balance by taking out of one scale as by adding to the other, and it is quite as easy to vary the effect of a will in any given direction by leaving words out as by putting them in. After much consideration, the following propositions commend themselves to the Court as rules which, since the statute, ought to govern its action in respect of a duly executed paper:– First, that before a paper so executed is entitled to probate, the Court must be satisfied that the testator knew and approved of the contents at the time he signed it. Secondly, that except in certain cases, where suspicion attaches to the document, the fact of the testator's execution is sufficient proof that he knew and approved the contents. Thirdly, that although the testator knew and approved the contents, the paper may still be rejected, on proof of establishing, beyond all possibility of mistake, that he did not intend the paper to operate as a will. Fourthly, that although the testator did know and approve the contents, the paper may be refused probate, if it be proved that any fraud has been purposely practised on the testator in obtaining his execution thereof. Fifthly, that subject to this last preceding proposition, the fact that the will has been duly read over to a capable testator on the occasion of its execution, or that its contents have been brought to his notice in any way, should, when coupled with his execution thereof, be held conclusive evidence that he approved as well as knew the contents thereof. Sixthly, that the above rules apply equally to a portion of the will as to the whole. The first and second of these propositions are amply established by the case of *Barry* v *Butlin* (1838) 2 Moo PC 480, and others of that class in the Privy Council. The third was also approved law in the Ecclesiastical Courts, for there must be an "*animus testandi*" to constitute a paper testamentary. The fourth requires no comment, and the last is justified by the case of *Allen* v *McPherson* (1847) 1 HLC 191. It remains to say a few words on the fifth. It is here that the right to derogate from the force of an executed paper approaches and receives its limit. And it is obvious enough, that if the Court should allow itself to pass beyond proof that the contents of any such paper were read or otherwise made known to the testator, and suffer an inquiry by the oath of the attorney or others as to what the testator really wished or intended, the authenticity of a will would no longer be set at large in the wide field of parol conflict, and confided to the mercies of memory. The security intended by the statute would thus perish at the hands of the Court. I have thus endeavoured to place the use of parol evidence in these matters on its true ground. The general rule for excluding it in our courts is based upon the proposition that written testimony is of a higher grade more certain, more reliable, – than parol, and that resort should be had to the highest evidence of which a subject is capable, to the exclusion of the inferior class. But it is one thing to admit evidence, and another to give effect to it. If a statute requires that a thing should be in writing and signed, in order to prove its validity, it precludes the Court from giving effect to parol testimony of that which is required to be so written and signed. And if it be said, why, they, admit parol evidence on the subject at all? The answer is, that if the scope of such evidence can be clearly known before it is heard, it should be excluded; but then only on the ground of immateriality, not because it is secondary. In actual practice a large number of cases are so presented that it is impracticable to reject evidence as immaterial before the details are known. Little need be added as to the operation of these principles upon the present case. The codicil was proved to have been read over to the testator before the execution thereof, she duly executed the same, and the Court conceives it to be beyond its functions or powers to substitute the oath of the attorney who prepared it, fortified by his notes of the testator's instructions, for the written provisions contained in a paper so executed. The probate will, therefore, be deliverd out to the plaintiffs in its present form.'

Hall* v *Hall (1868) 1 P & D 481 Probate Division (Lord Penzance)

Wills made under undue influence – definition of undue influence

Facts

The plaintiff, Ann Hall, propounded the will of her deceased husband, John Hall. The defendant, William Hall, the brother of the deceased, alleged that the will was obtained by the undue influence of the plaintiff in that she had used violence and made threats against the deceased and that the will had been made in consequence of these for the sake of peace and quietness and did not express the deceased's real testamentary intentions.

Held

In his summing up to the jury (which found that the plea of undue influence was proved) Lord Penzance said:

> 'To make a will a man must be a free agent. But all influences are not unlawful. Persuasion, appeals to the affections or ties of kindred, to a sentiment of gratitude for past services, or pity for future destruction, or the like – these are all legitimate, and may be fairly pressed on a testator. On the other hand, pressure of whatever character, whether acting on the fears or the hopes, if so exerted as to overpower the volition without convincing the judgment, is a species of restraint under which no valid will can be made. Importunity or threats, such as the testator has not the courage to resist, moral command asserted and yielded to for the sake of peace and quiet, or of escaping from distress of mind or social discomfort, these, if carried to a degree in which the free play of the testator's judgment, discretion or wishes, is overborne, will constitute undue influence, though no force is either used or threatened. In a word, a testator may be led but not driven; and his will must be the offspring of his own volition, and not the record of some one else's.'

Hastilow* v *Stobie (1865) LR 1 P & D 64 Probate Division (Sir J P Wilde)

Wills – need for testator to know and approve contents – presumption

Facts

The testator made two wills. The plaintiff, as executor of a will dated 10 February 1863, sought to propound it. The defendant, as executor of an earlier will, pleaded inter alia, that at the time of the execution of the will of 10 February 1863 the testator did not know and approve of the contents of that will.

Held

On the question of knowledge and approval Sir J P Wilde said:

> 'The defendant has pleaded to a declaration on a will that the deceased did not "know and approve of the contents thereof", and the question is, whether this plea is bad, not in form, but in substance? The main ground taken against it was indicated by Sir Cresswell Cresswell in the two cases which have been cited, where he is reported to have said, as an abstract propostion, that a man might make a good will without knowing anything of its contents. But he never had occasion expressly to decide this point. This proposition is certainly rather a startling one, because it conflicts with the natural and popular idea of the nature of a will, and it is at variance, besides, with the universal practice of mankind in such matters. For, however much men have been in the habit of yielding to the pressure and opinions of others in disposing of their property, I suppose no case ever yet to have occurred in which a man in possession of his full faculties handed over the making of his will to another, and was content to execute it without so much as the curiosity even to know what it contained. But still the question remains whether a will so made, if duly executed, would be good in law; and I am constrained to come to the conclusion that it would not. It might be enough to say, as the books abound with discussions as to the testator's intentions and state of knowledge, all based upon the foundation that a will is the act of a man's own intelligence and volition,

the burden of showing by authority that such a will as is now in question would be valid lies upon those who assert it, and that no text writer, modern or ancient – no judgment of any tribunal, here or elsewhere – and no dictum even, save the two to which I have referred, has been adduced in its support. It is extremely difficult in such a case to prove the negative; and the more completely such a notion is novel and out of question in our law, the less likelihood there is of meeting with a case against it. But there are considerations drawn from the undoubted law which go a long way to refute it. First, there is the practice of this court. Rule 71, which provides that in the case of blind and illiterate persons the registrar must be satisfied that the testator "had knowledge of its contents". Then there is the definition of a will to be found in Swinburne and adopted by Mr Justice Williams in his book on Executors: "*Testamentum est voluntatis nostrae justia sententia de es quod quis post mortem suam fleri relit*" ... Assuming then, that it is necessary that a testator should know the contents of his will, it cannot be doubted that he must also approve them ...'

Morris, Re [1971] P 62 Family Division (Latey J)

Wills – court's power to omit words included through mistake or misunderstanding

Facts

The testatrix made a long will, clause 7 of which contained 20 pecuniary legacies, each preceded by a Roman numeral in brackets. Shortly after executing the will she wished to alter certain bequests to a certain employee of hers which were clause 3 and clause 7 (iv) of the will. The testatrix's solicitor prepared a codicil in response to her wishes which, owing to his error, contained the clause 'I revoke clauses 3 and 7 of my said will'. This had the effect of defeating the testatrix's intentions by revoking all the bequests in clause 7 instead of merely sub-clause (iv). The executors of the will sought a grant of probate of the codicil with the omission of the numeral '7'. Evidence showed that the testatrix had read the codicil before executing it in the sense of casting her eye over it.

Held

1. The fact that the testatrix had read over the will herself was, *prima facie,* evidence that she knew and approved of the contents of the will. However, there was no rule of law or evidence which precluded the court from considering all the evidence in order to arrive at the truth whether fraud was suggested or merely mistake. It was clear from the evidence that she did not in fact know and approve its contents and the codicil would be admitted to probate with the omission of the number '7'.
2. Where a testator delegated to a draftsman the task of drafting an instrument and executed it as drafted, the cases showed that he would normally be bound by a mistake which the draftsman had made. However, in the present case this rule did not apply because the mind of the draftsman had never really been applied to the words introduced and never adverted to their significance and effect. There was a mere clerical error on his part, a slip. He knew what the testatrix's intentions and instructions were, and that he was outside the scope of his authority. This he did without knowing and approving of it himself. Assuming there was a principal/agent relationship one could not impute to the principal the agent's knowledge and approval which the agent himself had not got. Therefore, the testatrix was not bound by the mistake of the draftsman which was never brought to her notice and on this basis also, the numeral '7' would be omitted.

Parfitt v *Lawless* (1872) LR 2 P & D 462 (Lord Penzance, Pigott B and Brett J)

Probate and equitable doctrines of undue influence distinguished

Facts

The plaintiff, a Roman Catholic Priest, propounded the will of the testatrix under which he was the residuary legatee. The defendant alleged that the will was obtained by undue influence of the plaintiff. The plaintiff had been chaplain for many years to the testatrix and her husband and for part of the time he was their confessor. To carry out these duties he resided with them. At the time the will in dispute was made he was confessor to the testatrix. There was no evidence that the plaintiff had interferred in the making of the will, or that he had procured the gift of residue to himself, or that he had brought such gift about by coercion or dominion exercised over the testatrix against her will, or by importunity not to be resisted. Moreover, it was not shown that the testatrix was under the plaintiff's control or dominion in the common affairs of life or in business.

Held

There was no evidence to go to a jury on the issue of undue influence. Further, there was no presumption of undue influence in the case of gifts by will, and the rules of the courts of equity in relation to gifts inter vivos, which raises a presumption of undue influence where natural influence is used by a person to obtain a benefit for himself, are not applicable to the making of wills.

Lord Penzance:

> 'This rule was granted in order to consider a suggestion strongly pressed that the rules adopted in the Courts of Equity in relation to gifts *inter vivos* ought to be applied to the making of wills. In equity persons standing in certain relations to one another – such as parent and child, man and wife, doctor and patient, attorney and client, confessor and penitent, guardian and ward are subject to certain presumptions when transactions between them are brought in question; and if a gift or contract made in favour of him who holds the position of influence is impeached by him who is subject to that influence, the Courts of Equity cast upon the former the burden of proving that the transaction was fairly conducted as if between strangers; that the weaker was not duly impressed by the natural influence of the stronger, or the inexperienced overreached by him of more mature intelligence. Applying this view of the subject to the making of a will, it was contended in this case that it was enough to show that a legatee fell within the class emunerated, having done so, the onus was cast upon him of proving that his legacy was not obtained by undue influence. It would be an answer to this argument to say that this has never been, and is not the law in this or any other court regarding wills; and that, if this court should presume to make a new law on the subject, it would establish one rule in regard to personalty, while another would remain the existing rule in regard to realty. "One point, however, is beyond dispute" said Lord Cranworth in *Boyse* v *Rossborough* (1856-57) 6 HLC at p49, "and that is, that where once it has been proved that will has been executed with due solemnities by a person of competent understanding, and apparently a free agent, the burden of proving that it was executed under undue influence is on the party who alleges it. Undue influence cannot be presumed." But in truth the cases in equity apply to a wholly different state of things. In the first place, in those cases of gifts or contracts *inter vivos* there is a transaction in which the person benefited at least takes part, whether he unduly urges his influence or not; and in calling upon him to explain the part he took, and the circumstances that brought about the gift or obligation, the Court is plainly requiring of him an explanation within his knowledge. But in the case of a legacy under a will, the legatee may have, and in point of fact generally has, no part in or even knowledge of the act; and to cast upon him, on the bare proof of the legacy and his relation to the testator, the burden of showing how the thing came about, and under what influence or with what motives the legacy was made, or what advice the testator had, professional or otherwise, would be to cast a duty on him which in many, if not most cases, he could not possibly discharge. A more material distinction is this: the influence which is undue in the cases of gifts *inter vivos* is very different from that which is required to set aside a will. In the case of gifts or other transactions *inter vivos* it is considered by the Courts of Equity that the natural influence which such relations as those in question involve, exerted by those who possess it to obtain a benefit for themselves, is an undue influence. Gifts or contracts brought about by it are, therefore, set aside unless the party benefited by it can show affirmatively that the other party to the transaction was placed "in such a

position as would enable him to form an absolutely free and unfettered judgment": *Archer* v *Hudson* (1844) 7 Beav 551.

The law regarding wills is very different from this. The natural influence of the parent or guardian over the child, or the husband over the wife, or the attorney over the client, may lawfully be exerted to obtain a will or legacy, so long as the testator thoroughly understands what he is doing, and is a free agent. There is nothing illegal in the parent or husband pressing his claims on a child or wife, and obtaining a recognition of those claims in a legacy, provided that that persuasion stops short of coercion, and that the volition of the testator, though biased and impressed by the relation in which he stands to the legatee, is not overborne and subjected to the domination of another.

The influence which will set aside a will, says Mr Justice Williams:

> "must amount to force and coercion destroying free agency; it must not be the influence of affection or attachment; it must no be the mere desire of gratifying the wishes of another, for that would be a very strong ground in support of a testamentary act; further there must be proof that the act was obtained by this coercion; by importunity which could not be resisted; that it was done merely for the sake of peace, so that the motive was tantamount to force and fear." (*Williams' Executors*, pt I, bk 2, ch1, s2)

This difference, then, between the influence which is held to be undue in the cases of transactions *inter vivos*, and that which is called undue in relation to a will or legacy is all-important when a question arises of making presumptions or adjusting the burden of proof. For it may be reasonable enough to presume that a person had obtained a gift or contract to his own advantage and the detriment of another by way of personal advice or persuasion has availed himself of the natural influence which his position gave him. And in casting upon him the burden of exculpation, the law is only assuming that he has done so. But it is a very different thing to presume, without a particle of proof, that a person so situated has abused his position by the exercise of dominion or the assertion of adverse control.

For these reasons it seems to me that it would be improper and unjust to throw upon a man in the position of the plaintiff, without any proof that he had any hand whatever in the making of this will, the onus of proving negatively that he did not coerce the testatrix into devising the residue of her land to him. I say coerce, for this is the only matter involved in a plea of undue influence. Lord Cranworth appears in the case above cited to have regarded fraud as a species of undue influence. It is a mere question of terms; but by the rules of pleading established in this court since December 1865, fraud, which includes misrepresentation, is the subject of a separate plea, and undue influence as a term used in a plea in this court raises the question of coercion, and that only.'

Parke, In the Estate of [1954] P 112 Court of Appeal (Singleton, Birkett and Hodson LJJ)

Tetamentary capacity – test for unsoundness of mind

Facts

The deceased, a successful shipping and forwarding agent, became very lonely and depressed on the death of his wife in January 1948. To recuperate he decided to go on a voyage to South America and on returning he executed a will dated 1 March 1948. In May 1948 the deceased suffered a stroke which was brought on by hardened arteries. Although the deceased recovered from the stroke his behaviour thereafter was slightly eccentric. On 30 May 1949 he married the plaintiff and on the same day he executed an elaborate will under which the plaintiff benefited to a modest extent in the deceased's £120,000 estate. In a probate action before a jury (*In re Parke; Culross* v *Parke* (1950) The Times, 2 December) the executors sought determination of the question whether the deceased had the necessary testamentary capacity at the time he made the will dated 30 May 1949. The will was pronounced against. In the present action the plaintiff sought a declaration that her marriage to the deceased on 30 May was a valid marriage which had revoked the will dated 1 March 1948 and that he had therefore died intestate.

Held

The marriage was valid. The test to be applied in cases such as the present is whether the person was capable of understanding the nature of the contract into which he or she was entering, free from the influence of morbid delusions on the subject.

Hodson LJ

> '... in my opinion, there is no sliding scale of soundness of mind by reference to which different matters of which the law is required to take cognisance may be measured. The authority of Sir James Hannen in *Broughton* v *Knight* (1873) LR 3 P & D 64 and *Burdett* v *Thompson* (1873) LR 3 P & D at p72 do not, I think, support such a proposition. Indeed in the latter case Sir James Hannen was at pains to point out that it had been erroneously supposed that he had said it required a greater degree of soundness of mind to make a will than to do any other act. He said he never said that or meant to say that. He repeated that if you are at liberty to draw a distinction between various degrees of soundness of mind, then whatever is the highest degree of soundness of mind is required to make a will. In *Broughton* v *Knight* he had pointed out that, in considering the question whether the testator is of sound disposition, you cannot put aside the contents of the will and the surrounding circumtances therewith, and this passage indicates that you cannot consider unsoundness of mind in the air (so to speak) but only consider it in relation to the facts and the subject matter of the particular case.
>
> ... The contents of a will vary greatly from one case to another, and also the surrounding circumstances, and similar considerations apply to any transaction which a man may seek to carry through. It is true as Sir James Hannen P said in *Durham* v *Durham* (1885) 10 PD 80 that the contract of marriage is a very simple one which does not require a high degree of intelligence to comprehend ...'

Parker* v *Felgate (1883) 8 PD 171 Probate Division (Sir James Hannen P)

Testamentary capacity – time for satisfying the test

Facts

The deceased, a woman of 28, became affected with Bright's disease in 1882 and consulted her solicitor about making her will and in the course of several interviews she gave the solicitor instructions as to the contents of the will. Before the will was finally prepared the deceased became very ill and a will was quickly prepared for her to sign. At this time the deceased was falling into a deep coma but her doctor aroused her and said 'This is your will. Do you wish this lady (a Mrs Flack) to sign it?' The deceased said 'Yes'. The will was signed in the presence of the deceased and attested. The question arose whether at the time of signing the deceased had the necessary testamentary capacity.

Held

If a testatrix has given instructions for her will and it is prepared in accordance with them, the will will be valid though at the time of execution the testatrix merely recollects that she has given those instructions but believes that the will which she is executing is in accordance with them.

Sir James Hannen:

> '... the law applicable to the case is this: If a person has given instructions to a solicitor to make a will, and the solicitor prepares it in accordance with those instructions, all that is necessary to make it a good will, if executed by the testator, is that he should be able to think thus far, "I gave my solicitor insructions to prepare a will making a certain disposition of my property. I have no doubt that he has given effect to my intention, and I accept the document which is put before me as carrying it out".'

Phelan, Re [1972] Fam 33 Family Division (Stirling J)

Wills – court's power to omit words included through mistake or misunderstanding

Facts

The testator made a home-made will in June 1968 by which he appointed his landlady and her husband to be executors and beneficiaries of his estate. In July 1968 he executed three further home-made wills on printed will forms obtained from a stationer. Each of these three wills appointed the landlady and her husband as executors and beneficiaries and disposed of an investment in a unit trust. There was evidence that the testator believed that he had to make a will to dispose of each such investment. All three wills were attested within a few minutes of each other and all contained a printed revocation clause. The effect on the testator's death of these clauses was to render all the wills revoked save that which was last executed. The executors sought to have the revocation clause in the last three wills omitted from probate.

Held

The court had power to omit words which the testator had included in his will through inadvertance or through a misunderstanding if by their omission effect could be given to his true intentions. Since it was clear that the testator intended to give the interests in the unit trusts to the beneficiaries under the first will all the wills would be admitted to probate without the revocation clause in the last three wills.

Posner, In the Estate of [1953] P 277 Court of Probate (Karminski J)

Wills – effect of fraudulent representation as to status or relationships

Facts

By his will the deceased named 'my wife Rose Posner' as residuary legatee. Rose Posner was not in fact the deceased's wife. On 2 August 1945 she went through a form of marriage with the deceased while her husband was alive. At the time of the execution of the will, which was about one year before the deceased's death, the deceased did not know that Rose Posner was not his wife. There was no allegation of fraud.

Held

The bequest was valid because a false description of a legatee is not itself sufficient to invalidate the gift; there must also be a fraudulent assumption of that character by the legatee and the testator must furthermore have been deceived by that fraud.

Simpson* v *Simpson (1989) 19 Fam Law 20 Family Division (Mowitt J)

Wills – presumption of undue influence

Facts

The case concerned the mental capacity of a testator and undue influence. The plaintiffs in the case were the testator's children by a former marriage. The defendant was his third wife. By the provisions of his will the deceased's estate was to devolve on the defendant on trust, subject to the payment of the income and capital to the plaintiffs on the death of the defendant. The testator had developed a malignant brain tumour; as a result his mental processes had become impaired. The testator transferred substantial sums of money from bank and building society accounts into a joint account held with the defendant.

By the time of his death, the testator had disposed of approximately 70 per cent of his estate in this way. The plaintiffs claimed that:

a) The testator did not have the mental capacity to make these dispositions in favour of the defendant; and
b) The defendant must be presumed to have exercised undue influence over the testator.

Held

a) The testator did not have the mental capacity to make the dispositions.
b) In the absence of any evidence to the contrary, there was a presumption of advancement in favour of the defendant. However, the presumption was in this case rebutted by evidence of intention. The evidence was that the transfer into the joint account made by the testator was only for convenience to facilitate the payment of bills and expenses by the defendant and was not an outright gift.
c) Although the relationship existing between spouses did not itself give rise to a presumption of undue influence, it was possible in certain circumstances that such a presumption might arise. It did in these circumstances because of the illness and dependency of the testator.

Tyrell v Painton [1894] P 151 Court of Appeal (Lindley, A L Smith and Davey LJJ)

Wills – effect of generally suspicious circumstances

Facts

The testatrix, in 1880 and again 1884, made a will in favour of the defendant. Afterwards she became dissatisfied with him, and from 1888 to 1892 wrote repeatedly to her solicitor making serious complaints against him. On 7 November 1892 she made a will leaving her property to the plaintiff. On 9 November a son of the defendant brought to her a will prepared by himself, leaving her property to the defendant. This will was executed by her in the presence of and attested by the defendant's son, and a young friend of his, no one else was present and the existence of the will was not known to anyone else until after the death of the testatrix on 23 November. The defendant sought to propound the later will by orally examining the witnesses to it who disposed clearly that the will was read over to the testatrix and that she appeared to understand and approve of it. Probate was granted to the will. The plaintiff appealed.

Held

The evidence of the attesting witnesses was not sufficient to remove the suspicion arising from the circumstances under which the later will was prepared and executed, and therefore the former will must be established.

Lindley LJ:

> 'The rule in *Barry* v *Butlin* (1838) 2 Moo PC 480, *Fulton* v *Andrew* (1875) LR 7 HL 448 and *Brown* v *Fisher* (1890) 63 LT 465 is not in my opinion, confined to the single case in which a will is prepared by or on the instructions of the person taking large benefits under it, but extends to all cases in which circumstances exist which excite the suspicion of the Court; and wherever such circumstances exist, and whatever their nature be, it is for those who propound the will to remove such suspicion, and to prove affirmatively that the testator knew and approved of the contents of the document, and it is only where this is done that the onus is thrown on those who oppose the will to prove fraud or undue influence, or whatever else they rely on to displace the case made for proving the will. Here the circumstances under which the will of the 9th was prepared and signed are such as to cause the gravest suspicions. The doubt which they raise is not, to my mind, removed by the evidence on behalf of the defendants, and I should go further if it were necessary ...'

Wingrove* v *Wingrove (1885) 11 P & D 81 Probate Division (Sir James Hannen P)

Wills made under undue influence – definition of undue influence

Facts

It was alleged that the revocation of certain gifts by a codicil to the testatrix's will had been procured by the undue influence of the defendants.

Held

In addressing the jury on the subject of undue influence Sir James Hannen P said:

> 'Gentlemen of the jury, I must ask your particular attention to the exposition which I am about to give you of the law upon this subject of undue influence, for I find, from a now long experience in this Court, that there is no subject upon which there is a greater misapprehension.
>
> The misapprehension to which I have referred arises from the particular form of the expression. We are all familiar with the use of the word "influence", we say that one person has an unbounded influence over another, and we speak of evil influences and good influences, but it is not because one person has unbounded influence over another that therefore when exercised, even though it may be very bad indeed, it is undue influence in the legal sense of the word. To give you some illustrations of what I mean, a young man may be caught in the toils of a harlot, who makes use of her influence to induce him to make a will in her favour, to the exclusion of his relatives. It is unfortunately quite natural that a man so engaged should yield to that influence and confer large bounties on the person with whom he has been brought into such relation; yet the law does not attempt to guard against those contingencies. A man may be the companion of another, and may encourage him in evil courses, and so obtain what is called an undue influence over him, and the consequence may be a will made in his favour. But that again, shocking as it is, perhaps even worse than the other, will not amount to undue influence.
>
> To be undue influence in the eye of the law there must be – to sum it up in a word – coercion. It must not be a case in which a person has been induced by means such as I have suggested to you to come to a conclusion that he or she will make a will in a particular person's favour, because if the testator has only been persuaded or induced by considerations which you may condemn, really and truly to intend to give his property to another, though you may disapprove of the act, yet it is strictly legitimate in the sense of its being legal. It is only when the will of the person who becomes a testator is coerced into doing that which he or she does not desire to do, that it is undue influence.
>
> The coercion may of course be of different kinds, it may be in the grossest form, such as actual confinement of violence, or a person in the last days or hours of life may have become so weak and feeble, that a very little pressure will be sufficient to bring about the desired result, and it may even be, that the mere talking to him at that stage of illness and pressing something upon him may so fatigue the brain, that the sick person may be induced, for quietness' sake, to do anything. This would equally be coërcion, though not actual violence.
>
> These illustrations will sufficiently bring home to your minds that even very immoral considerations either on the part of the testator, or of someone else offering them, do not amount to undue influence unless the testator is in such a condition, that if he could speak his wishes to the last, he would say, "This is not my wish, but I must do it."
>
> If therefore the act is shown to be the result of the wish and will of the testator at the time, then, however it has been brought about – for we are not dealing with a case of fraud – though you may condemn the testator for having such a wish, though you may condemn any person who has endeavoured to persuade and has succeeded in persuading the testator to adopt that view – still it is not undue influence.
>
> There remains another general observation that I must make, and it is this, that it is not sufficient to establish that a person has the power unduly to overbear the will of the testator. It is necessary also to prove that in the particular case that power was exercised, and that it was by means of the exercise of that power, that the will such as it is, has been produced.'

Wintle v _Nye_ [1959] 1 WLR 284 House of Lords (Viscount Simonds, Lords Reid, Tucker, Keith of Avonholm and Birkett)

Wills – affirmative proof to remove suspicion – proof of 'righteousness of the transaction'

Facts

The testatrix, who had a large fortune, instructed her solicitors to make a will for her in January 1937. The instructions were that certain bequests and annuities should be made to her relatives and that the residue of her estate should be divided equally between eight hospitals. The solicitor and a bank were appointed executors. In April 1937 the testatrix ordered her solicitor to make certain alterations to the will, these included appointing him sole executor and leaving the residue of the estate to him, a clause being included requesting him to apply the same in accordance with a letter not yet written. The residuary gift was of substantial value. The whole will was drawn and executed in the solicitor's office and the testatrix received no independent legal advice on the matter although the solicitor had asked her to do so with regard to the residuary estate. In 1939 the solicitor wrote to the testatrix advising her to revoke the gifts of certain annuities to charities since there was a possibility that depreciating estates may have been inadequate to meet these. The testatrix acted on this advice and a codicil was executed revoking the annuities which in consequence fell into residue. The testatrix died in 1947, her estate was valued at £155,000 for estate duty purposes, the lion's share being the residue. The testatrix's next-of-kin (also a solicitor) brought an action to revoke a grant of probate to the will on the ground that the testatrix did not know and approve of the contents of her will. At the trial of the action the judge directed the jury correctly on the law but did not scrutinisethe evidence tendered by the solicitor. The jury found that the testatrix knew and approved the contents of the will. The Court of Appeal dismissed the next-of-kin appeal. On appeal to the House of Lords:

Held

The burden of proof was on the solicitor to establish that the testatrix knew and approved of the contents of her will and codicil so far as they benefited him. This burden was a very heavy one which required the jury to take a very critical approach to the solicitor's evidence. As the trial judge had not given such a direction the appeal would be allowed and the grant of probate revoked accordingly.

Viscount Simonds:

> '... it is not the law that in no circumstances can a solicitor or other person who has prepared a will for a testator take a benefit under it. But that fact creates a suspicion that must be removed by the person propounding the will. In all cases the court must be vigilant and jealous. The degree of suspicion will vary with the circumstance of the case. It may be slight and easily dispelled. It may on the other hand, be so grave that it can hardly be removed. In the present case the circumstances were such as to impose on the respondent as heavy a burden as can well be imagined. Here was an elderly lady who might be called old, unversed in business, having no-one upon whom to rely except the solicitor who had acted for her and her family; a will is made by him under which he takes the bulk of her large estate; a will made it is true, after a number of interviews extending over a considerable time, during which the details of her property and of her proposed legacies and annuities were said to have been put before her, but in the end of a complexity which demanded for its comprehension no common understanding: on her part, a wish disclosed in January 1937, to leave her residuary estate to charity which was by April superseded by devise of it to him, and, on his part, an explanation of the change which was calculated as much to aggravate as to allay suspicion: the will retained by him and no copy of it given to her; no independent advice received by her and, even according to his own account, little pressure exercised by him to persuade her to get it: a codicil cutting out reversionary legacies to charities allegedly for the benefit of annuitants but in fact, as was reasonably foreseeable, for the benefit of the residuary beneficiary. All these facts and others that I do not pause to enumerate demanded a vigilant and jealous scrutiny by the judge in his summing-up and by the jury in the consideration of their verdict.'

4 Revocation, Alterations, Revival and Republication

Adams, Re [1990] 2 WLR 924 High Court (Francis Ferris QC)

Revocation – will otherwise destroyed?

Facts

The testatrix made a will in 1976. In 1982 she telephoned her solicitor instructing him to destroy the will: he sent it to her saying that it would be better if she destroyed it. After her death in 1987, the will was found among her possessions; the typescript had been scribbled upon in many places with a blue-black ball point pen and the signature of the testatrix and attesting witnesses had been scored out particularly heavily. Had the testatrix intended to revoke the will and had she succeeded in 'otherwise destroying' it within s20 of the Wills Act 1837?

Held

She had. As material parts of the will had been destroyed with the intention of revoking it, the will as a whole had been revoked.

Francis Ferris QC:

> 'The question before me seems to come down to this: has this will been revoked in the words of s20 by the burning, tearing or otherwise destroying of the same with the intention of revoking of the same? I have already dealt with the question of intention and as I have said I find that whatever was done to this will was done with the intention of revoking it. There is, of course, no question of burning or tearing in this case. What it comes to, therefore, is whether what has happened comes within the words "otherwise destroying the same" ...
>
> I conclude that the question whether there has been a destruction of a material part of the will in the circumstances of this case depends on whether the original words of a material part of the will are or are not apparent as the will stands at the moment. The test which is to be applied for the purpose of deciding whether the original words are apparent when that question arises under s21 appears from *Ffinch* v *Combe* [1894] P 191 at 201 where Jeune P said:
>
> > "The result of the authorities, therefore, appears to be that the words beneath obliterations, erasures, or alterations on a testamentary document are 'apparent' within the meaning of the Wills Act, if experts, using magnifying-glasses, when necessary, can decipher them and satisfy the Court that they have done so; but that it is not allowable to resort to any physical interference with the document, so as to render clearer what may have been written upon it."
>
> As I have said, I consider that the same test applies for the purpose of determining whether an obliteration constitutes destruction for the purposes of s20.
>
> I therefore return to an examination of the present will. So far as the signature of the testator is concerned I have to say that initially I had the greatest difficulty in seeing at what part of the page this signature had been placed, although the heaviness of the underscoring acted as some sort of guide. Having examined the will further I can now, I think, just discern where the signature was originally placed

but to my eye the only part of that signature which I can decipher at all is part of what I think is the initial letter; this may well be an initial letter "A", which would, of course, be consistent with the first name of the testatrix, which was Almena, but if I had not known that fact I think I might well have been minded to say that what I can read is part of some other initial letter or perhaps that I had no idea what initial letter it is part of. Beyond that, although I think I may just be able to say that there is some further writing, I cannot read with my eye what that writing is, whether it is a further part of the testatrix's signature and what that signature is I am just unable to tell. No expert evidence has been put before me which would enable me to consider whether my inability to see what is there is attributable to my own deficiencies rather than to the heaviness of the overscoring.

In all the circumstances I have to say that I conclude that the signature, if that is what it was, of the testatrix on this will is not any longer apparent. I could only reach the conclusion that it was a signature by inference from other circumstances.

To some extent the same goes for the signature of at least the first attesting witness. Here I think I can just see that there is a signature beneath the underscoring, but whose signature it is and what form it takes is virtually impossible to make out. The same goes to a large extent but in a lesser degree for the signature, if that is what it is, of the second witness.

In all these circumstances it seems to me that applying the test which I have indicated I have to reach the conclusion that a material part of this will has been destroyed and accordingly the will as a whole has been revoked by the testatrix and ought not, therefore, to be admitted to probate.'

Bell* v *Fothergill (1870) LR 2 P & D 148 Probate Division (Lord Penzance)

Wills – presumption of revocation by destruction – circumstances

Facts

On the death of the deceased his will was found with the signature cut out, apparently by a pair of scissors, but the paper so cut out had been placed in position again and gummed there. The will had been in the custody of the testator up until the time of his death. Declarations of the deceased made subsequent to the date of the will were proved of an intention to benefit his wife by will. There was no other will.

Held

The presumption that the deceased had cut out the signature animo revocandi was not rebutted, and the gumming of the signature in its orignal place did not revive the will.

Lord Penzance:

'... the question is, what is the legal result of this state of things. In *Davies* v *Davies and Evans* (1756) Lee 445 the marginal note is "a will with the seal torn off, in the repositories of the deceased: held that the act was done *animo cancellandi*". I merely refer to this case for the general proposition contained in it, namely, that when a will has always remained in the custody of the deceased and is cancelled, the Court will presume that it has been cancelled *animo revocandi* by the deceased himself. The same doctrine is laid down in *Williams on Executors*, pt 1, bk 2, ch 3 Ss1 vol 2, p151, 6th Ed:

> "If a testament was in the custody of the testator, and upon his death it is found among his repositories mutilated or defaced, the testator himself is to be presumed to have done the act, and it has already appeared that the law further presumed that he did it *animo revocandi*."

See also *Lambell* v *Lambell* (1831) 3 Hag Ecc 568. These authorities establish the proposition that in the absence of evidence to the contrary, this Court is bound to presume that the testator did this act, the cutting out of the name, himself. If the paper had not been gummed on again, it is clear the Court must have further presumed that he did the act with an intention to destroy the will, and the question is, whether the presumption is altered because the name has been pasted on again, even assuming that it was pasted on by the deceased himself. I think not. Probably at one time the testator came to the determination to destroy his will, and subsequently have altered his mind, he thought, by pasting on the signature again, he could resuscitate it. The law does not upohold such a course. Lastly, is the presumption that the deceased did this act himself rebutted by his subsequent declarations? It is not necessary I should state at length the nature of these declarations. It is sufficient to say that they were general declarations, that he intended to benefit his wife by will, and they did not refer to the will as still in existence. With much reluctance I pronounce against the will. The costs of all parties will be paid out of the estate.'

Brunt* v *Brunt (1873) 3 P & D 37 Probate Division (Sir James Hannen)

Wills – revocation by destruction – mental capacity

Facts

The testator, a publican, made a will in November 1869. In October 1871 his doctor found that the testator was suffering from delirium tremens, and that during such an attack he was incapable of transacting business and was not responsible for his actions; but after the attack passed off he was perfectly normal. During the month that his doctor was in attendance upon him the testator went up to his bedroom one day at 2 am very drunk and opened his iron safe in order to put away the money he had taken during the previous day. Seeing the will in the safe, he deliberately tore it up into fragments and threw them on the table muttering to himself. The testator's wife collected the bits and locked them up. Afterwards the testator told some friends that he must have been insane when he tore up the will.

Held

That the will was not revoked.

Sir James Hannen:

> '... I am of the opinion that under these circumstances there was no revocation of the will by destruction. The act done by the testator can in no sense be considered his act, for he was then taken out of his mind; so that there has never been anything at all amounting to a revocation. After his recovery he expressed his regret, and proposed to make a fresh will. The circumstances are exactly the same as those in *Borlase* v *Borlase* (1845) No 4 of Ca 106. At page 139 Sir H Jenner Fust says:
>
> > "The deceased was at the time (of the destruction of the paper) in a state of mental excitement, and insane, and not master of his actions, and consequently not responsible for his act, as if it had been the act of a competent person and consequently the attempt of destruction, or even the actual destruction of the codicil by a person in such a state of mind, has no effect. The pieces of paper were saved and sealed in an envelope, with a memorandum setting forth the fact of the tearing by the deceased. This attempted destruction, therefore, cannot have the effect of a revocatory act. The deceased is said to have immediately recovered his faculties and to have expressed his regret at the act. I think this is not improbable looking at the nature of the attacks he was subject to; but whether or not this be so whether he did recover himself immediately or not if at the time of the attempted destruction he was not of sound mind, the act can have no effect upon the instrument he attempted to destroy; and therefore nothing, it appears to me, can in any way affect the disposition contained in the codicil".'

Bryan, In the Estate of [1907] P 125 Probate Division (Gorell Barnes P)

Wills Act 1837 s20 – revocation by implication.

Facts

The testatrix made a will in 1864 with a codicil thereto executed in 1865 leaving all her property to two named persons subject to the payment of debts and expenses. The gift of property was certain legacies on trust for the testatrix's sister for life, then on trust for the testatrix's niece for life with remainder to the children of the niece. The testatrix made another will in 1867 which in substance repeated the will and codicil of 1864 except that the trusts in favour of the niece and the niece's children were omitted and a specific legacy to the niece was cut down. The 1867 will also contained a legacy of £500 to a person not named in the 1864 will but there was no express clause of revocation and no gift of residue unlike the 1864 will.

Held

The later will could revoke the earlier testimony documents even if these disposed of all the deceased's estate and even if the last document contained no revocation clause. Whether it did so was a matter of construction of the document in question in each case and in the present case the last will was on its face a revocation of the earlier documents.

Gorell Barnes P:

> '... if this question were dealt with by a Court of construction, I do not think that the second lot of legacies would be treated in this case as cumulative on the first. Moreover, the matter is somewhat different where the Court dealing with it is the Probate Court and not a Court of construction dealing simply with two or more admitted instruments.
>
> Then, coming to decided cases, *Dempsey* v *Lawson* (1877) 2 PD 98 is an authority for saying that the fact that a later will does not dispose of the whole property of the deceased, and contains no express clause of revocation, will not necessarily prevent it from being treated as revocatory of an earlier document which did dispose of the whole property. Sir James Hannen said (1877) 2 PD 98 at 105:
>
> > "In support of this contention, *Williams on Executors*, 6th ed. p 150, 10th Ed P 102 and the cases there cited, were relied on. I assent to the principle expressed in the passage referred to, and I have had occasion to act upon it in the case of *In the Goods of Petchell* (1874) LR 3 P & D 153, but it becomes necessary on the present occasion to consider more minutely the nature and extent of the inconsistency of a later testamentary instrument, which will have the effect of revoking an earlier will. In this investigation the Court is necessarily called upon to put a construction upon the language of the instrument in question. The intention of the testator conveyed in that language has to be ascertained by reference to the facts in connection with which it is used; but in seeking for the true meaning of the testator, the substance and not the form of the instrument must be regarded. If it can be collected from the words of the testator in the later instrument that it was his intention to dispose of his property in a different manner to that in which he disposed of it by the earlier document, the earlier document will be revoked, and this, although in some particulars the later will does not completely cover the whole subject-matter of the earlier. This was decided by Sir Herbert Jenner Fust in *Plenty* v *West* (1845) 1 Rob Ecc 264."
>
> The decision in *Gould* v *Lakes* (1880) 6 PD 1 does not touch anything of importance in the present case.
>
> In *Lemage* v *Goodban* (1865) LR 1 P & D 57 it was perfectly obvious from the consideration of the testamentary papers themselves that the testator intended all his property to go to his sister. Another case cited was *Chichester* v *Quatrefages* [1895] P 186 [the learned President read the judgment from the report of that case].
>
> In regard to the further proposition contended for by Mr Priestly and Mr Stone that, if a perusal of the docouments themselves does not satisfy the Court, external evidence may be looked at, I doubt whether this means anything more than that the court may put itself in the same position as the deceased was in when she sat down to sign the last will in other words, to enable the Court to ascertain what the deceased knew at that time. In the case of *Jenner* v *Ffinch* (1879) 5 PD 106 I doubt whether the Court looked at anything more than was needed to put it in possession of the facts known to the testator at the time the will in question was signed.

Sir James Hannen there said [at 111]:

> "In *Dempsey* v *Lawson* I relied solely on the contents of the second instrument, taken in connection with the earlier one, and with the facts with reference to which the second was made, and which might, therefore, afford a guide to the testatrix's meaning. In the present case, although I think that the will of February 2, 1879, does contain some internal evidence of the intentions of the testatrix that it should be in substitution of the first, I think it is desirable, if I can properly do so, to have recourse to external evidence to show whether or not the testatrix intended the last instrument to constitute her sole will, and so by implication to revoke the first. This makes it necessary that I should consider the question which I advisedly left undetermined in *Dempsey* v *Lawson*, whether such external evidence is admissible, and under what circumstances. By the Wills Act (1 Vict c26, s20) it is enacted that 'no will or codicil or any part thereof shall be revoked otherwise than aforesaid (ie by marriage) or by another will or codicil executed in manner hereinbefore required'. This leaves untouched the question what will being duly executed will revoke an earlier one. I think it clear that no express words of revocation are necessary. The authorities appear now to establish that revocation by implication is sufficient. On this point I refer to what I said in *Dempsey* v *Lawson*."

Summed up in the report of *Jenner* v *Ffinch*, it is thus stated:

> "The question what instruments are to be admitted to probate, as together or separately constituting the testator's last will, is solely for the Court of Probate, as it was formerly for the Ecclesiastical Court."

In considering this question the Prerogative Court did in some circumstances admit parol evidence with respect to the factum of the instrument in order to investigate *quo animo* the act was done by the testator. The subject was very fully discussed by Sir H Jenner in *Thorne* v *Rooke* (1841) 2 Curt 799, and he came to the conclusion that where there is something on the face of the instrument raising doubt or ambiguity as to whether it was intended by the testator to be in substitution for or addition to a previous will, the Court is justified in having recourse to external evidence to ascertain the testator's intentions. In the cases before him the learned judge thought there was no such doubt or ambiguity, but the case of *Methuen* v *Methuen* (1817) 2 Phill 416, commented on and not disapproved of by Sir H Jenner, may be referred to as showing what doubt arising on the face of the instrument, and taken in connection with the facts known to the testator, will be sufficient to justify the admission of external evidence. There the testator, having made one codicil, under which his wife and daughters took certain benefits, after the marriage of one of the daughters made a codicil in which, after reciting that he had made a provision for the daughter, he proceeded to make dispositions in favour of the wife and daughters differing from those in the first codicil. There was nothing making it absolutely impossible that the testator meant their disposition to be cumulative, but, as Sir H Jenner points out, it did appear that if both the codicils had been acted upon, "the property of the deceased would not have been equal to the payment of all the legacies that had been given". It was upon this state of facts that Sir J Nicholl said:

> "The first instrument remains uncancelled and there are no revocatory words in the second. It is contended that the Court has no power to inquire further, but the same rules do not apply in a case relating to the factum of the will which would apply if the inquiry were concerning the construction of it. In the Court of Porbate the whole question is one of intention. The *animus testandi* and the *animus revocandi are* completely open to investigation in this Court. It is admitted that if there is doubt on the face of the instrument the Court may admit parol evidence."

That is the authority for the proposition that in cases of doubt external evidence is admissible. In the present case it is not necessary to refer to any such evidence. I am of opinion that on the face of these documents themselves the last will is a revocation of the earlier document. But if that were not so, and if this case fell within the decision of *Jenner* v *Ffinch*, it is made absolutely clear beyond all doubt that the testatrix intended the last will alone to operate. The effect is that there is an intestacy as to the residue.

It would be strange indeed if, when the testatrix had deliberately struck out the residuary legatees from the earlier will, they should be put back again by implication, through the admission of all three documents, merely because she did not dispose of the residue in the later will.

Champion, Re [1893] 1 Ch 101 Chancery Division (North J)

Wills Act 1837 s34 – effect of republication of will

Facts
The testator made his will in April 1873 and by it he devised his freehold cottage and the land thereto belonging 'now in my occupation' to trustees on trust for his wife for life and then to his children in equal shares. In September 1873 the testator purchased two fields adjoining the cottage and occupied them with the cottage till his death. In 1877 he made a codicil by which he changed the executors, and cofirmed his will in other respects.

Held
The effect of the codicil was to republish the will and to include in the devise all land belonging to the cottage at the date of republication. The two fields purchased between the date of the will and the date of the codicil passed thereunder.

Cheese v *Lovejoy* (1877) 2 PD 251 Court of Appeal (James, Baggalley and Cotton LJJ)

Wills Act 1837 s20 – recovation by destruction – need to prove intent to destroy and an effective act of destruction

Facts
A testator had drawn a pen through the lines of some parts of his will, leaving the words perfectly legible, and had written on the back 'All these are revoked'. A housekeeper who had been nine years with the testator said that about 11 years before the testator's death she had first seen the document in the testator's sitting room under a cushion of the sofa, that about seven or eight years before the testator's death the testator had kicked it into a corner of the sitting room among a quantity of other papers, and that she had eventually retrieved it from beside a coal-box and took it into the kitchen where she put it on the table. The document remained lying round the kitchen until the testator's death and he neither asked for it nor had it produced to him. The question arose whether the will had been revoked.

Held
The will was not revoked; the words 'or otherwise destroying' in s20 had not been satisfied because, whatever the testator intended, the will had not actually been injured.

James LJ:

> 'We cannot allow the appeal in this case. It is quite clear that a symbolical burning will not be, a symbolical tearing will not do, nor will a symbolic destruction. There must be the act as well as the intention. As it was put by Dr Deane in the Court below, "All the destroying in the world without intention will not revoke a will, nor all the intention in the world without destroying: there must be the two".'

Collins v *Elstone* [1893] P 1 Probate Division (Sir Francis Jeune P)

Wills Act 1837 s20 – revocation – effect of testator's misunderstanding as to effect of revocation clause

Facts

A testatrix left two wills, and a codicil to the first will. The second will, which disposed of only a small policy of insurance on her life, was prepared for her on a printed form by one of her executors. The form commenced with a clause revoking all previous testamentary dispositions; but when this was read over to her she objected to it, saying she did not wish to revoke her first will and codicil. The person who prepared the will assured her that as it only related to the insurance policy the words of revocation would not apply to her former testamentary dispositions, and that to make an erasure might invalidate the will.

Held

The testatrix must be taken to have known and approved of these words of revocation and therefore they must be included in probate of the last will.

Sir Francis Jeune P:

> 'Misinformed by this statement, she allowed the clause to remain. The question is, under these circumstances, can I strike it out consistently with the authorities? I am afraid I cannot. There are three cases to which I have been referred. The first is the case of *Guardhouse* v *Blackburn* (1866) LR 1 P & D 109, where Lord Penzance's words lay down a canon which no doubt completely covers this case, because Lord Penzance says that, subject to a question of fraud, the fact that a will has been read over to a capable testator on the occasion of its execution, or its contents brought to the testator's notice in any other way, should, when coupled with his execution thereof, be held conclusive evidence that he approved of as well as knew the contents. Then there is the case of *Atter* v *Atkinson* (1866) LR 1 P & D 665 to which I need not refer further, because Lord Penzance's view of the law is fully expressed in the case of *Guardhouse* v *Blackburn*. The case of *Guardhouse* v *Blackburn* is commented on *Fulton* v *Andrew* (1875) LR 7 HL 448; but I do not think that any material difference with it was expressed. All that the Lord Chancellor seems to me to have pointed out is, that when that case was left to the jury it was not clear that the jury did not believe then that there was some fraud with regard to the insertion of the particular clause, or that they were satisfied that it was read over so that it was fully before the mind of the testator. Therefore, I do not think that on these cases I should strike out these words. Then Mr Bray refers me to the case of *Morrell* v *Morrell* (1882) 7 PD 68, and it seems to me that the language used in that case expresses the law which is applicable to this case, and expresses what is some reason for it, because the view of Lord Hannen in that case is this, that if a testator employs another to convey his meaning in technical language, and that other person makes a mistake in doing it, the mistake is the same as if the testator had employed that technial language himself. Now, that view appears to me exactly to meet the present case. This lady thought it right to employ this gentleman to make her will for her; she thought it right to trust to him. No doubt he was mistaken; but, according to the view of Lord Hannen, his mistake was her mistake. For a moment I felt some doubt as to whether it might not be possible to extend the doctrine of fraud as to include this mistake. But I am afraid there is no authority to make such an extension. There is, of course, a distinction between fraud and anything else; and taking the view of Lord Hannen which I have just referred to, it seems to me that where there is the interposition of fraud between the principal and agent, it may be, to follow out Lord Hannen's view, that the agency is thereby rendered invalid, and that the person is not bound by the act of the agent. Under those circumstances, I feel bound to say that I am unable to strike these words out of the will, and probate will go of the will of October 17, 1889, with these words of revocation included. The will of 1875, with the codicil of 1885, will not be admitted to probate.'

Dadds, In b (1857) Dea & Sw 290 (Sir John Dodson)

Wills – revocation by destruction – effect of destruction by person other than testator

Facts

The deceased, who died in 1856, made a will with a codicil executed thereto in 1852. A week before her death the deceased expressed a desire to revoke the codicil but decided to delay this until she consulted her executor. On the day on which one of the executors was present she expressed her intention to revoke the codicil and directed that her will and codicil, which were locked in a drawer in a room beneath where she was lying, should be fetched. The codicil was brought up and in the presence of the two witnesses she desired that the codicil should be burnt; but as there was no fire in the bedroom at the time, she directed that it should be taken back to the room below for the purpose. The codicil was thrown in the fire in that room and burnt in the presence of several people but not in the presence of the deceased. The executor read through the codicil before putting it on the fire.

Held

The requirements of s20 of the Wills Act 1837 had not been complied with and the codicil was not revoked. The executor would therefore be required to give evidence of its contents, which would be admitted to probate.

***Dixon* v *Treasurer Solicitor* [1905] P 42 (Gorell Barnes J)**

Conditional revocation – destruction under mistake of law

Facts

A testator instructed his solicitor to draft a will for him and then cut his signature off his old will under the misapprehension that the new will could not be made until the previous one had been cancelled. He died before he got round to executing the new will.

Held

The old will had not been revoked.

***Doe d Perkes* v *Perkes* (1820) 3 B & Ald 489 (Abbot CJ, Bayley and Best JJ)**

Wills – revocation by destruction – effective act of revocation

Facts

The testator had a quarrel with one of the devisees named in his will and in anger he began to tear it with the intention of destroying it. Having torn the will into four pieces he was prevented from proceeding further, partly by the efforts of a bystander who seized his arms, and partly by apologies from the devisee. Upon this he became calm and folded the will and put it in his pocket then pulled it out again and on examining it said 'It is a good job it is no worse.' The will was found after the death of the testator, in four parts.

Held

That the testator had not completely finished all he intended to do for the purpose of destroying the will and it had not been revoked.

Best J:

> '... tearing is one of the modes by which a will may be cancelled; but it cannot be contended that every tearing is a cancellation; for if it were a testator, who took his will into his hands with intent to tear it, must, if he should tear it in the smallest degree and then stop, be considered as having cancelled it. The real question in these cases is, whether the act be complete. If the testator here, after tearing it twice through, had thrown the fragments on the ground, it might have been properly considered that he intended to go

no further, and that the cancellation was complete; but here there is evidence, that he intended to go further, and that he was only stopped from proceeding by an appeal made to his compassion by the person who was one of the objects of his bounty ...'

Dunn* v *Dunn (1866) LR 1 P & D 277 Probate Division (Sir J P Wilde)

Wills Act 1837 s22 – revival by re-execution in accordance with formalities

Facts
In 1837 a testatrix made her will, which was duly executed. In 1861 she decided to deliver the deeds of her property and her will to her nephew for safe keeping. On doing this she signed her name at the foot of the will in the presence of two witnesses who attested it. No reason was given for doing this.

Held
That this was not a re-execution of a will and that the will was entitled to probate by virtue of the original execution. It was likely that the testatrix wished the delivery of her deeds and will to the nephew to be witnessed and nothing more.

Durance, In the Goods of (1872) LR 2 P & D 406 Court of Probate (Lord Penzance)

Wills Act 1837 s20 – revocation – need to show intention to revoke

Facts
The deceased made a will on 14 March 1871 setting out a number of bequests to his brother and sisters and a friend. On 13 September 1871 he sent a letter to his solicitor, Mr Denman, authorising him to deliver up his will to his brother, Joseph, and also sent a letter to Joseph in the following terms:

> 'My dear Joe, – Enclosed, I hand you an order to get my will from Mr Denman, which please burn as soon as you receive it without reading it ...'

The letter to Joseph was signed and witnessed by two witnesses.

Held
The letter revoked the will as a writing duly executed declaring an intention to revoke the same.

Lord Penzance:

> 'The question is, whether the will is not revoked by the letter. If a man writes to another "Go and get my will and burn it," he shows a strong intention to revoke his will. In the language of the 20th section of the Wills Act, the letter is a writing declaring an intention to revoke the will, and it is duly executed. It is also of a testamentary character, and therefore I shall grant administration with it annexed ...'

Everest, Re [1975] Fam 44 Family Division (Lane J)

Wills – revocation by destruction – effect of destruction on non-essential part

Facts
The testator executed a will in August 1958 and deposited it with his bank for safe keeping. In 1960 he withdrew the will in order to make certain amendments but never returned it. After his death in September 1973 his widow found the will among his papers. The will contained a bequest of personal chattels to the testator's widow for life and directed that all his real estate and the residue of his personal estate

should be held by his bank on certain trusts. These trusts could not be ascertained because that part of the will had been cut away. However, in all respects the will was complete and was properly executed and attested. The executors sought a grant of probate to the will as it stood.

Held

The proper conclusion was that the testator himself cut off the missing part of the will. This mutilation was such as to raise an inference that it was done animo revocandi of the whole will. Probate would therefore be granted of the mutilated will.

Finnemore, Re [1991] 1 WLR 793 (Micklem J)

Wills – effect of failure of testator to comply with formal rules of execution

Facts

The testator had made three wills in succession. Each one contained substantial gifts, in identical form, to X. Also, each one contained a clause revoking previous wills. The first will had no problem, but the second and third wills were witnessed by X's husband. On the face of it X was deprived of any benefit: she could not claim under the last – the third – will since her husband had witnessed it as a result of s15 of the Wills Act 1837. Further, she was concerned that she could not claim under the first will because it had been revoked.

Held

The revocation clauses in the second and third wills could be read distributively and therefore, under the doctrine of dependent relative revocation, the gifts to X in the first will remained unrevoked.

Fraser, In the Goods of (1869) LR 2 P & D 40 Court of Probate (Lord Penzance)

Wills Act 1837 s20 – revocation by an express clause

Facts

The deceased duly executed a will on 24 July 1866, but in 1869 he wrote the following memorandum at the end of the will:

> 'Florence October 19th 1869. This will was cancelled this day, in the presence of Dr Roderick Fraser, physician, and Margaret Riley, nurse, who witnessed the signature of Thomas Fraser, Esq, both being present, and signed it as witnesses.'

The names of the deceased and the witnesses appeared at the end of this memorandum in the will. The deceased did not execute any other will.

Held

The will of 1866 was revoked by the note executed in 1869.

Lord Penzance:

> '... by the 20th section of the Wills Act it is enacted that a will or codicil may be revoked by another will or codicil duly executed, or by "some writing declaring an intention to revoke the same" and executed in the manner a will is theretofore required to be executed. There is a distinction, therefore, in this section, between a will or a codicil and some writing. I am clearly of the opinion that this memorandum is merely a writing, and not a will or codicil. The deceased does nothing by it, in no way disposes of any property, he only revokes the paper to which it is attached ...'

Gilligan, Harry, In the Goods of [1950] P 32 Court of Probate (Pilcher J)

Wills Act 1837 s18(2) – power of appointment and subsequent marriage

Facts

In 1890 the deceased, Gilligan, made a settlement of funds in contemplation of his marriage. The settlement provided that in the event of there being no children of the marriage the deceased should have a general power of appointment in one moiety of the trust fund to be exercised by will and that in default of the exercise of this power such moiety of the trust funds should be held 'in trust for such person or persons as would have been entitled thereto under the statutes for the distribution of the personal estates of intestates on the death of the said Harry Gilligan had he died possessed thereof intestate and without having been married'. There were no children of the marriage and in 1902 the deceased's wife died. In 1910 the deceased made a will, which in fact was his last will. By this will he exercised the power of appointment over the first moiety of the fund granted to him in favour of his nephews and nieces, and as to £500 thereof in favour of his executors so that such sum should form part of his personal estate. In 1912 the deceased married again and by a settlement made in contemplation of his second marriage he granted his second wife a life interest in the settled fund, There were no children of the second marriage. The deceased died in 1916 and his second wife in 1946. The successors of the appointees under the deceased's will and the second wife contended that that part of the will which exercised the powers of appointment remained unrevoked by the second marriage.

Held

The part of the will exercising the power of appointment was unrevoked by the deceased's subsequent marriage in 1912. The words 'and without having been married' indicated an intention by the settlor and grantor of the power that the fund should not pass as on an intestacy (in which case the exception in s18 would not apply). In the circumstances the portion of the will exercising the power of appointment in favour of the nephew and nieces were preserved. However, since the settlor had excluded any wife of the appointee from taking any portion of the fund, the moiety appointed to the widow passed as an intestacy as she would as the deceased's next of kin received that part in any event on intestacy.

Pilcher J:

> 'As I understand it, the meaning of s18 of the Wills Act 1837, so far as I need to consider its terms for the purposes of the present case, is as follows: namely, that the only exception to the rule that a will is wholly revoked by subsequent marriage in so far as such will exercises a power of appointment and then only when the instrument conferring upon the testator the power of appointment provides that in default of the exercise of the power by him the fund which is the subject matter of the power shall devolve other than to the next of kin of the testator under the Statute of Distributions 1670.
>
> The power of appointment which Gilligan purported to exercise by his will was conferred upon by the settlement of November 29, 1890. The material terms of the settlement provided in effect that in default of the exercise by Gilligan of the power of appointment granted to him the trust fund should pass to the person or persons who would on his death have been entitled to it under the statutes for the distribution of the personal estate of intestates had he died intestate, and without having been married.
>
> These last five words make it clear that in default of the exercise of the power of appointment granted to him the parties to the deed did not intend any widow of Gilligan to take the share to which she would otherwise have been entitled under the Statute of Distributions. To this extent therefore the provisions of the settlement expressly make it clear that in default of appointment the widow shall be excluded from the portion of the fund to which she would have been entitled on an intestacy. It would seem therefore that the words in the settlement "and without having been married" necessarily involve that the estate will not, to use the words of s18, "In default of such appointment pass to … the person entitled as his … next of kin under the Statute of Distributions" provided that a widow can be properly called a "next of kin" under the Statute of Distributions.

I was referred to *Garrick* v *Lord Camden, Patton and Jones* (1807) 14 Ves 372. In that case the testator David Garrick by a residuary clause in his will provided that the residue of his estate was "to be divided amongst my next of kin as if I had died intestate". It was held that the testator's widow was not one of his "next of kin" in the ordinary sense or in which the testator must be taken to have used the words. In that case Lord Eldon said:

> "It is competent to, and required from, the court to look through the whole will; and to see, whether from the whole an intention is manifested to include the wife among those who are to be taken more strictly as next of kin: a description *prima facie* excluding her."

Having reviewed the position of the widow under the other provisions of the will, Lord Eldon arrived at the conclusion that in the circumstances it would be wrong to conclude that the testator had intended his widow to take any part of the residue and that as a widow is not "of kin" to a deceased husband, Mrs Garrick was not entitled to any share of the residue.

I was informed that there was no reported decision as to the meaning to be given to the words "next of kin under the Statute of Distributions", in s18 of the Wills Act. Looking at this statute, the words "next of kindred" are used several times. Section 3, subs3, provides for orders being made for the distribution of estates, after payment of all debts etc "amongst the wife and children, or children's children, if any such be, or otherwise to the next of kindred to the dead person in equal degree ...."

Section 5 provides for the distribution of the estate to the wife and children, and by s6:

> "And in case there be no children nor any legal representatives of them, then one moiety of the said estate to be alloted to the wife of the intestate, the residue of the said estate to be distributed equally to every of the next of kindred of the intestate, who are in equal degree and those who legally represent them."

Section 7 of the Act contains a further passage in which a clear distinction is drawn between the wife and the "next of kindred" of the intestate [The numbering of the sections cited is that given in Statutes Act Large (Danby Pickering) 1763. In Statutes of the Realm, s3(3) is s1 and ss5 and 6 are s3 and s7 is s4.]

Looking therefore to the wording of the Statute of Distributions, it would not perhaps be unreasonable to assume that in using the words "next of kin under the Statute of Distributions", the framers of the Wills Act 1837, intended that a will exercising a power of appointment should be wholly revoked by a subsequent marriage, if the instrument conferring upon the testator the power of appointment provided, as did the settlement of November 28, 1890, that in default of appointment the fund should pass to those who would have been entitled to it under the statute for the distribution of the personal estate of intestates had the testator not been married or died a widower – that is, to his true next of kin to the exclusion of his widow.

Whilst it is not strictly material for my purpose, it is interesting to observe that the Administration of Estates Act 1925, which repeals the Statute of Distributions, provides by s50, subs1, as follows:

> "References to any Statutes of Distribution in an instrument *inter vivos* made or in a will coming into operation after the commencement of this Act, shall be construed as references to this Part of this Act; and references in such an instrument or will to statutory next of kin shall be construed, unless the context otherwise requires, as referring to the persons who would take beneficially on an intestacy under the foregoing provisions of this Part of this Act."

It would seem therefore that in documents to which this section applies, references to statutory next of kin will now be construed as including widows.

I was referred to *In the Goods of Russell* (1890) 15 PD 111. In that case upon facts somewhat similar to those which I have had to consider in the present case, Butt J granted administration with the will annexed to the widow of a testator who had before marriage, executed by will a power of appointment where the instrument creating the power provided that in default of appointment the fund should be divided amongst the testator's brothers and sisters who were in fact his true next of kin. It appears to have been assumed in this case that the words of s18 of the Wills Act, 1837, "next of kin under the Statute of Distributions", included the widow, and Butt J decided the case as he did on this basis. The point that the widow was not "next of kin" under the Statute of Distributions was not argued or apparently considered, but the court without argument accepted the proposition that the words of s18 of the Wills Act, "next of kin under the Statute of Distributions", are not confined to persons who are strictly "of kin" to the testator but include a widow who is entitled to her portion on an intestacy.

Although no argument was addressed to the point, I am naturally influenced by the fact that Butt J accepted the proposition in question without query. In the circumstances I may perhaps be permitted to consider shortly the purpose and effect of s18 of the Wills Act. The section provides that wills shall be revoked by subsequent marriage except in so far as they exercise powers of appointment where the instrument creating the power provides that in default of appointment the fund subject to the power passes other than to the heir at law or "next of kin under the Statute of Distributions". If these last words are ambiguous, and it seems to me that they may be, it is right that consideration should be given to the whole purpose of the section and such interpretation given to the potentially ambiguous words as shall carry out the intentions of the legislature if these can be ascertained.

The event which the section contemplates is the remarriage of a person who has made a will and the circumstances in which a will so made shall be revoked by such subsequent marriage. If the instrument creating the power of appointment provides that in default of appointment the fund shall pass to named persons or, as in the present case, that a widow shall be excluded from all shares in the fund, this manifests an intention by the settlor and grantor of the power that the fund shall not in default of appointment pass as on an intestacy. If on the other hand the instrument creating the power provides in terms that in default of appointment the fund shall pass as on an intestacy the settlor has not thereby manifested any intention actively to control the ultimate destination of the fund. It is the marriage of the testator which revokes his previously made will so that if after marriage he dies withou making another will his widow will take her portion on an intestacy under the Statute of Distributions. In so far as the exercise by will of powers of appointment is concerned there would seem logically to be no reason why a will exercising such powers should not be revoked by marriage where in default of the exercise of the power the aftertaken wife is entitled tt her widow's portion. Where, however, the settlor under the instrument creating the power has provided that in default of appointment no wife of the appointee shall take any portion of the fund it seems not unreasonable to adopt a construction of the words in the Act which will give effect to the wish of the settlor and will preserve such portion of the will as exercise the power of appointment. I have accordingly come to the conclusion that the words in s18 of the Wills Act 1837, "next of kin under the Statute of Distributions" were intended to include a widow. I think the intention of the section was that a will exercising a power of appointment should only be wholly revoked by the subsequent marriage of the testator in those cases in which the instrument creating the power provides that in default of appointment the funds shall devolve as on an intestacy, in which event the widow of the deceased will take her portion of the fund.

This construction gives to the material words in s18 the meaning which has been assigned to them by Butt J in *In the Goods of Russell* to which I have referred. It is also the meaning which they necessarily have since 1925 in documents in which s50 subs1 of the Administration of Estates Act applies.

I accordingly order a grant of administration to the applicant with that part of the will which remains unrevoked annexed.'

Gullen, In b (1858) 1 Sw & Tr 23 (Sir C Cresswell)

Wills Act 1837 s20 – revocation through destruction of essential part of will.

Facts

The deceased made a will on six or eight detached sheets of paper and at the time of execution he signed his name at the foot of each sheet in the presence of the attesting witnesses who subscribed in his presence each sheet. On his death two of the middle sheets of the will only were found amongst his papers, and there was no trace of the remaining sheets.

Held

That the signatures at the end of the will, being the only ones that satisfied the Wills Act, having been destroyed, the will must be presumed to have been revoked.

Sir C Cresswell:

> 'You would have been in a very different position, if no more than these two sheets had been executed. The signatures at the end of the last sheet were the only ones made in compliance with the statute. You cannot convert signatures not made in due compliance with the statute into valid signatures. The only execution in compliance with the statute having been destroyed. I cannot grant the motion.'

Hardyman, Re [1925] Ch 287 Chancery Division (Romer J)

Wills Act 1837 s34 – effect of republication of will

Facts

In 1898 the testatrix made her will by which she bequeathed a legacy of £5,000 'in trust for my cousin his children and his wife, failing his children upon his death and that of his wife or until she marries again …' The cousin referred to was one Colonel McClintock who was, at the date of the will, married to his first wife who died in January 1901. In November 1901 the testatrix, knowing of the death of the first wife, made a codicil, to her will which did not refer to this legacy but did refer to the will. In 1903 Colonel McClintock married again and in 1924 he died without issue to either marriage. The question arose whether the second wife could claim the £5,000 legacy under the testatrix's will.

Held

The legacy passed to the second wife as it was necessary to read the will and the codicil together, and these indicated that the testatrix was referring, after the execution of the codicil in 1903, to any wife Colonel McClintock might have in the future.

Romer J:

> '[Counsel] says that I must take the will first of all and substitute for the word "wife" the name of Colonel McClintock's first wife, and then, he says, having done that, the testatrix has by her codicil only republished a will in which she has given benefit to his first wife by name and that, as his first wife predeceased the testatrix, the second wife cannot possibly take under the devise. It appears to me that to adopt such such a course would not be to apply the rules as to republication with good sense and with discrimination, but to construe the will as though it had not been republished. I cannot substitute a Christian name of the first wife for the word "wife" unless I disregard the fact of the republication of the will and construe the will as though there had been no republicaton. What I have to construe is a will which has been republished and which, as I say, is a will which the testatrix tells me expressed her wishes as they were at the date of her codicil …
>
> Now he had no wife at that time, therefore, if those were the testatrix's wishes at the date of her codicil, the only person who could take under that provision would be and is, the lady whom Colonel McClintock married after the testatrix's death in 1903. It appears to me, therefore, that I ought to answer the questions that have been asked by the summons by declaring that according to the true construction of the will and codicil, and in the events which have happened, the second wife of Colonel McClintock has an interest for her life or until she marries in the sum of £5,000.'

Hobbs v *Knight* (1836) 1 Curt 768 (Sir Herbert Jenner)

Wills – revocation by destruction of part only of a will

Facts

The deceased made a will in 1835, and at some time after 1 January 1838, when the Wills Act 1837 was law, he cut his signature from it. The question arose whether the will had been effectively revoked by destruction under s20 of the Wills Act 1837.

Held

The will had been revoked.

Sir Herbert Jenner:

> 'Assuming that the statute applies to the case before the Court, the next question is, does the cutting out of the signature of the testator, the rest of the paper remaining entire, amount to a revocation of the will? In order to determine the effect of this act (the excision of the name of the testator) we must consider what is necessary to create a valid will under the statute. The ninth section of the statute is to this effect,
>
> > "that no will shall be valid, unless it shall be in writing and executed in manner hereinafter mentioned (that is to say), it shall be signed at the foot or end thereof by the testator, or by some other person in his presence, and by his direction; and such signature shall be made or acknowledged by the testator, in the presence of two or more witnesses present at the time, and such witnesses shall attest, and shall subscribe the will in the presence of the testator; but no form of attestation shall be necessary."
>
> It appears, then, that the signature of the testator is necessary to the validity of the will, that no will is valid without it, so that it is not only a material part, but an essential part, without which a will cannot exist.
>
> A will being so executed, the next question is how it is to be revoked? The 30th section provides, "that no will or codicil, or any part thereof, shall be revoked, otherwise than as aforesaid" (that is, by marriage, under the 18th Section) "or by another will etc" (which does not apply in this case), "or by burning, tearing, or otherwise destroying the same by the testator, or by some person in his presence, and by his direction, with the intention of revoking the same". Assuming then that this act was done by the deceased, it must be taken to have been deliberately done; the effect of that act is now to be considered. The signature of the testator being, as I before said, an essential part of a will, it is difficult to comprehend when that which is essential to the execution of a thing, is destroyed, how the thing itself can exist. There can be no doubt that if the name of the testator had been burnt or torn out, the revocation would have been as complete as if the will had been torn into twenty pieces. If this were not the case, it would lead to many to many absurd consequences. But it has been argued, that as the present act of Parliament has pointed out certain modes with regard to the revocation of wills, the Court cannot go beyond the express terms of the act; that the words being confined to burning, tearing or otherwise destroying, omitting the terms "obliterating" and "cancelling" used in the statute of frauds; there must be an actual burning or tearing, or as to "otherwise destroying," that the whole instrument must be destroyed; that the cutting, in the present case, is not tearing (burning is out of the question) and that instrument not being destroyed, that there is no revocation; and upon this part of the argument, the case of *Doe dem Reed* v *Harris* (1837) 6 Ad & Ell 209 in the Queen's Bench was referred to, in which the testator had thrown his will on the fire, with the intention of destroying it, and a part of the cover was burnt, but there being no burning on the instrument itself, the judges of that Court held that the will was not revoked; that the words of the statute of frauds had not been complied with. But that case is not applicable to the present point, for here a part of the will, the most essential part, is removed, and if in that case, the name of the testator had been burnt or torn off, I think the Court of Queen's Bench would have held that to be an effectual revocation by burning or tearing, for, according to the judgment in that case, it was not required that the whole will should be burnt or torn. The learned judges do not say how much it is necessary should be burnt, but Mr Justice Coleridge says it is sufficient if the entirety of the will is destroyed; his expressions are these:
>
> > "We were pressed with the argument; must the whole of the document be destroyed? I say no: but there must be a destruction of so much as to impair the entirety of the will, so that it may be said that the will does not exist in the manner framed by the testator."

So I say here is not the entirety of the will destroyed by the removal of the signature of the testator? It is true this is not an act of tearing, in the strict sense of that term, but, if the circumstances of this case required it, I think it would not be difficult to show that a will might be revoked by cutting with an instrument as well as tearing, if a corresponding effect be produced by the one act as by the other. The Latin equivalent for the verb "to tear" is *lacerare*, but I find, upon looking into the dictionaries, that *excindere,* "to cut out", is also used in the sense of "to tear", and Cicero uses the phrase *exscindere epistolam* (which is remarkable) with regard to the destruction of a document. But it is unnecessary to enter further into the consideration of this point, for, consistently, with the true construction of the act of Parliament, and the decision of the learned judges of the Court of Queen's Bench, it is not necessary, in order to bring the act within the meaning of the words "otherwise destroying", that the material of the will should be destroyed; it is sufficient as it appears to me, if the essence of the instrument (not the material) be destroyed. Suppose a will to be written in pencil, and the words were removed by means of Indian rubber; could there be any doubt that that would be a sufficient revocation? Cutting is a mode of destroying as effectual as tearing, and it appears to me that if tearing a will to this extent be a sufficient destruction of it, the same effect must be attributed to the act of cutting it: what would be the consequences of a different construction? Suppose a will torn into two or more pieces, the will no doubt, would be revoked; but if it were cut into twenty pieces with a knife that would be no revocation, and if the pieces could be collected and pasted together, the will must be pronounced for by the Court. I cannot conceive it possible that it was the intention of the legislature to leave the law in that state. The question then comes to this: whether this be or be not a destruction of the will. I consider the name of the testator to be essential to the existence of the will, and that if the name be removed, the essential part of the will is removed and the will is destroyed; otherwise the statute does certainly not deserve the title it bears, namely "An act to amend the laws with respect to wills".

It was said in the argument (perhaps it is not very material) that a will cannot now be revoked by obliteration, the term obliterations having been advisedly omitted by the legislature; but I am not prepared to say (although I now merely throw this out) that a will may not be revoked in that way, for I see no reason why, if the obliteration amounts to a destruction of the will, (that is, if the name of the testator, which is essential to a will, be so obliterated that it cannot be made out), a will may not be revoked in that way as well as any other. Suppose a testator had so obliterated his name from a will as to render it impossible to make it out, and I am not at liberty to supply it by evidence *aliunde*, how would this operate with respect to the 21st clause of the Act, which enacts "that no obliteration interlineation, or other alteration, made in any will after the execution thereof shall be valid, or have any effect", except so far as the words, or clause, as I understand it, where words are so obliterated that they do not appear, it is a good revocation *pro tanto.* Would not the same rule be applied with respect to the name of the testator? I think that it was the intention of the legislature that it should be sufficient if the name of the testator was so obliterated that it could not be made out; it never could be intended that a testator might revoke his will *pro tanto,* and yet not be at liberty to revoke the whole will.'

Lushington (Counsel for Knight):

'What does the Court say as to the names of the two witnesses? By a parity of reasoning there would be a revocation by the obliteration of the names of the attesting witnesses.'

Sir Herbert Jenner:

'I think so too; and if any such case should occur, I should think that if the names of the attesting witnesses were erased by the testator *animo revocandi,* it would be a sufficient revocation. It might be difficult to make it appear that the names of the witnesses were erased *animo revocandi;* but if it could appear, I should be of opinion that it would amount to a destruction of the will, within the meaning of the Act of Parliament. I do not think that the words "otherwise destroying" mean that the material of the will must be destroyed, but that it must be something which would amount to a destruction of the will itself.

I am then of opinion that the 34th section of the Act of Parliament did not exempt the deceased in this case from the necessity of complying with the requisites of the act, as to the manner in which this will

> was to be revoked; and secondly, that the act done to the will (the excision of the name) amounts to a destruction of the will within the meaning of the statute. With respect to the futher point, whether the excision of the name was intended only as a revocation, upon a new will being duly executed, I am of opinion that the case of *Onions* v *Tyrer* (1716) 1 P Wms 345, referred to in the argument does not apply to the circumstances of this case, because in that case the deceased believed that the last will was a valid will, and on that supposition he proceeded to annul the former will; while in the present case, it is pleaded in the allegation that the deceased knew that two witnesses were necessary to the due execution of the will, and therefore that the paper before the court could not have any effect.'

Hope-Brown, In the Estate of [1942] P 136 (Langton J)

Conditional revocation – condition in express revocation clause

Facts
The testator made in 1934 a will which completely disposed of his estate. In 1939 he made a holograph will with a revocation clause. In this will he directed that the residue should be disposed of among a number of beneficiaries, but no names were inserted in the space left for that purpose.

Held
The doctrine of conditional revocation applied since the revocation clause had been put into the 1939 will on the condition that this will would be complete. The two wills should therefore be admitted to probate with the revocation clause excluded.

Horsford, In the Goods of (1874) LR 3 P & D 211 Probate Division (Sir James Hannen)

Wills Act 1837 s21 – effect of alterations by total obliteration of words

Facts
At the testator's death a codicil to his will was found with a bequest in the following terms 'I leave and bequeath *ten* pounds, *which will be found* with my photograph, to Emily Bush ... as a rememberance for kindly coming to see me when she was a little girl.' The words in italics were written on pieces of paper pasted over the original writing. Certain parts of the will were pasted over also. The witnesses to both his will and codicil had no opportunity of observing the pages of the will and did not see if the strips of paper were pasted on at that time. The question arose whether the words under the pasted paper ought to be ascertained and included in probate.

Held
Where a testator, at a time which is unknown, has pasted over a whole legacy a piece of paper and has written on top a new bequest, the Court will not order the pasted paper to be removed and will direct probate to issue in blank as to that legacy. However, if the testator has covered over the amount of the legacy only, leaving the legatee's name untouched, the case may be one of dependent relative revocation and the Court will attempt to discover the amount of the legacy originally bequeathed by removing the paper.

Sir James Hannen:

> '... it is clear that words so written on strips of paper must follow the fate of ordinary alterations, and in the absence of evidence showing when they were made, it must be presumed that they were so added after the execution of the will and codicil. But ought I to treat the words over which the pieces of paper are

pasted as effectually obliterated, and grant probate of the will or codicil with the hidden passages in blank, or ought I to endeavour to ascertain what words have been covered up, and include them in probate? As to the will, the answer to these questions depends upon the construction to be put on the 21st section of the statute 1 Vict C26, by which it is enacted that no obliterations, interlineation, or other alteration made in any will after the execution thereof, shall be valid or have any effect, except so far as the words or effect of the will before such alteration shall be executed in like manner as hereinbefore is required for the execution of the will. Soon after the passing of the Act, Sir H J Fust, in *Townley* v *Watson* (1844) 3 Curt 761, decided that the construction to be put upon the words of the 21st section was that the effect of the will before the alterations must be apparent on the face of the instrument itself. He said:

> "What is an obliteration? Is it not by some means covering over words originally written, so as to render them no longer legible? I cannot understand, if the legislature really intended that extrinsic evidence should be admitted, why a few more words were not added, which would have freed the section from all doubt; for instance, why was it not thus penned: 'unless the words shall be capable of being made apparent'?"

I think it is impossible to read the words of the statute, and not to say that it was an intention of the legislature that, if a testator shall take such pains to obliterate certain passages in his will, and shall so effectually accomplish his purpose that those passages cannot be made out on the face of the instrument itself, it shall be a revocation as good and valid as if done according to the stricter forms mentioned in the Act of Parliament. Mr Justice Williams (*Executors* p139, 6th ed., in a note) says:

> "In a case before Sir H J Fust, he ordered that the erasures in a will should be carefully examined in the registery with the help of glasses, by persons accustomed to writing, to ascertain whether the words could be made out and directed that probate should pass with the erased passages restored, unless they could not be made out, and then with those parts in blank. Generally speaking, the Ecclesiastical Court will not in the first instance take upon itself to decide whether the obliterated words can or cannot be made out. It must be proved."

But it has not been the practice to adopt any means of ascertaining what the words attempted to be obliterated were, other than mere inspection by aid of glasses. Chemical agents have not been resorted to in order to remove any portion of the obscuring ink, and I do not think it would be proper to adopt such means. I think "apparent" in the 21st section means apparent on the face of the instrument in the condition in which it was left by the testator, and that if he had recourse to extraordinary means to obliterate what he had written, then this court is not bound to take any steps to undo what he had done … assuming that the words covered over cannot be ascertained by inspection, the probate must go with those parts in blank.'

Itter, In the Goods of [1950] P 130 Court of Probate (Ormrod J)

Wills Act 1837 s21 – effect of illegible writing – need to show 'apparent words'

Facts

A testatrix pasted slips of paper over the amounts of certain legacies in her will and then wrote on them certain sums of money. The new sums were signed by her but were not attested as required by the Wills Act 1837. Evidence was given that it was impossible to decipher the writing under the slips of paper otherwise than by taking infra-red ray photographs.

Held

The photographs were not admissible to show what was written under the slips of paper. 'Apparent' meant that the words must be apparent on the face of the 'instrument itself' and not be creating a new document.

Ormrod J:

> 'It is fair to say that it appeared to be the clear intention of the testator to bequeath to the respective legatees the amounts written on the slips of paper. But her signatures on these slips were not attested as required by the Act of 1837. Before the hearing an examination of the codicil had been made by a handwriting expert appointed for the purpose. He took photographs of the document by the use of infra-red rays and was able to produce to the court a photograph of the parts of the codicil which were under the slips of paper. I accepted his evidence of the original figures, and indeed there was no dispute between counsel on either side on this point. He said, however, that he was only able to find out what was under the slips by taking the photograph: he could not, by the assistance of any other modern scientific means in his possession or known to him, see what was on the codicil by looking at the document itself without removing the slips. It is contended by the plaintiffs that in these circumstances the words and figures under the slips are "apparent" within the meaning of s21 of the Wills Act 1837. I cannot accept this contention. "Apparent" must mean, to quote the words of the judge in *Townley* v *Watson* (1844) 3 Curt 761, 786 which concern this point, apparent on the face of the "instrument itself". If the words of the document can be read by looking at the document itself, then I think that they are apparent within the meaning of the section, however, elaborate may be the devices used to assist the eye and however skilled the eye which is being used; but if they can only be read by creating a new document, as in this case by producing a photograph of the original writing on the codicil then I cannot find that the words are apparent. They may be discoverable; in this case they have been proved to be so; but that is not the word used in the statute ...'

Jones, Re [1976] Ch 200 Court of Appeal (Buckley, Roskill and Goff LJJ)

Conditional revocation – effect of intent to make a will at time of destruction of existing will

Facts

The testatrix had a large number of nephews and nieces. By her will dated 12 July 1964 she devised a smallholding to the plaintiff and his sister, a nephew and a niece, in equal shares and left the residue to be divided equally between her other nephews and nieces. The testatrix at all times had the will in her custody. In 1970 the testatrix decided to change her will since she did not see the plaintiff and his sister very often and they had acquired property of their own. On 23 September 1970 she visited her bank manager about making changes in her will and told him she was thinking of leaving her smallholding to her nephew Jim, the first defendant. She then went on to see her solicitor, but he was unavailable; she arranged an appointment for the following week so that he could take her instructions for a new will. In the meantime, on 27 September 1970 the testatrix was taken seriously ill; she sent for her nephew William, as she thought she was dying. He asked if she had made a will and she replied in the negative. On 5 October the testatrix died without having made a new will. After her death the will dated 12 July 1965 was found in a mutilated condition, as if cut up by a pair of scissors, and several clauses were missing as well as the testatrix's signature and the witnesses' signatures. The missing parts were never found.

Reeve J, at first instance, held that the testatrix had mutilated the will and therefore revoked it with the intention of making a new will and that since this intention had not been effectively carried out the will had not been effectively revoked. On appeal:

Held

The will had been effectively revoked because from the facts it was clear that the testatrix did not intend that the revocation of her will of 1965 should be conditional or dependent or her making a new one, but that it should be absolute. This conclusion was not inconsistent with her intention to make a new will, and therefore in the circumstances she had died intestate.

Goff LJ:

'On the facts in this case, the question is whether the 1965 will was effectively revoked, or whether, no subsequent will having been executed, it is saved and stands good by virtue of the doctrine of dependent relative revocation.

Very often the applicability of that doctrine comes in question when an act *prima facie* revoking a will is done in circumstances where, to use a neutral expression for the moment, a further will is in contemplation, but it is not confined to such cases. It arises also, for example, where the testator has made a mistake as to the material facts, or as to the result in law of an intestacy, or has acted in the erroneous belief that by revoking a will he can, without more, thereby revive a previous will which that will had itself revoked.

In whatsoever way it arises, however, the principle on which it falls to be decided is, in my judgment, the same and well settled by authority. It is this: was the revocation absolute and unqualified, in which case it takes effect whatever happens, or conditional, in which case it does not take effect unless the condition be satisfied? I agree that each case must turn on its own facts and that reference to the authorities is of use, therefore, only insofar as they establish, as in my judgment they plainly do, the principles which I have just stated.

The principal authority for that purpose is, of course, the decision of this court in *Re Southerden* [1925] P 177. I do not think it is necessary for me to take up time reading citations from the judgments in that case, as the passages on which I would rely have already been cited by Buckley LJ.

I would, however, wish to refer briefly to *Dancer* v *Crabb* (1873) LR 3 P & D 98 where Sir James Hannen said [at 104]:

"Or, to state the proposition in different language, if the testator's act can be interpreted thus 'Whatever else I may do, I intend to cancel this as my will from this time forth', the will is revoked: but if his meaning is, 'As I have made a fresh will my old one may now be destroyed', the old will is not revoked if the new one be not in fact made."

I would further point out that in *Dixon* v *Treasury Solicitor* [1905] P 42 which has been cited by Buckley and Roskill LJJ, Gorell Barnes J made the position very clear indeed, because in the course of his judgment, before leaving the question to the jury, he said [at 45]:

"There is no doubt that the testator did what he did because he was making a new will."

He concluded:

"The questions I leave to you are (1) whether the testator cut his signature off the will with the intention of revoking the will; or (2) whether the testator cut his signature off the will with the intention that the will should be revoked conditionally on his executing a fresh will."

In *Re Botting* [1951] 2 All ER 997 at 1001 Havers J said:

"It seems to me that in the circumstances of this case I am bound to make that *prima facie* presumption, and then it is open to the plaintiff to bring before me, if he can, evidence to rebut it and to show what the intention of the testator was in destroying the will. If I am satisfied on the whole of the evidence that the destruction was conditional on another will being made, then the doctrine of dependent relative revocation applies ..."

The only other reference I would make to authority is the case of *Re Bromham* [1951] 2 TLR 1149. I would point out that there was a particular factor in that case tending strongly to support the view that the revocation was indeed conditional, and that was that the testator in that case was illegitimate. Lord Merriman P said [at 1153]:

"Of course, if, without any reference to the intention, at some later time after the discussion about the new will, and when he was in a state of complete oblivion of any such intention, or had firmly cast that intention aside, the deceased destroyed his will with the intention of revoking it, one also has to assume that he intended to be intestate, which would mean, on the facts of this particular case that instead of either Miss Mabel Wass, or Miss Doris Wills, or both, getting anything, he really intended the Chancellor of the Exchequer to get it all."

There was some discussion in the argument before us whether the doctrine was or indeed could have been, conceived to give effect to the intention of testators and whether it is necessarily excluded if it does not. In my judgment, however, that is not the right approach. Sometimes, as in *Re Southerden*, it clearly does give effect to the testator's intention, which would otherwise have been defeated. In many cases however, it cannot do so, because the testator wished to make dispositions which could only be effected by a valid new will which he failed to make.

The testator's testamentary intentions, as far as ascertainable, are of course relevant and important considerations in determining on the evidence as a whole whether the revocation is conditional or not, but that is as far as it goes.

There are also some arguments about the onus of proof, but I do not think that is really of importance, in all events where both sides have called evidence. It remains a question, what is the proper inference on the evidence as a whole?

It was further argued for the plaintiff that the learned judge's findings of fact should not be disturbed and that in reality he had found that the revocation was conditional. I do not think he had. Certainly he found that this was a classic case of dependent relative revocation, but in my judgment that was a conclusion based on a wrong test. He said this:

> "I have then to ask myself this question, did she cut her will with the intention of revoking it and dying intestate, or did she do so because she was determined to make some fresh testamentary dispositions?"

However, in my judgment, the fact that the testatrix revokes her will absolutely and not conditionally does not necessarily involve her having decided to die intestate; nor does the fact that she revoked the will because she is determined to make some fresh testamentary disposition necessarily involve the revocation being conditional.

In any case, although this court ordinarily does accept the trial judge's findings as the primary facts, it is free to draw its own inferences from them. We are able to do that as well as the trial judge himself. I therefore proceed to consider on the facts as found by the learned judge whether the revocation was unqualified or conditional, and I am satisfied that the correct inference is that it was unqualified.

My reasons for this conclusion are as follows: first, there is no evidence that the testatrix had a belief that it was necessary to revoke an existing will before one could make a new one. In the absence of such belief, however, it is difficult to see any reason why she should have mutilated the 1965 will, save for the purpose of getting rid of it forthwith and in any event.

Secondly, whether she cut off her signature and that of the witnesses and thereby also removed cll 3, 4 and part of cl 5 of the will, as the learned judge found and as I must accept, or whether as has been accepted she cut the paper the other way round, the fact remains that she did remove the signatures and a large part of the willl including the all-important cl 4, which devised the smallholding which formed substantially the whole of her estate. Moreover she apparently destroyed the part cut off. Why do this, I ask myself, if she had any idea that the document retained any capacity for life?

Thirdly, although she vacillated and as late as early September showed a clear intention to leave the smallholding to the plaintiffs, yet by 23rd September she had definitely decided to leave it to the children of the first defendant. She gave the bank manager, Mr Davies, three reasons for this decision. One was that the first defendant's parents had been very good to her, which is consistent with the revocation being solely for the purpose of changing the gift of the smallholding, and so tending to the inference that it was conditional. The other two, however, were personal to the plaintiff and her sister; one that they no longer needed the smallholding because they had bought a place of their own, which they had, and the other that they were not showing any proper interest in or regard for her, which may well have been unfair, but which was the view she had formed. In my judgment, these two reasons strongly support the inference that the revocation was not conditional.

There is another indication also pointing in the same direction, which is that on the morning of Sunday, 27th September, she told the second defendant, William George Harries, that she had not made a will. Too much reliance ought not to be placed on that, because she may have been merely telling him that, untruthfully, to stop any further discussion or questioning, but if she was stating the position as she understood it, then in my judgment it becomes another strong indication that the revocation was not conditional. With respect, I am unable to agree with the learned judge's view that this piece of evidence told the other way. He said:

> "I can find no possible motive for the deceased to have told anyone that she had not made a will at all, which would have been a completely untrue statement."

In my view, a person who has revoked her will may really quite accurately say, "I have not made a will", rather than, "I did make a will, but I revoked it." On the other hand if, in her view, the revocation had not yet taken effect and was conditional on the completion of her new testamentary dispositions, I cannot see how, if she meant to speak the truth, she could possibly say, "I have not made a will ..."

For those reasons, in my judgment, the mutilation of the will was done *animo revocandi*, and absolutely not conditionally.'

May, In b (1868) LR 1 P & D 575 at 581

Wills Act 1837 s22 – revival by codicil – need to prove intention to revive

Facts

The testator made a will on 11 January 1860. On 18 August 1860 he married and on the same day made a new will revoking the earlier one in express terms. In September 1860 he tore his signature from the first will. In July 1861 he made a codicil which was described as 'a codicil to the last will and testament of me, John May, of etc, and which will bears the date of the 11th day of January 1860'.

Held

The evidence of surrounding circumstances failed to show that the intention of the testator was to revive his former will. Everything pointed towards there being a mistake by the testator's attorney in drafting the will.

Mills* v *Millward (1890) 15 PD 20 Probate Division (Butt J)

Wills – unauthorised destruction – effect of attempt to ratify destruction

Facts

The testatrix made her will in 1888 leaving legacies to various relatives. She retained the will in her custody and shortly before her death gave it to her sister-in-law, Mrs Millward, to read, who on finding that neither her's nor her husband's name appeared in it lost her temper tore it up and threw the fragments into the fire in the presence of the testatrix telling her that unless she made a new will her property would go to her brother and not as she wished. The sister-in-law apologised and urged the testatrix to make another will, but she refused, saying 'I shall never make another will let it remain as it is.' The testatrix died a few days later without making another will.

Held

There was no sufficient evidence of a subsequent ratification of the destruction of the will so as to constitute it an act done by the direction and by the authoritty of the testatrix and probate would be granted of the will as contained in an affidavit of the executor.

Butt J:

> '... in order to establish revocation it is contended on behalf of the defendant that though Mrs Millward had no authority to destroy the will, and was in fact diametrically against the will of the testatrix in

> destroying it, yet as the testatrix afterwards expressed her satisfaction with the state of things which had been brought about by destruction, that amounts to a ratification of Mrs Millward had done, and that such ratification was tantamount to a destruction by the testatrix and by her authority. I doubt very much whether it is a tenable argument in any circumstances, but it is not necessary for me to decide the point, as I hold that the words attributed to the testatrix do not amount to a ratification of the destruction by Mrs Millward …'

Moore, In b [1892] P 378 Probate Division (Sir Francis Jeune P)

Wills Act 1837 s20 – need to prove knowledge and approval of revocation

Facts
A testatrix by her will constituted her illegitimate son her universal legatee and one of her executors. After the execution of the will, and shortly before her death, she expressed a wish to bequeath part of her furniture and other personal effects to her sister, her sole next of kin and heiress at law, and proceeded to write out a bequest giving effect to such wish on a printed form of will, which was duly executed. The form commenced by a clause of revocation; but the testatrix did not fill up the blanks in this part of the form, and the clause was not read over to her at the time of execution, though the rest of the will was, and there was evidence that she knew of the clause.

Held
In the circumstances probate would be granted of the paper omitting the revocation clause, as a codicil to the original will.

Moore, Re [1907] 1 IR 315 Chancery Division (Ireland) Barton J

Wills Act 1837 s34 – effect of republication of will

Facts
A testator devised certain lands to the Presbyterian Orphan Society, a registered charity. By the Charitable Donations and Bequests Act 1884 a devise of land to a charity was invalid unless the will in which it was contained was executed at least three months before death. The deceased had made his will more than three months before death but he executed a codicil to his will republishing it within three months of death. The question arose whether the devise to the charity was caught by the 1884 Act.

Held
The courts have never allowed republication to contradict or frustrate the intentions of the testator and therefore the gift to the charity could take effect.

Barton J:

> '… it is contended that the republication of the will, by bringing it down to the date of the codicil, caused this devise to be contained in a will executed less than three months before the testator's death and so invalidated it. That contention is, in my opinion, unsustainable. The devise did not infringe either the language of the section or its policy, which was to prevent the mischief of improvident alienations or dispositions by languishing and dying persons. The Wills Act affords no support to the objection, which rests upon what I think is a misunderstanding or misapplication of the rules about republication of wills.
>
> It is well settled that for many purposes republication brings the will down to the date of the codicil and makes it speak as a new will of that date and take effect as if it had been reinserted in the codicil and re-executed at the date of the codicil. But, it is equally well settled that there are limits to this doctrine.

"The rule is subject to the limitation that the intention of the testator is not to be defeated thereby" – per Patterson J, in *Doe d Biddulph* v *Hole* (1856) 15 QB 848. "It does not necessarily operate as if the will had been originally made at the date of the codicil" – per Lord Campbell C in *Hopwood* v *Hopwood* (1859) 7 HLC 728. The effect of the decision of the Court of Appeal in *Mountcashel* v *Smyth* [1895] 1 IR 346 is that republication republishes the will with all its contents, including its original date. It is as if the old document with its old date, were translated into the codicil. Republication gives to the will a fresh starting point, but it does not erase the old date. Nor does it, in my opinion, falsify the fact that the will contained a particular devise and was executed at a particular time. The authorities which have been cited lead me to the conclusion that the Courts have always treated the principle that republication makes a will speak as if it had been re-executed at the date of the codicil not as a rigid formula or technical rule, but as a useful and flexible instrument for effectuating a testator's intentions by ascertaining them down to the latest date at which they have been expressed.

A glance at a few of the best known cases will, I think, support this view of the effect of republication. The Court has, by regarding a will as re-executed by republication, been enabled to validate a legacy to a witness to the original will: *Anderson* v *Anderson* (1872) LR 13 Eq 381; to add to the will unattested papers which were sufficiently referred to in the will for the purposes of identification and incorporation, but were not written and signed until after its execution: *Truro's case* (1866) LR 1 P & D 201; to include in a number of cases under the old law, after-acquired lands in a devise, from which they would otherwise have been excluded; and since the Wills Act, to ascertain whenever it is necessary to do so, intention as regards after-acquired property by reference to both will and codicil. See *Re Farrer* (1800) 8 Ir CLR 370 and *Re Champion* [1893] 1 Ch 101. Again, where a husband purported by his will to exercise in his wife's lifetime a power which had been given only to the survivor of the husband and wife, and the wife died after the will but before the codicil, the republication was held to validate the exercise of the power: *Re Blackburn* (1890) 43 Ch D 75. Where a legacy was given subject to legacy duty, and a subsequent statute substituted succession duty for legacy duty, republication after the passing of the statute enabled the Court to give effect to the presumed intention of the testator that the legacy should be subject to the substituted duty: *Re Rayner* [1903] 1 Ch 685. Where a legatee of a legacy which was excepted from a general bequest, died after thewill, the contents of a subsequent codicil republishing the willenabled the court to infer a continuance of intention to except the legacy from the general bequest: *Re Fraser* [1904] 1 Ch 726.

On the other hand, the Courts have never allowed the republication of a will to contradict the acts or frustrate the intentions of a testator. Republication does not revive a legacy which has in the interim been revoked, adeemed or satisfied: *Powys* v *Mansfield* (1837) 3 My & Cr 359; *Hopwood* v *Hopwood.* Again, republication has been held not to render a power less beneficial to the grantee on account of a subsequent departure from a custom referred to in the will as regulating the power: *Doe d Biddulph* v *Hole* (1856) 15 QB 848. It has also been held that the date of the original execution remains a factor for the construction of the will, for example, when it is necessary to determine the date to which the adverbs of time occuring in the will are referable: *Mountcashel* v *Smyth.*

In short, the aim of the court has always been to apply the rules as to republication, with goods sense and discrimination, for the purpose of as far as possible, effectuating up to date the intentions of the testators ...'

Powell* v *Powell (1866) LR 1 P & D 209 (Lord Penzance)

Conditional revocation – conditional destruction

Facts

The testator made a will in 1862 and another will in 1864. By the later will he revoked all former wills. In 1865 he got out the two wills and had them read to him. He then placed the will of 1862 under his arm and said that was the will he intended to stand. He then tore up the will of 1864, and it was by his request put in the fire and burnt in his presence.

Held
The act of destruction by the testator was referable solely to his intention to validate the will of 1862, and that the act being conditional, and the condition being unfulfilled, there was no revocation.

Lord Penzance:

> 'In both cases the act is referable, not to any abstract intention to revoke, but to an intention to validate another paper; and as in neither case is the sole condition upon which revocation was intended fulfilled, in neither is the "*animus revocandi*" present.'

Roberts, Re [1978] 1 WLR 653 Court of Appeal (Buckley and Goff LJJ)

Wills Act 1837 s18(1) – revocation by marriage – effect of voidable marriage

Facts
The deceased made a will in 1973, when he was aged 60. In 1974 he married the plaintiff, and he died in 1976. On his death the plaintiff sought a grant of letters of administration to his estate on the ground that he died intestate. The defendant, who was a beneficiary under the 1973 will, alleged that the deceased suffered from senile dementia and other mental illnesses and claimed the marriage was void since the deceased lacked the necessary mental capacity and that he could not have revoked his will under s18.

Held
Under s12(c) of the Matrimonial Causes Act 1973 the marriage was merely voidable. A voidable marriage always revoked a will which was made by a party prior to the marriage whether or not the marriage was subsequently annulled. This was because the annulment of a voidable marriage was not retrospective in effect and was a valid marriage for the purpose of revoking any prior wills.

Comment
Contrast the position where the marriage is void as opposed to voidable. A void marriage will not revoke a will for the purposes of s18 because, as Lord Greene MR explained in *De Reneville* v *De Reneville* [1948] P 100 at 111:

> 'The substance, in my view, may be thus expressed. A void marriage is one that will be regarded by every court in any case in which the existence of the marriage is in issue as never having taken place and can be so treated by both parties to it without the necessity of any degree annulling it; a voidable marriage is one that will be regarded by every court as a valid subsisting marriage until a degree annulling it has been pronounced by a court of competent jurisdiction.'

Examples of void marriages are bigamous marriages and those where the parties are related within the prohibited degrees.

Rogers* v *Goodenough (1862) 2 Sw & Tr 342 Court of Probate (Sir Cresswell Cresswell)

Wills Act 1837 s22 – revival of will – impossibility of revival of will revoked by destruction

Facts
The deceased made one will in 1858 and another in 1859. The 1859 will expressly revoked the 1858 will which was later actually destroyed. A codicil was afterwards made to the 1858 will, and the question arose whether this revived the 1858 will.

Held

The 1858 will having been entirely destroyed could not be revived.

Sir Cresswell Cresswell:

> 'When the instrument had been destroyed, it no longer existed either in law or fact; it did not exist as a will from the time the second will was executed; it no longer existed as a written instrument, as a paper writing, from the time it was burnt. Not being either a will or a writing, how could it again become a will? That question seems to be decided by the statute, the 9th section says, "that no will shall be valid unless it be in writing and executed in the manner hereinafter mentioned". It has been said that it could again become a will, because it was revived by the codicil; but it could not be revived in its original condition of a written instrument, and thus the very first thing required by the statute that the expression "no will shall be valid" applies equally to an original will and a revived will.'

Southerden, In the Estate of [1925] P 177 Court of Appeal (Pollock MR, Warrington and Atkin LJJ)

Conditional revocation – destruction under incorrect assumption or belief

Facts

The testator made a will leaving all his property to his wife before they both went on a journey to United States of America. On their return the testator destroyed the will by burning it after saying to his wife: 'This is no good now. We have safely returned and it is all yours. We might as well burn it.' The testator had an incorrect belief that his wife would receive all his property under the rules of intestacy.

Held

The testator had destroyed the will on the basis of an assumption or belief which was incorrect and that the revocation was no use and was ineffective.

Pollock MR (adopting a passage from the judgments of Lord Meredith MR in the Irish case of *Re Faris (No 2)* [1911] 1 IR 469):

> 'The true view is that a revocation grounded on an assumption of fact which is false takes effect unless, as a matter of construction, the truth of the fact is the condition of the revocation, or in other words, unless the revocaton is contingent upon the fact being true: see *Thomas* v *Howells* (1692) 1 Salk 170'

Steele, In b (1868) LR 1 P & D 575 Probate Division (Sir J P Wilde)

Wills Act 1837 s22 – revival by codicil – need to prove intention to revive

Facts

A testator made a will dated 16 January 1866. On 25 October 1866 he made a fresh will revoking the former. On 12 January 1868 he made a codicil 'to his last will and testament which bears the date the 16th day of January last past', ie 16 January 1867. The testator then affirmed his last will.

Held

There was a latent ambiguity in the codicil which permitted the court to look at evidence of intention but this did not show any intention to revoke the later will and revive the former one. The will of October 1866 was therefore never revoked and was entitled to probate.

Comment

In b Steele was really three cases in one. Sir J P Wilde had to deal with the same point in each. The other two cases were *In b May* (see above) and *In b Wilson* (see below).

***Sugden* v *Lord St Leonards* (1876) 1 PD 154 Court of Appeal (Cockburn CJ, Jessel MR James and Mellish LJ and Baggalley JA)**

Wills – presumption of revocation by destruction – circumstances

Facts

Lord St Leonards made a will and several codicils, all holograph, and these documents were kept in a small black box of which the deceased had the key. It was possible for any one of a number of persons to have obtained the key to the box. After the death of the deceased, although the codicils and some other papers were found in the box, the will was not there. Immediately after the will was found to be missing from the box, a daughter of the deceased who was also one of the plaintiffs, and who had been the constant companion of her father during his last years, and who had ample means of becoming acquainted with the contents of the will, wrote out from memory, without reference to the codicils and other papers which were in the box, a statement of the contents. The daughter's integrity was not disputed, and her recollection was supported by the codicils and other documents. The evidence pointed to the testator's having died in the belief that he would not die intestate, and there was no evidence of the revocation of the will. No evidence was called for the defendants and interveners.

Held

The contents of the lost will, like those of any other lost instrument may be proved by secondary evidence. This may consist of declarations, written or oral, made by a testator, both before and after the execution of the will or by the evidence of a single witness, though interested, whose veracity and competency are unimpeached. So much of the contents of a lost will as are proved in this manner wlll be admitted to probate. In the present case the evidence of the daughter and certain declarations were accordingly admitted to probate.

Cockburn CJ:

> 'When the idea of Lord St Leonards having himself destroyed the will is disposed of, the next question which presents itself is, whether, the will, having been lost, secondary evidence can be given of its contents. Now that matter is disposed of by the authority of *Brown* v *Brown* (1858) 8 E & B 876, which, I think has been recognised as perfectly sound. There Lord Campbell says, "Parol evidence of the contents of the lost instrument may be received as much when it is a will as if it were any other document", and in that I, for one, most entirely concur. The consequence of a contrary ruling would be in the highest degree mischievous, it would enable any person who desired, from some sinister motive, to frustrate the testamentary disposition of a dead man, by merely getting possession of the will to prevent the possibility of the will of the deceased being carried into execution. No doubt the absence of the will is a serious fact, and one which may place the Court, which has to decide whether the parol evidence of the contents is right or wrong, in a position of considerable difficulty; but with that difficulty it is the business of the Court to grapple, in order that effect may be given to the will made according to the requirements of the statute, and which after the testator's death ought to be carried into effect.'

***Sykes, In b* (1873) LR 3 P & D 26 Probate Division (Sir James Hannen)**

Wills Act 1837 s21 – unattested alteration after execution but before codicil

Facts

The testator's will was made in 1869, with a codicil thereto in 1870 which referred to the will by date. About 1871 the testator put the will and codicil in a sealed envelope and deposited it with a Major-General Balfour for safe-keeping. After his death the packet was opened for the first time. In the will Dr John Scott was appointed one of the executors, but his name was written on an erasure. There was no evidence when his name was written on the erasure but Major-General Balfour swore that two years before the sealed packet was deposited with him the testator told him that Dr John Scott was one of his executors.

Held

The presumption that alterations were made after the will was executed was rebutted; the declaration of the testator as to whom he had appointed executor was admitted as evidence that the alteration was made before the execution of the codicil.

Sir James Hannen:

> 'This is a question as to an alteration in the will of the deceased. Was it made before or after the execution of the will, or before or after the execution of a subsequent codicil? The will is dated the 9th of November, 1869 and the appointment of Dr Scott as executor is written on an erasure. The question arises, whether this alteration is effectual. In the absence of evidence there is, in general, a presumption that all alterations made in a will were made after the execution. The authority for this is *Cooper* v *Bockett* (1846) 4 Moo PC 419. But the rule is somewhat differently expressed by the late Vice Chancellor, then Sir W P Wood, in *Williams* v *Ashton* (1859) 1 J & H 115. He there said:
>
> > "I do think that it is quite a correct mode of stating the rule of law to say that alterations in a will are presumed to have been made at one time or another. The correct view is that the onus is cast upon the party who seeks to derive an advantage from an alteration in a will, to adduce some evidence from which a jury may infer that the alteration was made before the will was executed. I do not consider that the Court is bound to say that it will presume such alterations to have been made, either before or after execution. With regard to a will, I do not see any necessary presumption of the kind."
>
> The onus, therefore, lies on those who assert the alteration to show that it was made before the execution of the will. Stated, however, as the rule generally is, that there is a presumption that alterations on the face of a will were made after its execution, this presumption may be rebutted by evidence of declarations made before and not after the execution: *Doe d Shallcross* v *Palmer* (1851) 16 QB 747. There the evidence was of declarations of an intention of the testator, which appeared to have been carried into effect by the will as altered, and not as it originally stood. In that case, as well as in *Williams* v *Ashton*, the Court dealt with the alterations on the will itself, and without any question as to the effect of the execution of a subsequent codicil.
>
> Now a codicil is the republication of a will, and usually the presumption remains the same as regards the codicil as the will; so that it will be presumed, without any evidence to the contrary, that alterations appearing on the face of the will were made not only after the execution of the will, but also of the codicil: *Lushington* v *Onslow* (1848) 6 N of C 183. It would appear, however, that as the declarations of a testator, made before the execution of a codicil, which republishes the will, may be admitted to show that the alterations in the will were made before the execution of the codicil. In the present case the affidavit of Major-General Balfour states, that on an occasion before the execution of the codicil the testator told him that he had appointed Dr Scott as his executor. This is a much more positive and stronger declaration than that made in *Doe d Shallcross* v *Palmer*, because it might be said that a statement by a man that he intends to make a bequest to a certain individual, leaves open the question whether the corrections, to carry out such intention, were made after the execution of the will, the document as originally executed having failed to do so. In this case the declaration is as to an act already done, and can only be correct if it be assumed that the appointment had been then made. The execution of the codicil was the confirmation of the will in its altered state, with the appointment of Dr Scott on it. I decree probate to him.'

Townsend* v *Moore [1905] P 66 Court of Appeal (Vaughan-Williams, Romer and Cozens-Hardy LJJ)

Wills – effect of two inconsistent wills of uncertain date

Facts

A testatrix executed two codicils, both of which were dated the same day but which contained some inconsistences in their provisions. The evidence of an attesting witness was that the two codicils were executed on the same occasion and practically simultaneously. Gorell Barnes J refused to admit either codicil to probate on the grounds that each was intended to operate only if the testatrix survived her husband a condition which had not been fulfilled. On appeal:

Held

1. On the true construction of the codicils they were not conditional but intended to operate in any event.
2. Where two testamentary documents are of the same date and it cannot be ascertained which of them was executed first, and their provisions are so inconsistent that they cannot stand together, the presumption in favour of admissibility will be rebutted and neither document will be admitted to probate. However, in the present case the provisions of the two codicils were not so inconsistent that they could not stand together, both ought, therefore, to be admitted to probate.

Vaughan-Williams LJ:

> '... the question now arises whether either or both of these codicils ought to be admitted to probate. In my opinion both ought to be admitted. *Prima facie* every document purporting to be be testamentary, and signed and witnessed in accordance with the provisions of the Wills Act, ought to be admitted to probate. When, however, there are more testamentary documents than one, the presumptive admissibility to probate of the documents may be displaced, because it may be that there is a sequence in date of the execution of the documents, which, coupled with the words of the later documents, or the inferences to be drawn from those words, leads to the conclusion that the later document was intended as a revocation of the earlier, or, it may be intended to revoke partially or to modify the earlier document, or, lastly, it may be that, apart from any question of revoction, the Court has to deal with documents which are proved to have been executed on the same date and occasion, or which are undated, and as to which it is impossible to affirm that the one has any priority in time of execution over the other. In this last case, if the documents are so inconsistent that they cannot stand together, in my opinion probate becomes impossible, because the presumption of admissibility to probate of a testamentary document executed in accordance with the Wills Act is displaced.'

White, Re, Barker* v *Gribble and Another [1991] Ch 1 Chancery Division (Andrew Park QC)

Wills Act 1837 s21 – effect of failure by testator to sign variation

Facts

The testator's signature to the variation of this will was signed by witnesses in the proper manner. Unfortunately the testator failed to sign again. The question arose whether the variation was valid in accordance with the requirements of the Wills Act 1837 c26, ss9, 15, 21. The testator, who died on 26 February 1985, made his original will on 2 January 1981. He attempted to alter the will on 14 December 1984 by, inter alia, decreasing the proportion of shares of X and Y and increasing the share of Z. In fact, however, the testator thereby created an intestacy under which X took a greater share. Z and another person witnessed the alterations and, in the presence of the testator at his request, placed their signature near the original signature of the testator and beneath the words 'alterations to will dated 14.12.84 witnesses:–'. However, the testator did not sign the will again. X argued for probate of the amended will claiming the alterations to be valid; Y and Z for probate of the original will (Z being aware of the possibility of the forfeiture of his entire share under s15 of the Wills Act 1837 because he was both a witness and a beneficiary), claiming that the amendments were invalid.

Held

Granting probate in solemn form of the original will, that the amendments were invalid because:

1. For the alterations to be valid under s21 of the Wills Act 1837 they must be effected 'in like manner as ... required for the execution of the will'. However, the alterations in this case were not signed by the testator or by someone under his direction;
2. The question arises of whether what took place on 14 December 1984 amounted to the creation of a valid will. The answer here was that it did not, because the formal requirements of s9(a)(b) and (d) were not complied with. In particular regarding s9(a) the new will was not signed by the testator as the signature already existed at the time of the alleged re-execution. As to s9(b) the testator did not by his existing signature intend to give effect to the new will, and as to s9(d) there was no conclusive evidence that the witnesses were attesting the will as opposed to merely attesting the alteration (*In the Goods of Martin* (1849) 1 Rob Ecc Rep 712; *In the Goods of Shearn* (1880) 43 LT 736 followed; *In the Goods of Dewell* (1853) 1 Ex & Ad 103 not followed and disapproved).

Wilson, In b (1868) LR 1 P & D 575 at 582

Wills Act 1837 s22 – revival by codicil – need to prove intention to revive

Facts

The testator made a will on 24th September 1858. On 16 July 1861 he made a fresh will disposing of all of his property. After his death the first will was found with the signature torn off, and it was clear it had been used as a draft for the second will. A codicil was also executed on 20 December 1864 which was stated to be a codicil to 'his last will and testament dated 24 September 1858'. However, the contents of the codicil showed that the testator was referring to the 1861 will.

Held

Despite the clear reference to the 1858 will there was no express intention to revive it; on the contrary the intention was to add to the 1861 will, and probate would be granted to that.

Sir J P Wilde:

> 'The occurrence of no less than three instances within a short period in which this question has arisen, makes it desirable to pass in review some of the decisions by which the judgment of the Court ought to be guided. The following appear to be the propositions established by previous authority: Unless there be a latent ambiguity in the codicil, evidence of the testator's real meaning must be excluded. This is in obedience to the well-known common law doctrine with respect to written instruments, as was decided in *Walpole* v *Cholmondeley* (1797) 7 TR 138, which was acted upon *In the Goods of Chapman* (1844) 1 Rob Ecc 1. It may be proper on some future occasion to consider the doctrine upheld in courts of equity, where mistakes, if proved to demonstration to be so, have been rectified even in written documents. This subject is well discussed in Storey's *Equity Jurisprudence*, 156, 157.
>
> The next proposition is this: that, although evidence of the testator's intention is excluded, the Court ought always to receive such evidence of the surrounding circumstances as, by placing it in the position of the testator, will the better enable it to read the true sense of the words he has used. This is a doctrine

constantly acted upon at common law in relation to written documents, and notably in cases of written guarantees. It is affirmed in the fifth proposition of Sir James Wigram's excellent book on this subject.

Thirdly, it has been decided by no less than three very remarkable cases, that if the codicil refers to a will with the intention of reviving it, and it turns out that such will had been entirely burnt or destroyed by the testator *animo revocandi,* the codicil cannot effect its revival.

The circumstances of these three cases of course varied, but in all three there were two wills, the later one revoking the former, and a subsequent codicil referring by date to the former will. They all had this further feature, that the first will was not only revoked, but destroyed. The earliest was the case of *Hale* v *Tokelove* (1850) 2 Rob Ecc 318, decided by Dr Lushington in 1850. He held that the codicil would not in law revive the first will, because the will "was gone, destroyed *animo revocandi*", but that the second will "was revoked by necessary implication because a prior will was confirmed". The only paper entitled to probate he held to be the codicil. The next was the case of *Newton* v *Newton* (1860) 5 LT (NS) 218, determined in Ireland by Mr Justice Keatinge in 1860. He held, like Dr Lushington, that the codicil could not revive the first will, but that the second will was entitled to probate as the intention to revoke the second was dependent upon the establishment of the first. His decision on this last head was reversed by the Court of Appeal in 1861 (1861) 12 Ir Ch Rep 118, and the testator declared to have died intestate. The last case was that of *Rogers* v *Goodenough* (1862) 2 Sw & Tr 342, decided by Sir Cresswell Cresswell in 1862. He held, as in the other cases, that the codicil could not revive the will that had no existence, but that, there being no words in the codicil expressing the intention to revoke the second will, and no dispositions of property inconsistent with that will, there was no ground for affirming that in any of the modes pointed out by the statute a revocation of the second will had been effected; and he granted probate of the second will and the codicil as together containing the will of the deceased. This last case, it will be observed, is an authority for this further proposition, that a codicil refers by date, and for which the testator intended as a codicil to whichone will, may be entitled to probate with another will.

Assuming, then, upon these authorities, that a codicil may, by referring in adequate terms to a revoked will, revive that will if it be in existence, and that in ascertaining whether the testator intended such revival, the Court is precluded, unless there is a latent ambiguity in the codicil, from receiving any evidence except what may suffice to place it in the position of the testator, the next question will be, what is the effect of the statute?

The words of the section (1837) 1 Vict c 26, s22 are as follows:

> "No will which shall be in any manner revoked shall be revived by a codicil, unless it be a codicil duly executed, and showing an intention to revive the same."

It is necessary to bear in mind the law as it stood when they were enacted. The theory of the law is and always was, that a codicil forms part of a will, and consequently that to make a codicil to your will is first to affirm the existence of that will; and secondly, to republish it or re-affirm its validity. It was, therefore, before the Act, an inference which the law drew from the making of a codicil, that the testator intended to re-affirm his will, and, if the will had been revoked, by re-affirming it to revive it. In brief, it would not be wrong to say that before the Act passed all codicils to wills were held to revive the wills in which they were respectively codicils, if such wills had been previously revoked. As soon, therefore, as it could be ascertained that the codicil in question was a codicil to a particular revoked will, that will was revived. The difficulty with which the courts in the contested case had to grapple, was to ascertain to which or what will the disputed paper was intended as a codicil.

Such being the state of the law before the Act, I hesitate to accept the conclusion, that the express words of the section meant to leave the matter in the same state in which it would have stood if they had never been introduced. If the merely declaring that a particular paper was to be taken as a codicil to a particular will, all that the legislature required, when it enacted that the codicil should "show an intention to revive" a revoked will, the words "showing an intention to revive the same" were quite needless, for every codicil to a revoked will, by force of being a codicil to such a will, so showed it. I therefore infer that the legislature meant that the intention of which it speaks should appear on the face of the codicil, either by express words referring to a will as revoked and importing an intention to revive the same, or by a disposition of the testator's property inconsistent with any other intention, or by some other expressions conveying to the mind of the Court, with reasonable certainty, the existence of the intention in question. In other words, I conceive that it was designed by the statute to do away with the revival of wills by mere implication. It is proper here to take note of the case of *Payne* v *Trappes* (1847) 1 Rob Ecc 583. In that case there would seem to have been but little beyond the reference by date to show the intention to revive a former will. But the Court did not lay down the proposition that the date alone was sufficient; on the contrary, the learned judge said he must "gather the intention from the codicil itself", "that the intention to revive the former will was clearly shown"; and "that the testator had taken great pains to describe the instrument to which the paper was intended as a codicil". The decision proceeded upon the ground that the judge was convinced of the testator's intention, not that he felt bound by the language in the face of an opposite conviction. On the other hand, I am much fortified in the view I take of the meaning of the statute by the remarks of Sir C Cresswell in the case of *Marsh* v *Marsh* (1860) 1 Sw & Tr 528. I allude to his statement that the words "last will" and "*prima facie*" refer to the real last will, and particularly to the opinion he there expressed, that "it appears to have been the object of the legislature to put an end equally to implied revocations and implied revivals".

The due result of the documents in each case, and of such external facts as may be admitted in evidence, must of course be gathered from the language of the documents themselves read in the light of such facts. Some general views however present themselves – some general probabilities of intention attend all such cases as those now under judgment. It may in the outset, I think, be doubted whether any testator who bore in mind that he had revoked his will, and substituted another for it, ever really sat down with the purpose of revoking his last will and reviving the former one, and set about the execution of that purpose by simply making a codicil referring by date to his first will without more. Would any lawyer advise such a course, or would any unskilled testator imagine he could achieve the end by such a method? The leading idea of revoking the one and reviving the other in its place would surely find expression by some form of words in a paper designed mainly for that object. On the other hand, I conceive that, in the vast majority of cases, when a man declares his intention that a particular paper, varying his previous dispositions, shall be taken as a codicil to "his last will and testament", he means that which really is his last will and testament, his then *existing* will, and the dispositions of his property then in force. In like manner, when he goes on to declare, in the common language of codicils, that "in all other respects he ratifies and confirms his last will and testament", he really means to confirm that which exists, and not to bring to life a paper which has ceased to be testamentary or revive dispositions which have no existence and are therefore not properly speaking, capable of being ratified.

... I am therefore of the opinion that the Court ought to be slow to conclude that a testator has manifested in this indirect way a desire to revoke his last will, and that it should scrutinise narrowly the language of a codicil which is said to show such an intention, lest in the desire to follow the testator's wishes too blindly it should set them at nought altogether.'

5 Devises and Legacies

Ashburner v *Macguire* (1786) 2 Bro CC 108 (Lord Thurlow LC)

Specific legacies – ademption

Facts
By his will made in September 1778 the testator bequeathed to his sister the interest on a bond for a debt of £3,500, owed by the sister's husband to the testator, for life. This amounted to £175 per annum and after her death the principle of the bond to be divided amongst her four daughters equally or the survivors of them. The testator also left to one Beawes, 'my capital stock of £1,000 in the India Company's stock'. In 1780 the sister's husband went bankrupt and on proving his debt of £3,500 in bankruptcy the testator received 4s 3d in the pound. The testator died in 1781 and after his death another 2s 9d in the pound was received. At the time of making the will the testator possessed £1,000 East India Stock but he sold the whole of this stock before his death. After his death his sister and her four daughters claimed such part of the £3,500 as due from the sister's husband, should be paid by his assignee and the remainder paid out of the testator's personal estate. They also claimed that the personal representatives of the testator should purchase £1,000 East India Stock for Beawes.

Held
1. The legacy of the interest and the principal of the bond was specific and had been partially adeemed by the testator receiving part of the debt after proving bankruptcy. The sister and daughters could only claim the remainder.
2. The legacy of 'my £1,000 East India Stock' was specific and adeemed into by the testator selling the stock.

Lord Thurlow LC:

> '... the claim of Mrs Ashburner and her daughters depends on two questions: First whether the bond was given as a specific legacy: which depends on this, whether the manner in which the sum is mentioned, turns it to be a pecuniary legacy, or, as civilians call it, a demonstrative legacy, that is a legacy in its nature a general legacy, but where a particular fund is pointed out to satisfy it; or whether it can be what they call a *legatum nominis* or *legatum debiti*. I shall not stand long on that point ...
>
> ...if the testator receives payment on the debt, the legacy is gone, unless it appears from the manner of his disposing of the money afterwards that he means to preserve it for the legatee. Lord Camden in *The Attorney-General* v *Parkin* (1769) Amb 566 held there was no distinction between voluntary payment and payment on a demand, and that in both cases the legacy was extinguished; he added, that where the sum is specified in the bequest, it is a general legacy, as I shall mention on the other point. But the distinction between "I bequeath *the £500 due on a bond from A B*" and "I bequeath *the bond from A B*", is very slender: and so admitted to be by his Lordship.
>
> In the civil law there is distinction taken between a deemonstrative legacy, where the testator gives a general legacy, but points out the fund to satisfy it, and a specific legacy, where he bequeaths a particular thing.
>
> On the first point, I am clear this is a specific legacy. If the fortune of the testator had failed, so as not to satisfy all the pecuniary legacies, and the question had been, whether this legacy should have been contributive to the pecuniary legacies, I believe no man in the profession would have doubted.

When the testator made his will, £3,500 was due to him from William Ashburner, by bond: he meant to relinquish that bond for the benefit of the family; not by way of release to the husband, but by way of settlement; and that this debt, whether it turned out ill or well, should go to the family: the interest to his sister for her life, the principle among her daughters. In this case, the bequest must be considered as specific, although the sum be mentioned: *for I cannot agree to Lord Camden's distinction.*

As to the legacy of East India Stock to the plaintiff Beawes, there is no case to countenance his claim. The testator says, "I give *my* capital stock to," etc: the pronoun *my* has been relied on, in many cases, in deciding the legacy to be specific.

The testator, after making his will, sold his stock, which made it as if it had never existed; *the legacy is adeemed*, according to all the cases.'

Bothamley* v *Sherson (1875) LR 20 Eq 304 Chancery Division (Jessel MR)

Specific legacies – definition

Facts

By his will the testator bequeathed 'all my shares or stock in the Midland Railway Company'. The question arose as to whether this was a specific or a general legacy.

Held

The legacy was specific.

Jessel MR:

'... I think one may arrive at a tolerably clear idea of what a specific bequest is. In the first place it is a part of the testator's property. A general bequest may or may not be a part of the testator's property. A man who gives £100 in money or £100 stock may not have either the money or the stock sufficient to discharge the legacy, in which case the executors would probably discharge it out of the actual money or stock. But, in the case of a general legacy it has no reference to the actual state of the testator's property, it being only supposed that the testator has sufficient property which on being realised will procure for the legatee that which is given to him, while in the case of a specific bequest it must be part of the testator's property itself. That is the first thing.

In the next place, it must be a part emphatically, as distinguished from the whole. It must be what is sometimes called a severed or distinguished part. It must not be the whole, in the meaning of the totality of the testator's property, or the totality of the general residue of his property after having given legacies out of it. But if it satisfies both conditions, that it is a part of the testator's property itself, and is a part as distinguished, as I said before, from the whole, or from the whole of the residue, then it appears to me to satisfy everything that is required to treat it as a specific legacy. I hope the definition which I have attempted to give will be more successful than those which have been attempted before, but I can only express that hope with some degree of trepidation.

Now there is no question, as I understand the authorities, that the part may be defined in any way which distinguished it. If a testator gives "the black horses which I now have", or "the black horses of which I shall be possessed at the time of my death", or at any other specified time, the gift satisfies the definition of a specific legacy. If authority were wanted there is plenty. I have been referred to a great many cases, and I will mention on that point one or two. There is the very singular case, to which I shall refer for another purpose, of *Stewart* v *Denton* (1785) 4 Doug 219, where a gift was of "any-stock-in-trade of wines and spiritous liquors which I shall be possessed at the time of my death". That was held to be specific. Again, in the case of *Fontaine* v *Tyler* (1821) 9 Price 81 at 98, Chief Baron Richards says,

> "A gift of all the horses which I may have in my stable at the time of my death, would be specific. Therefore, the mere fact of death being referred to as the period for ascertainment does not make the gift less specific; and those cases get rid of the observations made by Sir Thomas Plumer in the case of *Parrott*

> v *Worsfold* (1820) 1 Jac & W 594, that a specific legacy must necessarily be subject to ademption. That cannot, of course, be so when the time of death is the time for ascertainment: for a man does not live after his own death, and therefore there is no period at which ademption can take place. It is not necessary therefore that a specific bequest should be subject to ademption ..."

... in the case of *Fielding* v *Preston* (1857) 1 De G & J 438, there were two gifts: one was of "my leaseholds", and the other of "my funded property and other personal estate not hereinbefore bequeathed". Lord Cranworth was clearly of the opinion that both would have been specific except for the circumstances that the gift "of my funded property" was followed by a gift of all the rest of the estate. His Lordship says:

> "My mind has fluctuated on this point, but at last I have arrived at the conclusion that this is not a specific gift of the funded property; and I come to that conclusion because I think it would be very dangerous to hold that in a will where there is a gift of the residue, and the testator unnecessarily chooses to enumerate some particular things in that residuary gift, such a circumstance was sufficient to constitute the things so enumerated specific gifts. It rarely happens that in the gift of residue something is not mentioned specifically. For instance, a testator may give his horses and all his other personal estate, or his stock in trade and the rest of his personal estate. Such bequests could not, I think, be properly held to be specific. Suppose the will to be worded thus: 'I give to Henrietta, her executors, administrators, and assigns, all my other personal estate, including my funded property', that would not have been specific."

Therefore, when you come within that line of cases such gifts are not specific not because the word "my" would not make the bequest specific, but because it is the mere enumeration of particulars making up the residue, and it is not intended by the testator to be a gift of part of the property itself to be taken by the legatee in that shape.

I think, then, that ... gifts either "of my shares or stock in a railway company", or "of the stock of shares in the railway company which I shall be possessed of at the time of my death", or, as it was in *Stewart* v *Denton,* "of all my stock in trade which I shall be possessed of at the time of my death", are specific legacies.

... one class of specific bequests is ... the class of specific bequests described as generic, that is, a specific bequest which points to a class of objects given by the testator, and which from their nature would not naturally be referable to the date of the instrument. A good illustration of this class of bequests is gift "of my household furniture". There are very few persons not in articulo mortis who would not expect that some articles of household furniture would wear out, or be broken, or otherwise be parted with, and be replaced with articles of a similar kind. It would not be natural to assume that a man giving that kind of legacy intended to restrict it to the property of that description which he had at the date of the will. It has been held in *Goodlad* v *Burnett* (1855) 1 K & J 341, and in some other cases to which reference has been made, that in cases of that description the new law (ie section 24 Wills Act) brings down the specific bequest to the date of death; in other words, the new law makes a specific bequest of "my furniture", to mean not "the furniture which belongs to me at the time of making this my will," but "the furniture which shall belong to me at the time of my death".'

Brooke, Lord v *Warwick, Earl of* (1863) 2 De G & Sm 425

Specific legacies – chattels in a particular place

Facts

The testator made a bequest of household furniture, pictures and books which might be at his decease in or about his mansion.

Held

This bequest passed all pictures removed from the mansion and in the hands of a picture cleaner to be cleaned, and books sent to be repaired. But it did not include articles which had been purchased for the mansion by the testator but not delivered to it at his death.

Clarke v *Bruce Lance and Co* [1988] 1 All ER 364 Court Appeal (May and Balcombe LJJ)

Professional responsibility

Facts

In 1973 a testator had executed a will which was prepared and drawn up by the defendant solicitors. The plaintiff was entitled to the residuary estate under the provisions of that will as drafted. Some months later the testator granted a lease of a commercial property owned by him for 21 years. In 1978 the solicitors acted in the drawing up of a deed of variation of the lease. This deed included a provision that the lessee should have the option to purchase the property at the fixed price of £28,000 after the death of the testator or his wife, whichever was the later. The testator died in 1981. By this time inflation had caused a vast appreciation in the value of the property. The plaintiff sued the solicitors claiming negligence, and alleging that they had been in breach of their duty to the testator and to the beneficiary. Their claim was that the solicitors knew that the beneficiary's interest under the will would be adversely affected and yet they had not advised the testator that the fixed price option amounted to an uncommercial transaction.

Held

In the Court of Appeal a solicitor who has acted for a testator in preparing a will owes no duty of care to a beneficiary under the provisions of that will when acting for the testator in a subsequent transaction which decreases the value of the beneficiary's interest.

Clifford, Re [1912] 1 Ch 29 Chancery Division (Swinfen Eady J)

Specific legacies – stocks and shares – whether ademption

Facts

T bequeathed 'twenty-three of the shares belonging to me' in a certain company. At the date of the will T had 104 £80 shares in the company. Before his death the company changed its name and sub-divided each of its £80 shares for four shares of £20 each. At his death T had 416 £20 shares in place of his 104 £80 shares.

Held

There was no ademption; a change in name and form only had occurred and not a change in substance.

Swinfen Eady J:

> '... the residuary legatees ... contend that the bequest speaks from death and only passes twenty-three new £20 shares. In the alternative they contend that if the bequest speaks from the date of the will and refers to the old £80 shares then existing it is adeemed, as those shares had disappeared before the testator's death.
>
> Now s24 of the Wills Act 1837 provides that:
>
> "Every will shall be construed, with reference to the real and personal estate comprised in it, to speak and take effect as if it had been executed immediately before the death of the testator, unless a contrary intention shall appear by the will."
>
> Is there such a contrary intention on the face of the will?

... in the present case the bequest of "twenty-three of the shares belonging to me in the London and County Banking Company Limited" is a specific bequest of a thing incapable of increase or diminution, and there is in my opinion a sufficient contrary intention to show that the testator meant the bequest to be construed as at the date of the will.

The residuary legatees contend that if so construed the bequest has been adeemed, as the £80 shares no longer exist ... Here I find the twenty-three shares bequeathed by the will changed in name and form only, but substantially existing in their sub-divided form, and each original share traceable into its four sub-divided shares. The subject-matter of the bequest remains in substance, though changed in name and form. There is therefore no ademption, and ninety-two of the new shares, identical in all but name and form with the twenty-three original shares, pass by the bequest ...'

Davies, Re [1957] 1 WLR 922 Chancery Division (Vaisey J)

Acceleration – application to class gifts

Facts

A testatrix gave and bequeathed her residuary estate equally between her two sons and her stepdaughter and directed that the share of the stepdaughter should be 'hers for life and then to be divided equally between her issue'. The testatrix died in 1955 and in 1956 the stepdaughter disclaimed by deed the life interest conferred on her by the will. At the date of disclaimer she had three children none of whom had had any issue. The question arose as to how the disclaimed share ought to be dealt with.

Held

The principle of acceleration applied and the fund went to the three children of the stepdaughter to the total exclusion of other members of the clauss who might come into existence in the future, ie any grandchildren or remoter issue.

Vaisey J:

'One view, which I will call the first view, is that the principle of acceleration now falls to be so applied as to give the fund to those three children to the total and final exclusion of all the other at present non-existent members of the class, that is to say, Mrs Mackintosh's grand-children and remoter issue. It seems rather suprising that the purely gratuitous act (that is, disclaimer) of one of the beneficiaries, Mrs Mackintosh, should operate to deprive and dispossess a number of other beneficiaries, namely Mrs Mackintosh's grandchildren and remoter issue, of the interest which she, the testatrix, had given them by her will. It is clear, however, that acceleration may and does sometimes alter the constitution of a class of beneficiaries from what it would have been if the gift had not been accelerated: see *In re Johnson* (1893) 68 LT 20. Another view, which I will call the second view, is that, as the disclaimed life interest must be treated as struck out of the will and as not having been thereby effectively disposed of, the obvious consequence is a partial intestacy in which case the income of the fund during the residue of the life of Mrs Mackintosh is divisible equally between the two sons of the testatrix, leaving the capital of the fund to be divided strictly in accordance with the plain terms of the will. I have mentioned two possible views, but a third one is that the three children of Mrs Mackintosh should be treated as possessing vested interests liable to be divested by the birth of further issue to Mrs Mackintosh during her life. Between those three views, I am bound to say that the choice is to my mind difficult, as it is, in my view, not supported by any clear authority.

On the whole, I decide this case in favour of the first view, which treats the class of Mrs Mackintosh's first issue as now finally closed, this view being, in my judgment, supported by *Jull* v *Jacobs* (1876) 3 Ch D 703. In that case there was a gift to a testator's daughter of real and personal estate during her life-time, and after her decease the property was to be equally divided between her children on their coming of age. It was held that the gift to the daughter being void on account of her having witnessed the will, the gift to her children was accelerated and took effect immediately. The report seems to make it clear that it was possible for the daughter to have had further children. In the course of his judgment, Malins V-C said at [712]:

> "I am clearly of opinion that the remainder is accelerated, and the children take just as if the mother had died immediately after the testator."

To the same effect, I think, is *In re Townsend's Estate* (1886) 34 Ch D 357, of which the headnote reads:

> "Gifts by will of real and personal estate upon trust to convert and pay the income of the proceeds to A, for life, and after A's death to pay the capital or income thereof unto the child or children of A, in equal shares with gifts over in case A should die without leaving issue living at his death. The will had been attested by A's wife so that the gift of a life interest to her was void under section 15 of the Wills Act. There were no children of A's marriage. The personal estate was exhausted and the trust funds represented real estate only.
>
> ... until A had a child the gifts upon the determination of A's life estate could not be accelerated, and that during the life of A and so long as he had no children, the income of the trust funds was undisposed of, and belonged to the heir-at-law, and could not be accumulated for the benefit of persons contingently entitled to remainder."

Jull v *Jacobs* was distinguished and other cases were explained. And see also *In re Johnson.*

What I have called the second view, which is that there is no acceleration, and an intestacy as regards the income during Mrs Mackintosh's life, may have some support from *In re Vernon* (1906) 95 LT 48 but this is far from being conclusive. For the third view, which seems logical, though it may be awkward to work out in practice, I can find no authority at all ...'

Gibson, Re (1866) LR 2 Eq 669 Court of Chancery (Wood V-C)

Wills Act 1837 s24 – effect on specific bequests

Facts

A testator possessed at the time of making his will £1,000 of guaranteed stock in the North British Railway. By his will he bequeathed to his son, 'my one-thousand North British Railway Preference Shares'. After making his will he sold his North British Railway guaranteed stock and died possessed of shares and stock in the North British Railway acquired by several successive purchases, exceeding the amount bequeathed to the son.

Held

The bequest was of a specific thing which had been sold by the testator, the legacy had adeemed and the son was not entitled to have his legacy satisfied out of the shares and stock purchased since the will. Section 24 could not be applied so as to read the bequest as to the testator's death.

Wood V-C:

> 'Suppose a man to have, at the date of his will, a picture of the Holy Family by some inferior artist, and to give by his will "my Holy Family". He afterwards disposes of this picture, and subsequently acquires by purchase or gift a very much better one, on the same subject, painted by an eminent artist. Would it not be a monstrous construction to hold, that the picture existing in the testator's possession at the time of death, would pass? When there is a clearly indicated intention upon the face of the will, to give the single specific thing and nothing else, it would be a very narrow construction of the words of section 24 of the Wills Act to hold that you must sweep in everything to which the words might be held to apply, without the slightest reference to the state of things existing at the date of the will. It is true that the testator had not at the date of his will 1,000 shares, but £1,000 guaranteed stock. But he had nothing else too which the words of the will could be applied, and no one could doubt that his stock was the thing pointed out

by the will. After the date of his will he sold this £1,000 stock, and purchased not *uno ictu,* but bit by bit a number of other shares or stock. I adhere to my view, that where there is a distinct reference to a distinct and specific thing and not to a genus, there is a sufficient indication of "a contrary intention" to exclude the operation of the rule established by the 24th section of the Wills Act, and the limit of the operation of the will and the state of things existing at the date of the will.'

H (deceased), Re [1990] 1 FLR 441 (Gibson J)

Forfeiture Act 1982 – scope of application in cases of manslaughter

Facts

The plaintiff, who was severely depressed and on anti-depressant drugs, had killed his wife. At the trial it was found that he bore no responsibility for his actions. Since he was the sole beneficiary under his wife's will the question arose of whether he could benefit. Therefore, by an originating summons, he raised the question of whether the forfeiture rule applied, thereby disallowing claims by a person benefiting from his own criminal act, and if so whether the court would exercise its power to modify the application of the rule.

Held

Public policy did not require the application of the forfeiture rule in every case of manslaughter; the test was whether there had been deliberate, intentional and unlawful violence or threats of violence. In this case there was no such violence. Therefore the provisions of the Forfeiture Act 1982 would not apply. Even if the forfeiture rule had been applicable the court would have used its power under s2(1) of the Act to modify the application of the rule in the plaintiff's favour (*Gray* v *Barr* [1971] CLY 6012 applied).

Harker's Will Trusts, Re [1969] 1 WLR 1124 Chancery Division (Goff J)

Acceleration – effect of surrender of life interest on class gift

Facts

Funds were settled on trust for the will of a testatrix for her son for life, and on his death the capital was to to go to the son's children in equal shares on their attaining 21. The son surrendered his life interest by deed to the trustees. The question arose, as to whether the surrender of the son's life interest had the effect of destroying it so as to cause acceleration of the gift and close the class under the rule in *Andrews* v *Partington* (see below, Chapter 6) since at the date of the summons one child of the son had attained 21.

Held

The deed of surrender destroyed the son's life interest but it did not result in the class closing rules applying so that the class closed on the first child attaining 21. This rule was to be adopted only to reconcile inconsistent directions in a will. In this case there was no inconsistency and the class remained open until the son's death.

Hickman* v *Peacey [1945] AC 304 House of Lords (Viscount Simon LC, Lords MacMillan, Wright, Porter and Simonds)

Law of Property Act 1925 s184 – presumption of survivorship in regard to claims to property

Facts

At 6.30 pm on 14 September 1940, when the Battle of Britain was at its height, a small house, No 5 Upper Cheyne Row, Chelsea, was struck by a high-explosive bomb which fell to the basement of the house and then exploded. In the basesment there was a small air-raid shelter. At the time of the explosion five persons were in the house: (1) Mrs Price-Jones, aged 52, the owner of the house (2) her daughter (3) Miss Parke, aged 70, the housekeeper of some neighbours (4) Mr Randolph Grosvenor, aged 73, a neighbour and the first testator (5) Mr Edward Grosvenor, aged 66, a neighbour and the second testator. It was the regular practice of these persons to go down to the air-raid shelter in the basement when the air-raid alert was sounded. The house was completely ruined and all five persons were killed and buried in the debris. By his will the first testator left property in which his brother, the second testator, would share if the latter were one of his brothers 'surviving at the date of my decease', and also his housekeeper Miss Parke if she survived him. Under the will of the second testator Mrs Price-Jones, Miss Parke and the first testator would benefit if they survived him. The question arose whether under s184 the deaths of these persons ought to be presumed to have occurred in the order of seniority. The Court of Appeal (Lord Greene MR and Goddard LJ, Luxmoor LJ dissenting) took the view that s184 only applied where the proper inference was that the deaths took place consecutively and it was uncertain which took place first and not where the deaths took place simultaneously. On appeal:

Held

All that is necessary in order to invoke the statutory presumption in s184 is the presence of an element of uncertainty in the circumstances as to which of the deceased survived the other or others. As it was impossible to prove if two people died at exactly the same time, then in circumstances where such an inference would be justified s184 applied.

Lord Macmillan:

> 'My Lords, in this appeal your Lordships are called upon for the first time to consider the interpretation and application of an enactment which has introduced an entire novelty into the law of England. It first appeared in s107 subs3 of the Law of Property Act 1922, and is now in identical terms embodied in s184 of the Law of Property Act 1925. It reads as follows:
>
> > "In all cases where, after the commencement of this Act, two or more persons have died in circumstances rendering it uncertain which of them survived the other or others, such deaths shall (subject to any order of the court), for all purposes affecting the title to property, be presumed to have occured in order of seniority, and accordingly the younger shall be deemed to have survived the elder."
>
> The problem with which the legislature has thus dealt has long been familiar to lawyers. Rights of succession, alike testate and intestate, depend on the survivance of one person to another. The living succeed to the dead. In the ordinary case there is no difficulty in ascertaining which of two persons died first. But in the vicissitudes of human life there occur instances in which, owing to the absence of any positive evidence, it is not possible to arrive at a conclusion and the matter is left in uncertainty. The most familiar case is where two or more persons meet their death in a common calamity, the case of commorientes, as lawyers designate it. Two or more persons perish together and there is no evidence to show which survived the other or others. Yet rights of high importance may depend thereon. The Roman Law provided a solution for the dilemma in certain cases by means of presumptions founded on what I may call biological considerations. Thus a grown up son is presumed to have survived his parent. *Cum explorari non possit uter prior extinctus sit, humanis est credere filium diutius vixisse.* Dig Lib XXXIV Tit V De Rebus Dublis. The presumption takes the place of proof. The topic has been discussed with much learning by continental jurists and is specificially dealt with in the Code Napoléon by means of detailed presumptions. For the continental law I may refer to Burge's *Commentaries on Foreign and Colonial Laws*, 1st ed. vol IV, pp 11–29. But, says Chancellor Kent in his *Commentaries on American Law*,

> "The English law has hitherto waived the question, and perhaps prudently abandoned as delusive all those ingenious and refined distinctions which have been raised on this vexed subject by the civilians." (14th Ed, Vol II, p435).

In the absence of any presumptions the English courts had to find some way of extricating the difficulty. What they did was to fall back on the principle that the plaintiff must prove his case – *actori incumbit onus probandi.* If a plaintiff's claim depended on showing that A survived B then the plaintiff must establish the fact affirmatively by evidence; if sufficient evidence was not forthcoming the claim failed: *In Re Phene's Trusts* (1869) LR 5 Ch 139. This important conclusion was not a solution of the problem but rather an admission of its insolubility. Where the deceased persons had mutual claims to succeed the one to the other and there was no evidence that one survived the other, the fiction was adopted of hoping that they died together at one and the same time; *In the Goods of Beynon* [1901] P 41. This expedient of assuming the deaths to have occurred simultaneously did not proceed on any proof of the fact or on any presumption, but was merely a method of solving an otherwise insoluable problem which had to be solved somehow. Such a state of law was far from satisfactory. The results which may follow from the absence of any aid from presumptions are well illustrated in a recent case in Scotland, where the common law remains as it was in England: *Drummond's Judicial Factor* v *Lord Advocate* (1944) SC 298. In that case the whole savings of one of the victims of a calamity almost identical in the circumstances with that which this House has now under consideration were carried off by the Crown.

It was to remedy this imperfection of the law that the legislature came to the aid of the courts by enacting a statutory presumption in the terms which I have quoted. Unfortunately, the wording of the section is such as to have given rise to controversy. Two views have been advanced as to its meaning and effect. According to one view, which is the view of Lord Greene MR and Goddard LJ, the statutory presumption is strictly limited in its application to cases in which:

> "the court is satisfied as to two things – one that the proper inference from the circumstances is that the deaths took place consecutively, the other, that the circumstances leave the court in uncertainty as to which death took place first" [1944] Ch 138 at p146.

That is to say, all that the statute does is to fix artificially the order of sequence among consecutive deaths, where that order cannot in fact be ascertained. If the circumstances are such as to justify an inference that all the parties concerned died simultaneously then the circumstances are not such as to render it uncertain which of them survived the other or others, for it is certain that none survived the other or others. This, according to Goddard LJ [1944] Ch 138 at p152, is the literal construction of the plain words of the enactment. The other view is that when the circumstances are such that it cannot be ascertained that one of the deceased survived the other then the uncertainty which the section postulates exists and the statutory presumption applies. One reason why it cannot be ascertained that one survived the other may well be that the deaths occurred so closely in time that there is a high probability that they were practically simultaneous. I say "practically" for reasons which will appear later. Having carefully weighed the arguments in support of each of these rival constructions I pronounce unhesitatingly in favour of the latter. It would be indeed unfortunate if the former were to prevail. For one thing it would mean that the legislature has signally failed to provide any remedy for an admitted defect in the law in a large and unahppily increasing number of cases in which evidence that the victims died consecutively is not available. Having set out, as I think may be reasonably assumed, to remedy the law as to commorientes, or persons dying together, the legislature is ironically found not to have made any provision for the case of commorientes who die together but to have dealt only with persons proved to have died consecutively. In the next place, I would observe that where two persons perish in a common calamity and there is no evidence as to which died first it is necessarily left uncertain whether they died consecutively or simultaneously, although the circumstances may point with high probability to their not having both died at the same moment. The operation of the statutory presumption is, in the view of the learned Master of the Rolls, made dependent on the ascertainment of the fact, namely, that the deaths were consecutive, which is itself necessarily conjectural in the absence of any positive evidence. The only case in which can be demonstrated that the deaths were consecutive is where one of the persons concerned is proved to have been alive after the other is proved to have died; but in such a case there is no need for any presumption of survivorship. Nevertheless, it is said that unless the court is satisfied that one of two victims of a common calamity survived the other the circumstances are not such as to render it uncertain which victim survived the other. I prefer to read the enactment as meaning that where the circumstances are such that it is no possible to say with certainty that one of the victims survived the other there is then uncertainty as to which survived the other. Clearly you cannot say with certainty that one of the victims survived the other if your belief is that both died at the same time, if that be possible. The decision of the Court of Appeal, if it were affirmed, would almost inevitably lead to every case having to come into court for determination of the obviously contentious and often really insoluble question whether the deaths were consecutive or simultaneous. The view of the learned Master of the Rolls involves two things, first, that it is possible by legal proof to demonstrate that two persons died at precisely the same moment of time, and second, that intentionally or inadvertently the legislature omitted to deal with this case. I gravely doubt whether the legislature envisaged as a practical consideration the existence of the possibility of simultaneous deaths. The draftsman in addressing himsel to the formulation of this remedial enactment may be assumed to have read at least the leading case of *Underwood* v *Wing* (1860) 4 De GM & G 633, 661. There he would find at p661 this pronouncement by Lord Cranworth LC:

> "It cannot be assumed to be proved, or probable, or possible, that two humans beings would cease to breathe at the same moment of time, for that is hardly within the range of imagination, and to adjudicate on such a principle would, I think, be proceeding on false data, but the real ground to proceed on is that it cannot be proved which died first."

It is easy to involve oneself in logical and metaphysical subleties, and perhaps fallacies, in handling such a topic as this. It is true that time is infinitely divisible and also that it is theoretically possible that the deaths of two persons may be absolutely coincident in time. "This is, of course, a profound and impressive truth", as Lord President Robertson once said in another context, and then proceeded to add "but there are times and places for everything, and I should hardly have thought a Tramway Act exactly the occasion which Parliament would choose for teaching business men metaphysics unawares." *Edinburgh Street Tramways Co* v *Edinburgh Magistrates* (1894) 21 R 688, 704. I prefer, therefore, to judge the language of the present enactment by a more commonplace standard. I think that it poses a practical question – Can you say for certain which of these two dead persons died first? If you cannot say for certain, then you must pre-sume the older to have died first. It is immaterial that the reason for your inability to say for certain which died first is either because you think they both died simultaneously or because you think they died consecutively but you do not know in what sequence. I note with interest that the learned Master of the Rolls himself in the course of the argument in the Court of Appeal [1944] Ch 138 at p145 "suggested that the section on its true construction might cover the case of simultaneous deaths". The reasons which he gives for rejecting his suggestion do not, with all respect, convince me, despite their verbal logical cogency.

I would add only a few words regarding the term "uncertain" which occurs in the enactment and which was so much canvassed in the course of the argument. The basis of belief may range from mere conjecture throuh all degrees of probability to absolute demonstration – possibility, probability, certainty. In seeking to arrive at a conclusion in fact in ordinary human affairs the law rejects mere possibility as an insufficient basis of proof, but on the other hand it does not exact absolute or mathematical proof. It is content to proceed on probability, if it is sufficient, and the test of sufficient probability is that the direct evidence, with all legitimate inferences, is such as ought to satisfy the mind of a person of reasonable intelligence. But the result of a decision on a question of fact by a judge or a jury is not certainty. It is finality, not certainty. Your Lordships in considering a verdict of a jury on a question of fact have often declared that it is not to be disturbed because there was evidence on which a reasonable person could so find but that it is not to be taken that your Lordships would have reached the same conclusion. Can it be said that in such circumstances the fact found by the jury has been ascertained with certainty? It has been determined with finality in law, but but not with certainty in fact. In my opinion the legislature in employing the word 'uncertain' in the section which the House has to construe was not thinking of the kind of certainty with which the law has to be content but was using the word in its ordinary acceptation as denoting a reasonable element of doubt.

So, coming at last to the facts of the present case so far as known, I put the question thus: Can it be said for certain if any of the five persons involved in this tragic occurrence that one did or did not survive the other? All that is certain is that a high explosive bomb fell on a small house, No 5 Upper Cheyne Row, Chelsea, on September 14, 1940 about 6.30, that it exploded within the house and reduced it to a heap of ruins, that five dead bodies, severely mutilated, were subsequently recovered from the debris and that there was a shelter in the basement of the house to which the deceased were in the habit of resorting when there was an aid-raid. No technical evidence was led on the action of blast from high explosives or its effect on the human body. Now I do not for the purpose of my argument need to say that, if a judge or jury had to try the issue whether in these circumstances all the victims of the calamity perished at precisely the same instant, and were to find as a matter of fact that this was so, the finding would on appeal be set aside on the ground that there was no evidence on which a reasonable man could reach that conclusion – pace Lord Cranworth LC who thought that the simultaneous death of two human beings was insusceptible of proof. Two most eminent and most reasonable judges have so found in this case. But, with all respect, that is not an issue which the statute requires to be determined in order to bring it into operation or exclude its operation. All that is necessary, in order to invoke the statututory presumption, is the presence in the circumstances of an element of uncertainty as to which of the deceased survived the other or others. I can imagine a juryman saying:

> "I really cannot answer this question. It may be that they died one after the other or it may be that they all died at the same moment, but in any case I cannot say for certain which, if any, was the survivor."

That is also my state of state of mind on the facts of the present case. Without resorting to fantastic or far-fetched conjectures it is perfectly possible that the blast of the explosion did not annihilate the whole of these five victims at the same instant. Thus, one of them may quite well have been out of the shelter in another part of the house at the moment of the impact of the shell and the blast, though by an infinitesimal interval, may have struck him sooner or later than the others. I simply do not know. Nobody can know. When everything depends, as Lord Cranworth said in *Wing* v *Angrave* (1860) HLC 183 at p207, on "survivorship for a second" I cannot accept the view that in the circumstances of this case there was no element of uncertainty, legal or other, on the cardinal issue.

My opinion, accordingly is that the statutory presumption applies and that the appeal should be allowed.'

Jones (John Keith) v *Roberts (John Ronald)* (1994) 19 April Chancery Division (H H J Kolbert [Ex rel Jeffrey Terry, Barrister])

Manslaughter – diminished responsibility – killing of parents by paranoid schizophrenic – whether excluded from benefiting from estates of intestate victims

Facts

J pleaded guilty to the manslaughter of his parents but not guilty to their murder on the grounds of diminished responsibility. He had battered his parents to death with a hammer during a period when he was suffering from paranoid schizophrenia. At the time he was under the impression that they were both KGB agents who had been instructed to kill him. J now applied for determination of the question whether he was precluded, by his conviction, from any entitlement to benefit from their estates. Both parents died intestate.

Held

1. J was subject to the forfeiture rule and was not entitled to benefit from his crime;
2. if public policy was to be reshaped so as to allow a person convicted of manslaughter on the grounds of diminished responsibility to benefit from his crime in the way in which Gibson J had sought to

do in *Re H (decd)* [1990] CLY 4656, that was a matter for a higher court. Furthermore, *Re H* was distinguishable because it had been held on the special facts of that case that the killer bore no responsibility for his crime notwithstanding that he had been convicted of manslaughter on the grounds of diminished responsibility; and

3. it was not clear whether the test laid down by the Court of Appeal in *Gray* v *Barr,* that the rule would apply where the offender had been 'guilty of deliberate, intentional and unlawful violence or threats of violence', applied to cases of diminished responsibility. However, if it did, the wielding of the hammer was a deliberate, intentional and unlawful act of violence by J notwithstanding his diminished responsibility for his actions. The test was accordingly satisfied.

Jull* v *Jacobs (1876) 3 Ch D 703 Chancery Division (Malins V-C)

Acceleration – scope and operation

Facts

By his will the testator devised and bequeathed certain real and personal estate to his daughter 'during her lifetime, and after her decease the property to be equally divided between her children on their becoming of age'. The daughter was an attesting witness to the will and the question arose whether the interests of the children had accelerated.

Held

The interests in both the real estate and personal estate were inthe remainder and as the daughter's interest was void on account of her having attested the will, the gift to the children accelerated and took effect immediately.

Malins V-C:

> '... but then comes the question whether the Wills Act by taking away the life estate of the daughter causes an intestacy during her life, so as to carry the property to the heir at law, or accelerates the remainder. It is perfectly clear, in the first place that the children are postponed to the mother simply because the mother is to have the property for her life, but if the mother cannot have the property for her life, why are the children to be postponed? The reason of their postponement altogether ceases: they are not to have it until after her death, because the testator assumed that she would have it during her life.'

K (deceased), Re [1986] Ch180 Chancery Division (Vinelott J) Court of Appeal (Ackner, Griffiths and Browne-Wilkinson LJJ)

Forfeiture Act 1982 – application to case of manslaughter

Facts

The deceased and his widow were married in 1974 when the deceased was 63 and the widow 52. The first two years of the marriage were satisfactory but thereafter the deceased began to show signs of violence on the widow. The widow said nothing about the attacks but contemplated leaving the deceased and was only dissuaded from doing so because the deceased agreed to see a doctor. The attacks continued and the deceased began to abuse the widow in public. She thought of leaving again but considered that the deceased must have a brain tumour and needed looking after. On 30 September 1982 the deceased attacked the widow in the kitchen and she picked up a shotgun, which was kept there to shoot rabbits in the garden, in order to deter him from making further attacks. As she pointed the gun at him it went off without warning, killing the deceased. By his will the deceased had bequeathed his residuary estate to the widow for life with remainder to four named beneficiaries. The estate was worth £412,000. The widow was also entitled to succeed to the deceased's half share in the matrimonial home which was valued at £80,000. The question arose whether the Forfeiture Act applied to the widow and, if so, whether she was entitled to relief thereunder.

Held

1. The forfeiture rule applied to the widow because she had been guilty of deliberate threats of violence towards the deceased in holding the shotgun at him. Whether she intended the consequences of her behaviour was not a relevant matter in deciding if the forfeiture rule applied.
2. The widow would be permitted to take the benefits conferred upon her by the will and the deceased's half share in the matrimonial home because she had been a loyal wife who had suffered considerable violence and there were no other persons for whom the deceased had a moral duty to provide.

Vinelott J:

> '... section 2(2) requires that before making any order under that section modifying the effect of the forfeiture rule the court must be satisfied that, having regard to the conduct of the offender and of the deceased and to such other circumstances as appear to the court to be material, the justice of the case requires the effect of the rule to be so modified in that case ... It is clear, I think, that the relative financial position of a person claiming relief under the 1982 Act and of others with claims under the testator's will or intestacy are circumstances which the court is entitled to take into account in the exercise of its discretion ... However, in a case where reasonable provision is made by the will, the first question is whether, having regard to the conduct of the deceased and of the claimant in particular in relation to the unlawful killing, justice requires that the claimant should be relieved against forfeiture in respect of all or any interests accruing on the death. The 1982 Act was clearly passed with the decision of Pennycuick V-C and earlier decisions in mind. In *Re Giles* [1972] Ch 544 Pennycuick V-C declined to enter into any investigation of the degree of moral culpability attending the killing. The purpose of the 1982 Act as I see it is to entitle and indeed require the court to form a view on that very matter.
>
> I have reached the conclusion after anxious consideration that in the very unusual circumstances of this case it would be unjust that the widow should be deprived of any of the benefits which the deceased chose to confer on hereby his will or which accrued to her by survivorship. As Lord Salmon observed in *DPP* v *Newbury* [1977] AC 500 at 507, it being unnecessary in cases of manslaughter to prove that the accused knew that the act causing death was unlawful or dangerous, cases of manslaughter necessarily vary infinitely in their gravity. Despite the revulsion which any person must feel at conduct which leads to the death of another human being it is impossible in the tragic circumstances of this case not to feel sympathy for the widow. If the cases vary infinitely in their gravity, for this, I think, one of the cases which weighs least heavily. The widow, as I have said, was a loyal wife who suffered grave violence at the hands of the deceased. When she took hold of the gun and released the safety catch she was in a state of great distress and feared further violence. She must accept the blame for what happened but she should not, in my judgment, suffer the further punishment of being deprived of the provision which her husband made for her which was, it seems to me, wholly appropriate having regard to the fact that the widow gave up a worthwhile and satisfying career when she married him, to her conduct towards him to the very end of his life and to the fact that there were no other persons for whom he was under any moral duty to provide.'

Kebty-Fletcher's Will Trusts, Re [1968] 2 WLR 34 Chancery Division (Stamp J)

Acceleration – whether application to class gifts

Facts

By her will the testatrix left a share of her residue on trust for each of her nephews and nieces for life and after their deaths on trust for such of their child or children who attained 21 in equal shares. In 1960 a nephew, who had children who had fulfilled the contingency, released his life interest so that the property could be dealt with as if he were dead. The children alive in 1960 claimed that they were entitled to the capital to the exclusion of any children who might be born thereafter.

Held

There was no acceleration nor was the composition of the class altered by the release of the life interest.

Stamp J:

> '... my attention has also been called to a number of cases where a gift to A for life has been followed by a gift to his children and the gift to the children has, by reason of disclaimer or invalidity of the prior gift, been accelerated. I must refer to some of them.
>
> In *Re Davies, Davies* v *Mackintosh* [1957] 3 All ER 52 there was, as here, a gift to A for life followed by a direction for division equally between his issue. A disclaimed the life interest. Vaisey J held that the disclaimer operated to acclerate the gift to issue. He also held that the acceleration operated to exclude after-born children and issue of A. The judge treated the problem as simply one of acceleration and did not explain the process by which he came to the conclusion that afterborn children and issue were excluded, relying primarily on *Jull* v *Jacobs* [1876] 3 Ch D 703 for that conclusion. I have read *Jull* v *Jacobs* more than once. There the gift was a gift to a lady who [attested the will] for life and after her death to be equally divided between her children on their becoming of age. Sir Richard Malins V-C held that the gift to the children was accelerated by reason of the fact that the lady could not take, and that the income was not undisposed of during their mother's life. I can find no indication in the judgment, and the point does not appear to have been argued, that the effect of the acceleration was to exclude children born after the eldest, for the time being in existence, had attained a vested interest.
>
> That question would indeed have been a future question which may never have arisen, and it does not seem to be that the fact of acceleration involves the corollary that the class intended to take is altered. If, as a matter of construction, the testator intended all the children of the lady born in her lifetime to take, it would, so I think, be after the acceleration just as if the gift had been an immediate gift to the chldren of the lady living at the testator's death who attained twenty-one and those thereafter born who attained that age (see for example *Scott* v *Earl of Scarborough* (1838) 1 Beav 154 and the terms of the declaration made in that case). Again, in *Re Townsend's Estate, Townsend* v *Townsend* (1886) 34 Ch D 357, which Vaisey J treated as to the same effect as *Jull* v *Jacobs,* there was no suggestion that all the children of the life tenant, whenever born, would not take. Therefore having given the matter the best consideration that I can, I conclude that neither *Jull* v *Jacobs* nor *Re Townsend's Estate* are authority for the view that acceleration has the effect indicated by Vaisey J and I am left with the decision in *Re Davies* itself. In *Re Taylor* [1957] 1 WLR 1403 Upjohn J expressed approval of the decision in *Re Davies,* but it was not necessary for him to do so and he was at pains to point out that the doctrine of acceleration does not permit one to misconstrue a will. The latter remark was, I think, part of the ratio decidendi of the decision of Upjohn J.
>
> I am content to treat the decision of Vaisey J as one applicable only to a case of acceleration. I am not prepared to extend it to such a case as the present where there has been no acceleration. The doctrine of acceleration is that all interests which fail or are undisposed of are captured by a residuary gift or go on an intestacy, but that a testator is presumed to have intended an acceleration of subsequent interests where a life interest fails in consequence of the donee being prevented by law from taking (see *Re Crowther's Trusts* [1916] IR 53). As a matter of construction a similar result may follow where the testator himself by a codicil revokes the prior life interest. And in that case, and again as a matter of construction, the testator may be presumed to have intended the period of distribution among the class to be his own death so as to bring a further role of construction known as *Andrews* v *Partington* (1791) 3 Bro CC 401 into operation. *Re Johnson* (1893) 68 LT 20 – on which Vaisey J in *Re Davies* relied as supporting the proposition that acceleration may, and does sometimes, alter the membership of the class – falls into the latter category. It does not, however, in my judgment follow that because the revocation by the testator of a life interest may bring about both the results I have indicated, so will a disclaimer; and I confess to a doubt whether *Re Davies* was correctly decided.

It is, however, sufficient for me to say that although a disclaimer being sometimes within the contemplation of the testator, may, on the authority of *Re Davies* operate not only to accelerate the subsequent gift to the class but also, as a matter of construction of the will, alter the composition of that class, it does not in my judgment follow that a disposition of a life interest, the terms of which cannot have been envisaged by the testator, and which may not have the former effect, nevertheless has the latter. The dispositions of the nephews' life interests under the will of the testator could not operate over the capital of their shares or alter in any way the construction of the will. If one of those dispositions had extended to a nephew's life interest in half his share instead of the whole of it, the question which has been discussed would have arisen with regard to that half, and no authority has been cited to me requiring this court to attribute to the testator such a prophetic vision as would enable me to hold that if the disposition by one of his nephews had operated over half instead of the whole of the income of his settled share, that half would be divisible to the exclusion of the nephew's children, born after a child attained twenty-one but that the latter children would participate in the other half.'

Land* v *Devaynes (1793) 4 Bro Ch 537

Specific legacies – chattels in a particular place

Facts

The testator gave all his plate and linen in his house in S (with the lease) to his wife. The testator had one set of plate and one set of linen, which was usually removed as the family went from house to house. At the death of the testator the plate was at the testator's country home at B.

Held

The plate passed to the wife; the reference to the place was merely to identify the plate at the date of the will.

Mytton* v *Mytton (1874) LR 19 Eq 30 Chancery Division (Malins V-C)

General legacies – definition

Facts

By her will the testatrix bequeathed 'the sum of £3,000 invested in Indian Security' to her nephew. The question arose whether the legacy was specific or general.

Held

The will as a whole showed that the testatrix intended that the legacy should be general.

Malins V-C:

'... the authorities which were cited, and others which might have been referred to, show that in order to determine this question the court will look at the whole will for the purpose of ascertaining the intention of the testatrix in making this provision.

What was the intention of the testatrix? She begins with a specific legacy of certain parts of her estate to her trustees. It is certainly specific to some extent, though not so much so as Mr Glasse and Mr Renshaw contended. I think it would have passed any balances at her bankers. She then charges her debts upon this fund, then makes the gift in question ...

Now, did she merely intend to give shares in Indian funds? If she had used the word "my" the gift must have been held specific and have failed, because she had no property answering that description at the time of her death. If she intended to give a legacy, at all events the words descriptive of the fund make it simply a demonstrative legacy.

In this case I am so clearly satisfied that it was the intention of the testatrix to give £3,000 irrespective of the kind of investment she might have at her death, that I would look carefully at everything in the will tending to show that it was not specific. If she had said: "I give £3,000 which is now invested in Indian securities", the gift would be simply demonstrative. Now, looking at the whole will, I am so clearly of opinion that it was her meaning to give the £3,000 which was then invested in Indian Securities, that I think it ought not to fail, because at her death there was no fund invested in Indian securities, and I am perfectly satisfied that this decision will be in accordance with her real intention.'

O'Connor, Re [1948] 1 Ch 628 Chancery Division (Roxburgh J)

General legacies – distinguished from specific legacies

Facts

The testator made a will dated 5 August 1942. By clause 5 he gave his son 'ten thousand preference shares of one pound each fully paid in the capital of J & K O'Connor Ltd'. By clause 6 he bequeathed five pecuniary legacies to named persons and by clause 7 he made a disposition of his residuary estate upon certain trusts. In clause 8 of the will there was a direction to the executor to pay his debts and liabilities and the pecuniary legacies bequeathed by clause 6 out of the residuary estate. At the date of the will and at his death the testator had only 9,000 preference shares in J & K O'Connor Ltd. The question arose whether the bequest of the preference shares to the son in clause 5 was a specific or a general legacy.

Held

The bequest was a general legacy.

Roxburgh J:

'The question which I have to determine is whether this legacy of ten thousand preference shares of £1 each is a general legacy or a specific legacy, and there are two points in that there is nothing in the language of cl 5 itself to indicate that the testator is describing specific property of his. For example, the testator does not use the word "my" or any possessive word. The second point in favour of a general legacy – and, in my judgment, a very strong point – is that the testator never had ten thousand preference shares either at the date of his will or at the date of his death, but only nine thousand, and accordingly, if he did intend by this clause to make a specific disposition of existing property of his, he must have been misinformed as to its extent. Those are the two points in favour of a general legacy.

The two points in favour of a specific legacy are these: First, there is the circumstance that the bequest is one of shares of a private company of which the testator was the manager and governing director, a company in which the shares were subject to the restrictions on transfer usual in such a case. Secondly – and this is a very important point – the testator did not include the bequest of the preference shares among the bequests which his executors and trustees were to satisfy out of the residue ...

... There is no doubt that the court leans strongly in favour of a general legacy. How strongly is apparent from the decision in *Re Willocks* [1921] 2 Ch 327, yet if the testator, instead of referring to the ten thousand preference shares had referred to nine thousand or less preference shares, I should have held that there was sufficient context here to carry me to the other side of the line ... I decide ... that this is a general legacy ...'

Paget* v *Huish (1863) 1 H & M 663 Court of Chancery (Page Wood V-C)

Demonstrative legacies – definition

Facts

By his will a testator gave five annuities to named persons and then directed: 'And I declare that each of the said five annuities shall be paid by the trustees of this my will out of the rents of my real estate hereby devised half-yearly, and the first payment thereof shall be due and be made at the end of six calendar months from my decease. And I give the said five annuities free of legacy duty, which I direct to be paid out of the rents of my real estate.' The question arose whether the annuities were demonstrative legacies and thus chargeable on the general personal estate of the testator insofar as the rents were insufficient to meet them or were only to be taken from the rents and, if these were insufficient, to abate.

Held

The gifts were demonstrative legacies in nature.

Page Wood V-C:

> '... the first class is where you have a simple gift of a legacy of annuity, with a mere charge upon real estate; and there the personal estate is not only not exonerated, but remains primarily liable; just as the case of a charge of debts.
>
> Another class is where the legacy or annuity is a specific gift out of real estate, which is assumed to be sufficient to cover the amount. There the personal estate is in no way liable, and if the specific fund fails the gift must fail with it.
>
> The third class is intermediate to these where a legacy or annuity is, as it is termed, demonstrative, there being a clear general gift, but a particular fund pointed out as that which is to be primarily liable, on failure of which the general personal estate remains liable.
>
> The point in all these cases is to ascertain whether the testator has merely pointed out a particular fund which he desires to have applied in paying the legacy, or whether the legacy itself is given only as a portion of the specified fund.
>
> These are, therefore, the three classes of gifts: First, a general gift, in which no special fund is pointed at for payment; secondly, a specific gift out of a particular fund alone; and, thirdly, a gift where a particular fund is pointed out as primarily applicable, but where the gift is not to fail by the failure of the particular fund. In this case I think there is a clear intention that the gift should take effect in any event ...'

Ross* v *Caunters [1980] Ch 297 Chancery Division (Megarry V-C)

Wills Act 1837 s15 – gifts to attesting witnesses – solicitors' negligence in failing to warn of invalidity of such gifts

Facts

A testator gave his solicitors instructions for his will and asked them to post the will to the plaintiff's home, where he was staying, to be signed and attested. The solicitors sent a covering letter with the will giving instructions as to how the will was to be executed but failed to warn the testator as to the effect of s15 of the Wills Act. The plaintiff, who received benefits under the will, sued the solicitors for damages because her husband was one of the attesting witnesses. The solicitors admitted negligence but denied that they were liable to the plaintiff because either they were only liable in contract or in tort on grounds of public policy they ought not to be held liable in negligence.

Held

Under the 'neighbour' principle in *Donoghue* v *Stevenson* there was a duty of care owed by the solicitors to a beneficiary under a will since the beneficiary was someone within their direct contemplation as a person so closely and directly affected by their acts and omissions that they could reasonably foresee that she would be likely to be injured by those acts or omissions. There was a breach of this duty of care and the plaintiff had suffered loss as a direct result of that breach of duty and was entitled to succeed.

Megarry V-C:

'That, I think, disposes of the issues before me. It may be of assistance if I summarise my main conclusions:

1) Despite the dicta in *Robertson* v *Fleming* (1861) 4 Macq 167 and what was said in *Groom* v *Crocker* and other cases in that line, there is no longer any rule that a solicitor who is negligent in his professional work can be liable only to his client in contract; he may be liable both to his client and to others for the tort of negligence.

2) The basis of the solicitor's liability to others is either an extension of the *Hedley Byrne* principle, or, more probably, a direct application of the principle of *Donoghue* v *Stevenson*

3) A solicitor who is instructed by his client to carry out a transaction that will confer a benefit on an identified third party owes a duty of care towards that third party in carrying out that transaction, in that the third party is a person within his direct contemplation as someone who is likely to be so closely and directly affected by his acts or omissions that he can reasonably foresee that the third party is likely to be injured by those acts or omissions.

4) The mere fact that the loss to such a third party caused by the negligence is purely financial, and is in no way a physical injury to person or property, is no bar to the claim against the solicitor.

5) In such circumstances there are no considerations which suffice to negative or limit the scope of the solicitor's duty to the beneficiary.

From what I have said, it follows that the plaintiff's claims succeeds, and she is entitled to damages against the defendants for the loss of benefits that the 1974 will would have carried to her but for the negligence of the defendants.'

Rowland, Re [1963] Ch 1 Court of Appeal (Lord Denning MR, Harman and Russell LJJ)

Law of Property Act 1925 s184 – presumption of survivorship in situation of common disaster

Facts

The testator and his wife were drowned when their small boat sank in the Pacific Ocean. The actual date when the boat sank was unknown, but a Commission of Inquiry concluded that it was between 10 and 18 July 1958. By his will the testator left all his estate to his wife but also stated that his estate should pass to other named persons if the death of his wife 'preceded' his or 'coincided' with his.

Held

On the facts the testator's use of the words 'preceded' and 'coincided' merely indicated that he intended to make provision in the event of his wife not surviving him. This did not, however, show that he had contemplated the situation where they died together. Accordingly s184 LPA applied and as the wife was the younger she was assumed to have survived the testator so her estate was entitled. Further, even if it could be shown that the word 'coincided' was used to cover their deaths simultaneously the evidence did not show that this was the case.

Harman LJ:

'... the testator and his wife were thus involved in a common disaster, and the question is whether his death and hers can be said to have coincided. The testator has by his will given all his estate to his wife, and this is, of course effective if and only if, she survives him. He has, on the other hand, provided that in the event of her death preceding his, the estate is to go to the second and third defendants. All events in time are thus provided for except one, that of neither surviving the other. There is nothing in the will about the cause or the occasion of death; it is simply a question of time.

... so here it is attractively argued that this testator setting out on the adventure offered by this post in the Southern Pacific contemplated, as did his wife, the very event which happened, namely, that both of them should be involved in the same calamity. The learned judge did not feel able to reach this conclusion. It is for those claiming under the gift over to prove their case that the deaths of the testator and his wife were coincident. This word in the context in which it appears can in my judgment only be a reference to the time and not the occasion of death. In other words, "coincident" is equivalent to "simultaneous". That was the only event which the testator on the language he used could have contemplated. He had already made gift to his wife if she survived him and to the defendants if she did not. Can these deaths on the evidence be held to have been simultaneous, using the word not in the philosopher's sense but as it was used by the testatrix in *Pringle's case* [1946] Ch 124? I am satisfied that it cannot. Not enough is known. It is not even known at what date, within a week, the ship went down, nor is the whereabouts of either the testator or his wife at that time certain. One or other of them may easily have survived the going down of the ship and the event is too uncertain to infer a simultaneous death, as was possible for Cohen J in the case of two persons killed in close proximity to each other by the same bomb.

If this meaning of the word be out of the question, it is argued that "coincident" is a little looser and can mean in this will, "at about the same time and as a result of the same catastrophe". This in my opinion is an impossible view. The will has provided for both possibilities of survivorship and there is no warrant for introducing a reference to something other than time, namely, the same catastrophe. I am, therefore, of the same opinion as the learned judge and would dismiss this appeal.'

Scott, Re [1975] 1 WLR 1260 Chancery Division (Walton J)

Acceleration – impossibility while a contingency remains unfulfilled

Facts

The testatrix, who died in 1973, left a will dated 1964 by which she left her residuary estate upon trust for her sister Ruth and her brother, Colonel Scott, in equal shares, during their joint lives and then to the survivor during his or her life and after the death of the survivor for all or any of the children of her brother 'who shall be living at my death or born afterwards and being male attain the age of twenty one years or being female attain that age or marries': there was then an ultimate gift to two named organisations for the benefit of clergymen. At the testatrix's death her brother was aged 78 and her sister aged 82 and neither had children. The brother and sister disclaimed their interests in the residuary estate. The question arose whether there was an acceleration to the two named charities who took under the ultimate remainders.

Held

There could be no acceleration in favour of those entitled under the ultimate remainders because it was clear that the testatrix did not intend these charities to benefit should her brother have children who satisfied the contingencies. As it was still possible that the brother might have children the doctrine of acceleration was excluded.

Walton J:

'... on the facts of this case, the result of acceleration might be startling. The charities might get the income which they were never intended to have at all until the birth of a child (who subsequently attained 21, or, being a female, married) to Colonel Scott. And it is quite clear that it was never the testatrix's intention that if there was such child the charity should touch a penny of her money. Of course, one may equally say that it was never the intention of the testatrix that the income should go anywhere else than to her sister, Ruth, her brother, Colonel Scott, and Colonel Scott's children, and so on, but of course, if as a result of something completely unforeseen, in the event that the estate is not disposed of, well, that is carried by law in certain directions, and whether the testatrix wanted it or not, that is something which is imposed on her by law. But never has the doctrine of acceleration been used, nor in my judgment, can it ever be used, to carry an interest to somebody to whom the testatrix never intended it to go, if something else happened, and that something else is still capable of happening.'

Sinclair, Re [1985] Ch 446 Court of Appeal (O'Connor and Slade LJJ, Bristow J)

Wills Act 1837 s18A – effect of dissolution or annulment of marriage on wills

Facts

The testator made a will in November 1958 which devised and bequeathed all his estate to his wife but also directed that if she predeceased him or failed to survive him for a period of one month his estate was to pass to the Imperial Cancer Research Fund. The testator and his wife were divorced in September 1962 and the testator died on 26 October 1983 without having revoked or altered the 1958 will. There was no dispute as to the effect of s18A on the former wife's interests under the will, these clearly failed under the provision. However, the question arose whether the estate should devolve on the Imperial Cancer Research Fund or pass to the testator's next of kin on intestacy on the ground that the will made no effective gift of the estate.

Held

The word 'lapse' in the context of s18A(1)(b) meant that the devise or bequest to the former spouse failed and without regard to the consequences which this might have upon other dispositions in the will. In particular, the word lapse was not to be construed as meaning that the devise or bequest to a former spouse failed with the same consequences as if the former spouse had died in the testator's lifetime. Thus, on the failure of the gift to the former wife the gift in favour of the Imperial Cancer Research Fund could not take effect because neither of the contingencies upon which this gift would take effect had happened. Accordingly, the estate passed to the next of kin on intestacy.

Slade LJ:

'... on no possible footing can one read the opening words of the new s18A(1)(b) as meaning simply "any devise or bequest to the former spouse shall fail by reason of the death of the legatee during the testator's lifetime". For, in the cases dealt with by s18A(a)(b), the former spouse is ex hypothesi still alive at the date of the testator's death.

In the more developed stages of his argument, Mr Rawson had to contend and did context that, in the context of s18A(1)(b), the word "lapse" means something more than this. He contended that (unlike the word as used in other provisions in the 1837 Act) the single word "lapse" in this context is in truth a deeming provision. He submitted that the opening words of s18A(1)(b) should be read as meaning "any devise or bequest to the former spouse shall fail with the same consequences as if the former spouse had died in the testator's lifetime". It is thus an essential part of the fund's case on this appeal that the single word "lapse" in s18A(1)(b) should be read as not only importing a failure of the relevant gift in favour of the former spouse, but as designating also the consequences of such failure in relation to the other provisions contained in the will ...

... for my part, I find it impossible to read the opening words of s18A(1)(b) in this manner. First, as I have said, it must be and is accepted that the word "lapse" is, in an appropriate context, perfectly apt to cover the happening of any event in a testator's lifetime which prevents the intended legatee from being entitled to the legacy, and thus to mean nothing more than fail. In my opinion the word "lapse" in the context of s18A(1)(b) is to refer to the happening of an event, namely divorce, in the testator's lifetime which is to prevent the intended legatee, the former spouse, from becoming entitled to the legacy. The natural meaning of the word "lapse" in this particular context is that, in the relevant contingency, the devise or bequest to the former spouse shall fail, no more and no less.

Second, if the legislature had intended that s18A(1)(b) should have the effect, not only of preventing the former spouse from receiving the gift in cases such as this, but also of designating the consequences which would ensue in relation to the other provisions of the will, it would in my opinion inevitably have said so. To spell out a deeming provision from this one word "lapse" would in my opinion be impermissible according to any proper principles of statutory construction.

Third, the conclusion that the legislature did not regard s18A(1)(b) as designating the consequences that would ensue from the failure of the gift to the former spouse, in relation to the other provisions of the will, is in my opinion clearly supported by the presence of subsection (3). For this subsection does designate such consequences in those cases where the will has given the former spouse a life interest. The provisions of subsection (3) would have been wholly unnecessary if s18A(1)(b) had itself been intended to provide that the effect of the failure of the gift on all theother provisions of the will was to be the same as if the former spouse had died in the testator's lifetime ...'

Slater, Re [1907] 1 Ch 665 Court of Appeal (Cozens-Hardy MR)

Specific legacies – stocks and shares – whether ademption

Facts

The testator made a bequest of 'the interest arising from money invested in *(inter alia)* the Lambeth Waterworks Company'. Between the date of the will and the date of the death, the undertaking of this company was acquired by the Metropolitan Water Board in pursuance of an Act by which it was provided that the Metropolitan Water Board should pay to the company as compensation for the acquisition of its undertaking, a sum to be determined, but the sum so payable might, if the Water Board and the company so agreed, be satisfied wholly or partly in stock. Under a scheme made in pursuance of this provision the Metropolitan Water Board stock in question was issued to the testator.

Held

As the company's undertaking had been sold for cash, and the price was paid in stock under a scheme agreed to by the company, and as the security for the new stock was very different from that of the old, the new stock did not pass under the bequest. There was an absolute annihilation or extinction of the interests in the Lambeth Waterworks Company, and the compensation awareded was in the shape of an allotment of different stock in a different concern on a different footing altogether.

Cozens-Hardy MR:

'But, supposing I am wrong in that, and that the appellant is right on this point, and that by construction I am to read this bequest as meaning "I bequeath the interest during her life arising from the money invested in the following particulars which I now hold", then you are face to face with the question, "Has not this gift, so far as the Lambeth Waterworks Company's stock is concerned, been adeemed by the subsequent transaction?" Speaking for myself, altough it may not be absolutely necessary for the decision of this case, I think it has been. There was a time when the Courts held that ademption was dependent on the testator's intention, on a presumed intention on his part: and it was therefore held in old days that when a change was effected by public authority, or without the will of the testator, ademption did not follow. But for many years that has ceased to be law, and think it is now the law that where a change has occurred in the nature of the property, even though effected by virtue of an Act of Parliament, ademption will follow unless the case can be brought within what I may call the principle of *Oakes* v *Oakes* (1852) 9 Hare 666 in which Turner V-C held that a bequest of shares in a railway company was not revoked by the subsequent change of those shares into stock by reason of a vote of the company under the powers of their special Act. At the end of his judgment the Vice-Chancellor says this (at p672):

> "The testator had this property at the time he made his will, and it has since been changed in name or form only. The question is, whether a testator has at the time of his death the same thing existing, it may be in a different shape – yet substantially the same thing".

Remembering the extraordinary accuracy of the language used by Turner V-C, I think there is a great force in those words which he used "changed in name or form only ... yet substantially the same thing". Applying that to the present case, in the first place the Lambeth Waterworks undertaking was sold, and sold for cash – sold, that is, for cash in the sense, that the price was ascertained in cash and could only be paid otherwise than in cash if both the vendors and purchasers agreed to a scheme providing for satisfying the purchase money otherwise. That agreement was obtained in the present case. A scheme was prepared, and the Water Board B stock was allotted to the testator in respect of his shares in the old company. But can it possibly be said that is the same thing? Instead of having shares in a company dependent for its profits upon water rates which they, and they alone, were able to demand from the limited area within the ambit of their Act of Parliament, the Water Board B stock is a stock which is payable out of water rates levied not merely upon the Lambeth Waterworks area, but upon the whole of the metropolitan area, and I think, also on some districts even outside the metropolitan area. But, more than that, in the event of the water rates being insufficient to provide for the interest the present stock has a claim upon the rateable property in London, and any deficiency has to be made good out of the general rates. I cannot bring myself to say that is the same thing. I feel bound myself to adopt the view taken not in one case only, but in many, that you have to ask yourself, where is the thing which is given? If you cannot find it at the testator's death, it is no use trying to trace it unless you an trace it in this sense, that you find something which has been changed in name and form only, but which is substantially the same thing. One authority has been adduced to us which is certainly very near the present case: it is the case of *In Re Grey* (1887) 36 Ch D 205 decided by Kay J. It is quite true that the observations made by that learned judge were not necessary for the decision of the case, for he first held that the legacy in that case was general not specific, but he went on to discuss the question of what would happen assuming that the gift was specific. In that case the testator bequeathed certain shares in an old unlimited bank. It is in the interval between the date of his will and of his death the company was registered under the same name with the addition of the word "Limited" and the shares were sub-divided up, each £100 being converted into two shares of the nominal value of £60, and the learned judge held that, even assuming the legacy had been specific, the shares in the limited company were not so completely identified with the old shares as to prevent the application of the doctrine of ademption.'

***Stanley* v *Potter* (1789) 2 Cox 180 (Lord Thurlow LC)**

Specific legacies – debts – ademption by payment by debtor

Facts

By his will the testator bequeathed a debt of £2,000 to the debtor. However, during the lifetime of the testator the debtor repaid the debt in full. The question arose whether he could, after the testator's death, claim the £2,000 legacy.

Held

The legacy had been adeemed.

Lord Thurlow LC:

> '... when the case of *Ashburner* v *Macguire* (1786) 2 Bro CC 108 was before me, I took all the pains I could to sift the several cases upon the subject, and I could find no certain rule to be drawn from them,

except this, to inquire whether the legacy was a specific legacy (which is generally the difficult question in these cases) and if specific, whether the thing remained at the testator's death; and one must consider it in the same manner as if a testator had given a particular horse to AN. If that horse died in the testator's lifetime or was disposed of by him, then there is nothing on which the bequest can operate. And I do not think that the question in these cases turns on the intention of the testator. The idea of proceeding on the *animus adimendi* has introduced a degree of confusion in the cases which is inexplicable, and I can make out no precise rule from them upon that ground. As to the case of *Attorney-General* v *Parkyns*, I collect from the note I read of that case that Lord Camden would have had great difficulty in making those legacies contributory in the event of a deficiency of assets: and if so, I cannot conceive how they are to be taken as general legacies for any other purpose; they must have had all the consequences of general legacies, or none; they could not be specific to one purpose, and general to another. This I cannot understand. And I believe it will be a safer and clearer way to adhere to the plain rule which I before mentioned, which is to inquire whether the specific thing given remains or not. For where a testator gives by his will a particular sum of money, and he afterwards receives and spends it, I see no end to the confusion arising from the following any other line.'

Sweeting (deceased), Re [1988] 1 All ER 1016 Chancery Division (Nicholls J)

Devises – ademption through conditional contracts of sale

Facts

The testator made a will dated 18 July 1978 which, inter alia, devised a yard adjoining his dwelling house under two separate gifts. On 16 March 1981 the testator entered into two contracts of sale, one for his house and one for the yard. The testator died on 9 April 1981 before either contract was completed. After the testator's death his executors completed both contracts. The question then arose whether the proceeds of sale of the yard ought to be paid to the devisees thereof in the will or whether the devise had adeemed by reason of the contract of sale so that the proceeds of sale should pass into the residuary estate. This was because completion of the contract for the sale of the yard was conditional on simultaneous completion of the contract for the sale of the house. The latter was also conditional on certain releases being made by the testator's widow and the cancellation of a land charge.

Held

The devises of the yard were adeemed by the contract of sale and the fact that they were conditional did not avoid ademption. This was because the testator's widow had in fact given her consent to the sale and could have been compelled to furnish the releases and cancel the land charge as a consequence. Thus, the contract for the sale of the yard was specifically enforceable by or against the testator. Further, under the rule in *Lawes* v *Bennett* (1785) 1 Cox Eq Cas 167, it was provided that where a testator devised property by his will and subsequently granted another an option to purchase that property at the same time after his death and the option was duly exercised, the gift adeemed. This rule applied to conditional contracts with the effect that when the conditions were fulfilled and the contract completed after the testator's death the devises adeemed.

Trotter, Re [1899] 1 Ch 764 Chancery Division (Byrne J)

Wills Act 1837 s15 – gift to attesting witness to codicil but not will itself

Facts

By his will the testator gave a legacy to an attesting witness in the will, one John Trotter. Subsequently, the testator executed a codicil to the will but John Trotter was not an attesting witness thereto. A second codicil was made at a later date, John Trotter was an attesting witness to it but he received no benefit thereunder. The question arose whether he could benefit under the original will.

Held

He was entitled to receive his benefit under the will; s15 only affected benefits given by the instrument attested where it was not in any way republished or confirmed at a later date by another instrument unconnected with the attesting beneficiary.

Byrne J:

> '... in *Gurney* v *Gurney* (1855) 3 Drew 208 the testator had given benefits by his will to two persons who did not attest the will, but who did afterwards attest two codicils. Kindersley V-C decided that the word "thereby" in s15 of the Wills Act must be construed to mean "by the same testamentary instrument which is attested" and that it does not apply to the case where a legatee has not attested the same instrument under which he takes. This points to the will and codicil being treated as separate instruments for the purpose of ascertaining whether or not an attesting witness to either of such instruments can take ... I think that these points in respect of wills made since the Wills Act have been thus established. (1) that a will invalid in itself may operate as a valid instrument when referred to and incorporated in or with a subsequent and validly-executed codicil. (2) That a valid gift by a will to a legatee is not rendered invalid by reason of his subsequently attesting a codicil, although the codicil has the effect of republishing and incorporating the will. (3) That although a gift by a valid will to an attesting witness is utterly null and void, such gift may be rendered effectual if the will is republished by a codicil referring to the will but not attested by the legatee. (4) That the legatee must be able to point to an instrument giving him his legacy not attested by himself before he can establish his right to his legacy. Bearing in mind these principles, the question appears to be whether or not John Trotter can point to an instrument not attested by himself and giving him the benefit he claims. It cannot be to the will alone, for though a valid instrument it is utterly null and void so far as the disposition in his favour is concerned. But just as had the original will been altogether void he would have been able to point to a codicil republishing and incorporating the whole of it, and as validating the whole of the dispositions intended to be made by the will so in like manner I think he can point to the first codicil republishing and incorporating an instrument valid as to some of its dispositions, but invalid as to the dispositions in his favour, as being the instrument under which he claims. I think that the true view is that, where the original gift is by the operation of s15 of the Wills Act utterly null and void, the will is pro tanto null and void, as it would have been, if unattested, null and void altogether; and that, just as in the latter case the whole will would, if referred to in a duly-executed and duly-attested codicil, operate in its entirety as from the date of the codicil, so where void in part as to its dispositions by reason of improper attestation, it will, so far as void, operate for the first tme by the incorporation and republication effected by the due execution of the codicil. I think that John Trotter is entitled here to point to the first codicil as the instrument conferring upon him the benefit in question, inasmuch as that codicil incorporates the whole will, including the originally void disposition, and that this being so, upon the authority of *Gurney* v *Gurney* and *Re Marcus* (1887) 57 LT 399 he has not lost this benefit by reason of his having subsequently attested the second codicil.'

Wilson, Re [1967] Ch 53 Chancery Division (Pennycuick J)

Residuary gift – definition

Facts

A testatrix left several pecuniary legacies and then left 'all my real estates and the residue of my personal estate' to her daughter. As the will contained no express directions on the payment of debts and setting aside a fund for the pecuniary legacies the rules in Schedule 1 Part II of the Administration of Justice Act applied which made, on the facts, the residuary estate primarily liable for these. The question therefore arose whether the gift of real estate to the testatrix's daughter was to be classed as a specific devise or a residuary devise. If it were the former it would be exempt from payment of the debts of the pecuniary legacies fund.

Held

The gift was a residuary gift.

Pennycuick J:

> '... apart from authority, the natural view, so it seems to me, is that where a testator makes a general or universal gift of his real estate, that is "all my property", the subject-matter of that gift falls under the second head (para 2 of Sched 1), that is, as being property not specifically devised but included "in a residuary gift ...". A gift in this form does not indicate any particular items of property but covers all items of real property which the testator may be entitled to at his death. In ordinary language today lawyers would, I think, not inaptly describe such a gift as a residuary devise. They would certainly not describe it as a specific devise.
>
> [Counsel] for Mrs Lambert advanced certain arguments to the contrary. His first argument was that all devises are from their nature specific. It seems that this was indeed so, at any rate until 1925: see in particular *Hensman* v *Fryer* (1867) LR 3 Ch App 420 and *Lancefield* v *Iggulden* (1874) LR 10 Ch App 136.
>
> On the other hand, as I have said, it is clear that Part II of the Schedule contemplates that real property may be capable of being comprised in a residuary gift. I do not think that in the context of the First Schedule to that Act one should put a construction on the words "specifically devised" and "residuary gift" as would in effect deprive the class of residuary gifts of realty of any possible content at all.
>
> ... [Counsel's] second point was that a devise is residuary only if there has been a previous devise, so that the residuary devise operates on what remains after the previous devise has taken effect. That is grammatically a good point. On the other hand, the expression "residuary gift" is habitually used to denote a general or universal gift and, as I have said, it seems to me natural so to treat the words "residuary gift" here.
>
> The only alternative in the context of para 2 is to treat the general or universal gift as a specific gift, and that I should have thought certainly it was not. This construction would produce a wholly illogical result as regards payment of debts. On the one hand a residuary gift devise following a specific devise would be a residuary gift for the purpose of para 2. On the other hand, a general or universal devise would be a specific devise and would fall not within para 2 but para 6. I cannot think that that is right.
>
> I conclude, therefore, that the devise of "all my real estate" to Mrs Lambert in this will is a residuary gift for the purpose of para 2 of Pt 2 of Sch 1 to the Administration of Estates Act 1925.'

Zouche, Baroness, Re [1919] 2 Ch 178 Chancery Division (PO Lawrence)

Specific legacies – permanent removal of property from named place

Facts

A testatrix made a bequest of 'the furniture, picture, plate, articles of virtue and curiosities at Parnham House at the time of my decease'. At the testatrix's death a quantity of plate belonging to her was at her bankers for safe custody. It had been placed at the bank some years before by the testatrix's predecessor in title, when the house was let furnished, and was allowed to remain after the tenancy determined. The testatrix also moved some rare books and MSS which were lent to the British Museum for exhibition and were still there when she died.

Held

Neither the plate at the bank nor the books and MSS at the British Museum passed under the specific bequest. The period of time over which they were absent tended to show that they were no longer to be considered part of the contents of the house.

PO Lawrence J:

> '... if any part of this plate had been sent to a shop for repair at the time of the death, and was only temporarily absent for that purpose, or had been deposited at the bank by the testatrix for a temporary purpose, eg, while she was absent from town on a visit, there could not be any reasonable doubt that it would have passed by the gift. But, to my mind the facts in this case are wholly different. The testatrix herself did not deposit this plate at the bank. The temporary purpose for which it was originally deposited by her predecessor in title had expired many years before her death. Neither her predecessor nor the testatrix ever fetched the plate away from the bank, and it is a matter of pure speculation what her intention with regard to the destination of the plate would have been if she had ever thought of taking it away from the bank. In my judgment, the testatrix, knowing it was not at Parnham House at the time she made her will, did not intend that it should pass by the specific gift in her will ... That leaves only the rare books and MSS at the British Museum, and I think the judgment I have just given with regard to the plate covers the articles which were lent to the British Museum for exhibition purposes ...'

6 Construction of Wills

Abbott* v *Middleton (1858) 7 HLC 68 House of Lords (Lord Chelmsford LC, Lords Cranworth, St Leonards, Wensleydale and Brougham)

Construction of a will – words given their ordinary meaning

Facts

A testator gave an annuity of £2,000 to his widow, and set apart, out of his personal property, a sum sufficient to provide for its payment. He then directed that, on the death of his widow, the sum so set apart should

> 'become the property of my son George, so far as he shall receive the interest during his life, and on his death the principal sum to become the property of any children he may leave, in such sums as he shall direct, but in the event of my son dying before his mother, then the principal sum to be divided among the children of my daughters, the deceased Jane Ricketts and Mary Paxton and of my now surviving daughter Eliza Middleton (should she leave any issue) in equal portions'.

George married after the date of the will, had one son and died before the testator. The question arose whether George's son took a vested interest at the testator's death in the capital of the fund set apart to provide for the payment of the widow's annuity, subject to her life interest therein. The Master of the Rolls declared that according to the true construction of the will George's son was entitled to such an interest. The children of the daughters appealed.

Held

The appeal would be dismissed since on the death of the testator's widow, the son of George became entitled to the fund which had been set apart to provide the annuity, for that the property vested in it vested in the children of George, independently of their father, who merely took a life interest in it.

Lord Chelmsford:

> 'The whole question turns upon one clause in the will, or it may rather be said, upon the meaning of a few words in one of its clauses. It is impossible to entertain any moral doubt of the testator's intention, and there is, therefore, great danger of the mind being strongly and improperly influenced by this consideration. But disclaiming all right to act upon any conjectural interpretation, I have arrived at a satisfactory conclusion that in the will itself there can be found an ample justification for the Decree which has been pronounced.
>
> I entirely agree in the rule for the construction of wills laid down by my two noble and learned friends (Lords Cranworth and Wensleydale) in the case of *Grey* v *Pearson* (6 H L Cas 61). This rule, however, is applicable only when the language of the will is clear and unambiguous. Where there is an uncertainty as to the meaning of any part of a will, the right of a court of construction even to introduce words, in case of necessity, is clearly stated by Lord St. Leonards, in the passage quoted from *Eden* v *Wilson* (4 H L Cas. 284). A power of this kind must, of course, be very cautiously exercised, to use the language of Mr Jarman (*on Wills*, 2d vol, 680), "not merely on a conjectural hypothesis of a testator's intention, however reasonable, in opposition to the plain and obvious sense of the language of the instrument."
>
> In applying these general rules to the will in question, I have not the smallest doubt that it can be fairly

and legitimately collected from the whole will to have been the intention of the testator not to permit the capital fund, provided for the payment of his widow's annuity, to go over to his daughter, and to the children of his deceased daughters, if his son should have a child. The general scheme of his will seems to have been to benefit all his children and grandchildren, by distributing his property amongst them, in different proportions, the whole amount having been stated by him in a paper accompanying his will. In this distribution, it was evidently his intention that the son and his children should receive the largest share, as he not only gives them the fund provided for the annuity, but also makes his son his residuary legatee. According, however, to his statement of the amount of his property, the residue would be nearly exhausted by the specific legacies and the annuity fund, so that a very small residue would have been enjoyed by the son, and he would have been in a less favourable position than his sister and his sister's children till the death of his mother. It is stated, that at the time of the testator's death, his property had very largely increased. But, although a will is said to speak from the death of a testator, yet, in construing his intention, you must necessarily refer to the period of making the will. If the Appellants are right in their construction of the will, the son of the testator's son, the principal object of his regard, would derive scarcely any benefit from the dispositions of the will, but would be superseded by all the other members of the family, themselves already the objects of distinct and independent provisions. This appears to me to be utterly inconsistent with the obvious meaning of the testator. The dispositions of his will are perfectly clear down to and inclusive of the bequests to the children of his son. A fund is set apart for the annuity to the widow. The interest of that fund on her decease is to be received by the son during his life, "and on his decease the principal sum to become the property of any child or children he may have born in lawful wedlock, and in such sums as he shall will and direct". The son of the testator, therefore, had a life estate given to him in the fund, with a contingent interest to his children in the principal. But the son was then unmarried, and it was, of course, uncertain whether he would ever marry or have children, and so the bequests, both of the interest of the fund and of the fund itself, might have failed together. The testator, then, having the possibility of the death of his son while a bachelor, in his view, provides upon its occurrence for the distribution of the fund amongst all the rest of the family, even to the issue of his daughter, Mrs Middleton, who had no children at the time, and is now childless, and without any reference to the possible children of his son, for whom he had provided so immediately before. The words which he used to express his intention were, "but in case of my son dying before his mother". This peculiar mode of describing the gift over, does not necessarily imply that, in that event, the son's children, to whom just before the principal sum had been given, were to be supplanted by the daughter and the other grandchildren of the testator. It may mean, and, consistently with the previous gift to the children of the son, would more properly mean that they were to take the capital fund in no other event than the death of George, in the lifetime of his mother, not necessarily that the fund was to be theirs absolutely on that event happening. This appears to me to leave it open to attribute a meaning to the language of the will which will render it consistent throughout, instead of confining the construction to the narrow limits of the few words introductory of the gift over.

This is not like the case put at the Bar, of a gift to A, and if B should go to Rome, or if some insignificant act should be done, then over. There the event described is wholly collateral to and unconnected with the previous limitations, and however capricious and whimsical such a bequest may be, the testator has expressed it in clear and unambiguous terms, and it must prevail. But here, the event, on which the gift over depends, is implicated and involved in the prior limitations; it is not, as in the case supposed, self-interpreting, but itself creates an ambiguity which, without it, would not have existed.

There are few of the cases cited in the argument which are of much assistance in determining the construction which ought to be adopted in this case. All those on which an estate was to commence, or to take effect upon certain specified events, which never occurred, and in which the gift therefore altogether failed, are obviously inapplicable. This is a case in which a gift, either absolute or contingent, is clearly and distinctly made, and the question is whether the words, on which the doubt arises, take it away again, on the happening of an event not consistent with it, but upon which the determination of a prior gift depended.

That appears to me to be a safe and reasonable principle of construction which was stated by Lord

Brougham, in the case of *Horne* v *Pillans* (2 Mylne and K 25), "that where there is a clear gift, it can only be altered and retracted by the most plain, and unambiguous, and unequivocal words, and the Court will, *in dubio*, justly prefer that construction of any subsequent clause which will make it consistent with the intention plainly expressed in the preceding part".

But it was strongly insisted by the Appellants' counsel, that it was impossible for your Lordships to decide in favour of the Respondents in this case without overruling the case of *Holmes* v *Cradock* (3 Ves 317), which was alleged to be a case where there was a bequest in derogation of a previous absolute gift, which was allowed to prevail. But *Holmes* v *Cradock* was a case which ranges under the head of those to which I have already alluded, where an interest was to take effect upon an event which never happened. There the bequest was, "if my son shall die, leaving my wife, without leaving a widow or any child; after his death and my wife's, I give and bequeath to Mr Holmes £500". The son survived the wife, and died without leaving a widow or child, and it was held that Mr. Holmes was not entitled to the legacy, as all the events had not occurred upon which it was to take effect, one of them being that the son should die leaving the wife. This was not the case, then, of a previous gift taken away by subsequent words, but a gift upon certain conditions, which were not fulfilled.

Here there is, first, a plain and unequivocal gift, and then there are words immediately following which at once produce an inconsistency, and therefore an ambiguity in the dispositions of the will. By reading the will as if it had said, "But in case of my son dying before his mother without leaving a child", the whole is rendered plain and consistent. Are your Lordships then at liberty to supply these words as the expression of a necessary implication? Various authorities have been cited in favour of such a course; one of the earliest of which was *Spalding* v *Spalding* (Cro Car 185). That was a case very similar to the present, because if the clause had been read as it stood in the will, it was expressed in clear and unambiguous words, and reasons might readily have been suggested as in this case, why if John died leaving Alice, the estate should go over to William, although John had left children; but there the very words which are wanting here (or equivalent ones), were supplied, and the clause was read, "If John die without issue, leaving Alice." I do not think that the application of that case can be weakened by the observation that the Court proceeded upon the whole context of the will in aid of the construction. This only shows that you are at liberty to resort to the rest of the will, to discover a different meaning from that which the words taken by themselves would convey. And the importance of this case is very much increased, in my mind, by the view of it which was taken by Lord Hale in *King* v *Melling* (Ventr 225), by Lord Harcourt in *Kentish* v *Newman* (1 P Will 234), by Lord Macclesfield in *Hewet* v *Ireland* (1 P Will 427), and by Lord Ellenborough in *Doe* v *Micklem* (6 East, 486).

The case of *Targus* v *Puget* (2 Ves 194) is also a strong authority for supplying words similar to those which are required to be understood in this case, nor can those who consider that you are bound to adhere to the words used as conclusively expressive of a testator's meaning, object that this case and that of *Kentish* v *Newman*, are cases of marriage articles in which a provision may be expected to be made for the children of the marriage, because the same presumption may be raised in favour of the children of the testator's son under the present will. It is to be observed that in this case the property is vested in the children of the son, independently of their father, who merely takes the interest of it for his life; and the event upon which the gift over depends, is one which affects the father's life interest only, and does not touch the estate of his children. I do not see why the construction suggested by the Respondents should not be adopted; that there are two contingent independent dispositions which are attached to the bequest to the son; so that if one takes effect the other fails. This renders the whole will sensible and consistent, while on the contrary "the opposite construction (to use the words of Vice-Chancellor Wigram in *Hillersdon* v *Lowe* (2 Hare, 355, 370), is capricious and irrational, and subverts the scheme of the will which is expressed in clear and unambiguous language in all other parts of it".

It appears to me, my Lords, that without going out of the will in search of any conjectural intention, but gathering the testator's meaning from a consideration of the whole of his dispositions, and more especially from the context of the particular passage upon which the question arises, your Lordships will not be frustrating, but fulfilling, the testator's intention, by determining that the Appellant took a vested interest in the capital of the fund, set apart to answer the annuity to the testator's widow, and that the decree of the Master of the Rolls should therefore be affirmed.

I think it right to add, that my noble and learned friend, Lord Brougham, who heard the first argument upon this case, at the conclusion of it agreed with me in the view which I then took, and which I have now expressed. Of course my noble and learned friend is not to be bound at all by that opinion as a final opinion, inasmuch as he has not heard the second argument which was ordered by your Lordships, much less of course can he be bound by the reasons which I have expressed for the opinion which I have formed, and in which opinion, as I have stated, he concurred.'

Allgood* v *Blake (1873) LR 8 Exch 160 Court of Exchequer (Blackburn, Keating, Mellor, Grove and Honyman JJ)

(Note: nothing turns on the facts of this case, which are in any case very complex.)

Blackburn J:

'The general rule is that, in construing a will, the Court is entitled to put itself in the position of the testator, and to consider all material facts and circumstances known to the testator with reference to which he is to be taken to have used the words in the will, and then to declare what is the intention evidenced by the words used with reference to those facts and circumstances which were (or ought to have been) in the mind of the testator when he used those words. As is said in *Wigram on Extrinsic Evidence* p9:

"The question in expounding a will is not what the testator meant, as distinguished from what his words express, but simply what is the meaning of his words."

But we think that the meaning of words varies according to the circumstances of and concerning which they are used.

In *Doe d Hiscocks* v *Hiscocks* (1839) 5 M & W 363 at p369, in the judgment of the Court of Exchequer it is said:

"The object in all cases is to discover the intention of the testator. The first and most obvious mode of doing this is to read his will as he has written it, and collect his intention from his words. But as his words refer to facts and circumstances respecting his property and his family, and others whom he names and describes in his will, it is evident that the meaning and application of his words cannot be ascertained without evidence of all those facts and circumstances. All the facts and circumstances, therefore, respecting persons and property to which the will relates are undoubtedly legitimate and often necessary evidence to enable us to understand the meaning and application of his words."

No doubt in many cases the testator has for the moment forgotten or overlooked material facts and circumstances which he well knew. And the consequence sometimes is that he uses words which express an intention which he would not have wished to express, and would have altered if he had been reminded of the facts and circumstances. But the Court is to construe the will as made by the testator, not to make a will for him; and therefore it is bound to execute his expressed intention, even if there is great reason to believe that he has, by blunder, expressed what he did not mean. And the general rule, we believe, is undisputed, that, in trying to get at the intention of the testator, we are to take the whole of the will, construe it altogether, and give the words their natural meaning (or, if they have acquired a technical sense, their technical meaning), unless when applied to the subject matter which the testator presumably had in his mind, they produce an inconsistency with other parts of the will, or an absurdity or inconvenience so great as to convince the Court that the words could not have been used in their proper signification, and to justify the Court in putting on them some other signification which, though less proper, is one which the Court thinks the words will bear.

The great difficulty in all cases is in applying these rules to the particular case; for to one mind it may appear that an effect produced by construing the words literally is so inconsistent with the rest of the will, or produces an absurdity or inconvenience so great as to justify the Court in putting on them another signification, which to that mind seems a not improper signification of the words, whilst to another mind the effect produced may appear not so inconsistent, absurd or inconvenient as to justify putting any other signification on the words than their proper one, and the proposed signification may appear a violent construction.

Grey v *Pearson* (1857) 6 HLC 61 is an example of this: Lord Cranworth, Lord St Leonards, and Lord Wensleydale laid down the general rule in terms not substantially differing from each other; but when they came to apply them to the case in hand, there was a marked difference of opinion. We apprehend that no precise line can be drawn, but that the Court must, in each case, apply the admitted rules to the case in hand, not deviating from the literal sense of the words without sufficient reason, or more than is justified; yet not adhering slavishly to them, when to do so would obviously defeat the intention which may be collected from the whole will.

Let us, then, in the first place, see what were the material circumstances known to the testator in the present case …'

Andrews* v *Partington (1791) 3 Bro CC 401 (Lord Loughborough LC)

Class gifts – fixing maximum size of class to achieve certainty

Facts

A grandfather made a bequest of residue to the children of his son Robert Andrews

> 'equally to be divided between and among them; if more than one share and share alike, and if but one, then to such only child; the parts of shares of such child or children to be paid in the manner following: [ie] the daughter's shares at her or their age or ages of twenty-one, or day or days or marriage, which should first happen; and the son's share or shares, at his or their age or ages of twenty-one; or to be sooner advanced, for his or their preferment in the world, or benefit, if the trustees, or the survivors of them should think fit … .'

The grandfather died in 1763. In 1781 Robert Andrews' wife died and at that time they had twelve children. The question arose as to what children ought to take under the bequest.

Held

(per Lord Loughborough LC). The fund was divisible when the eldest child attained 21 and the division was to be among those then in esse.

Battie-Wrightson, Re [1920] 2 Ch 330 Chancery Division (Astbury J)

Construction of wills – punctuation in original will – relevance

Facts

In September 1917 the testatrix instructed her solicitor to prepare a new will. On 3 October 1917 he attended her with a draft copy of the will which included the following:

> 'I give the following legacies (to be paid out of the money standing to my credit at the National Provincial Bank of England, Bishopsgate, EC., and not out of my other monies, namely) to Mrs Annie Stevens. … I give to the said Annie Maria Middleton in addition to the legacy which I have already given to her the undisposed balance which may be to my credit at the said bank …'

By the testatrix's direction the solicitor struck out the words in the brackets and because of her state of health the testatrix decided to execute the altered draft as her will without waiting for a fair copy or an engrossment, this was done with the alteration being duly attested. The testatrix died on 29 October 1917 and her will was proved in September 1918, the cancelled words being omitted from the probate which was engrossed clean so as to read without any blank. As no bank was mentioned in the probate copy the question was whether the 'said bank' could be identified by reference to the original will which was produced from Somerset House.

Held
In order to ascertain what bank was intended the Court was entitled to look at the original will, in which the clause, immediately preceding the specific bequest and containing the name of the bank had been formally erased.

Astbury J:

> '... I have no doubt myself that it is not only the right but the duty of the court in this case to have regard to this erased portion of the will. That being so, it is clear that the expression "undisposed of balance which may be to my credit at the said Bank" means the balance at the only bank mentioned by name. The passage mentioning it was erased, not, as the residuary legatee contends, for the purpose of rendering it doubtful which bank the testatrix was referring to, but for some totally different purpose, because it is perfectly obvious that she intended to give a particular balance for a particular specified purpose ... There is, however, another ground upon which this case can be decided, although I prefer the one that I have already dealt with. On the second point the question is whether "undisposed of balance at the said bank", no bank being mentioned by name, is in the circumstances a patent or a latent ambiguity; the testatrix gave, and unquestionably intended to give, a bank balance, and the only ambiguity arises as soon as evidence is admitted that she had more than one bank. The word "said" points to her having some particular balance in her mind, especially when evidence has been admitted that she had more than one balance standing to her credit. The particular extrinsic evidence which is necessary and sufficient in this case is the original will. That is admissible under the extrinsic evidence rule as well as under the general rule I have already dealt with ...'

Berkeley Leisure Group v *Scott and The Spastics Society* (1992) 29 October Chichester County Court (ex rel Paul Ashwell, Barrister) (Baker J)

Estate including mobile home bequeathed to charity – whether pitch agreement also passes

Facts
The testator bequeathed his entire estate to The Spastics Society, a registered charity. Among the assets was a mobile home with the benefit of a pitch agreement subject to s3 of the Mobile Homes Act 1983. A preliminary point referred to whether or not the agreement came to an end on the death of the testator.

Held
The Spastics Society was a person entitled to the mobile home by virtue of the deceased's will. The agreement enured for the benefit of the charity under s3(3)(b) of the Act.

Charter v *Charter* (1874) LR 7 HL 364 House of Lords (Lord Cairns LC, Lords Chelmsford, Hetherley and Selbourne)

Wills – construction – admissibility of extrinsic evidence

Facts
By his will the testator gave the residue of his estate to 'my son Forster Charter' and appointed him as his executor. The testator had three sons; one named Forster died as a boy long before the will was made. Of the two sons who survived the testator one was called 'William Forster Charter' and the other

'Charles Charter'. Probate of the will was granted to William Forster Charter but an application was made by Charles Charter to have it revoked. At first instance extrinsic evidence was admitted by Lord Penzance which showed that the testator had been on bad terms with William Forster Charter, that he lived over 100 miles away from the testator and only visited him occasionally. Evidence also showed that Charles Charter had lived at home with his mother and his father, the testator, on his farm and helped the testator there and that the testator had always referred to Charles as 'Forster' and William Forster as 'Willie'. There was also evidence in the will which contemplated that the executor and the testator's widow would live together and evidence of declarations of intention by the testator to benefit Charles which were also admitted by Lord Penzance. On appeal:

Held

The evidence of the facts and circumstances surrounding the testator at the time he made his will was admissible, therefore the Court could hear the evidence on the relationship of the testator with his sons William Forster and Charles and on the names he habitually used to refer to them. However, the declarations of intention were not admissible but despite this the evidence was sufficient to show that the testator made a mistake and in fact intended to refer to Charles Charter (Lords Chelmsford and Hatherley dissenting).

Lord Cairns LC:

> 'My Lords, the consideration of this case has been attended, to me, with much anxiety, and that anxiety has not been diminished when I find that I have come to a conclusion upon it different from that at which some of your Lordships have arrived.
>
> My Lords, upon one part of the case I have never entertained any doubt. I hold it to be clear, as I think all your Lordships do that this is not a case in which any parol evidence of statements of the testator, as to whom he intended to benefit, or supposed he had benefited by his will, can be received. The learned Judge of the Probate Court, Lord Penzance, appears to have admitted evidence of this description, although he states that his judgment would have been the same if the evidence had been excluded. I am of the opinion that it ought to have been excluded. The only case in which evidence of this kind can be received is where the description of the legatee, or of the thing bequeathed, is equally applicable in all its parts to two legatees or to two things. That clearly cannot be said of the present case.
>
> But my Lords, there is a class of evidence which in this case, as in all cases of testamentary dispositions, is clearly receivable. The Court has a right to ascertain all the facts which were known to the testator at the time he made his will, and thus to place itself in the testator's position, in order to ascertain the bearing and application of the language which he uses, and in order to ascertain whether there exists any person or thing to which the relevant description given in the will can be, reasonably and with sufficient certainty, applied.
>
> I may refer, as well-known authorities for these propositions, to the cases of *Doe d Hiscocks* v *Hiscocks* (1839) 5 M & W 363, *Bernasconi* v *Atkinson* (1853) 10 Hare 345, and *Drake* v *Drake* (1860) 8 HLC 182 in this House ...'
>
> [His Lordship then referred to the facts of the case and continued:]
>
> 'I now turn to the will of the testator. It commences:
>
> > "The last will and testament of Forster Charter ... I nominate and appoint my son Forster Charter as the executor of this will, and to him I give, devise, and bequeath all my messuages, etc, ... for his use and benefit, and for the use and benefit of the persons hereinafter to be named."
>
> The name here given to the person whom he describes as his son is clearly inaccurate. His son Forster Charter was dead. The younger of his two surviving sons was Charles; the elder was William Forster; but Forster was not his first or leading name, nor was it the name by which he was generally or ever called or spoken of by the testator. There is, therefore, here clearly a mistake. It is possible that if nothing else was found in the will, yet, inasmuch as Forster formed a part of the name of the elder son, and no

part of the name of the younger son, the elder son must have taken, there being no description nor demonstration to rectify or explain the mistake in the name.

But the testator continues:

> "My will is that my executor, Forster Charter, shall annually pay to Elizabeth Charter, my wife, the sum of ten pounds sterling, and at the time (time) allow my said wife her *ordinary* maintenance *so long as they reside together in the same house, but should they think proper to live separately*, then my will is that besides paying my wife the above-named annuity of ten pounds, the said Forster Charter shall allow my said wife, rent free, the use of the cottage at Woodburn Hill now occupied by David Wood, and shall also supply her gratis with a reasonable quantity of bread, corn, potatoes, coals, butter, cheese, and garden produce. Also my will is that should any difference of opinion arise between my said executor and my said wife with regard to the quantity or quality of the above-named bread, corn, potatoes, etc the matter shall be laid before Walter Davison, shoemaker, and his decision shall be final."

These words appear to me to be very important. They do not give to the widow an annuity and maintenance "if" she and the son should reside together, or "provided" the son should live with his mother, or the mother with the son, but it is a direction to the executor to pay an annuity and allow maintenance "so long as they reside together in the same house", with farther directions should they "think proper to live separately". It appears to me that these words are intelligible and appropriate when applied to persons who were living together at the time, but that they are entirely inappropriate if applied to persons not so living together, and if intended to provide a joint residence to commence for the first time at a later period.

Moreover, it was in the highest degree natural for the testator to contemplate the continuance of a conjoint residence which then existed, and had existed so long, but it was in a high degree improbable that he should assume that his eldest son would not merely leave the place where he was settled in life, but also take his mother to live with him. The words "so long as they reside together", appear to me to be equivalent to the words "so long as they continue to reside together", and have, in this sense, involved in them the statement that the persons spoken of did reside together at the time. Farther than this, the maintenance to be allowed the widow is termed "ordinary maintenance", which is put in marked contradistinction to the "reasonable quantity of bread, corn, potatoes, coals, butter, cheese and garden produce", which if she were to live separately, and occupy the cottage, she was to receive, and any difference as to the amount of which she was to be referred to the arbitration of Davison. I understand the terms "ordinary maintenance" to mean the usual or accustomed maintenance which she had hitherto had in the testator"s home, which was to be judged of, not by the decision of Davison, but by the standard of what had been customary during the joint residence of the father and mother and the son Charles.

The result, therefore, is, that I find the testator speaking of a "son" as the object of his bounty. He has but two sons, and the name he gives is not the name of either. It is part of the name of one, but not his first name, or the name by which he is known and called. The testator is not accurate in the names of his children, for he calls his daughter, whose name was Barbara, only "Barbara Forster". To the inaccurate name of his son I find him adding a provision, which, although in terms a gift of an annuity and maintenance to his wife, is, in substance, a description or demonstration, as I read it, of the son who was to be executor and devisee.

The case, therefore, appears to me to become one of those in which there is an erroneous or inaccurate name, and a description or demonstration sufficiently clear to correct the error or inaccuracy. The name and the description cannot, as it appears to me, stand together. In *Drake* v *Drake*, where there was an accurate name, "Mary Frances Tyrwhitt Drake", but an inaccurate description, "niece", and which, therefore, was a much stronger case than the present, for there the name was wholly accurate, the Lord Chancellor, in moving the judgment of this House, expressed himself thus:

> "I see nothing that can warrant us in saying that the testator intended that his sister, Mary Frances Tyrwhitt Drake, should take the residuary estate under his will, unless the maxim which is contended for by the Appellant should govern the case, that without any evidence whatever to prove error of demonstration here is a rigid rule that the name should prevail. But, my Lords, I deny there there is any such rule. There

> is a maxim that the name shall prevail against an error of demonstration; but that you must first show that there is an error of demonstration, and until you have shown that, the rule *verotas nominis tollit errorem demonstrationis* does not apply. I think that there is no presumption in favour of the name more than of the demonstration. Upon referring to the numerous cases have been cited at the Bar, it will be found that there are are more instances in which the demonstration prevailed than in which the name prevailed."

There are some observations upon the same subject by the Vice-Chancellor, my noble and learned friend here present (Lord Hatherley), in *Bernasconi* v *Atkinson*, which, I think, are worthy of our Lordships' attention. The Vice-Chancellor says:

> "It certainly does appear, singularly enough, that the description of the legatee has, in most of the cases referred to, prevailed over the name. Thus, in *Adams* v *Jones* (1852) 9 Hare 685, the description of 'wife', and in *Bradshaw* v *Bradshaw* (1836) 2 Y & C 72, the description of 'second son' were held to designate the respective legatee. In *Doe d* v *Huthwaite* (1820) 3 B & Ald 632, also, the name of the legatee was wrongly expressed, and the description of second son determined the title to the legacy. The selection of the second son showed that the attention of the testator was directed to that description of the object of his bounty, although the name was misplaced, the name of the third son being mentioned in priority to that of the second. So, again, in *Lord Camoys* v *Blundell* (1848) 1 HLC 778, the gift was to a person not named, but described as the second son of Edward Weld of Lulworth, although there was no such person as Edward Weld, the possessor of Lulworth being Joseph Weld. There, the description of 'second son' prevailed, and has held to designate clearly the second son of Joseph. Lady Stourton was mentioned as one of the sisters of Edward Weld. She was a sister of Joseph, and the only person answering the description was the second son of Joseph. But, although this had happened in some cases, they do not say 'take the description in preference to the name'. Far from it; the principle of the cases is, that where there are two descriptions where the testator specifies in two different ways the object of his bounty, the Court adopts that which, in each instance, appears to be the least open to error."

Applying the principle of these authorities, it appears to me that we have here a name in which there is obviously an error, and a description or demonstration which, as I read it, is clear and intelligible, and applies satisfactorily to the younger son, and does not apply to the elder, and therefore corrects the error of the name. My Lords, my noble and learned friend who addressed your Lordships last has said he knows of no authority which would authorise the Court to transfer the property from a person named by a christian name and surname which he bears, to another not bearing the christian name, merely because the full christian name of the devisee is not given. My Lords, I must submit to my noble and learned friend that this is the assumption of the whole question. The question is not one of transferring property from a devisee. The question is, who is the devisee? And that question must be answered by an examination of the whole will, and of all the circumstances of the case legitimately in evidence, an examination which becomes proper and even necessary as soon as it is found that the name inserted in the will is not the correct name of any person in existence.

My Lords, I think that the judgment of the Court below ought to be affirmed. But I further think that, as the case is one of great difficulty, and difficulty caused by the testator himself, your Lordships would do well to follow, with regard to the appeal, the course taken by the Court below, and order the costs of both parties to be paid out of the estate.'

Chartres, Re [1927] 1 Ch 466 Chancery Division(Astbury J)

Class gifts – nature and effect of closing rules

Facts

A testator provided in his will for the disposal of his income 21 years from his decease. At the end of that period two-fifths of the residue of the trust funds were to be held in trust for R's children as R should by will appoint and in default of appointment for all R's children who attained 21. The testator died in 1905 and the 21-year period expired in 1926. R had one son A who attained 21 in 1916. In 1924

R released his power and in 1925 A died having appointed R one of his executors and bequeathing all his property to R. R claimed he was entitled to the two-fifths of the fund.

Held

When R released his power of appointment A had attained 21 and the class in default of appointment closed, so that the whole fund passed to R and any future born children were excluded.

Astbury J (after stating the facts):

> 'The question is whether what has been described as a rule of convenience, for the purpose of ascertaining the class to take under a gift of the fund in order that the beneficiaries may know what their shares are and that the executors may distribute the fund, ought to be applied in the circumstances of the present case.
>
> There can, of course, be little doubt that the testator intended the two-fifths of his residue to go to all Richard's children who being sons should attain twenty-one or being daughters should attain that age or marry, unless Richard, by exercising his testamentary power, gave the property to his children or remote issue or some or one of them. In other words, there really can be no doubt that the tesator intended that any child of Richard who should come into existence in his lifetime should take in default of appointment, although Richard by exercising that power could distribute the two-fifths in the way I have mentioned; and the question I have to decide, and which in my judgment is an extremely difficult one, is whether this so called rule of convenience in the events that have happened entitles the personal representatives of Archibald who died after acquiring a vested interest subject to its being divested or altered in amount either by the exercise of the power or in default of appointment by other children being born to Richard is now, by reason of the rule, entitled to defeat the plain intention of the testator.
>
> The principle of this rule is that the class to take is to be ascertained as soon as possible in order that the beneficiaries may know what their shares are and that the fund may be distributed. The rule is, of course, obviously convenient to those who take under it to the exclusion of others intended to benefit, but the irony of the rule is no doubt more apparent to those who are by its application excluded from taking what the testator intended them to take. The rule is so well established and its ambit so clearly laid down that if the present case did not raise a point of equity, which I do not think has ever been directly decided, there would be little more to say. Having regard, however, to this point of equity I will endeavour to state very shortly what this rule is in general though not in exhaustive terms.
>
> The rule may be divided into three heads. First, if there is an immediate gift in a will to A's children the rule lays down that only those children in existence at the testator's death shall take, although his intention was obviously different. By way of exception to this first head, if there are no children of A in existence at the testator's death then the rule of convenience ceases to operate, and all subsequently born children take in accordance with the testator's intention. The second head of the rule may be stated as follows: if the gift is in future, as for instance to A for life with remainder to B's children, the rule provides that only those children of B shall take who come into existence before A's death. Here again there is an exception that if there are no children of B in esse before A's death, then the rule ceases to operate, and all subsequently born children take. The third head may be stated as follows where there is a gift to A for life and after his death to B's children who atain twenty-one, then if at A's death there are children of B who have attained twenty-one or the representatives of such children, the rule applies and the class closes. If at A's death there are only infant children of B who subsequently attain twenty-one then again the class closes when the first child so attains that age; and in all cases the rule is excluded if there is an express intention of the testator to the contrary …
>
> … before proceeding, it is interesting to try to ascertain the origin of the rule in the circumstances in which it came to be made. As far as the text-books are concerned it is, I think, throughout treated as a rule of convenience, by which a person having a vested interest at a date is entitled to be paid and those who come into existence afterwards are excluded in order to permit a distribution at a vested date of payment, but that does not satisfy me as to why it should ever have been made at all. If a man leaves his property to A B's children why it should be a rule of convenience that one child shall take and another be excluded is difficult to see, especially if one considers the interest of the second child. The only

explanation that I can find of the origin of this rule and application is a difficult case in a statement by Buckley J in *In re Stephens* [1904] 1 Ch 322, 328. The learned judged said:

> "When the rule is adopted the solution arrived at is the result of an endeavour by the Court to reconcile two apparently inconsistent directions – the one that the whole class of children shall take, and the other that the fund shall be divided at a moment when the whole class cannot be ascertained."

That is the most intelligible reason for this rule that I have been able to discover. If it be the fact in any case that a testator has given two apparently inconsistent directions, the one as to when his fund shall be divided and the other as to who shall take, then there seems little inconsistency or hardship in the Court trying to give effect to the testator's intention to be derived, although with difficulty, from two apparently inconsistent directions. And it seems to me, with great respect to many decisions in the past, that if you can discover from a testator's will a direction or intention that the fund in question shall be distributed at a certainn time and a direction that the class of people who shall take it are such that at that particular time of distribution they cannot be wholly ascertained, there only being some in existence, then it does not seem very difficult to appreciate the reason for cutting the knot in the way that has been done. Whether that explanation is consistent with all the decisions in which the rule has been applied I do not propose to state or inquire.

In *In re White's Trusts* (1860) John 656, 659, a case where a power existed, Wood V-C said:

> "In a case where the donee of the power survives the tenant for life, there would be a possible ground for arguing that the class must be kept in suspense long enough to let in all who might be born while the power was in existence."

This is a very striking passage, because it apparently refers to a case where a testator gave property to AB for life with remainder to the children of CD as X should appoint, and one would have thought that in that case, as long as the power of appointment existed, it would really be impossible to apply the rule in favour of any particular children of CD who were in existence before AB's death. However, there is this doubt expressed; but speaking for myself I should have thought that if the power had been such as I have suggested it would have been quite impossible to apply the rule to the children of CD in esse before AB's death, so long as the power is in existence which might alter the people who may ultimately take. I mention that as showing the extraordinary force that has come to be given to this so-called rule of convenience.

The fact that the rule when applied more or less defeats the intention of the testator does not seem to be disputed. Many judges have commented upon it and some have deplored it. In *In re Emmet's Estate* (1880) 13 Ch D 484 a testator gave the income of his property to HE for life, and after his death he gave one-third of his property in trust for all and every of the children of G, the shares to be conveyed and paid to them at twenty-one or marriage. HE, the tenant for life, died a bachelor. At his death G was a widower with two children. He married again, and when his eldest child attained twenty-one he had six children, all of whom lived to attain that age. Another child was born afterwards, and it was held by Hall V-C and the Court of Appeal that the six children or their representatives were entitled and the after-born child was excluded. That is an instance of the third head of the rule to which I referred. Hall V-C says [at 488]:

> "The rule which permits any future born child to be let in until the time when one child attains the age at which he is entitled to call for an actual payment over of his share, may, as Lord Loughborough said in *Andrews* v *Partington* (1791) 3 Cro CC 401 at 404, occasion wonder to any person who is not trying a case according to legal decisions."

... Whether anyone can or cannot understand the rule, it is one founded upon convenience: as it would not allow the going beyond the particular time when one of the children could say "actually pay me over my shares".

Later on he says:

> "The authorities seem to me to amount to this: that where, upon looking at the whole will, the testator must be considered to have made it upon the basis or footing of adopting or taking a certain time as the

period of distribution or division, the Court must, taking that period, construe the will accordingly, although possibly it is not the period for the actual distribution of the fund."

That I think is in exact accordance with the views expressed by Buckley J. That case went to the Court of Appeal, and Jessel MR said [at 490]:

"Under that will any layman would understand that all the children of George Nelson Emmet, at whatever time they were born, would become entitled, and in the absence of authority so should I. There has, however, been established a rule of convenience, not founded on any view of the testator's intention, that since a child wants its share it is convenient that the payment of the share should not be deferred, it shall be made payable by preventing any child born after that time from participating in the fund. The rule is, that, so soon as any child would, if the class were not susceptible of increase, be entitled to call for payment, the class shall become incapable of being increased. That rule of convenience, being opposed to the intention, is not to be applied where it is not necessary, there being a rule that you let in all who are born up to the time when a share becomes payable."

Then he discusses the particular case before him.

Now assuming as I do that this rule originated in attempting to solve two apparently inconsistent directions, one must find, in order to apply it, period of distribution fixed or pointed to by the testator and a class to take at that period which may subsequently be extended beyond its then numbers. In the present case, having regard to the fact that one is asked to depart from the testator's intention, clause 13, upon which the present question turns, may be looked at from many points of view. There is no doubt that the testator points to a period of distribution which he refers to as "from and after the expiration of 21 years", but it is extremely difficult to say that he takes that as a period when anybody will be entitled to call for anything while Richard is living, because from and after the expiration of twenty-one years subject to the prior interests he gave and bequeathed this fund in trust for the child or children and remoter issue of Richard as he should by will appoint. And it is difficult for me, at all events, to imagine that this testator dreamt for a moment that during Richard's lifetime one of his children should take to the exclusion of others, if any, who might be born. But the matter does not end there, because in default of such appointment and so far as the appointment shall not extend, the testator bequeathed this fund in trust for all the children of Richard who being sons should attain twenty-one or being daughters should attain that age or marry ...'

Cook, Re [1948] Ch 212 Chancery Division (Harman J)

Construction of wills – use of technical words – rebuttal of the presumption

Facts

The testatrix made her will on a printed form, and the dispositive part consisted solely of a gift of 'all my personal estate' to her nephews and nieces. The greater part of her estate consisted of realty and it was unlikely that she intended to dispose only of her personalty.

Held

The realty did not pass under her will but devolved as on her intestacy.

Harman J:

'... this is a case where a layman has chosen to use a term of art. The words "all my personal estate" are words so well known to lawyers that it must take a very strong context to make them include real estate. Testators can cause black to mean white if they make their intention sufficiently clear, but this testatrix has not done so. It may well be that she thought "personal estate" meant "all my wordly goods". I do not know. In the absence of something to show that the phrase ought not to be construed I must suppose that she used the term "personal estate" in its ordinary meaning as a term of art.'

The meaning of the words in the will will be controlled by context. Thus, the intention collected from the whole will prevails and can fix the sense of ambiguous words, control the sense of clear words and supply the place of express words. The general principle was stated by Lord St Leonards in *Grey* v *Pearson* (1857) 6 HLC 61 at 99:

> "Nobody is more disposed than I am to abide by clear words, and to give them their natural and grammatical meaning, but I never did and I never can come to this conclusion, that the words of a will cannot admit of modification according to the real intention of the testator, as you find it from other expressions, or from the whole context of the will. It is difficult to lay any abstract rule upon the subject, but where I find the intention, and I find words pointing out the intention, and that if I give to the words their simple meaning according to grammar and according to their plain *prima facie* import, I defeat the intention, I hold that I am bound, by every rule of law and equity, to see whether I cannot give them, by natural construction, an import which will effectuate and not defeat the intention".'

Doe d Hiscocks v *Hiscocks* (1839) 5 M & W 363 (Lord Abinger CB)

Wills – equivocation – the best evidence rule

Facts

The testator devised lands to his son John Hiscocks for life and then after his death to his, the testator's, grandson John 'eldest son of John Hiscocks' and on his death to the first son of the body of his grandson in tail male. At the date of the making of the will the testator's son had been twice married. By his first wife he had one son Simon and by his second wife an eldest son John and other children. The lands devised had come to the testator from the father of the testator's son's second wife. At the trial of the action to decide which grandson was entitled to the devise Bosanquet J admitted evidence of the instructions given by the testator for his will and declarations of intention, to show that Simon was intended to be the object of the testator's bounty. On appeal:

Held

Evidence of intention as admitted at the trial was not admissible to show which of the two grandsons was intended by the will. It was quite clear from the evidence of surrounding circumstances who was intended and that being the case no evidence of intention was admissible.

Lord Abinger CB:

> '... it must be admitted that it is not possible altogether to reconcile the different cases that have been decided on this subject; which makes it the more expedient to investigate the principles upon which any evidence to explain the will of a testator ought to be received. The object in all cases is to discover the intention of the testator. The first and most obvious mode of doing this is to read his will as he has written it, and collect his intentions from his words. But as his words refer to facts and circumstances respecting his property and his family, and others whom he names or describes in the will, it is evidence that the meaning and application of his words cannot be ascertained, without evidence of all those facts and circumstances. To understand the meaning of any writer, we must first be apprized of the persons and circumstances that are the subjects of his allusions or statements; and if these are not fully disclosed in his work, we must look for illustration to the history of the times in which he wrote, and to the works of contemporaneous authors. All the facts and circumstances, therefore, respecting persons or property, to which the will relates, are undoubtedly legitimate, and often necessary evidence, to enable us to understand the meaning and application of his words.
>
> Again, the testator may have habitually called certain persons or things by peculiar names, by which they were not commonly known. If these names should occur in his will, they could only be explained and construed by the aids of evidence to show the sense in which he used them, in like manner as if his will

were written in cipher, or in a foreign language. The habits of the testator in these particulars must be receivable as evidence to explain the meaning of his will.

But there is another mode of obtaining the intention of the testator, which is by evidence of his declarations, of the instructions given for his will, and other circumstances of the like nature, which are not adduced for explaining the words or meaning of the will, but either to supply some defiency, or remove some obscurity, or to give some effect to expressions that are unmeaning or ambiguous.

Now, there is but one case in which it appears to us that this sort of evidence of intention can properly be admitted, and that is, where the meaning of the testator's words is neither ambiguous or obscure, and where the devise is on the face of it perfect and intelligible, but, from some of the circumstances admitted in proof, an ambiguity arises, as to which of the two or more things, or which of the two or more persons (each answering the words in the will) the testator intended to express. Thus, if a testator devise his manor of S to AB and has two manors of North S and South S, it being clear he means to devise only one, whereas both are equally denoted by the words he has used, in that case there is what Lord Bacon calls "an equivocation", ie the words equally apply to either manor, and evidence of previous intention may be received to solve this latent ambiguity; for the intention shows what he meant to do; and when you know that, you immediately perceive that he has done it by the general words he had used, which, in their ordinary sense, may properly bear that construction.

It appears to us that, in all other cases, parol evidence of what was the testator's intention ought to be excluded, upon this plain ground, that his will ought to be made in writing; and if his intention cannot be made to appear by the writing, explained by circumstances, there is no will.'

Doe d Winter* v *Perratt (1843) 6 M & G 314 House of Lords (Lords Brougham and Cottenham, Parke B, Tindal CJ Bayleey B, Coltman J, Moule J, Littledale J, Bosanquet J, Taunton J, Patterson J and Williams J)

Construction of wills – use of technical words and expressions

Facts

A devised Whiteacre to B for life, remainder to C or his male heir, if any; and if no male heir lawfully begotten by C then to fall to 'the first male heir' of D's family, paying unto such of the daughters of D who should be living £100 each, at the time of taking possession of the estate. C died in the lifetime of B leaving a daughter, who also died in the lifetime of B leaving a son E. Previously to the date of the will D had died leaving five daughters; viz. F with a daughter; G with two sons; M and N; H with one son, O; I with one son, P; K with one son, Q. After the death of A, the daughter of F had a son L; after which F died, then I, then B. The question arose whether the expression 'first male heir of the branch of D's family' was to be considered as having been used in a technical sense or in a popular sense, applicable to an heir apparent and an heir presumptive.

Held

(Lord Brougham, Parke B, Cottman J and Moule J) The expression was to be considered as having been used in its technical sense. (Lord Cottenham, Tindall CJ Bayley B, Littledale J, Bosanquet J, Taunton J, Patterson J and Williams J) The expression was to be considered as having been used in its popular sense.

Parke B:

'My Lords, my answer to the first question proposed by your Lordships, is, that in my humble opinion the expression "the first male heir" was not used by the testator to denote a person of whom an ancestor might be living. It is a rule in the judicial exposition of wills, that technical words, or words of known legal import, are to be considered as having been used in their technical sense, or, according to their strict acceptation, unless the context contains a plain indication to the contrary. Such is the rule laid down by

Eyre CJ in *Buck* v *Nurton* (1828) Hudson & Brookes' Rep 684, by Lord Alvanley MR in *Thellusson* v *Woodford* (1809) 12 East 293 and in *Poole* v *Poole* (1851) 1 De GM & G 502 citing *Goodright* v *Pulleyn* 14 Com B 385; and lastly by Lord Redesdale in *Jesson* v *Wright* (1855) LJ CP 71, and other authorities. That this rule is well established admits of no doubt; and it is a sound and salutory principle of construction – which affords the best chance of obtaining a reasonable degree of certainty in the exposition of testamentary papers – to abide steadily by general rules, and not to indulge in conjectures of the supposed intent of the testator. Upon this subject I cannot forbear referring to a passage in Mr Fearne's work, page 136, in which this doctrine is ably enforced:

> "Certain established maxims as to the legal import and effect of technical expressions will render the decisions of titles to property a little dependent, as the nature of things will admit, upon the occasional opinion, humour, ingenuity, or caprice of the judge, and are therefore most proper and sure grounds for titles to rest and depend upon. Titles so founded may be easily and clearly ascertained; and under them, a permanent peaceful enjoyment may be expected." [Comparing the supposed difference of construction in deeds and wills]

Adopting, then, this rule of construction, the word "heir", in its strict legal acceptation, cannot be applicable to any one whose ancestor is living; *Nemo est hoeres viventis* [Strictly speaking, perhaps no one is an heir except a person who has succeeded to some property, or to some liability of an ancestor.] That word must, therefore, be read in the will in question with its appropriate meaning, unless the context contain a plain indication to the contrary. No one can take "by a devise to an heir, who is not an heir indeed, without demonstration plain", to use the language of a marginal note in Hobart, [Hobarts Reports (1603-1625) 33], sanctioned by Bridgman CJ [(1620) Bridgman 413] and Eyre CJ in the cases referred to. It seems to me that there is nothing in the context of this will which amounts to "demonstration plain", or anything like a plain indication, or indeed any indication, that the testator meant to use the word heir in any other than its primary acceptation.

There is no doubt that the word "heir" is capable of being applied to one whose ancestor is living; and there are cases where the context has been, in the opinion of the court, sufficiently clear to call upon it to construe the word in its improper or secondary acceptation; such as the case of *Long* v *Beaumont* (1700) 2 Peere Williams 229 and *Brooking* v *White* (1780) 2 W Blackstone 1010. Whether, in all those cases, the circumstances relied upon amount to a clear indication of the intent of the testator to use the word heir in other than its strict sense, so as to satisfy the rule laid down in the cases above referred to, and now established, it is not necessary to inquire. In the present case no similar circumstances exist; and it appears to me to be a mere conjecture, and that upon a slight foundation, that the testator intended to make any but a very heir the object of his bounty.'

Dorman (deceased), Re [1994] 1 WLR 282 Chancery Division (David Neuberger QC sitting as Deputy Judge of the High Court)

Will – bank account – gift of moneys in numbered account at bank – transfer to higher interest account in ignorance of terms of will – whether moneys in second account at date of testatrix's death pass as specific legacy or to residuary estate

Facts

Where the transfer of moneys, in ignorance of the terms of a will, to a second bank account was a change in form only, the moneys passed as a specific legacy rather than to the residuary legatees.

By clause 2 of her will made on 29 September 1987, the testatrix stipulated that the balance of a numbered deposit account was to be added to the capital of a trust fund from which she received income. Prior to her death, and in ignorance of the terms of the will, on 16 July 1990 the account was closed and a new account was opened to take advantage of better interest rates. The entire moneys in the first account were transferred. After her death on 27 January 1991, the court was asked to decide whether the moneys in the second account passed to the specific legatees named in clause 2, or to charities named as residuary legatees.

Held

On a true construction of the will the moneys passed as a specific bequest under clause 2 rather than into the residuary estate. The arrangements under the new account were in effect identical to the old account. It was to be inferred that the change to the second account was a change in name and form only.

David Neuberger QC:

> 'The only case in English law on the bequest of moneys in a bank account to which I have been referred is *In re Heilbronner decd, Nathan* v *Kenny* [1953] 1 WLR 1254. The testator in a home-made will bequeathed his "bank deposit at the Midland Bank" to his nurse. A few days before he died he withdrew all moneys from his only bank account with the Midland Bank. Roxburgh said, at p1259:
>
> > "In my judgment, it is going too far to say that 'my bank deposit at the Midland Bank' has not got a reasonably clear meaning. It is quite true, in one sense, that no money is really deposited at a bank because the relations between the banker and customer is that of debtor and creditor. The actual money which is deposited is, of course, free for the bank to spend as it thinks fit. But that is a legal notion. It is common to speak of 'deposit account' and 'current account', but there is no difference between a deposit account and a current account except that, in one case, interest is usually paid and, in the other case, it is usually not paid, though that is not invariable. In the case of a deposit account notice is required, though it is very often waived, and in the case of a current account it is never required. Those are the differences in the terms of loan and nothing else. The relationship between the banker and the customer is that of debtor and creditor. Therefore, there is no great art in the words 'deposit account' and, in my judgment, when a man says 'my bank deposit' at a particular bank, primarily he means 'the money which I have on current or deposit account'."
>
> On the basis that the money was removed from the bank only on a temporary basis, Roxburgh J concluded that the money which had been standing in the account shortly before the testator's death passed under a specific request.
>
> Bearing in mind these principles, I have after considerable hesitation reached the conclusion that the moneys in the second account did pass under clause 2(e) of the will in the instant case. I reach that conclusion for two reasons which are to an extent connected. First, the money in the first account represented, on the very unusual facts of this case, money in the nature of a fund; all, or at any rate virtually all, of the money in that account had been paid to the deceased by the trust, and it is an inference that the money was effectively intended to be repaid by the deceased to the trust on her death insofar as it had not been spent by or on her during her lifetime.
>
> It seems to me that the deceased intended that the trust was to receive back the moneys which it had paid to her since its inception in 1985, and insofar as she did not spend the money during her lifetime. It is difficult to see how she could have more conveniently produced this result if she intended to bequeath to the trust the funds she had received from the trust and had not spent. If, as seems to me likely in view of the value of her estate and the pecuniary bequests, she had other sources of income and possibly other accounts in banks or building societies, it would have involved a complex task of tracing the moneys she intended to bequeath to the trust, unless she kept them in some sort of separate account. I think it likely on the balance of probabilities from the evidence, albeit not very full evidence, in this case that this is what she did.
>
> Accordingly, consistent with what I might call the lay approach to bank accounts as described in *In re Heilbronner decd* [1953] 1 WLR 1254, I consider that, on the special facts of this case, the reference in clause 2(e) of the will to the balance in the first account was effectively reference to a fund of money.
>
> Secondly, the arrangement embodied in the second account was very similar to that in the first account. In legal terms, each involved the same creditor, that is the deceased; the same debtor, that is Barclays Bank

plc; the same branch of the debtor; the same loan subject to withdrawals by the deceased or payments by the trust; and very similar terms. The only differences were the improved rate of interest in the second account and the need for 30 days' notice for withdrawal on the second account.

At close of business on 16 July 1990 it seems to me that the money in the second account was substantially the same thing (to use the words in *In re Slater* [1907] 1 Ch 665) as the money in the first account had been when the bank opened for business that morning. I do not see why that should cease to be the case some six months later when the deceased died.

The interest of the deceased was practically the same in the second account as it was in the first account, and the change from the first account to the second account was substantially a change in name and form only, to quote the words of Neville J in *In re Leeming* [1912] 1 Ch 828, 830.

On 16 July, if the bank account is to be characterised as a loan from customer to bank or a debt from bank to customer it appears to me that the change of accounts involved a change of name which was equivalent to, and a change of terms which was less substantial than, the change of name and of terms in *In re Kuypers* [1925] Ch 244 as described in the judgment of Tomlin J. ...

In those circumstances, with gratitude for the arguments which were skilfully and succinctly put before me, I have reached the conclusion that the order I should make on the originating summons before me is that on the true construction of the will and in the events which have happened, moneys at the death of the deceased held in the name of capital advantage account No 00327786 at the 10, Church Street, St Austell, Cornwall, branch of Barclays Bank plc do pass under clause 2(e) of the said will and not under clause 4 thereof.'

Freeman, Re [1910] 1 Ch 681 Court of Appeal (Cozens Hardy MR, Buckley and Kennedy LJJ)

Construction of codicils – narrow construction

Facts

By his will made in 1907 the testator appointed X to be one of his executors and bequeathed to him, if he should prove the will, a legacy of £1,000 and then gave him a share of the residue. By a codicil made in 1908 the testator after referring to the appointment of X as executor and the £1,000 legacy to him, revoked the appointment and the legacy, and appointed Y as an executor instead and gave him a legacy of £200. At the end of the codicil the testator directed that his will should be construed as if Y's name was inserted throughout the will instead of X's. The question arose whether this direction affected the gift of residue to X.

Held

The direction did not revoke the gift of residue to X since a clear gift in a will is not to be cut down by anything subsequent which does not with reasonable certainty indicate the intention of the testator cut it down. The court will not allow a plain gift in a will to be cut down by something ambiguous in a codicil.

Gauntlett* v *Carter (1853) 17 Beav 586 Court of Chancery (Sir John Romilly MR)

Construction of wills – relevance of punctuation marks

Facts

A testator devised his freehold estate 'situate in Bullen Court, Strand, and Maiden Lane, in the County of Middlesex, unto ...'. At the time of his death the testator owned certain freehold houses and premises, situate in Bullen Court (off the Strand) and others in the Strand but not in Bullen Court. The question arose whether the word 'Strand' was part of the description of Bullen Court or whether it operated to pass the freehold estates of the testator in the Strand.

Held

The words should be construed as passing the property in Bullen Court, and in the Strand, and in Maiden Lane.

Sir John Romilly MR:

> '... upon examining the clause itself more attentively, I observe that he is not disposing of his houses, but of his estate though he points out the parcels. He says "my freehold estates situate in Bullen Court, Strand and Maiden Lane", and there was a large block of property belonging to him situate between Maiden Lane and the Strand and bounded by Bullen Court. Again, the introduction of the commas before and after the words "Strand" is a circumstance of importance; and though it is unusual to use the word "Strand" by itself, without the article "the", yet, where there are preceding words of enumeration and it is used as part of a sentence, the custom of prefixing the article "the" is not always followed, for it is frequently used without it, in the enumeration of places.
>
> I am of the opinion, that the best construction of this clause of the will is, that the testator not only meant to dispose of the freehold estates situate in Bullen Court, but also in the Strand and Maiden Lane. At the same time I cannot say that this is not a question of considerable obscurity, and another mind might very possibly come to an opposite conclusion on it.'

Hammond, Re [1938] 3 All ER 308 Chancery Division (Simonds J)

Wills – irreconcilable provisions – The 'Rule of Despair'

Facts

By his will the testator left legacies to several institutions and in each case the amount of the legacy was stated both in words and in figures. However, one legacy read 'I bequeath ... to Miss May's Mission the sum of one hundred pounds (£500).'

Held

The later of the two provisions must prevail so that the legacy should be read as being £500.

Simonds J:

> 'The question is whether the gift to Miss May's Mission is one of £100 or £500. I think it is a case in which I should apply the maxim *cum duo inter se pugnatia reperuintur in testamento ultimum ratum est,* which is to say that an intention is to be attributed, sometimes arbitrarily to the testator that, where in a will there are two inconsistent provisions, the later one is to prevail. It is an arbitrary rule in the sense that one can only give effect to the intention of the testator, but it is better to follow a general rule than to rely upon fine distinctions which can be of no substance. In this case therefore, I shall adopt the principle. No doubt there is a *prima facie* rule that, where words and figures conflict, the words ought to prevail, but no case has been brought to my notice where that rule has been applied, otherwise than in the case of commercial documents. The rule must of course, give way to the context, but the context here justifies the view that the testator intended £500 and not £100."

Hancock* v *Watson [1902] AC 14 House of Lords

Wills – inconsistent provisions – reconciliation

Facts

The testator gave his residuary personalty in trust for his wife for life, and after her death to be divided into five portions. Two portions were allotted 'to SD I give two of such portions', and he directed that these two portions should remain in trust for her for her separate use and after her decease for her children upon attaining 25, if sons, or upon attaining 21, or marrying, if daughters. In default of any such issue the two portions were to be divided among the children of C, subject to the same conditions as to age or marriage. SD died without having had a child. At her death there were children of C, daughters who had attained 21 or married.

Held

1. The gift over at the death of SD was void for remoteness.
2. The original gift to SD was absolute; and by reason of the invalidity of the trusts granted onto it, the original absolute gift remained, and upon her death passed to her personal representatives.

Lord Davey:

> 'If you find an absolute gift to a legatee in the first instance and trusts are engrafted or imposed on that absolute interest which fail, either from lapse, or invalidity or any other reason, then the absolute gift takes effect as far as the trusts have failed, to the exclusion of the residuary legatee or next-of-kin as the case may be ...'

Henley* v *Wardell (1988) The Times 29 January Chancery Division (Mr John Mowbray QC)

Construction of a will – need for careful drafting

Facts

The testator's will gave a life interest to W and the remainder to the children when 21 years old. By clause 10 of the will the trustees were given the power to advance a capital from the fund created by the will. Clause 10 sought to vary s32 by the inclusion of the words:

> 'to the intent that the powers given to the trustees by s32 Trustee Act 1925 shall be enlarged so as to permit my trustees in their absolute and uncontrolled discretion to advance at any time the whole of any expectant or presumptive share to any of my children'.

Held

a) This clause merely increased the amount that could be advanced to a beneficiary under the provisions of the statute, namely one-half. It was not effective to remove the requirement that the life-tenant must consent to the advance under s32(1)(c).

b) The court indicated that if will draftsmen sought to exclude the necessity of obtaining the life-tenant's consent, they must say so expressly, for example, by such words as 'and s32(1)(c) of the Trustee Act 1925 shall not apply (to this will)'.

Howell* v *Howell [1992] 1 IR 290 (Carroll LJ)

Will – construction – lapse of gift – whether gift to other beneficiary residuary

Facts

By his will a testator left certain property to one brother J and 'all my stocks and any other assets I may have' to another brother, D. J predeceased the testator. Another brother, P, would benefit if the failed gift was distributed as an intestacy. P brought proceedings to determine whether the bequest to D should be regarded as residuary.

Held

The bequest to D was not residuary. The reference in the will to 'any other assets' meant any assets other than those already mentioned. The testator's intention had been to divide his estate between two of his brothers and the expression 'any other assets' was used in the context of distinguishing what the division was to be rather than in the context of a residuary gift.

Key v *Key* (1853) 4 De GM & G 73 Court of Appeal in Chancery (Knight Bruce and Turner LJJ)

Construction of wills – general intention of will prevails

Facts

A testator, before the Wills Act 1837 came into operation, devised his 'estate' as Ashby Folville in the County of Leicester to Samuel Key for life, charged with life annuities, but in case the annuitants, or any one of them, survived Samuel Key, he gave the aforesaid 'estate' to Samuel Key's eldest surviving son, charged with the annuities but in default of issue male he gave the aforesaid 'estate' to Thomas Key charged in like manner, and unto his eldest son upon the same conditions, but in default of issue male the premises were to descend to the testator's heirs charged as above. The testator died in 1789 leaving his only sister Jane Reeve as his heiress-at-law. Samuel Key died in 1835 intestate, having survived all the annuitants and leaving John Key, his eldest son, Samuel Key (the plaintiff) his second son, and other children. Thomas Key died in 1833 without having had a child. John Key died in 1850 and he devised all his freehold lands and hereditaments on trust to his brother Samuel Key and other trustees on trust for sale to pay the income to Jane Key, his widow, for life and after her death to his children. Samuel Key (the plaintiff) claimed the Ashby Folville estate as heir male of the body of his father.

Held

1. The limitation to Samuel Key's eldest surviving son ought not to be construed literally so as to make it dependent on Samuel Key being survived by one of the annuitants. Further, the words in default of issue male were not to be construed referentially as meaning in default of an eldest surviving son, but generally, so as to give Samuel Key an estate in tail male.
2. Where upon careful perusal of an instrument, it is impossible not to be satisfied that a strict and ordinary interpretation of its language would disappoint the intention with which it was framed, such an interpretation is not to be adopted.

Knight Bruce LJ:

> 'I agree, "*certa pro in certis non relinquenda*", but I also say, "*In obscuris quod versimilius*", and as "*Leges non es verbis sed ex mente intelligendas*" so of wills. In common with all men, I must acknowledge that there are many cases upon the construction of documents in which the spirit is strong enough to overcome the letter; cases in which it is impossible for a reasonable being, upon a careful perusal of an instrument, not to be satisfied from its contents that a literal, a strict, or an ordinary interpretation given in particular passages, would disappoint and defeat the intention with which the instrument, read as a whole, persuades and convinces him that it was framed. A man so convinced is authorised and bound to construe the writing accordingly.
>
> Such decisions upon controversies, "*ex scripto et sententia*" – as Cicero terms them De Inv Rhet Lib 2 c42, – "Script et voluntatis" – in the language of Quintilian Inst Orator lib 7 c6, sl, – who citing the *judicum Curianum,* says Ib s9, "*In testamentis et illa accidunt ut voluntas manifesta sit, scriptum nihil sit*", and

adds, "*Id quoque, quod huic contrarium est, accidit nuper up esset scriptum quod apparescriptorem noluisse.*" Ib s11, have been of course frequent and familiar when and wherever justice has been administered among civilised and enlightened men. This is a controversy of that cass; and though it may perhaps seem neither necessary nor very apt in a cause of the particular species of the present to refer to such cases as *Browne* v *De Laet* (1794) 4 Bro CC 527, *Church* v *Munday* (1810) 12 Ves 426, and *Bootle* v *Blundell* (1815) 1 Mer 193 yet the language of Lord Thurlow and Lord Eldon in those instances seems to me not without application. Nor does Lord Eldon's reference, with apparent assent, in *Wykham* v *Wykham* (1816) 18 Ves 395, and *Wilkinson* v *Adams* (1812) 1 V & B 466, to Lord Hardwicke's expression in *Coryton* v *Helyer* 2 Cox 340. The language, as given in *Wilkinson* v *Adams*, is

> "Necessary implication means, not natural necessity, but so strong a probability of intention, that an intention contrary to that which is imputed to the testator, cannot be supposed."

The phrases given in *Wykham* v *Wykham*, are "probable necessity" and "an implication so probable that the mind could not resist it". Mr Cox's report is thus: "There is hardly any case where an implication is of necessity, but it is called 'necessary' because the Court finds it so to answer the intention of the devisor." Finally, may I mention the present Lord Chancellor's opinion in a recent case of *Hart* v *Tulk* (1852) De G M & G 300 where it was held by his Lordship and myself that a schedule had been described in a will by a wrong number, and the authorities there referred to.'

Perrin* v *Morgan [1943] AC 399 House of Lords (Viscount Simon LC, Lords Atkin, Thankerton, Russell of Killowen and Romer)

Construction of wills – testator's intention – will must be read as a whole

Facts

A testatrix, by her will made on a printed form without legal assistance, directed that 'all moneys of which I die possessed of shall be shared by my nephews and nieces now living'. Her estate consisted of investments valued at £32,783; cash at bankers amounting to £689; dividends of £36; rents due prior to her death £82; income tax rebates due to her of £32; household goods valued at £62; freeholds specifically bequeathed valued at £1,445; and freeholds not mentioned in the will valued at £340. At first instance, Farwell J held that the term 'money' did not include the investments but included the cash at bankers, dividends, rents and income tax rebates only. The Court of Appeal affirmed his decsion, albeit reluctantly being bound by the principle of *Shelmer's Case* (1725) Gilb 200. The nephews and nieces appealed to the House of Lords.

Held

The bequest of 'all moneys of which I die possessed' included all the net personalty. In interpreting a will the court is not bound in the absence of special circumstances to adopt a fixed meaning of the word 'money' as being its 'legal' as opposed to its 'popular' meaning, but must ascertain as between various usual meanings which is the correct interpretation of the particular document in the light of the context and other relevant circumstances.

Viscount Simon LC:

> 'My Lords, the fundamental rule in construing the language of a will is to put on the words used the meaning which, having regard to the terms of the will, the testator intended. The question is not, of course, what the testator meant to do when he made his will, but what the written words he uses mean in the particular case what are the "expressed intentions" of the testator? In the case of an ordinary English word like "money", which is not always employed in the same sense, I can see no possible justification for fixing on it, as the result of a series of judicial decisions about a series of different wills, a cast-iron meaning which must not be departed from unless special circumstances exist, with the result that this

special meaning must be presumed to be the meaning of every testator in every case unless the contrary is shown. I agree, of course, that, if a word has only one natural meaning, it is right to attribute that meaning to the word when used in a will unless the context or other circumstances which may be properly considered show that an unusual meaning is intended, but the word "money" has not got one natural or usual meaning. It has several meanings, each of which in appropriate circumstances may be regarded as natural. In its original sense, which is also its narrowest sense, the word means "coin". Moneta was an appellation of Juno, and the Temple of Moneta at Rome was the mint. Phrases like "false money" or "clipped money" show the original use in English, but the conception very quickly broadens into the equivalent of "cash" of any sort. The question: "Have you any money in your purse?" refers presumably to bank notes or treasury notes, as well as to shillings and pence. A further extension would include not only coin and currency in the possession of an individual; but debts owing to him and cheques which he could pay into his banking account, or postal orders, or the like. Again, going further, it is a matter of common speech to refer to "one's money at the bank", although in a stricter sense the bank is not holding one's own money and what one possesses is a chose in action which represents the right to require the bank to pay out sums held at the call of its customer. Sums on deposit, whether with a bank or otherwise, may be included by a further extension, but this is by no means the limit to the senses in which the word "money" is frequently and quite naturally used in English speech. The statement: "I have my money invested on mortgage, or in debentures, or in stocks and shares, or in savings certificates", is not an illegitimate use of the word "money" on which the courts are bound to frown, though it is a great extension from its original meaning to interpret it as covering securities, and, in considering the various meanings of the word "money" in common speech, one must go even further, as any dictionary will show. The words may be used to cover the whole of an individual's personal property – sometimes, indeed, all of a person's property, whether real or personal. "What has he done with his money?" may well be an enquiry as to the general contents of a rich man's will. Horace's satire at the expense of the fortune-hunter who attached himself to childless Roman matrons, has its modern equivalent in the saying: "It's her money he's after". When St Paul wrote to Timothy that the love of money is the root of all evil, he was not warning him of the risks attaching to one particular kind of wealth but was pointing to the dangers of avarice in general. When Tennyson's Northern Farmer counselled his son not to marry for money, but to go where money is, he was not excluding the attractiveness of private property in land. These wider meanings of "money" are referred to in some of the reported cases as "popular" meanings, in contrast to the "legal" meaning of the term, but for the purpose of construing a will, and especially a home-made will, a popular meaning may be the more important of the two. The circumstance that a skilled draftsman would avoid the use of so ambiguous a word only confirms the view that, when it is used in a will, the popular as opposed to the technical use of the word "money" may be important. I protest against the idea, that, in interpreting the language of a will, there can be some fixed meaning of the word "money", which the courts must adopt as being the "legal" meaning as opposed to the "popular" meaning. The proper meaning is the correct meaning in the case of the particular will, and there is no necessary opposition between that meaning and the popular meaning. The duty of the court, in the case of an ordinary English word which has several quite usual meanings which differ from one another is not to assume that one out of several meanings holds the field as the correct meaning until it is ousted by some other meaning regarded as "non-legal", but to ascertain without prejudice as between various usual meanings which is the correct interpretation of the particular document.

I now turn to some of the reported cases, premising only that it seems to me a little unfortunate that so many of such cases should find their way into the books, for in most instances, the duty of a judge who is called on to interpret a will containing ordinary English words is not to regard previous decisions as constituting a sort of legal dictionary to be consulted and remorselessly applied whatever the testator may have intended, but to construe the particular document so as to arrive at the testator's real meaning according to its actual language and circumstances. It can rarely happen, I should suppose, that the interpretation of a word like "money" in one will provides a sure and certain guide to its meaning in another will, which is differently expressed. In *Abbott* v *Middleton* (1858) 7 HLC 68, 119, a decision of this House in which Lord Chelmsford LC, Lord Cranworth, Lord St Leonards and Lord Wensleydale all took occasion to expound the governing rule as to the interpretation of wills, Lord Wensleydale observed:

> "A great many cases were cited at the bar, as they always are, when the question is on the construction of wills. Generally speaking, these citations are of litte use. We are no doubt bound by decided cases, but when the decision is not upon some rule or principle of law, but upon the meaning of words in instruments which differ so much from each other by the context, and the peculiar circumstances of each case, it seldom happens that the words of one instrument are a safe guide in the construction of another ..."

Notwithstanding this long tradition I would urge the House to reject the view that, in construing a will, the court must start with a presumption in favour of a particular narrower meaning of the word "money" (though not, indeed, its narrowest meaning), and that, in the absence of contradictory context, the court is bound to apply this narrower meaning, even though the inference is that this is not what the testator really meant by the term. As I have already said, the word "money" has more than one meaning, and it is, in my opinion, a mistake to pick out one interpretation of the word and to call it the "legal" meaning or the "strict legal" meaning as though it had some superior right to prevail over another equally usual and not illegitimate meaning. The context in which the word is used is, of course, a main guide to its interpretation, but it is one thing to say that the word must be treated as having one particular meaning unless the context overrules the interpretation in favour of another and another thing to say that "money", since it is a word of several possible meanings, must be construed in a will in accordance with what appears to be its meaning in that document without any presumption that it bears one meaning rather than another. While disclaiming any idea of interpreting a document which is not before me, I should have thought that the mere fact that a will in a single sentence disposed of "all the money of which I die possessed" was a reason for interpreting "money" in a very wide sense, though there is no positive context.

In choosing between "popular" meanings, it seems to me that an interpretation which includes realty as well as personalty in the word "money" may often be going too far, though of course, everything turns on the language and circumstances of the particular will. An amateur will-maker, though using the word "money" loosely, may be drawing a distinction between "my money" and "my land", and indeed, may mean to include leaseholds as well as freeholds in the latter expression, if he owns both. In the present case, the testatrix owned no leaseholds so the question whether "all moneys" would have included leaseholds does not arise. On the other hand, the will deals separately with the more important of the freeholds, and this circumstance goes to show that "all moneys" in this will does not include the omitted freeholds. If the expression were "all remaining moneys" it might have been different.

I have felt it right to deal with this case in the wider aspect, but before parting from it I must add that I am much disposed to share the view which I understand commends itself to some of your Lordships, that even if the so-called rule of construction were to be left standing, there are some indications in this will which might justify the application of the so-called rule being displaced by the language used and the circumstances of the case. The testatrix directed that "all moneys of which I die possessed" should be "shared by my nephews and nieces" as named. The testatrix held very considerable investments to which she makes no separate reference in her will. If the state of her property when she made her will was anything like what it was at her death, she must, therefore, either have deliberately intended to die intestate in respect of her stocks and shares and to leave these nephews and nieces to share in what happened to be the balance at her bank at the moment of her death and little else, or else she must have used the phrase "all moneys of which I die possessed" as covering her investment also. But whether or not these considerations would be sufficient to overthrow the presumption which has for so long been regarded as *prima facie* forcing the court to apply a narrower meaning, it is clear that, when the rule is rejected and the present will is given its natural construction free from the restraining use of a judicial dictionary, the appeal should succeed.'

Tepper's Will Trusts, Re [1987] 1 All ER 970 Chancery Division (Scott J)

Administration of Justice Act 1982 s21 – extrinsic evidence of testator's intention

Facts

By his will the testator made a contingent gift of income from his residuary estate to be paid

> 'for the education and advancement of [my daughter's children] in equal shares and upon their attaining the age of 25 years to be paid to them absolutely provided they shall remain within the Jewish faith and shall not marry outside the Jewish faith'.

There followed a gift of a remainder interest in the residuary estate to

> 'all my grandchildren as shall be living at the date of my death such shares to be paid to them upon their attaining the age of 25 years provided however that they shall not marry outside the Jewish faith'.

The question arose which grandchildren would become entitled to share in the residuary estate. The testator had six grandchildren, four of whom married persons who were Jewish and two of whom married persons who were not Jewish. Was the relevant clause '... Jewish faith ...' void for uncertainty?

Held

On the evidence before the Court the provisos appeared to be void for uncertainty but that conclusion was not inevitable or final. The validity of the provisos depended on what the testator had meant by the use of the expression 'the Jewish faith' in his will, and while direct evidence of his intention was not admissible, extrinsic evidence of the Jewish faith as practised by the testator and his family might well be adduced which could make it possible to attribute to the expression a meaning sufficiently certain to enable the test as to certainty (which was that governing conditions subsequent) to be satisfied.

Whitrick, Re [1957] 1 WLR 884 Court of Appeal (Jenkins, Romer and Sellers LJJ)

Construction of wills – reading words in through necessary implication

Facts

A testatrix provided by her will that her whole estate should go to her husband but added 'in the event of my husband ... and myself both dying at the same time' then her estate should be held in trust for three named persons. The husband predeceased the testatrix leaving a will in similar terms to that of the testatrix and under which she took his whole estate. The question arose whether the court should read words into the will to enable the trust to the three named persons to take effect.

Held

It was clear that the testatrix had not expressed the whole contingency for which she intended to provide by the words 'in the event of my husband ... and myself both dying at the same time'. It was clear that she also intended to provide for the disposition of her estate if her husband predeceased her as well as if they died at the same time. The court would therefore supply the words to give effect to this clear intention.

Jenkins LJ:

> '... the reading of words into a will as a matter of necessary implication is a measure which any court of construction should apply with the greatest caution. Many wills contain slips and omissions and fail to provide for contingencies which any testator would obviously wish to provide. The court cannot rewrite the testamentary provisions in wills which come before it for construction. This type of treatment of an imperfect will is only legitimate where the court can collect from the four corners of the document that something has been omitted and, further, collect with sufficient precision the nature of the omission ...'

Williams, Re [1985] 1 WLR 905 Chancery Division (Nicholls J)

Administration of Justice Act 1982 s21 – extrinsic evidence of testator's intention

Facts

The testatrix made a will seven days before her death in which she appointed executors and then listed 25 names divided into three groups numbered 1, 2 and 3 but without any indication as to the purpose of the list. There were no words of gift as to whether those named were intended beneficiaries and, if so, what they were to receive. The will merely concluded that in the event of any of the 'beneficiaries' predeceasing the testatrix, their share was to pass to the residuary legatee. The will was admitted to probate in this state and the question arose whether a letter from the testatrix to her solicitor could be admitted as extrinsic evidence under s21(1)(b) AJA 1982. The letter asked the solicitor to 'organise' the bequests in her will and stating that the first, for example, should receive, say, £2,000 each; the second £1,000, and the third £500.

Held

1. There was an effective disposition by the testatrix of her estate to the 25 named beneficiaries but the will was ambiguous as to the purpose of dividing them into three groups. As two possible meanings could be attached to this division, there was an ambiguity on the face of the will and the letter could be admitted in evidence to assist in the construction of the will.
2. The letter was of no assistance in construing the will because it could only be used as an aid to construction when it showed which one of two or more meanings the testator attached to a word or phrase and that meaning was one which the word or phrase was capable of bearing in its context. In the circumstances the letter did not meet these criteria.
3. Rejection of the letter did not mean that the dispositions to the 25 named beneficiaries failed instead the will would be construed without the letter and the estate would therefore be divided equally between the beneficiaries.

Nicholls J:

> '... the testatrix placed her 25 beneficiaries into three groups, but her purpose in so doing is not apparent on the face of the will. The basis of the classification, if not the intended result, might have been apparent if the testatrix had, for example, placed her relations in one group, charities in another group and friends in a third group, but she has not done this ... Each of the testatrix's three groups included relations; each of the three groups included statutory next of kin; each of the three groups included individuals who were not relations; and charitable gifts were included in group 1 and group 3. From this the inference seems to me that the testatrix may have intended the grouping to be related, in some unexplained way, to the size of the benefits that the groups or the members of the groups were to receive. Turning to s21, I do not think that the numbering 1, 2 and 3 can be regarded as meaningless within s21(1)(a), namely without meaning. The difficulty is a different one, namely which of at least two possible meanings is to be attributed to the use of the numerals 1, 2 and 3 in the context of this unusual will, wholly devoid as it is of any relevant dispositive words.
>
> One possible meaning being contended for was that by the use of these numerals the testatrix intended to say that her estate should be divided into three equal shares, one share to go to the members of each group. Another meaning was that the testatrix was intending thereby to divide her list of beneficiaries into three parts and that she failed to spell out what the consequences of that division were to be (and hence the beneficiaries should take in equal shares). Thus the problem is one of ambiguity, not of meaninglessness ... On this basis the letter was admitted in evidence under para (b) ...
>
> I have found the letter to be of no assistance, for several reasons. First, the letter does not support either ... construction. second, as to other possible constructions, it is necessary to keep in mind thepurpose of s21. Section 21 is concerned with the admission of evidence as an aid to construction.

Subsection (2), when read with the material paragraph (para (b)) of subs(1), provides that, insofar as the language used in any part of the will is ambiguous on the face of it, extrinsic evidence including evidence of the testator's intention, may be admitted to assist in its interpretation. The evidence may assist by showing which of two or more possible meanings a testator was attaching to a particular word of phrase. "My effects" and "my money" are obvious examples. That meaning may be one which, without recourse to the extrinsic evidence, would not really have been apparent at all. So long as that meaning is one which the word or phrase read in its context is capable of bearing, then the court may conclude that, assisted by the extrinsic evidence, that is its correct construction. But if, however liberal may be the approach of the court, the meaning is one which the word or phrase cannot bear, I do not see how, in carrying out a process of construction (or interpretation, to use the word employed in s21), the court can declare that meaning to be the meaning of the word or phrase. Such a conclusion, varying or contradicting the language used, would amount to rewriting part of the will, and that is a result to be achieved, if at all, under the rectification provisions in s20. (In passing, I note that there is no claim for rectification in the present case. it was suggested in the course of argument that s20 could not apply to a home-made will such as the one before me, because "clerical error" in s20(1)(a) suggests a clerk. I do not accept this. A testator writing out or typing his own will can make a clerical error just as much as someone else writing out or typing a will for him). Again, if extrinsic evidence shows that a testator was unclear, or undecided, on what he meant by the ambiguous word or phrase, I do not see how that can require or enable the court to reject the word or phrase altogether if the court is able to construe the word or phrase without the aid of extrinsic evidence.

Applying that approach to the evidence admitted under s21(b) in this case, I reject the submission that the contents of the letter can lead to the conclusions that the gift to the 25 beneficiaries fails altogether. Likewise, I do not accept the contention that the gifts are to be construed primarily as pecuniary legacies,or as gifts to individuals or groups of shares in the estate in the proportions of 4:2:1. Even if the contents of the letter clearly supported these constructions (which I do not think they do), such constructions seem to me to be outside any meaning which the simple dividion in this will is capable of bearing.

My third reason for rejecting the letter as an aid is that I do not think that in any event it is or affords an explanation of what the testatrix meant by what she had written in her will. It was a letter of instruction to solicitors to prepare a new will, telling them what were the provisions she wished them to include in her new will regarding the three categories of beneficiaries. What the letter did not do is to explain, nor does it assist in understanding, what the testatrix meant to be achieved by the divisions she had made in the will she had already executed when the letter was posted to the solicitors.'

7 Intestacy

Black* v *Yates (1989) The Times 11 May Queen's Bench Division (Potter J)

Adoptive children – foreign element

Facts

The plaintiff was the widow of the deceased. She was the joint administratix of his estate, as well as the mother of his adoptive children. The deceased had been killed during his holiday in Spain when he travelled as the defendant's pillion passenger on a motorcycle.

English solicitors acted for the plaintiff in respect of her various claims (for herself and for her children) under the Fatal Accidents Act 1976 and the Law Reform (Miscellaneous Provisions) Act 1934. They retained Spanish lawyers to represent her in the Spanish district court hybrid proceedings in respect of the criminal element of the case, in which it the court could award compensation. The English solicitors only sought to establish the defendant's liability: they did not know that they had to expressly decline the exercise by the Spanish court of its powers of disposition where action in another jurisdiction was proposed. A compensation order was made. In the subsequent English proceeding for damages, the defendant raised the defences of res judicata and the fact that payment had been made pursuant to the Spanish judgment under the provisions of the Civil Jurisdiction and Judgements Act 1982. In Spanish law the jurisdiction of cases relating to the authority of a parent to act for a minor was a matter for the law of the parent's domicile, in this case the mother.

Held

The plaintiff failed in her own claim. However, as regards the children's claim the case of *Jeffrey* v *Kent CC* [1958] 1 WLR 927 was cited.

In that case Paull J had held that the court had no power to enter into an agreement which compromised the interests of children in an action unless (a) each who was sui generis and wished to claim had approved the agreement; and (b) the court had sanctioned the agreement as being for the benefit of the infants.

The up-to-date position was that Order 80 rules 10 and 11 governed such a compromise, whether made before or after the institution of proceedings in England. The immediate purpose of s34 of the 1982 Act was to extend the doctrine of merger to foreign decisions.

In considering the interests of the children the court went behind the foreign judgment to look at the position at the time of the grant of the power of attorney. In its view this was necessary to protect the interests of the children. Accordingly judgment was given in favour of the children and the deceased's estate.

Bowen-Buscarlet's Will Trusts, Re [1972] Ch 463 Chancery Division (Goff J)

Administration of Estates Act 1925 ss46 and 49 – distribution on partial intestacy

Facts

By his will the testator gave his widow a life interest in his residuary estate but did not provide what was to happen after her death. The result was a partial intestacy as regards the remainder. The question arose whether, under ss46 and 49 of the AEA 1925, the widow was entitled to an immediate payment of her statutory legacy or whether it would only become payable on her death to her personal representative as part of her estate.

Held

The provisions of s46 had to be read into the will in accordance with s49. Therefore, the joint effect of the will and the statute was to give the widow a life interest and after that the residuary estate was charged with the payment of her statutory legacy. She was, therefore entitled to receive the statutory legacy forthwith.

Goff J:

> 'I would think that on a true analysis the joint effect of the will and the statute is a bequest to the widow for life and subject thereto to raise and pay the statutory legacy to her. Perhaps it is not very significant whether one says it is only the reversion which is charged or that the whole estate is charged subject to the life interest, but I can see no warrant for making the charge a charge in favour of her personal representatives only, and the reasoning of Lord Hanworth MR *In Re McKee* [1931] 2 Ch 145 at pp 157-158, supports my analysis. There he said:
>
> > "By section 49 which is found in Part IV (of the Administration of Estates Act 1925) it is provided: 'Where any person dies leaving a will effectively disposing of part of his property, this part of this Act shall have effect as respects that part of his property not so disposed of subject to the provisions contained in the will and subject to the following modifications.' This section, therefore, applies to the present case and operates in substance – as pointed out by Lord Cairns in *Cooper* v *Cooper* (1874) LR 7 HL 53, 66 in relation to the Statute of Distributions – to make a will for the intestate in those respects in which he failed himself to do so; and the subclause and the part of it that is here effective is: '(b) The personal representative shall, subject to his rights and powers for the purpose of administration, be a trustee for the persons entitled under this part of this Act in respect of the part of the estate not expressly disposed of ...' Turning then to section 46 which is also in Part IV, the widow is entitled to take the personal chattels absolutely, and in addition the residuary estate is to stand charged with the payment of £1,000 to her with interest at five per cent from the date of the intestate's death until it is paid or appropriated. But does the trust imposed on the personal representative under subclause (b) above impose a duty of immediate sale of the reversion expectant upon the widow's life interest in order to pay this £1,000 charged in the widow's favour, and to give her the benefit of the income from the balance produced by this sale?"
>
> Lord Hanworth MR thus returned to the question of the sale of the reversion, but if, on the principle of *Cooper* v *Cooper*, you read into the will the statutory charge under section 46 and do not alter it you give her an immediate interest, not a charge in favour of her personal representatives as part of her estate, and it is also observed that in *In Re McKee* Lawrence LJ himself thought the matter operated in accordance with the principle of *Cooper* v *Cooper*.
>
> There is no question here of competition between deferred legatees. It is simply a case in which the widow is entitled to say:
>
> > "I am the only person having any interest under this charge. There is a charge in my favour postponed to a life interest it is true, but that life interest is mine and thereforee I merge it and claim payment."
>
> Why cannot she do that? It seems that the answer must be that she can, and I think that this is what Vaisey J meant when he said somewhat cryptically in *In Re Douglas' Will Trusts* [1959] 1 WLR 744 at 748:
>
> > "As regards that part of the Administration of Estates Act 1925 which gives her an absolute interest in undisposed property, I think that the widow, if she wants it, can claim to have paid over to her this portion

> which I am referring to of £1,000 with interest at five per cent from the death. I do not see how that can be surmounted."

It is also interesting to observe that Maugham J, in *In Re McKee,* felt himself fortified by the fact that whereas under the law as it stood then, certain persons had to bring into account interests which they took under the will, a widow was not so accountable. That has now been changed by section 49(1)(aa) of the Administration of Estates Act 1925 (an amendment made by the Intestates' Estates Act 1952).

If, of course, the decision in *In Re McKee* were authority, settling the law and binding upon me, I do not think I could regard that provision as amending the law by a sidewind, but it is, I think, a consideration which one is entitled to have in mind when the point comes to be argued that the provision which Maugham J thought helped him to his conclusion is not, now, open. There is moreover an indication in support of the conclusion I have reached in that the new section directs the widow to bring into account an actuarial valuation of her life interest. If Parliament regarded the law as being such that the widow had no beneficial interest and there was merely a charge in favour of her estate, one would have thought that the direction would have been to bring in the actual value of the life interest as ascertained on the date of her death, and the legislature would not have speculated where there could be certainty.

In the end it came back to this: in my judgment, the effect of the will and the statutory charge is to give the widow a right to the benefit of the charge and the right to the income, and therefore to give her an interest which I think is immediate.'

Chaplin, Re [1950] Ch 507 Chancery Division (Vaisey J)

Definition of personal chattels – 'articles of personal use'

Facts

A testator left 'all the residue of my personal chattels as defined by the Administration of Estates Act 1925 to my wife absolutely'. The question arose whether 'personal chattels' included a motor-yacht which the testator had used for pleasure.

Held

The yacht was an article of personal use within s55(1)(x) of the AEA 1925.

Collins, Re [1975] 1 WLR 309 Chancery Division (Pennycuick V-C)

Valuation of matrimonial home for purpose of appropriation

Facts

The intestate died in 1972 leaving surviving his second wife and his daughter of his first marriage. The estate was sworn at £11,494 at his death and of that the second wife had a charge on the estate for £8,750 the balance being the residue, half being held on trust for life for the second wife and the remainder going to the daughter. The second wife exercised the right under Sch 2 para 1 of appropriation in respect of the matrimonial home in which she resided. At the date of the death the house was worth £4,200 and at the date of appropriation it was worth about £8,000. The question arose as to what value the second wife was entitled to have the property appropriated towards satisfaction of her charge of £8,750.

Held

The value at which the house is to be appropriated is the date of appropriation and not the date of the intestate's death. Accordingly it was to be considered as worth £8,000.

Collin's Will Trusts, Re [1971] 1 WLR 37 Chancery Division (Brightman J)

Definition of personal chattels – 'personal effects' – stamp collections; car

Facts
By his will a testator made bequests of 'personal effects'. The question arose whether these included (1) stamp and coin collections and (2) a motor car.

Held
The term 'personal effects' prima facie included all of these articles since there was no sufficient context in the will to displace that meaning.

Comment
In *Re Collin's* Brightman J followed Stamp J in *Re Reynolds' WT*. However, the decision in *Re Reynolds'* is in need of qualification in the light of the Court of Appeal decision in *Re Crispin* where Russell LJ in delivering the judgment of the Court doubted the soundness of Stamp J's conclusion that a bought collection of stamps would not be considered to be articles of personal use for the purposes of the Act.

Crispin's Will Trusts, Re [1975] Ch 245 Court of Appeal (Russell, Stamp and James LJJ)

Definition of personal chattels – 'furniture' and 'articles of personal use or ornament'

Facts
A testator assisted a friend to build up a large collection of clocks and watches. The friend bequeathed the collection to the testator by his will and the testator bought a lager house to keep it in. The clocks were kept in locked rooms and the watches in special chests. However, the testator selected a watch to wear from time to time. On the testator's death the collection was valued at £50,000 and his total estate was valued at £80,000 (including the collection). By his will the testator bequeathed 'all my personal chattels' to his sister. The executors sought determination of the question whether the collection of clocks and watches should go to the sister or fall into residue. At first instance, Burgess V-C considered it improbable that the testator intended his sister to receive such a large share of the estate and held that they fell into residue. On appeal:

Held
1. The value of the collection was irrelevant in deciding if it was to be classed as personal chattels. The scope of the bequest would be decided in the same way as on intestacy.
2. As to the clocks – per Russell LJ:

   '... in our opinion a clock, whether in a long case or a bracket, is an article of furniture in the ordinary sense of the word, and it matters not whether it is keeping good or bad time or no time at all, whether it is standing in the room in the testator's house which is in everyday use or stored in a locked room therein, or stored at a repository, or on loan to a museum. The fact that it is one of a collection of clocks brought by the testator or inherited by the testator from another seems to us nothing on the point. Nor, to our minds, is the fact that it is one of a collection which could be said to be a hobby of the testator; if anything, that fact would incline us to think that it was not only an article of furniture but also an article of personal use ...'

3. As to the watches – per Russell LJ:

   '... a watch is in its nature an article of personal use: and in the present case we regard the cherishing by eye and hand of the collection as well as the wearing of selected items from time to time as bringing them within the definition of articles of personal use.'

Edwards* v *Strong (1994) The Times 9 November Chancery Division (Mr Stanley Burnton QC sitting as Deputy Judge of the High Court)

Intestacy – succession in title – effect of notice served on beneficiaries of estate

Facts

The deceased, who was A's father, gave B an option to purchase his house for valuable consideration after his death. The deceased died intestate and his daughters became entitled to his property. The option agreement stated that B could exercise his option by giving notice in writing to the deceased's successors in title and by completing within eight weeks. B delivered a letter to the daughters stating his intention to exercise the option. However, no action was taken to do so until B changed solicitors. The plaintiffs argued that the notice was invalid because it had not been served on the deceased's successors in title. Since the deceased had died intestate, his successor in title was the President of the Family Division. B argued that the phrase 'successor in title' included the deceased's daughters and that service on the President of the Family Division would have been pointless. He would have taken no action in the matter.

Held

The phrase 'successor in title' referred to the person/s in whom the property was vested and who were in a position to convey the property. Pending the grant of letters of administration the successor in title was the President of the Family Division. The plaintiffs had done nothing to give B reason to suppose that they accepted the notice and they were not successors in title for the purpose of the exercise of the option. Neither were they agents of the President of the Family Division. The option had not been exercised validly and the notice was ineffective.

Grover's Will Trusts, Re [1971] Ch 168 Chancery Division (Pennycuick J)

Administration of Estates Act 1925 s49(1)(a) – the distributive construction

Facts

The testator settled one moiety of his residuary estate on his widow for life and after her death for all her children who attained the age of 21 years. There was a partial intestacy as regards another moiety in the residue and the question arose whether the widow and children had to bring into account their interests which amounted to the entire capital of their moiety in the residuary estate.

Held

They had to bring these into account.

Pennycuick J:

> '... as has been pointed out in the cases to which I will refer in a moment, section 47(1)(iii) presents no particular difficulty. It imposes a straightforward provision under which, against the stirpital share of any child, there is to be brought into account any money paid by way of advancement on the marriage of the child or settled for the benefit of the child. That, of course, includes property settled on such trusts that the child takes a primary life interest but no more.
>
> On the other hand, section 49 presents great difficulties of language which have been considered in the two reported cases to which I will refer in a moment. Section 49 is by its express terms an annexe to section 47 and must be read in conjunction with section 47. Accordingly a member of the class of issue of the deceased, that is, a descendant of any degree, who acquires a beneficial interest under his will has to bring some subject-matter into account against the share which he takes under the partial intestacy. One

might have expected section 49, conformably with section 47, to provide that each child of the deceased should bring into account any legacy, including a share of residue, bequeathed to the child or settled by the will for the benefit of the child. But it is impossible so to read section 49 without a hopeless contortion of language. It may be observed, incidentally, that if that had been the effect of section 49, the exclusion of interests acquired by other persons at the end of sub-paragraph (a) would have been superfluous.

It is clear that the subject matter to be brought in under section 49 is beneficial interests acquired by descendants. The section is, however, singularly obscure as to what beneficial interests are to be brought into account as against the share of any given descendant. The section merely prescribes that the requirements of the previous section apply to any beneficial interests acquired by any issue of the deceased under the will of the deceased.

A possible construction of that provision, which was advanced in the cases to which I am going to refer, and which, I confess, appeals to me, was that it must be treated on some *reddendo singulis* principle, with the consequence that any descendant of the testator who acquires a beneficial interest under his will brings that interest, and nothing more, into account against his share under the partial intestacy. So, for instance, a child of the testator would bring into account any beneficial interest acquired by that child under the will, but nothing more, and similarly a grandchild of the testator would bring into account any beneficial interest taken by that grandchild. It is accepted, I think, on all hands, that that is so as regards a grandchild ...'

Hardy v *Shaw* [1976] Ch 82 Chancery Division (Goff J)

Administration of Estates Act 1925 s47(1)(iii) – the Hotchpot Rule

Facts

In 1952 a father who owned nearly all the shares in a family company made allotments to each of his three children, the plaintiff and the two defendants, to bring their holdings in the company up to 600 shares each. Shortly afterwards the plaintiff became engaged to a man of whom the father strongly disapproved. The father was further upset when, after her marriage, the plaintiff ceased to work for the family company, something which she had done in common with two defendants up until then. The father gave the plaintiff no further shares in the business and only regretted what he had already given her. The father died in 1954 leaving the whole of his estate, including the shares, in the family company to his widow. In 1957 the widow decided to give all her shares in the family company to the two defendants. On the advice of an accountant she gave 499 shares to each of the defendants and retained two shares for herself. The widow died intestate in 1971. The plaintiff sought a declaration that the transfer of the two blocks of shares was by way of advancement and should be taken as being transferred in or towards satisfaction of the respective shares of the defendants in the widow's estate under s47(1)(iii) of the AEA 1925.

Held

1. The word 'advancement' in s47(1)(iii) was not to be construed narrowly as being restricted to establishing a young person in life or, in the case of an older person a gift for the purpose of meeting some particular need, but as including any gift whereby the donor made some permanent provision for the donee. Since the transfer of shares by the widow to the defendants gave them a controlling interest in the company, they constituted permanent provision for them and were by way of advancement under s47(1)(iii).
2. There was no contrary intention shown by the widow to exclude the statutory direction for hotchpot. The test for determining whether such contrary intention existed was subjective and concerned with whether the inference could be drawn that the donor's intention was that the gift should not be brought into hotchpot. The widow had shown a clear intention to exclude the plaintiff from receiving

any further shares in the business but it could not be inferred from that that she also intended to exclude the plaintiff with regard to the whole of the expected inheritance since there was no evidence that she had directed her mind as to what should happen to her property on her death. Therefore, the blocks of 499 shares given to each of the plaintiffs had to be brought into hotchpot.

Goff J:

'... I therefore turn to the second question: does a contrary intention appear from the circumstances of the case? I would first observe that in my judgment the test is not objective; that is if the intestate thought of everything what would her intention be likely to have been? but subjective: looking at all the circumstances, do they require an inference that her intention was that the gift should not be brought into hotchpot? I have no doubt that is right, not only on the language of the section itself but because that was clearly the approach of the whole court in *Re Lacon* [1891] 2 Ch 482.

That, however, does not, in my judgment, mean that it must be shown that the mother's attention was specifically drawn to the section or its effect, or that she formed an intention expressly in relation thereto. The question, in my view, is whether the facts as a whole indicate an intention on her part not simply to anticipate as to the defendants the provision her children would get on her death, but an intention and desire to prefer them to the plaintiff not only in point of time but in point of the amount and nature of that provision. In saying that I am applying the language of Lindley LJ in *Re Lacon* with modifications to fit the case of an intestacy as distinct from double portions of ademption.'

Hutchinson, Re [1955] Ch 255 Chancery Division (Danckwerts J)

Administration of Estates Act 1925 s55(1)x – definition of personal chattels – 'horses'

Facts

The intestate owned at the date of his death 12 racehorses in training which were used entirely for recreational purposes. A summons was taken out to determine if they were 'personal chattels' within the meaning of s55(1)(X) and therefore passed to his widow absolutely.

Held

They were personal chattels and passed to the widow. Although the words 'horses' in the subsection was used in connection with the words 'carriage' and 'stable furniture', this did not restrict its meaning to horses used for domestic purposes but also included racehorses.

Danckwerts J:

'It is clear, and it is expressly stated in the subsection, that horses used for business purposes were not to be included, but I do not see why horses kept by the deceased purely for the purpose of recreation could not be included in the terms "personal chattels".'

McKee, Re [1931] 2 Ch 145 Chancery Division (Maugham J) Court of Appeal (Lord Hanworth MR, Lawrence and Romer LJJ)

Administration of Estates Act 1925 s33 – partial intestacy – effect of express trusts for sale

Facts

A testator devised and bequeathed the residue of his estate to his trustees upon trust for sale on trust to pay the income to his wife for life and after her death to divide the same between his surviving brothers and sisters. The last of the brothers and sisters died in 1930 and at that time the widow was still living. There was therefore an intestacy as regards the reversionary interest in the residuary estate. One of the questions which arose was whether s33 of the AEA 1925 applied and that therefore the reversionary interest had to be sold.

Held

The reversionary interest did not have to be sold. Section 33 of the AEA 1925 did not apply where there was an express trust for sale because this would override the statutory trusts.

Romer LJ:

> '... now, in connection with this matter, our attention was called to the provisions of s33 of the Act dealing with the case of a person dying intestate as to any real or personal estate. If that section applied to the present case, it would no doubt create much difficulty. In my opinion, however, the section is confined to the case of a person dying intestate as to some one or more specific items of his real or personal estate, and does not extend to a case like the present, where there is a will which deals with every item of the testator's estate, but omits to dispose of every interest in that estate. There is no provision in the Act that the words "real and personal estate" include any interest in real or personal estate. It is not, therefore, permissible to read s33 as referring to a person dying intestate as to any interest in his real or personal estate. Nor are the provisions of the section at all applicable to such a case. By way of illustration, let me take the case of a testator who has given the whole of his personal estate to his executors and trustees upon the usual trusts for conversion, payment of debts, funeral and testamentary expenses and legacies, and then to stand possessed of the residue upon trust for two persons in equal shares, of whom one predeceases the testator. If the one-half of the testators net residue is to be treated as personal estate of his, as to which he has died intestate then that half is to be held upon the trusts specified in sub-ss 1 and 2 of s33 of the Act. But the sale of the testator's personal estate will already has been effected, in order to produce the very residuary estate of one-half of which the testator has failed effectually to dispose.
>
> The section seems therefore quite inapplicable to such a case ...'

Ogilby, Re [1942] Ch 288 Chancery Division (Simonds J)

Personal chattels – distinguished from chattels used for business purposes

Facts

The question arose whether a herd of shorthorn cattle on a farm belonging to the intestate which was not worked at a profit were personal chattels within s55(1)(X) of the AEA 1925.

Held

Even if the farm was not worked at a profit, it was nevertheless a business and the cattle were 'used for business purposes'. They were not personal chattels.

Simonds J:

> '... it may be right to say that a person who keeps a cow or a pig or some other domestic animal for his own use does not do so for business purposes. It may sometimes be difficult to draw the line, but where you find farming on this scale, a home farm with a substantial acreage and live and dead stock valued for the purpose of probate at between £1,400 and £1,500 including thirty-one head of cattle and thirty-five head of sheep, there is no doubt on which side of the line the case falls. There is a farming business being carried on and the live and dead stock are being used for the purpose of that business ...'

Phelps, Re [1980] Ch 275 Court of Appeal (Buckley, Bridge and Templeman LJJ)

Transactions which are part appropriation, part sale

Facts

A husband died intestate in February 1971. His widow was entitled to appropriation under the intestacy. In June 1972 the widow gave notice requiring appropriation of the matrimonial home, which was at that time worth more than £8,750. She was willing to pay the difference between her entitlement and the actual value of the house. The question arose whether if, for example, the house was worth £12,000 on the date of appropriation, the widow could require the matrimonial home to be appropriated partly in satisfaction of her interest and partly in return for the difference in value between the interest and the matrimonial home. At first instance Foster J refused to allow such a transaction. On appeal:

Held

Sch 2 Para 1 (1) must not be construed in isolation but, instead, read in conjunction with Sch 2 para 5(2) which extended the meaning of 'power of appropriation' in s41 of the AEA 1925 to include a transaction which was part appropriation and part sale. Therefore the widow's notice was a valid exercise of the right in Sch 2 para 1(1).

Reynolds' Will Trusts, Re [1966] 1 WLR 19 Chancery Division (Stamp J)

Definition of personal chattels – stamp collection

Facts

The testator left 'the remainder of my personal chattels as defined by s55 (1)(X) of the AEA 1925, to my sons ... ' the question arose whether this included a stamp collection made by the testator as a hobby and valued at £1,848.

Held

Since the collection was made and kept by the testator as a hobby it was an article of personal use even if its value was such that it could be regarded as an investment.

Stamp J:

> '... it is conceded that in view of authority the stamp collection does not come within the words "books" which is included in the definition I have read, but it is contended ... that it was in truth an article "of personal use" within the meaning of that expression. If I were to regard the stamp collection in isolation and without regard to its history it seems to me that I would be bound to hold that it does not come within the definition. If the testator had gone into a shop of a stamp dealer and bought a collection of stamps and installed it in his flat it could hardly be said that the collection so bought was an article of personal use. But I have to put myself into the testator's armchair and look at the stamp collection in relation to the way in which he collected it and the way in which he used it. In my judgment, the collection made in the way I have described and kept by the testator as part of his only or principal hobby, can properly be described as an article of personal use.'

Spence (deceased), Re, Spence v *Dennis and Another* [1990] 2 WLR 1430; [1990] 2 All ER 827 Court of Appeal (Sir Nicolas Browne-Wilkinson V-C, Nourse and McCowan LJJ)

Legitimacy – child of void marriage

Facts

Addy Pidwell ('the mother') married Frederick Love in 1895; in 1911 she gave birth to twins, one of whom is the first defendant. Shortly thereafter she went to live with Thomas Spence, taking the first defendant with her. She gave birth to the intestate in 1912 and to the plaintiff in 1916. In 1934 she 'married' Thomas Spence – he, it was assumed, reasonably believing that the marriage was valid; in fact the mother's marriage to Frederick Love was never dissolved. The mother died in 1949, Frederick Love in 1953 and Thomas Spence in 1957. Following the death of the intestate in 1985, in that year the first defendant obtained a grant of letters of administration claiming to be a sister of the whole blood. In 1988 the plaintiff issued a writ claiming to be a legitimate brother of the whole blood of the intestate and the only person entitled to his estate. The Treasury Solicitor, the second defendant, contended that neither the plaintiff nor the first defendant was a legitimate brother or sister of the whole or half blood and accordingly that the intestate's estate devolved on the Crown as bona vacantia. As a preliminary issue, the question arose: could a person be treated as legitimate under s1(1) of the Legitimacy Act 1976 notwithstanding that he was born before his parents entered into a void marriage? Morritt J answered this question in the negative ([1989] 3 WLR 834); the plaintiff appealed.

Held

The appeal would be dismissed as the words 'child of a void marriage' in s1(1) of the 1976 Act meant those who were strictly 'of' the supposed marriage, that is, those who would be born in wedlock if the marriage were valid.

Whitby, Re [1944] Ch 210 Court of Appeal (Lord Greene MR, MacKinnon and Luxmore LJJ)

Definition of personal chattels – 'jewellery'

Facts

The question arose whether a quantity of cut but unmounted diamonds fell within the word 'jewellery' in the definition of personal chattels.

Held

Lord Greene MR

> 'The definition of "jewellery" in the Shorter Oxford Dictionary – and for present purposes the definition in the larger dictionary is the same – is as follows: "Jeweller's work, gems or ornaments made or sold by jewellers; jewels collectively or as a form of adornment". From that definition it seems to me clear that in the ordinary use of English language the word "jewellery" would cover jewels collectively and gems sold by jewellers just as it covers jewels made up into articles adornment such as a brooch. I cannot see any justification in this case for excluding from the meaning of that word the jewels collectively or gems sold by jewellers ...'

Young, Re [1951] Ch 185 Chancery Division (Harman J)

Administration of Estates Act 1925 s49(1)(a) – the stirpital construction

Facts

A testator directed his trustees to hold his residuary estate, after the death of his widow, in trust as to five-sevenths for his five children, A, B, C, D and E, in equal shares, another one-seventh share for the maintenance of X, another of his children, or any child or children of X, and after X's death to his children. X had two children. The other one-seventh share was left on trust for Y, a bachelor son of the testator, who had, unknown to the testator, died before the date of the will. The testator died on 9 January

1939 and X died on 26 January 1939. Since the testator had died intestate as to Y's one-seventh share, the question arose at the death of the widow whether X's personal represenatives were liable to bring into hotchpot the capital of the one-seventh share settled on X and his children or whether they could participate in Y's share without doing so.

Held

The one-seventh share settled on X and his children must be brought into hotchpot against Y's share on intestacy.

8 Family Provision

Beaumont, Re [1980] Ch 444 Chancery Division (Megarry V-C)

Family provision – being maintained immediately before death other than for valuable consideration

Facts

The plaintiff and the deceased lived together as man and wife from 1940 until the deceased's death in 1976. The deceased was 79 at her death and had been a civil servant. She retired in 1964 and had a civil service pension and a state pension. The plaintiff had a variety of jobs and he retired from full-time employment in 1966. The plaintiff and the deceased lived in a bungalow owned by the deceased. From 1945 onwards the plaintiff paid the deceased a weekly sum for accommodation and also contributed towards the weekly shopping bill which was about £5 per week from 1966 onwards. The plaintiff had his own car which he purchased and maintained with his own money; the deceased paid the insurance. The deceased paid all the outgoings and expenses of the bungalow and did the cooking and housework and other household chores. The plaintiff had done some household jobs and gardening. Prior to the deceased's death the plaintiff nursed her for some five weeks at home. By her will the deceased left nothing to the plaintiff. However, over a year before her death she nominated £550 worth of savings certificates in his favour. The plaintiff made an application under s1(1)(e) of the 1975 Act for reasonable financial provision.

Held

1. Where a claim was brought under s1(1)(e) it had to be qualified by ss1(3) and 3(4) of the Act; this required the plaintiff to show three things:
   a) that under s1(1)(e) he was being maintained 'immediately before' the death of the deceased. This was ascertained not by looking at the de facto state of maintenance immediately before the deceased's death but by looking at the arrangement then generally existing between the parties, using the date of death as the day on which that arrangement was to be considered.
   b) that under s1(3) the deceased had made a substantial contribution in money or money's worth towards his reasonable needs other than for valuable consideration. S1(3), however, barred not only claims where the distribution was for full valuable consideration but also claims where a couple living together make contributions towards the maintenance of each other by bearing the costs of the home equally. In such a case each would be maintaining the other for full valuable consideration and neither could make a claim against the estate of the other.
   c) that the deceased had 'assumed responsibility' for his maintenance under s3(4). This required an act which demonstrated an undertaking or assumption of responsibility.
2. In the circumstances the plaintiff was unable to show that he satisfied either 1(b) or (c) and his application must be dismissed accordingly.

Megarry V-C:

> 'I turn to the phrase "immediately before the death of the deceased was being maintained", in s1(1)(e), and particularly the word "immediately". Does this require consideration to be given only to the state of affairs

existing at the instant before the death of the deceased, or does it allow a wider approach? In particular, what if the state of affairs at that instant differs from the normal state of affairs? Suppose that C is being maintained by D, living in D's house, eating D's food and having clothes bought for him by D. C falls ill and goes to a national health service hospital. A day, a week, a month, or a year later D dies. At the instant before D's death, D had not been providing anything for C, whether food, lodging, clothing or anything else and had not been making any "substantial contribution in money or money's worth towards the reasonable needs of C. If only the instant before death is to be considered, C appears to have no claim. Yet if C had been discharged from hospital and had returned to D's home, however shortly before D's death, presumably C can claim against D's estate.

Again, suppose B has maintained C for years. B falls ill and her sister, D, fetches both B and C to live with her until B is better. If B dies the next day, must C's claim against her estate fail? If instead D dies the next day, can C claim against her estate? Other examples abound. Let me assume that the effect of s1(3) is that where two people share the expenses of a common home, the one whose contribution is substantially more valuable than the other's will be taken to be partly maintaining that other. That is a point that I shall have to discuss in due course; but for the moment I shall make an assumption broadly to that effect. Clearly the balance between the relative contributions made by the two is liable to be changed at any moment, sometimes suddenly. Suppose that C is contributing substantially less than D, in whose house they both live, and D is then taken ill. If C thereupon nurses D devotedly until D dies, the value of C's contribution to D's maintenance may then greatly outstrip that of D's contribution to C's maintenance, so that if matters are tested as at the moment before D's death, C's devotion may have destroyed any claim under the Act. But if the day before dying, D had been removed to hospital, this would make it possible to contend that the former position of D partly maintaining C had been restored, so that C could make a claim. Furthermore, if C and D have for years lived together on a basis of equality of contribution, both financially and in domestic work, C will have no claim. Yet if through illness or laziness or obstinancy C's contribution is reduced sufficiently, it may then be possible to say that D is maintaining C: and so long as this occurs before D's death, however short the period, C can claim under the Act. One may also take the case of two students who share accommodation, one poor and the other wealthy. If from generosity Dives is contributing substantially more than his fair share of the expenses just before his death, Lazarus may then be said to be entitled to claim against his estate.

The contemplation of possible examples such as these suggest certain consequences. First, it seems to me improbable that the word "immediately" in s1(1)(e) was intended to confine the gaze of the court to whatever was the state of maintenance existing at that precise moment. I very much doubt whether Parliament can have intended people to shuffle in and out of s1(1)(e) and 1(3) with every variation in the state of maintenance between them, so that last week C was partly maintaining D with substantial contributions, this week neither is maintaining the other, and next week D will be maintaining C with substantial contributions. Given that the moment at which the examination must be made is the moment before the death of the deceased, what has to be examined ought not, I think to be the de facto state or balance of maintenance at that moment, but something more substantial and enduring.

The question is what that something is. If at the moment before the death of the deceased there is some settled basis or arrangement between the parties as regards maintenance, then I think that s1 should be applied to this rather than to any de facto variation in the actual maintenance that may happen to exist at that moment. If the general arrangement between the parties is that D is substantially maintaining C, then matters ought to be decided on that basis. This should be so even if, at the moment before D dies, C is in fact making such contributions whether in personal services such as nursing or in the provision of money or goods, that on balance C is substantially maintaining D. The word "immediately" plainly confines the court to the basis or arrangement subsisting at the moment before death, and excludes whatever previously subsisted but has ended, and the state of affairs under it. The nature or the quality of the basis or arrangement in question is a matter that I shall consider in due course. At this stage I shall only add that under all the other heads of s1(1) the qualification is of an enduring nature. There must be a past or present marriage, paternity or maternity, or the treatment of the claimant as a child of the marriage of the deceased. If para (e) made no more than a transient and fluctuating requirement, it would be strikingly out of line with the other paragraphs.

Second, there is an assumption that I made a short while ago in relation to s1(3). What is the meaning of the parenthetic phrase "otherwise than for full valuable consideration" in the subsection? Does it merely mean, as I assumed, that you weigh up the value of the respective contributions in money or money's worth made by C and D towards the reasonable needs of the other, strike a balance, and then say whether the balance of contributions (if any) is substantial? One of counsel's contentions for the plaintiff was that this was wrong. Anything provided for full valuable consideration should be disregarded, he said, if it was provided under a contract; this was necessary in order to protect the proprietor of an old person's home for example, from being treated as maintaining all those in his home despite their paying in full for their board and lodging. But unless there was a contract, the parenthetic phrase did not apply.

I can see no justification for reading into the subsection a reference to a contract that does not appear in it. The reference to "valuable consideration" suggests that thoughts of contract were not likely to have been far from the draftsman's mind – and yet there is no mention of any contract in the subsection. Furthermore, if D is providing full board and lodging for C, but C, without being contractually bound to do so, regularly gives D, in money or money's worth, more than the value of the board and lodging, I find it difficult to see how, in any real sense of the words, it could be said that C "was being maintained" by D, or that D, by providing C with board and lodging worth less than C gives for it, was making "a substantial contribution in money or money's worth towards C's needs". Quite apart from language, it would be quite contrary to the whole tenor of the Act to allow C to make a claim under it in such a case.

One other consideration is that of the position of C and D if, without any contract, each makes contributions of equal value towards the maintenance of the other, one providing the home and the other the food and drink. Neither in any real sense of the word is maintaining the other, each is bearing a half share of the cost of the joint establishment. Yet if contributions are to be ignored only if made under contract, plainly each is making a substantial contribution in money or money's worth towards the reasonable needs of the other, and so whichever dies first, the other could claim under the Act againt the estate of the deceased. Yet if a contract could be spelled out of the arrangements which they made, neither could make such a claim. I cannot see why so much should turn on the presence or absence of a contract.'

Besterman, Re [1984] Ch 458 Court of Appeal (Oliver, Fox and Robert Goff LJJ)

Family provision – reasonable financial provisions for surviving spouse

Facts

The deceased and his wife were married in 1958 and the marriage was a contented one. The deceased was a millionaire and prior to his death in 1976 he and his wife lived in a large luxurious house in Oxfordshire, worth £350,000, and enjoyed an extremely high standard of living. There were no children of the marriage. The deceased died in November 1976 leaving a will under which the wife received his personal chattels and a life interest in some War Stock producing £3,500 per annum. He left the remainder of his estate, valued at about £1.5 million, mainly to Oxford University. The wife applied under s1(1)(a) of the 1975 Act on the ground that the deceased did not make reasonable financial provision for her. An interim order was made of £75,000 capital to enable the wife to buy a smaller house to live in and for a payment of £15,000 per annum income. At trial the judge increased the provision for the wife to a total sum of £259,000 taking into account the interim order and the provisions in the will. The wife appealed on the ground that the award was too low since it was less than she might have expected to receive under the Matrimonial Causes Act 1973 if the marriage had ended in divorce (See s3(2) 1975 Act) and that the judge had applied the wrong criterion in assessing the award by looking only at what was required for her maintenance.

Held

1. The judge had adopted the wrong approach because he had considered the wife's financial position only on the basis that the marriage had broken down and the financial needs and amount required for her maintenance in such circumstances. These were only some of the matters to be taken into account under s3(2).
2. Where the deceased left a very large estate and his only obligation was towards his widow who had been a faithful and dutiful wife and who was incapable of supporting herself, reasonable financial provision required that she should have access to a lump sum sufficient to ensure beyond reasonable doubt that she should be relieved of any anxiety for the future. In the circumstances an overall sum of £378,000 should be awarded.

Oliver LJ:

> '... these then are the factors to which the court is directed to pay regard and of particular importance in this case are, first, the plaintiff's resources (she has none apart from the will), second, the principal beneficiary's needs (there are none save those connected with the carrying out of the purposes described by the bequest), third, the obligations owed to the plaintiff as his widow, fourth, the fact that this is an exceptionally large estate of a testator who owed no obligation to anyone other than his widow, fifth, the plaintiff's age (she is clearly unable to fend for herself but nevertheless has a fair expectation of life), and, finally and very importantly, what she might reasonably have expected to receive if the marriage had terminated, not by death, but by divorce.
>
> Now the last factor is, of course, a further imponderable added to a list of imponderables, it must bring into the calculation a consideration of the provisions of s25 of the Matrimonial Causes Act 1973 ... In an application under s25 of the 1973 Act the court is directed, so far as it is practicable and is just to do so, to put the parties in the same financial position as they would have been if the marriage had not broken down. In that calculation, the concept of what is "reasonable" is nowhere mentioned, although the parties' financial needs, which have been construed to mean "reasonable requirements", constitute one element to be considered. In an application under their 1975 Act, however, the figure resulting from the s25 exercise is merely one of the factors to which the court is to "have regard" and the overriding consideration is what is "reasonable" in all the circumstances. It is, however, a very important consideration and one which the statute goes out of its way to bring to the court's attention. If, therefore, the provision which the court finds to be reasonable under the 1975 Act turns out to be very widely at variance with the figure which might be expected to be achieved on a divorce, one is immediately driven to ask what regard the trial judge did in fact pay to it ...
>
> ... there was also another consideration which, in my judgment, should have commanded considerable weight but to which the judge attached very little importance. Although he made provision for what he described as "a little over to allow for some inflation" he appears to have taken no real account of possible future contingencies ... houses decay, circumstances change, the cost of living increases and the value of money falls ... Furthermore, although, happily, the plaintiff appears to be in good health, there is an inevitable health hazard with advancing age and, having regard to the fact that this lady is the widow of a more than ordinarily wealthy man, reasonable provision would in my judgment require that she should have access to a sufficient sum to ensure beyond any reasonable doubt that she is relieved of any anxiety for the future ...'

Bishop* v *Plumley [1991] 1 WLR 582 The Times 11 July Court of Appeal (Purchas and Butler-Sloss LJJ and Sir Patrick O'Connor)

Contribution for full valuable consideration?

Facts

The applicant for financial provision had supported and cared for an elderly man, now deceased, with whom she had lived while he was in bad health. In return, she had received a secure home. Had the deceased made a substantial contribution towards the applicant's reasonable needs other than for full valuable consideration?

Held

The question would be answered in the affirmative and the case remitted for consideration as to whether an order should be made. Butler-Sloss LJ said that the test laid down in s1(3) of the Inheritance (Provision for Family and Dependants) Act 1975 was in two parts: (i) was the deceased making a substantial contribution in money or money's worth towards the reasonable needs of the plaintiff and, if so (ii) was the contribution made for full valuable consideration by the applicant? As the answer to (i) was 'yes' and to (ii) 'no', the applicant qualified as being maintained either wholly or in part. Her Ladyship did not consider that the applicant's evidence that she did everything for the deceased over a period of years could be assessed in isolation from the mutuality of the relationship. If a man or a woman living as man and wife with a partner gave the other extra devoted care and attention, particularly when the partner was in poor health, was he or she to be in a less advantageous position on an application under the Act than one who might be less loving and gave less attention to the partner? That could not have been the intention of Parliament in passing the legislation.

Bramwell, Re, Campbell v *Tobin* [1988] 2 FLR 263 High Court (Sheldon J)

Family provision – wife dying before proceedings commenced

Facts

In 1975 a widow aged 65 married a widower of 71: they parted company in 1979: the husband died in 1986, his wife six months later. Between the two deaths, the wife instructed solicitors to make a claim under the Inheritance (Provision for Family and Dependants) Act 1975. After the wife's death, the plaintiff sought to pursue such a claim: the defendants (the husband's executors) applied to have the proceedings struck out.

Held

The defendants' application would be successful as the plaintiff had no locus standi.

Sheldon J:

> '... in my judgment, it is clear – as has been recognised and acknowledged without recorded dissent for over 40 years – that in matrimonial proceedings a claim for financial provision neither gives rise to nor becomes a "cause of action" within s1(1) of the Law Reform (Miscellaneous Provisions) Act 1934 unless an order has been made in respect of it before the death of the deceased: until such an order has been made, therefore, it remains a mere hope or contingency which survives neither against nor for the benefit of the deceased's estate.
>
> In [the plaintiff's] submission, however, a similar principle is not to be applied to claims for financial provision under the 1975 Act; on the contrary, in the case of a wife or husband of a deceased spouse, such a claim contains not only a personal but also a proprietary element which is more than a mere hope or contingency and which, by s1(1) of the 1934 Act, survives the death of the claimant for the benefit of his or her estate. It is a submission, if I understand it correctly, which is based upon the facts, first, that the right to make a claim under the 1975 Act is given to others besides those properly to be found under the matrimonial umbrella – to "any person ... who immediately before the death of the deceased was being maintained, either wholly or partly, by the deceased" – and, second, that although others are entitled to apply for "such financial provision as it would be reasonable in all the circumstances of the case for the applicant to receive for his maintenance", the surviving spouse could ask for "such financial provision as

it would be reasonable in all the circumstances of the case for a husband or wife to receive whether or not that provision is required for his or her maintenance".

In my judgment, however, the fact that a stranger to the marriage, who was also being maintained by the deceased immediately before his death, was entitled under the 1975 Act to make a claim for maintenance does not affect the nature of the claim that can be made by the surviving spouse – though it might, of course, affect the quantum awarded. On the contrary, I agree with Booth J (in *Whytte* v *Ticehurst* [1986] 2 WLR 700) that, in the latter context,

> "... the purpose of this legislation was to enable the court to place the surviving spouse in the financial position he or she would have been in had a matrimonial decree been granted during the lifetime of the other."

This conclusion, indeed, in my opinion, follows or is supported by the express provision to such an effect in s3(2) of the Act and by the other terms of s3 which set out the matters to which the court is to have regard in exercising powers under the Act and by their similarity to the corresponding provisions of s25 of the Matrimonial Causes Act 1973.

It follows, therefore, that, in my judgment, a claim under the Inheritance (Provision for Family and Dependants) Act 1975 – as with a claim for financial provision under the Matrimonial Causes Act 1973 – neither gives rise to nor becomes a "cause of action" within s1(1) of the Law Reform (Miscellaneous Provisions) Act 1934 unless an order has been made in respect of it before the death of the surviving spouse or other potential claimant; until then it remains no more than a hope or contingency of no surviving value to a deceased's claimant's estate.'

Callaghan, Re [1985] Fam 1 Family Division (Booth J)

Family provision – effect of treating a child as a child of the family: 'adult children'

Facts

The plaintiff was born in 1937 and his father was killed on active service in 1943. After his father's death the plaintiff and his mother lived in a house in Bedford owned by his mother and which was given to her by the plaintiff's paternal grandfather. In 1950 the deceased came to live in the house as a lodger, eventually they started to share a room and live together as man and wife. In 1953 the house in Bedford was sold and a house bought in London, the plaintiff, his mother and the deceased all lived in this house and the deceased treated the plaintiff as if he were his own son. In 1960 the plaintiff married and he had his wife lived in the London house until 1969 when they went to live in Basingstoke. In 1972 the deceased and the plaintiff's mother married and in 1973 the London house was sold and another purchased in Basingstoke, the title to this being conveyed into the joint names of the plaintiff's mother and the deceased. The plaintiff's mother died intestate in May 1980 and the deceased died intestate in August 1980. The deceased's estate was worth £31,000 including the house valued at £18,000. The plaintiff was 47 with a modest income and no capital and living in a council house. He applied under s1(1)(d) of the 1975 Act. One of the questions which arose was whether s1(1)(d) included adult children or was confined to minors or dependent children.

Held

Section 1(1))(d) included adult children, and in view of the obligations and responsibilities the deceased assumed towards the plaintiff, the fact that he had no such obligations to the persons who would take his estate on intestacy and that the assets of the deceased derived mainly from the plaintiff's mother, it was appropriate to make reasonable financial provision for him and a lump sum of £15,000 would be awarded.

Booth J:

'... so it is argued, the words in s1(1)(d), "treated by the deceased as a child of the family", must be construed as treatment as a minor or a dependant child of the family and that it must be directly referable to the marriage, which means that it must have occured after the marriage had taken place.

I do not agree that the words in s1(1)(d) require such a narrow construction. "Child", for the purposes of s1, clearly includes an adult child. One of the persons who may apply by virtue of s1(1)(c) is "a child of the deceased", and it cannot be suggested that in that context "child" must be limited to a minor or dependent child. In s1(1)(c) "child" relates to the relationship between the deceased and the applicant. In my judgment this is precisely the same in s1(1)(d) of the Act, and no different meaning should be given to the word "child" in the context of the words "treated by the deceased as a child of the family". It is again a matter concerning the nature of the relationship between the deceased and the applicant, and it does not follow that treatment necessarily refers to the treatment of the applicant by the deceased as a minor or dependant child. in this case the acknowledgement by the deceased of his own role of grandfather to the plaintiff's children, the confidences as to his property and financial affairs which he placed in the plaintiff and the dependence on the plaintiff to care for him in his last illness are examples of the deceased's treatment of the plaintiff as a child, albeit an adult child, of the family. All these things are part of the privileges and duties of two persons who, in regard to each other, stand in the relationship of parent and child; it is the existence of that relationship that enables the plaintiff to apply under s1(1)(d) of the Act. My view of this is not altered by the fact that in considering an application by a person coming within s1(1)(d) the court is required to have regard to the education or training of the applicant and must also consider the extent to which the deceased has assumed responsibility for his maintenance. Those two considerations are in addition to the other matters specified in s3(1), to which the court must have regard in determining any application, and undoubtedly these matters are referable to minor or dependant applicants, but I cannot accept the argument that the additional duty laid on the court in the case of minor or dependant applicants limits the capacity of those who apply under s1(1)(d) to minor or dependant children. Equally, the court is required to consider the education or training of an applicant who claims as a child of the deceased, and, as I have already said, it cannot be suggested that such claims are limited to minors or dependants.'

Collins, Re [1990] 2 WLR 161 High Court (Hollings J)

Family provision – adopted child

Facts

At the date of death the deceased was married to the first defendant, although a decree nisi had been granted. Accordingly, as the deceased had died intestate and her estate was worth about £27,000, the first defendant was entitled to the whole of it, subject to any successful claim under the Inheritance (Provision for Family and Dependants) Act 1975. The deceased had two children, X (who was illegitimate) and Y (legitimate): Y had been adopted after the deceased's death but three months before the commencement of these proceedings in which X and Y claimed reasonable financial provision under s1 of the 1975 Act.

Held

An award (£5,000) would be made in favour of X, and Y's claim would be dismissed.

Hollings J:

I rely on *Whytte* v *Ticehurst* [1986] Fam 64 as indicating that what Y had, before he was adopted, was not a cause of action. A fortiori it was not an interest expectant, whether immediate or not.

For that reason, taken as a preliminary point, I do not make any award in his case ...

I turn now to the claim made by X ... I do not consider that the fact of support from the DSS precludes consideration of whether the intestacy has or has not made reasonable financial provision for her ...

And so in this case I have to look at the situation as it is today in the case of this young lady. She will obtain employment, no doubt, and the question is: what, if anything, does she need for her maintenance, bearing in mind the matters set out in s3 of the 1975 Act, which are relevant and material to this case?

I have to have regard to her financial resources and needs now and in the foreseeable future, to the size and nature of the net estate of the deceased, to the various other relevant matters set out in s3, and to any other matter, including the conduct of the applicant or any other person, which in the circumstances of the case I may consider relevant.

It is not appropriate, in my judgment, for an order for periodical payments to be made in her case, having regard (1) to the difficulty of assessing an appropriate amount, (2) to the comparatively small amount of the net estate in any event and (3) to the desirability of achieving finality …

There is one other matter which I should mention. I was told of an unexecuted will of the deceased; we are not told of its contents and, as I have said already, I did not admit it in evidence before me. I have not, therefore, taken into account the deceased's wishes expressed in any other way. But I can say that, in the circumstances of this case, I am quite satisfied that the failure of the deceased to make a will, which resulted in the rules of intestacy giving the benefit of her estate to her divorced or half-divorced husband, was plainly not her intention; and, if and in so far as that intention was relevant, I could have taken that into account; but there has been no need to do so.'

Coventry, Re [1980] Ch 461 Chancery Division (Oliver J) Court of Appeal (Buckley, Geoffrey Lane and Goff LJJ)

Family provision – reasonable financial provision for son – need to establish a moral claim

Facts

The deceased and his wife were married in 1927 and they subsequently acquired a house through their joint efforts. The applicant, a son was born in 1931 and he eventually joined the Navy. In 1957 he returned home when the wife left home for good and from then until 1961 he lived at home rent free, but by an arrangement he did the domestic work, paid for the food and paid the gas and electricity bills. In 1961 the son married and brought his wife to live in the house; she took over the domestic duties and they lived rent free. In 1975 the son's marriage broke up and in 1976 the deceased died intestate leaving a net estate of £7000 which under the intestacy rules the wife was entitled to absolutely. At the time the wife was aged 74 and lived on a pension in a council flat. She had received no maintenance or support since she left home nor applied for any. The son was aged 46 and earning £52 per week from which he had to pay £12 per week maintenance to his wife. The son applied under s1(1)(c) of the 1975 Act.

Held

1. In considering an application within s1(2)(b) the court was to interfere only if the deceased's dispositon or lack of them produced an unreasonable result in not making provision or greater provision for the applicant's maintenance. This required an applicant to establish a moral claim to be maintained over and above the claim of blood relationship and the mere fact that the applicant found himself in necessitous circumstances was not sufficient by itself to establish such a claim. On the evidence the plaintiff was not entitled to claim.
2. The court would not interfere or reform the deceased's dispositions merely because the deceased acted unreasonably, the Act was not to be used to provide a bounty for those who were related to the plaintiff but omitted from the provisions of the will.

Oliver J:

'… The 1975 Act may have been one to make "fresh" provision but it forms part of a continuum and the introduction of an expanded class of potential applicants does not of itself point to the adoption of any different approach to the exercise of the discretion, which remains restricted to "reasonable provision for maintenance". At the same time, I have to bear in mind that, in relation to all applications under the 1975 Act, s3 now lays down an expanded list of guidelines to which the court is directed to have regard both in relation to the question of whether it shall exercise its discretion at all and in relation to the extent to which, if it does so, that discretion is to be exercised.

I think, in these circumstances, that I ought not to approach this application with any preconceived notion that there is some especially heavy burden on a male applicant of full age beyond that which must, as a practical matter, necessarily exist when a person who applies to be maintained by somebody else is already capable of adequately maintaining himself. The matter was put succinctly by Buckley J in *Re Ducksbury* [1966] 1 WLR 1226 where he said:

> "It seems to me that the subsection does not put the burden of proof one way or another. It is for the court to decide on such evidence as it has before it whether or not the testator has made reasonable provision for the maintenance of the applicant, and I do not think that the court should start with a leaning one way or another either in favour of the view or against the view that the testator owed some sort of moral duty to provide for any particular applicant."

It seems to me, however, that, in regarding the circumstances and in applying the guidelines set out in s3, it always has to be borne in mind that the 1975 Act, so far as it relates to applicants other than spouses, is an Act whose purpose is limited to the provision of reasonable maintenance. It is not the purpose of the Act to provide legacies or reward for meritorous conduct. Subject to the court's powers under the 1975 Act and to fiscal demands, an Englishman still remains at liberty at his death to dispose of his own property in whatever way he pleases or, if he chooses to do so, to leave that disposition to be regulated by the laws of intestate succession. In order to enable the court to interfere with and reform those dispositions it must, in my judgment, be shown, not only that the deceased acted unreasonably, but that, looked at objectively, his disposition or lack of disposition produces an unreasonable result in that it does not make any or any greater provision for the applicant and that means, in the case of an applicant other than a spouse, for that applicant's maintenance.

It clearly cannot be enough to say that the circumstances are such that if the deceased had made a particular provision for the applicant, that would not have been an unreasonable thing for him to do and therefore it now ought to be done. The court has no carte blanche to reform the deceased's disposition or those which statute makes of his estate to accord with what the court itself might have thought would be sensible if it had been in the deceased's position. This may seem almost truism, but I mention it because some of counsel's submissions for the plaintiff, although he did not put it so in terms, seemed to me to be leading to the conclusion that because the deceased's intestacy and the inflation of property values had produced something of a windfall, which could reasonably have been disposed of by the deceased in favour of his son if he had thought about it, therefore the court ought to step in and divert it to where it would be most useful and appreciated.

That is not the purpose of this legislation at all. It cannot be enough to say,

> "Here is a son of the deceased, he is in necessitous circumstances, there is property of the deceased which could be made available to assist him but which is not available if the deceased's dispositions stand; therefore those dispositions do not make reasonable provision for the applicant."

There must, as it seems to me, be established some sort of moral claim by the applicant to be maintained by the deceased or at the expense of his estate beyond the mere fact of a blood relationship, some reason why it can be said that, in the circumstances, it is unreasonable that no or no greater provision was in fact made. This was the approach under the former legislation and it is reflected in the passage from the judgment of Buckley J in *Re Ducksbury* to which I have already referred, where, towards the end of his judgment, he says:

> "... it is not for me to try to effect the sort of testamentary dispositions which I think that a testator should have made or would have made had his mind not been affected, as I think it was, by his matrimonial disputes with his first wife. It is not for me to say what he ought to have done if he had been generously disposed towards the plaintiff. I have to consider what is reasonable in the circumstances of this case to

order that she should receive, having first of all satisfied myself that the testator had failed to make reasonable provision for her. He has in fact made no provision for her, and for the reasons that I have indicated I think that he was under a moral obligation to make some provision for her. I am, therefore, satisfied that he has failed to make a reasonable provision for her."

Turning to the circumstances of the instant case, undoubtedly if I look alone at the plaintiff's financial resources he does not live and has, in his present occupation, not expectation of living in a state of affluence. Counsel for the plaintiff put before me figures of estimated expenditure designed to show that the plaintiff, once he can no longer have the benefit of rent-free occupation of 41 Granville Road, will be unable to support life at all on the £40 per week net which remains after providing for the weekly maintenance payable for his children. I am bound to say tha I treat those figures with considerable reserve. They assume that the plaintiff when he leaves Granville Road (and it is, as I understand it, common ground that the property is in a condition in which it is no longer habitable with comfort in the absence of major repair work) will not be housed by the local authority pursuant to its statutory duties and that he will be obliged to seek a furnished flat in the private sector at a rent equal to, possibly three quarters of his available income. His own evidence is that he has not even enquired about the cost of a single furnished room. I am prepared to assume, however, in the plaintiff's favour that the necessity to provide accomodation for himself will leave him a considerably smaller margin for living expenses than he enjoys at the moment. A gross wage of £66 per week in present conditions is not, perhaps, quite on the breadline, but it is not far above it. In addition there are other commitments which have come into existence since the deceased's death and which the court is directed by s3(5) to take into account. The plaintiff owes some £70 for divorce costs and something over £300 for arrears of maintenance which arose during the period when he was unemployed. His only capital is about £200 most of which is represented by a tax repayment. Additionally, he has a potential liability, which has not yet crystallised and for which he appears to made no provision, for the continued use and occupation of 41 Granville Road since the death of his father.

If, therefore, the financial need were the sole criterion, then I think that undoubtedly, it exists although its stringency may have been to some extent the plaintiff's own responsibility. But the mere fact that the plaintiff finds himself in necessitous circumstances cannot, in my judgment, by itself render it unreasonable that no provision has, in the events which have happened, been made for his maintenance out of the deceased's estate.

Section 3(3) appears to me to point to the sort of circumstances in which it would be appropriate for an adult capable of earning his own living to seek provision under the 1975 Act, a case, for instance, in which the deceased died whilst his adult son was being supported in the process of acquiring some occupational qualification and in which no provisions were made by the dececased for its completion. But there is nothing of that sort in this case and I can see no other circumstances here which could be said to have put the deceased under any obligation during his lifetime to maintain or to contribute to the maintenance of the plaintiff. He appears to have had no particular affection for his son, and the evidence of the plaintiff's former wife indicates that there was no more than a perfectly sensible arrangement, which does not appear always to have worked entirely harmoniously, under which the deceased allowed his son and his family to have the benefit of the house in return for keeping him and paying a proportion of the outgoings.

Counsel for the plaintiff submits that a moral obligation in the deceased was created in this way. Because, he suggests, the plaintiff elected to stay at home and go out to work instead of re-enlisting to the Royal Navy (which he says he did because his father was not accustomed to looking after himself) the plaintiff gave up a career which might have led to his promotion and to his receiving an early pension on his retirement. Moreover, by the arrangement which was made while the plaintiff and his wife lived at the house, they were encouraged not to do what they might otherwise have done, that is to say, to acquire a house for themselves. There was thus, counsel submits, a moral obligation cast upon the deceased to ensure that after his death a home would be provided for his son, an obligation which can now only be fulfilled by transferring to the plaintiff the whole of the deceased's interest in the house.

Against this, however, I have already referred to the evidence of the plaintif's former wife, that the deceased frequently made it clear that he wanted the plaintiff to move out and that there were frequent arguments about the condition into which the house was being allowed to fall. Indeed the plaintiff, in his own evidence, agrees that he did indeed look for other accomodation but he does not seek to suggest that he was prevented from providing a home for himself or that the arrangement by which he enjoyed rent-free accommodation for himself and his family was not one which was at least as much to his advantage as it was to the advantage of the deceased. No doubt it could be thought that reasonable family affection might have prompted the father to make some provision for a son who, although earning an adequate living, was clearly not well-to-do; but there is no question of the plaintiff having given up work and disabled himself from earning an adequate living in order to devote himself to his father and I cannot see anything in the history of the relationship between them which could be said to impose any sort of moral duty on the father to provide for his son's maintenance, either during his lifetime or after his death.

So far as the defendant is concerned the master was, I think, rather influenced by the fact that the deceased's intestacy brought her a windfall ... Even assuming that to be so, this does not, in my judgment, involve as a corollary that some provision ought, in reason, to have beenn made for a son of full age to whom the deceased owed no obligation of or responsibility for maintenance. But in fact the "windfall", as it seems to me, was one to which the defendant can show some colour of entitlement and such obligations as the deceased may have had were, I should have thought, rather towards her than towards his son. After living with him for 30 years she was induced to leave by the joint conduct of the deceased and the plaintiff, abandoning a matrimonial home in which she had already acquired a substantial interest. She received from the deceased no maintenance at all at any time thereafter and no recompense for the continued use of her property which was enjoyed by the deceased and the plaintiff to her total exclusion for the next 19 years. And indeed the fact that the estate and the defendant's share in the property is not substantially larger than it is in fact is due to the continued failure by the deceased and the plaintiff, between them, to keep the property in a reasonable state with the result that its present value is approximately two-thirds of what it would be worth were it in a proper state of repair.

Under s3(1)(g) counsel for the plaintiff submits that one of the "other matters" which the court should take into account is that this is a case of intestacy in circumstances in which, so far as the evidence goes, the testator would, if he had thought about it, have preferred the property to go to his son. But the evidence on this is conflicting and the master has made no finding about it. The plaintiff says that his father had told him that the house would be his when he died, but the plaintiff's former wife says that one of the reasons why the plaintiff carried out so few repairs was that he was not willing to do work on a property which was not going to be his and indeed that between 1970 and 1975 the deceased expressed a desire that the house should go to his grandchildren. Moreover, I bear in mind the plaintiff's own evidence before the master of his father's refusal to trust him with the deeds.

In these circumstances, it is, I think, quite impossible to form any reliable conclusion about what the deceased may have intended and the probability is, since he never troubled to make a will, that he really did not care very greatly what happened to the property after his death.

In my judgment, the plaintiff's claim substantially rests on two limbs only, that is to say, (a) that he is a son of the deceased with whom it might be thought that there would be a bond of natural affection, and (b) that although he is in employment and capable of maintaining himself his circumstances leave him little or no margin for expenditure on anything other than the necessitiies of life.

I have every sympathy for any plaintiff who, on relatively slender earnings, has to meet a steadily rising cost of living, but, as I have said, I cannot regard the 1975 Act as one which entitled the court to interfere with a deceased person's dispositions simply because a qualified applicant feels in need of financial assistance.

I cannot in this case find any circumstances which satisfy me that it is an unreasonable result of the intestacy laws that no provision is made for the plaintiff's maintenance and in my judgment the application must fail.'

Davis v *Davis* [1993] 1 FLR 54 Court of Appeal (Sir Stephen Brown P, Stuart-Smith and Mann LJJ)

Family provision – claim by widow – whether life interest in majority of estate was reasonable financial provision

Facts

Just prior to his death the testator gave £15,000 to his second wife and executed a will bequeathing two pieces of furniture to his son from his first marriage and the remainder of his chattels to his wife, the residue of his estate to the trustees, with a life interest to the wife. The trustees bought a house for the wife.

At the time of the appeal the assets in the trust consisted of £12,000 in cash, a share in a farm worth £75,000 to be realised in two years, £20,000 due from the estate of the testator's uncle, as well as the expectation of a share from the estate of the deceased's father when the life tenant died.

The widow claimed that the will had failed to make reasonable financial provision insofar as no capital payment had been made. She claimed that the freehold of the house should be transferred to her. The judge dismissed her application.

Held

The Court of Appeal dismissed her application. The widow had been accommodated and proper and adequate provision had been made for her maintenance. The judge at first instance had taken into account all relevant considerations therefore there was no reason for the appellate court to interfere.

Fullard, Re [1982] Fam 42 Court of Appeal (Ormrod LJ and Purchas J)

Inheritance Act 1975 s25(1) – former spouse who has not remarried

Facts

On divorce between the plaintiff and the deceased in 1976 there was agreement that the deceased would transfer his interest in his property (worth £9,000) to the plaintiff for £4,500. The deceased went to live with a friend and made his will in 1977 leaving almost all his entire estate to her. He died in 1978 leaving an estate valued at approximately £7,000. The plaintiff applied under the 1975 Act as a former wife under s1(1)(b) for reasonable financial provision.

Held

As the plaintiff and the deceased had settled their financial affairs on the divorce, and had the plaintiff been satisfied she could have applied for ancillary relief in the divorce proceedings, it was reasonable for the deceased to make no financial provision for her in his will. In view of the existence in divorce legislation of powers to grant ancillary relief on divorce it will be rare for a former wife to be successful in an application under the 1975 Act.

Ormrod LJ:

> 'With the coming into effect of the Matrimonial Proceedings and Property Act 1970 with the new powers to make property adjustment orders and very much freer power to order lump sums, the court now has power to make appropriate capital adjustments as between spouses after divorce and those powers, although they are not necessarily comprehensive – that is plain from section 15 of the Act of 1975 which clearly contemplates that proceedings may be taken under the Inheritance (Provision for Family and Dependants) Act 1975 after divorce – nonetheless the number of cases in which it would be possible for an applicant to bring himself (or herself) within the terms of section 2 of the Inheritance (Provisions for Family and Dependants) Act 1975, in my judgment, would be comparatively small. Where the estate – like

this one – is small, in my view the onus on an applicant of satisfying the conditions of section 2 is very heavy indeed and these applications ought not to be launched unless there is (or there appears to be) a real chance of success, because the result of these proceedings simply diminishes the estate and is a great hardship on the beneficiaries if they are ultimately successful in litigation.

... the question is – and it is a simple question to my mind – is it unreasonable, or was it unreasonable, that this man made no financial provision by his will for his former wife. He thought he and the plaintiff had sorted out their financial claims as between each other when they reached the agreement about the house. It is right to say that if the plaintiff had been dissatisfied with that arrangement, she had her remedy. She could have applied to the court for an order and she might have succeeded in getting the whole of the house transferred to her without having to pay anything – or perhaps on payment of very much less.

The final irony of this case is to be seen in looking at the estate of the deceased which amounted to £7,100 the greater part of which consisted of the £4,500 which the plaintiff had paid for her share of the house. So, if she is right on this application, what she is in fact doing is asking for her money back. It is as simple as that. It does not get any less simple and any less stark by going through all the steps that section 3(1) of the Act of 1975 directs the court to do. We come back to the same position which is, is it reasonable to expect a husband with assets of this kind who has made arrangements with his former wife which settled their financial affairs, is it reasonable for the court in his place to make provisions for the wife out of his estate? To my mind the answer is plain and obvious. It is obviously "no".

As I mentioned at the beginning of this judgment it seems to me that the number of cases which, since the court acquired its wide powers under the Matrimonial Proceedings and Property Act 1970 to make property adjustments, which can now get in within the umbrella of the Inheritance (Provision for Family and Dependants) Act 1975 post divorce must be comparatively few. In the course of argument I suggested one case where a periodical payment order has been going on for a long time and the husband is found to have a reasonable amount of capital in his estate. That is one. Mr Reid suggested that there was another possible situation – where a substantial capital fund was unlocked by the death of the deceased, such as insurance or pension policies. Those are cases which could come within the Act of 1975. Apart from those, it seems to me there cannot be many cases which qualify.

Mr Reid rightly draws attention to the provisions of section 15 of the Act of 1975 which provides:

> "On granting a decree of divorce, a decree of nullity of marriage or a decree of judicial separation or at any time thereafter, the court may, if the court considers it just to do so and the parties to the marriage agree, order that either party to the marriage shall not be entitled on the death of the other party to apply for an order under section 2 of this Act."

Certainly that provides a form of security against such applications as this. On one view it might be said that the court, and legal advisers acting in these cases, might be well advised to remember section 15 and, if they can persuade the other side to agree, to write into an order the appropriate provisions. I regard section 15 as a form of insuring against applications under the Inheritance (Provisions for Family and Dependants) Act 1975 which some people may very reasonably wish to do having made financial provision of a capital nature for the former spouse. People obviously have other commitments – second wives (or husbands) and children and so on. I do not regard section 15 as materially affecting the question the court has to answer as the condition precedent to these applications.'

Jelley* v *Iliffe [1981] Fam 128 Court of Appeal (Stephenson, Cumming-Bruce and Griffiths LJJ)

Family provision – proof of 'assumption of responsibility'

Facts

The applicant had lived with his daughter up until 1971 when he went to live with the widow of his wife's brother in her house because she was afraid to live alone. The applicant shared the house with her and they pooled all their income, including their old age pensions to meet their living expenses. The applicant received rent free accommodation and had his washing and cooking done for him. In return he provided some furniture for the house, did odd household jobs and the gardening. The widow of the wife's brother died in 1979 and by her will, made in 1972, she left all her property, including the house, to her children and made no provision for the applicant. The applicant brought a claim under section 1(1)(e) of the 1975 Act. The registrar struck out the application and on appeal the judge upheld the registrar's decision. The applicant appealed to the Court of Appeal. The judge at first instance held that the provision of rent free accomodation for the applicant did not amount to an assumption of responsibility for the maintenance of the applicant for the purposes of section 1(1)(e) and section 3(4).

Held

The mere fact that the applicant was generally being maintained under an arrangement subsisting at the deceased's death generally raised a presumption that the deceased had assumed responsibility for the applicant's maintenance under s3(4) of the Act. However, the applicant had also made a contribution to the maintenance of the deceased. The appeal would be allowed as there was an arguable case and as it was not clear whether the applicant's contributions equalled or outweighed those of the deceased.

Stephenson LJ:

> 'Section 1(1)(e) defines one new class which qualifies for the right to apply for such provision. The question which, like the district registrar and Bush J, this court has to decide is whether on the evidence, which must be at this stage accepted as true, the plaintiff comes within the defined class and qualifies for that right. Whether there is anything else in the statute, particularly in sections 1(3) and 3(4) which affects that definition and that right is a question we have to consider. Whether the plaintiff will succeed in his application is not a question we have to consider except – an important exception – in so far as it might be plain that his application would be bound to fail.
>
> In answering the question whether the statute gives the plaintiff the right which the registrar and judge have denied him we, like the statutes, are concerned with dependency for support of that kind well-known to family law as maintenance. What may be called matrimonial maintenance is mainly if not exclusively of two kinds, financial provisions or the provision of accommodation in a house. A man maintains his wife and children by providing them with somewhere to live or by paying contributions of money or by both, and if he does that he maintains them, he assumes the responsibility of maintaining them and he discharges that responsibility as long as he continues to do so. That it seems to me is the background against which we have to consider the relevant provisions of the Act extending the right to apply for financial provision to those who have been maintained by a deceased person during his lifetime and immediately before his death, and to consider counsel's submissions upon those provisions and their true interpretation.
>
> I respectfully agree with Megarry V-C, for the reasons that he gives in his exposition of the statute in *In Re Beaumont* [1980] Ch 444, 450–458 on all points but one. (1) the deeming provision in section 1(3) exhaustively or exclusively defines what section 1(1)(e) means by "being maintained", and does not include in those words a state of affairs which is not within section 1(1)(e) and would extend its ambit. To qualify within section 1(1)(e) an applicant must satisfy section 1(3), as if before the words "if the deceased" the draftsman of section 1(3) had inserted the word "only". (2) In considering whether a person is being maintained "immediately before the death of the deceased" it is the settled basis or general arrangement between the parties as regards maintenance during the lifetime of the deceased which has to be looked at, not the actual, perhaps fluctuating, variation of it which exists immediately before his or her death. It is, I think, not disputed that a relationship of dependence which has persisted for years will not be defeated by its termination during a few weeks of mortal sickness. (3) Like Megarry V-C, I reject the contention that the parenthetical words in section 1(3) "otherwise than for full valuable consideration" apply only to full valuable consideration under a contract and agree with him and with

Arnold J that they apply whenever full valuable consideration is given, whether under contract or otherwise. Mr Goffe supported the plaintiff's argument against that interpretation by a reference to sections 10(2)(b) and 11(2) (c), where the same phrase is clearly used in the context of a disposition or contract for the benefit of a donee. But even without referring to the Law Commission's *Second Report on Family Property: Family Provision on Death* (1974) (Law Com No 61), on which the statute was based, the narrower construction which has so far been rejected would exclude from its benefits those family arrangements which it seems designed to recognise as often requiring a continuation of support after the death of the supporter.

Where, however, I feel bound to part company from Sir Robert Megarry V-C, is in his interpretation of assumption of responsibility for the maintenance of the supported person. I do not question his opinion that the requirement of section 3(4) that the court:

> "shall ... have regard to the extent to which and the basis upon which the deceased assumed responsibility for the maintenance of the applicant and to the length of time for which the deceased discharged that responsibility"

implies or "assumes" (in another sense), that at the first stage, when the court is considering the applicant's right to apply under section 1(1)(e), he must prove that the deceased did "assume responsibility" for his maintenance. But I cannot, with respect, agree with him, in spite of Mr Butterfield's submission for the defendants that I should, that the bare fact of maintenance raises no presumption that responsibility for it has been assumed. I am of opinion that it generally does. I would not disagree with Megarry V-C when he says:

> "The word 'assumes' ... seems to me to indicate that there must be some act or acts which demonstrate an undertaking of responsibility, or the taking of the responsibility on oneself."

And the Act, here and elsewhere, has drawn a distinction between assuming and discharging responsibility. But how better or more clearly can one take on or discharge responsibility for maintainance? than by actually maintaining? A man may say he is going to support another and not do it, promise to pay school fees but not pay; but if he does pay them, has he not both assumed and discharged responsibility for them whether or not he covenants to pay them? Surely A shoulders the burden of supporting B by supporting him. If B is A's mistress and he maintains her by providing her with accommodation or money or both, has he has not assumed or taken on responsibility for her maintenance. If it be said, as Mr Butterfield submitted, that he has a moral obligation which makes the assumption of responsibility easier to presume, is the presumption nevertheless not to be made where provision of a share in a home and/or financial support is made out of the donor's generosity of heart to a poor relation or friend; it may be tht the presumption can be rebutted by circumstances including a disclaimer of any intention to maintain. But here there is, in my judgment, a distinction to be drawn between an intention to maintain during the lifetime of the giver who has something to offer and an intention to provide continuing support after death. I cannot help thinking that there is some confusion between the two, if not in Megarry V-C's judgment in *In Re Beaumont*, at least in the judgment of Bush J and in the argument by which Mr Butterfield has sought to support it. If it is necessary, or relevant, to prove an intention on the part of the deceased to maintain a dependent, qualified to apply under section 1(1)(e), after the deceased's death, the only cases in which there will be the required qualification wll be those where the deceased's intention has been defeated by accident, eg by his dying intestate and leaving children or having made an invalid will in the dependant's favour.

I do not read the Act as expressing so limited a legislature intention. its object is surely to remedy wherever reasonably possible, the injustice of one, who has been put by a deceased person in a position of dependency upon him, being deprived of any financial support, either by accident or by design of the deceased, after his death. To leave a dependent; to whom no legal or moral obligation is owed, unprovided for after death may not entitle the dependent to much, or indeed any, financial provision in all the circumstances, but he is not disentitled from applying for such provisions if he can prove that the deceased by his conduct made him dependent upon the deceased for maintenance, whether intentionally or not.

Accordingly, I am of opinion that the court has to consider whether the deceased, otherwise than for valuable consideration (and irrespective of the existence of any contract), was in fact making a substantial contribution in money or money's worth towards the reasonable needs of the plaintiff, on a settled basis or arrangement which either was still in force immediately before the deceased's death or would have lasted until her death but for the approach and the consequent inability of either party to continue to carry out the arrangement. To discover whether the deceased was making such a contribution the court has to balance what she was contributing against what he was contributing, and if there is any doubt about the balance tipping in favour of hers being the greater contribution, the matter must, in my opinion, go to trial. If, however, the balance is bound to come down in favour of his being the greater contribution, or if the contributions are clearly equal, there is no dependency of him or her, either because she depended on him or there was mutual dependency between them, and his application should be struck out now as bound to fail. Where what B does gives full valuable consideration for the substantial contribution A makes, there is no dependency and B's claim under the Act should be struck out. The balancing of imponderables like companionship and other services, on which the court has somehow to put a financial value, against contributions of money or accommodation, is a hard task, as Arnold J found it in *In Re Wilkinson* [1978] Fam 22 a case of two arthritic sisters, in which he found "with considerable uncertainty" that the services of the sister who was taken into the deceased sister's house were just outweighed by what the deceased gave her in board and lodging enough to entitle her to go on with her application. In *Re Beaumont* which was on the facts much closer to this case, Megarry V-C did not weigh the contributions of man and mistress in a balancing operation because he held that there had been no assumption of responsibility for maintenance of the man by what the deceased mistress had contributed in accommodation and money. It is an operation which it may be said should be left to the later stage of trial, but if it can be done at this stage and plainly results in the scales ending level or the plaintiff's scale descending under the weight of his greater contribution then the right course is to save the costs of further proceedings, which will probably come out of the estate, may be charged to the legal aid fund, and are likely to leave little or nothing for the plaintiff or the deceased's estate. Such litigation in respect of small estates should be discouraged as far as justly possible, as this court recently repeated in *In Re Coventry* [1980] Ch 461.

Can this difficult operation be carried out at this stage and plainly produce that result? I have no doubt that the provision of free accommodation in these times is a substantial contribution to the needs of the accommodated and was a substantial contribution to the plaintiff's reasonable needs.

If in describing the deceased as one who "happens to own the house in which they live" the judge intended to treat that as an accidental and therefore insignificant circumstance, I cannot agree with him. It might qualify the plaintiff to pursue his claim because the pooling of their incomes and the remaining contributions of aid and comfort which each gave to the other cancelled out. In my judgment the statute, whether literally or purposively construed, requires the court to take a broad common sense view of the question whether the applicant for the statutory relief was a dependant of the deceased before death, and the ordinary man's answer to what, on this approach, is the right question, "Was this man dependent on this woman during her lifetime for maintenance, or did he give as good as he got?" might be (without regard to nice differences between the facts in this and other cases) that each was partly dependent on the other and he gave her, in companionship (whether or not it amounted to consortium) and help in money, and in furnishing her house and caring for her and her house and garden, as much as she gave him in companionship and rent-free accommodation and money and looking after him by cooking and cleaning.

I do not, therefore, agree with the judge that the plaintiff was the one who had been making substantial contributions, if by that he means that the plaintiff was the only one. Nor would I accept that the deceased's provision of rent-free accommodation was insignificant in relation to those acts of his. I find here, unlike the judge, maintenance in money and money's worth for a long time and an assumption of responsibility for such maintenance by the deceased to a considerable extent and on a settled basis. But I do not think her intention to continue such maintenance until *his* death (as the judge is noted as saying), or his awareness (or ignorance) that such was not her intention, is relevant to the question whether he qualifies for any financial provision after *her* death. And I find also that the plaintiff was helping to maintain her by his contributions financially and otherwise and so giving some valuable consideration for her contributions to their life together.

But how can we decide now whether the plaintiff was, on balance, being maintained in the sense required by the statute and so is a dependent qualified to claim that the deceased ought to have made some financial provision for him after her death? The qualifying status of dependency is a question of fact which can only be decided against an applicant if there is no evidence on which it could be answered in his favour and although we were told that the plaintiff is probably not in a position to call any further evidence I do not think we should rule out his application now and prevent the court to which the discretion has been given from exercising it after hearing all the evidence.'

Jessop* v *Jessop [1992] 1 FLR 591 Court of Appeal (Nourse and McCowan LJJ and Sir John Megaw)

Financial provision for dependants – severability of share of joint property

Facts

The applicant was a widow who made her application under the 1975 Act against a woman with whom the deceased intestate had been living. Apparently the deceased had been married and had maintained two families.

Originally the house in which the deceased lived with his second family had been owned by the respondent, with the financial assistance of her mother. In order to repay her mother she had subsequently borrowed from a building society. The house was then put into the joint names of the deceased and the respondent to enable the respondent to take through the right of survivorship when the deceased died.

By virtue of the intestacy provisions the applicant became entitled to a small amount of cash on the death of the deceased.

At first instance the judge had ordered that £10,000 should be paid to the widow by the respondent in respect of the deceased's severable share in the property.

Held

The Court of Appeal overruled the first instance decision. It held that on an objective basis the judge had to decide whether reasonable provision had been made by will or intestacy. In contrast to matrimonial proceedings, there were no broad powers under the 1975 Act proceedings, to make equitable distribution of any available assets.

Kusminow* v *Barclays Bank Trust Co Ltd [1989] Fam Law 66 High Court (Sir Stephen Brown P)

Financial provision – factors to be considered

Facts

The plaintiff, aged 78, had married in 1958; she was Polish in origin, her husband was Russian, but they had spent their married life in England. The plaintiff left her husband in 1984 and he died the following year. By his will, made in 1968, he divided his estate between his nephew and niece who lived in the Soviet Union. The plaintiff made a claim under s2 of the Inheritance (Provision for Family and Dependants) Act 1975 and, for the purposes of the hearing, it was agreed that the value of the deceased's estate was about £100,000. The plaintiff, an arthritis sufferer, lived in a rented flat; she had savings of about £20,000 and a retirement pension. The nephew and niece lived in conditions of some poverty.

Held
Taking into account the respective needs of all the parties, the plaintiff would be awarded a lump sum of £45,000.

Sir Stephen Brown P explained that when making an order under s2 of the 1975 Act the court had to have regard to the matters set out in s3. These included a provision that in the case of an application by the wife of the deceased the court should have regard to the provision which the applicant might reasonably have expected to receive if, on the day on which the deceased died, the marriage instead of being terminated by death, had been terminated by divorce. If the court had been dealing with the matter as if it were considering financial provision following the dissolution of the marriage it would have taken into account the fact of a long marriage in which the wife had worked hard for the benefit of both parties, and in the circumstances of the plaintiff would have calculated that she was entitled at any rate to a half share of the family assets of £120,000. Of course, that was not the only factor which had to be taken into account in dealing with the application of s3. His Lordship took the view that the widow was in need, and reasonably required a capital sum to provide for her at present and in the future. He also took the view that notwithstanding her age it was not a case where money should be placed on trust, bearing in mind the cost of administration and the fact that the beneficiaries were resident behind the Iron Curtain. This was a case where a final disposition should be made. The plaintiff would have to ensure that she had sufficient money to provide not only income but also accommodation of a satisfactory kind. Regard must be had too to the fact that there was need on the part of the beneficiaries who should each receive a substantial capital sum.

Lake* v *Lake [1989] STC 865 (Mervyn Davies J)

Deed of variation – effect of rectification – tax implications

Facts
The testator had left a will whereby most of his estate passed to his widow for life, then to his children and grandchildren. Since she was independently wealthy, the widow wanted to avoid an aggregation of the two estates. A deed of variation was executed whereby additional sums were given to the children. Unfortunately, due to a clerical error the gifts were expressed to be 'free of tax'. Although a second corrective deed was made this was held to be ineffective. The family applied for rectification of the first deed of variation.

Held
Rectification was granted. Since all the parties desired the order rectification of the deed should not be refused where the sole purpose was to enable the parties to obtain an advantage which had been their common intention at the time of the document's execution.

Leach, Re [1986] Ch 226 Court of Appeal (O'Connor, Slade and Robert Goff LJJ)

Family provision – effect of treating a person as a child of the family: 'adult children'

Facts
The plaintiff was born in 1928 and moved away from home in 1949. In 1959 the plaintiff's mother died and in 1960 her father married her stepmother. The plaintiff never lived in the same house as her father and stepmother and was never maintained by her stepmother but she enjoyed a close relationship with them. The plaintiff's father died in 1974 and by his will he left all his estate to the stepmother. The stepmother died intestate in 1981 leaving an estate of about £34,000. The plaintiff applied for reasonable

financial provision under s1(1)(d) of the 1975 Act. She was given £19,000. This next of kin appealed on the grounds that (i) the plaintiff was not eligible to apply under the 1975 Act; (ii) she had in any event failed to establish that the disposition of the estate was such that it did not make reasonable financial provision for her; (iii) the award of £19,000 was excessive.

Held

The plaintiff was eligible to apply under s1(1)(d) even though she was of mature years and had never lived with the stepmother or been maintained wholly or partly by her. This was because, on the evidence, the stepmother had assumed the position of a parent towards the plaintiff with all the attendant responsibilities and privileges of that relationship.

Slade LJ:

> '... in ... s1(1)(d) of the 1975 Act ... the phrase used is not "during the subsistence of that marriage"; it is the wider phrase "in relation to that marriage". It seems to me that the treatment of an applicant by a surviving spouse after the death of the other spouse may be a relevant factor in deciding whether the applicant qualifies under s1(1)(d), provided that such treatment is referable to or ... "stems from" the marriage. In a case where the marriage has been terminated by the death of one of the spouses I do not think it correct for the purpose of applying s1(1)(d) to regard the family unit created by that marriage as necessarily having come to an end on such death. That would be too rigid and technical a construction. To give one hypothetical example, let it be assumed that H who has one young child, A, who is living with a foster motherin Australia, marries W, who has four young children of her own. For the rest of H's life he and W and her four children share a happy household. After a short time H then dies. Subsequently, W learns that A's foster mother has died. W takes him into her home and, without formally adopting him, treats him as if he were one of her own children. In these hypothetical circumstances, on W's subsequent death, A could, in my opinion, claim to have been treated by W as a child of the family in relation to her marriage to H. I would accordingly hold that the court, in applying s1(1)(d) of the 1975 Act, is entitled to take into consideration, inter alia, the conduct of the testator or intestate after the death of his or her spouse, provided that such conduct can fairly be said to be referable to the relevant marriage.
>
> The second major problem of interpretation to which s1(1)(d) gives rise is this: what is the nature of the behaviour which will amount to "treatment as a child of the family"? ... the legislature cannot have contemplated that the mere display of affection, kindness or hospitality by a stepparent of the stepchild as a child of the family in relation to the marriage, for the purposes of s1(1)(d), so as to place the parent and his or her estate under a potential liability to provide for the stepchild. Something more is needed: reasonable stepparents can usually be expected to behave in a civilised and friendly manner towards their stepchildren, if only for the sake of their spouse ... I can see no reason why ... an adult person may not be capable of qualifying under that subsection, provided the deceased has, ... expressly or impliedly, assumed the position of parent towards the applicant, with the attendant responsibilities and privileges of that relationship ...'

McBroom (deceased), Re [1992] 2 FLR 49 Family Division (Eastham J)

Whether application before grant is possible

Facts

The deceased and the woman with whom he lived died in a car accident. As the woman was younger it was presumed that she survived the deceased. They were joint tenants of a property. The deceased's son applied for financial provision under s19 of the 1975 Act, and that the deceased's severable share be treated as part of the net estate. It was held by the district judge that the application was premature.

An appeal had been made against an order striking out an application made before a grant. The question was whether such an application was indeed valid.

Held

Eastham J dismissed the appeal. He applied an obiter dictum in *Re Bidie* [1949] Ch 121 although this was stated in a totally different context, and did not consider *Re Searle* [1949] Ch 73 where it was expressly decided that an application could be made before grant.

Malone v *Harrison* [1979] 1 WLR 1353 Family Division (Hollings J)

Family provision – assumption of responsibility

Facts

The deceased separated from his wife in 1939. In 1958 he met X, who moved into his house and whom he treated as his wife. In 1965 the deceased met the plaintiff, a girl of poor academic ability who had a job as a telephonist when he met her. He persuaded her to come with him on trips abroad. From that time forward the deceased paid all the plaintiff's living expenses; he took her on holidays to Malta and told her he would marry her if free to do so. The deceased took exception to the plaintiff working and he gave her a nominal job with his company, earning £68 in 1968. He also provided her with a car and bought her shares, a flat in England and a flat in Malta. The deceased told the plaintiff that he would make no provision for her in his will and he sent her a newspaper cutting on the provisions of the 1975 Act. When the deceased died the plaintiff had received from him property valued at £25,000 plus about £4,000 a year as income. The deceased made no provision for the plaintiff in his will but only for his wife, X, his son, and his brother. After his death the plaintiff had difficulty in finding a job and at the date of the application was caring for old people at £23 per week and had a substantial overdraft. She applied to the court for reasonable financial provision under the 1975 Act.

Held

1. That since the deceased had assumed full responsibility for the plaintiff's maintenance for 12 years, on the basis that he would not leave her unprovided for after his death the court should make an order for a lump sum payment out of the deceased's residuary estate.
2. In ordering reasonable financial provision for the plaintiff under s1(2)(b) and s1(3) the court had to have regard for the deceased's obligations and responsibilities towards other beneficiaries, particularly X, under s3. The plaintiff's resources were also material and her need to maintain herself reasonably in her present or a comparable flat. Since the plaintiff's earning capacity was limited the deceased had not made reasonable provision for her. It would be fair to provide her with an income of £4,000 per annum. In the circumstances taking into account her expectation of life, her earning capacity and her present capital resources £42,0000 ought to be awarded but £19,000 should be deducted from this to represent the capital the plaintiff already had.

Moody v *Stevenson* [1992] Ch 486 Court of Appeal (Mustill LJ and Waite J)

Family provision – reasonable financial provision for surviving spouse

Facts

The applicant was the widower of the deceased; they had married in 1971 when he was aged 61 and she was aged 66. The testatrix had lived with the applicant until 1984 when she moved into a nursing home. When she died in 1988 the testatrix left her modest estate by will to her stepdaughter. This included the house.

The applicant sought an order for 'reasonable financial provision' under ss1, 2 and 3 of the

Inheritance (Provision for Family and Dependants) Act 1975. In the county court his claim had been dismissed; the legatee had been granted an order for possession of the house.

The applicant appealed.

Held

The appeal was allowed; the provision was not reasonable. Mustill LJ said that the 1975 Act placed a claim by a surviving spouse on a new footing as a claim for 'reasonable financial provision'. Following s3(2) the court was to have regard to the provisions a spouse might reasonably have expected to receive if on the day of death the marriage had been terminated by divorce. The county court judge should have decided the case by asking: 'What would a family judge have ordered for the couple if divorce instead of death had divided them?' Had the judge applied this test – the proper test – he would have made an order permitting the applicant to remain in the house as long as he wished. This test, therefore, was an objective one, rather than a subjective decision from the point of view of the deceased. The court should address three questions:

1. What provision could a family court judge have ordered had the marriage ended in a divorce?;
2. What would be the effect of any other of the factors mentioned in s3 of the 1975 Act?; and
3. In the light of the answers to the above, whether or not the provision was reasonable under the will or intestacy?

Under s3 of the 1975 Act the factors that can be taken into account include, inter alia, actual and potential needs and resources of the applicant and any other applicants and 'any other matter' including the conduct of the parties as the court might consider relevant.

In holding that the provision was not reasonable it was noted that had there been a divorce the court would have given the husband a right of occupation of the property. The order was that the property should be settled on terms to enable his occupation.

Powell* v *Osbourne (1992) The Times 3 December Court of Appeal (Dillon and Simon Brown LJJ)

Financial provision for dependants – value of severable share – time of valuation

Facts

The deceased held property jointly. Its value was greatly enhanced by a life policy which redeemed the mortgage upon his death. What was the correct approach with regard to s9 which provides that the court may order that the deceased's severable share be taken 'at the value thereof immediately before his death' as being part of the net estate? At first instance the judge had considered that he was restricted by these words in s9 to deal only with the equity in the property prior to the policy monies redeeming the charge. In doing so the deceased's prima facie half share in the proceeds of the policy as applied to the mortgage could not be claimed by the applicant.

Held

The Court of Appeal held that the purpose of s9 was to make available, if appropriate, what could have been severed immediately before the date of his death. The last moment that severance can take place is immediately before death. The judge at first instance had treated the deceased's half share of the policy as, in effect, of no value at all. However, the Court of Appeal indicated that the imminence of the deceased's death meant that the value was in effect the same as the value upon death. Although, therefore, the building had been subject to a mortgage and it was a condition of that mortgage that a half share of the policy monies were to be applied to it, it was held that the policy monies formed part of the net estate. As a result, the applicant received an increased capital sum.

Salmon, Re [1981] 1 Ch 167 Chancery Division (Megarry V-C)

Inheritance Act 1975 s4 – time for application

Facts

A husband died in 1978, aged 83, leaving by his will his estate worth £75,000 to his elderly sister and two lady friends. He left nothing in his will to his wife (the widow) whom he married in 1932 and who left him in 1944 after an unhappy relationship, but never divorced him. There were no children of the marriage. Letters of Administration cumtestamento annexo were granted to the National Westminster Bank on 15 December 1978. On 14 February 1979 a friend of the widow wrote to the administrator's solicitors on her behalf asking for an ex gratia payment for her 'rather than consider proceedings under the Family Inheritance Act'. This request was met with a refusal. On 2 April 1979 solicitors were instructed on the widow's behalf to institute proceedings under the 1975 Act. At this time some 21/2 months of the six-month time limit for commencing proceedings under s4 of the 1975 Act remained unexpired, ie until 15 June 1979. Legal aid was applied for on the widow's behalf on 24 April 1979 but was not granted until 30 July 1979, six weeks outside the s4 time limit. An originating summons was not issued until 27 November 1979, some 51/2 months late. The widow's solicitors did not write to the administrator's solicitors until 31 October 1979 to warn them of a possible claim under the 1975 Act. At the end of the six months time limit the administrators consulted their solicitors to see if anything had been heard from the widow as regards a claim; as nothing had been heard they proceeded to distribute the estate. The bulk of the estate was distributed between 27 June and 11 November. The widow sought permission to make an application outside the six-month time limit in her summons.

Held

Permission for the widow to make an application out of time under s4 of the 1975 Act would be refused for the following reasons:

1. The delay was substantial and due to the fault of the widow;
2. There was no negotiation during the six month period and no indication given to the administrator that an extension of time was to be sought;
3. The bulk of the estate had been distributed and no warning had been given to the bank that a claim might be made;
4. It was likely that the widow had a claim in negligence against her solicitors;
5. It would be unjust to the beneficiaries to extend the time limit for an application when the widow had a remedy against her solicitors.

Megarry V-C (after reviewing previous decisions relating to the courts' jurisdiction to extend the time limit) laid down the following guidelines:

> 'I am anxious not to go further than is proper in attempting to discover guidelines in exercising the court's discretion under s4. I bear in mind what Ungoed-Thomas J said on this; and in saying what I do, I disclaim any intention to lay down principles, though I am not sure that it makes it much better to use the term "guidelines" in place of "principles". However, after 14 years I think that some progress can be made towards identifying some guidelines. A number of points seem reasonably plain. The first two are sufficiently supported by *Re Ruttle* [1970] 1 WLR 89. First the discretion is unfettered. No restrictions or requirements of any kind are laid down in the Act. The discretion is thus plainly one that is to be exercised judicially, and in accordance with what is just and proper. Second, I think that the onus lies on the plaintiff to establish sufficient grounds for taking the case out of the general rule, and depriving those who are protected by it of its benefits. Further, the time limit is a substantive provision laid down in the Act itself, and is not a mere procedural time limit imposed by rules of court which will be treated with the indulgence appropriate to procedural rules. The burden on the applicant is thus, I think, no triviality: the

application must make out a substantial case for it being just and proper for the court to exercise its statutory discretion and extend the time.

In addition to the two points which emerge from *Re Ruttle* there are orders which I think can properly be considered in deciding whether or not to extend time. In my view, a third point is that it must be material to consider how promptly and in what circumstances the applicant has sought the permission of the court after the time limit has expired. This is not, of course, a crude matter of simply looking at the length of time that has been allowed to elapse; it is not a mere matter of comparing, for instance, the six weeks of *Re Ruttle* with the $2^1/_2$ years of *Re Gonin* [1979] Ch 16. The whole of the circumstances must be looked at, and not least the reasons for the delay, and also the promptitude with which, by letter before action or otherwise, the claimant gave warning to the defendants of the proposed application. Thus if the warning was given within time, but for some good reason the proceedings were not commenced until a short while after time had run, I would expect the applicant's task to be relatively simple. Where there has been some error or oversight, an obvious question is whether the applicant has done all that was reasonably possible to put matters right promptly, and keep the defendants informed. As I have said more than once, it is not only Heaven that helps those who help themselves.

This leads to the fourth point: for the reasons that I have already given, I think that it is obviously material whether or not negotiations have been commenced within the time limit: for if they have, and time has run out while they are proceeding, this is likely to encourage the court to extend the time. Negotiations commenced after the time limit might also aid the applicant, at any rate if the defendants have not taken the point that time has expired.

Fifth, I think it is also relevant to consider whether or not the estate has been distributed before a claim under the Act has been made or notified. Section 20(1) provides that the Act is not to make a personal representative liable for distributing the estate after the six months has ended on the ground that he ought to have taken account of the possibility that the court might permit an application to be made after the six months; but this provision does not prejudice any power to recover, by reason of the making of an order under the Act, any part of the estate so distributed. The end of the six months thus marks a change from a period when any distribution by the personal representatives is made at their own risk (see *Re Simon* [1956] Ch 38) to a period where there is some statutory protection for a distribution.

So far as the beneficiaries are concerned, there will usually be a real psychological change when the estate is distributed. Before the distribution, they would have only the expectation of payment; and if they are entitled to a share of residue, they will often have a considerable degree of uncertainty as to the amount. After the distribution, they have the money itself, and know the exact amount. If an order is made under the Act, the difference will be the difference between the prospect of receiving in due course less than they had hoped, and on the other hand having something that they had already received and regarded as there own taken away from them. For most people, there is a difference between the bird in the hand and the bird in the bush. In addition, of course, the beneficiaries are more likely to have changed their position in reliance on the benefaction if they actually received it than if it merely lies in prospect. If it is always prejudicial to claimants not to receive money that they are entitled to receive at the earliest possible moment, it is likely to be even more prejudicial to have taken away from them money that they have actually received and begun to enjoy. The point is strengthened if they have changed their position in reliance on what they have received, as by making purchases or gifts that they otherwise would not have made. However, I shall not pursue this, as there is no evidence of any change of position in the case before me.

Sixth, I think that it is relevant to consider whether a refusal to extend time would leave the claimant without redress against anybody. In *Re Gonin* Walton J considered the possibility that the plaintiff might sue her solicitors in negligence if in fact it was due to their faulty advice that her claim was not made in time. Although the subject matter is different, there seems to me to be considerable force in the approach to be found in the line of cases associated with the name of *Allen v Sir Alfred McAlpine & Sons Ltd* [1968] 2 QB 229 on dismissing actions for want of protection. Even if the plaintiff personally is completely blameless, the delays of his or her solicitors must be treated as the delays of the plaintiff, though injustice to the plaintiff will often be avoided by the existence of the plaintiff's right to sue the solicitors for negligence [ibid at 256–257]. There may appear to be some logical difficulty in making the decision whether the defendants should escape liability under the 1975 Act depends in any degree on whether the responsibility for the delay was that of the plaintiff personally or was that of the plaintiff's solicitors: the liability of the defendants, it may be said, ought not to depend on the distribution of fault between the plaintiff and his or her solicitors. Nevertheless, however logic may affect the defendant's position there is a real and plain difference to a plaintiff between having a claim against his or her solicitors instead of against the defendants, and having no claim against anybody.'

Sehota, Re [1978] 1 WLR 1506 Chancery Division (Forster J)

Inheritance Act 1975 s1(1) – wife under a polygamous marriage

Facts

The plaintiff and her husband were married in India in 1937, and at that time the marriage was potentially polygamous under Indian law. In 1948 the husband married a second wife. At a later date the plaintiff and her husband acquired an English domicile of choice. The husband died in 1976 and by his will he left all his estate to his second wife. The plaintiff made an application for reasonable provision out of her husband's estate under s1(1)(a) of the 1975 Act. The second wife opposed the claim.

Held

The plaintiff was on the true construction of s1(1)(a) 'the wife ... of the deceased' and therefore entitled to make a claim for provision from his estate even though the marriage was polygamous.

The right of a surviving spouse to bring a claim under the 1975 Act is a personal right and is extinguished on the surviving spouse's death.

Smith* v *Clerical Medical and General Life Assurance Society [1993] 1 FLR 47 Court of Appeal (Parker and Scott LJJ and Sir Roger Ormrod)

Family provision – endowment policy – death of one policyholder

Facts

The deceased and the plaintiff purchased a property in joint names with a 100 per cent building society mortgage supported by an endowment policy, signed by both, which provided a fund from which the mortgage would be repaid at the end of its term or the earlier death of the lives assured. When the deceased died the building society did not claim the policy money. A dispute arose as to whether the money should go to the plaintiff on the basis that the policy had been to effect the payment of the mortgage despite the fact that the building society had not chosen to claim the policy money, or, alternatively, whether the policy money should go to the personal representatives of the deceased under the terms of the policy. The question was whether the policy money was due to the other policyholder or to the personal representatives as equity would not allow personal representatives to defeat the intention of the parties paying into an endowment policy whereby the mortgage debt could be discharged and on the basis of which they had entered into substantial financial commitments. The plaintiffs appealed against the first instance decision, where the judge had dismissed their claim on the ground that the intention of the parties with regard to the endowment mortgage had been deferred by the building society's decision to look to the proceeds of sale of the house rather than the proceeds of the policy.

Held

The plaintiff's appeal was allowed. The entire objective of the transaction was that the policy money should be used to discharge the mortgage so that the survivor would be left with an unencumbered property. If the building society elected not to demand the policy money as a means of discharging the mortgage there could be no ground upon which the personal representatives could claim to be beneficially entitled.

Whytte* v *Ticehurst [1986] Fam 64 Family Division (Booth J)

Inheritance Act 1975 – surviving spouse – nature of personal right to bring a claim.

Facts

The husband and wife were married in 1953. In 1982 the husband made a will leaving all his property, including the matrimonial home, to a charity, subject to the wife having a right to remain in the house during her lifetime. The husband died in February 1984; in July 1984 the widow made a claim under the 1975 Act, but she died in December 1984. The widow's personal representatives applied for leave to carry on the action for the benefit of her estate on the ground that it was a cause of action which survived for the benefit of the estate under s1(1) of the Law Reform (Miscellaneous Provisions) Act 1934.

Held

The basis of the right of action under the 1975 Act was, in the case of a married couple, one which arose from their relationship and was personal to the surviving spouse so that it ceased against the deceased spouse's estate on the death of the surviving spouse.

Booth J:

> '... to my mind the purpose of this legislation was to enable the court to place the surviving spouse in the financial position he or she would have been in had a matrimonial decree been granted during the lifetime of the other. The foundation of the jurisdiction is, as in the matrimonial legislation, the relationship of the two parties to the marriage, and the only right that the statute gives is the right to the survivor to apply for relief against the estate of the deceased spouse ... Further, in my judgment, both the 1973 Act (Matrimonial Causes Act) and the 1975 Act by their explicit terms and by the very purposes for which they were enacted restrict the claim for financial relief to a spouse or a surviving spouse. I do not think that by extending the power of the court to grant such relief to a surviving spouse Parliament intended to create a cause of action which insofar as it is related to provision not required for maintenance would survive for the benefit of his or her estate ...'

Wilkinson, Re [1978] Fam 22 Family Division (Arnold J)

Family provision – 'being maintained by deceased immediately before death'

Facts

In 1969 the applicant went to live with her sister, a childless widow, who was suffering from severe arthritis. At that date the applicant was 61. The sister provided the applicant with free board and lodgings and paid all her household expenses. In return the applicant looked after the deceased by helping her to dress etc and did some light housework and cooking. A home help was employed to do the heavy housework since the applicant had a hernia and also suffered from arthritis. Towards the end of the sister's life the applicant spent much time sitting up with her at night, and was constantly at her bedside. On the sister's death in 1976 the applicant brought a claim under s1(1)(e) of the 1975 Act on the ground that the deceased's will had not made reasonable financial provision for her. The registrar held that the applicant was a person who immediately before the deceased's death was being maintained by the deceased and therefore within s1(1)(e). The deceased's executor appealed.

Held

It was for an applicant under s1(1)(e) to show that a substantial contribution made by the deceased in money or money's worth towards her reasonable needs had been made otherwise than for full valuable consideration under s1(3) of the Act. In the present case the financial value of the services provided by the deceased and the detriments caused to her did not constitute a full valuable consideration for the board, lodging and expenses which the deceased had provided.

Arnold J:

> 'It is in my judgment plain that the onus of bringing the applicant within the definition of a person such as is described in s1(1)(e) rests squarely throughout on the applicant. It is thus necessary for an applicant under that paragraph to prove first that the deceased was making a substantial contribution in money or money's worth towards the reasonable needs of that applicant, and secondly that the deceased was doing otherwise than for full valuable consideration. It is moreover, in my judgment, plain that in order to determine whether that was so, one must look at the consideration, if there was any consideration, which was being provided by the applicant at the time at which the deceased was making the relevant contribution. From the language of s1(1)(e) it is plain that that time was the time immediately before the death of the deceased. Accordingly the question which I have to ask myself in this case, since there is no dispute that the deceased was making a substantial contribution in money or money's worth towards the reasonable needs of the applicant, is whether the consideration which the applicant was providing in the period immediately before the death of the deceased, was a full valuable consideration. That is how I understand the construction of the relevant parts of this section.'

9 Vesting, Collection, and Realisation of the Estate

Anker-Petersen* v *Anker-Petersen and Others [1991] LSG 1 May Chancery Division (Paul Baker J)

Trustees' powers of investment – scope of powers

Facts

The plaintiff was the tenant for life of a fund held on the trusts of his father's will. He applied for approval of the extension of the Trustees' powers of investment, either under section 57 of the Trustee Act 1925 or under section 1 of the Variation of Trusts Act 1958. As the terms provided that moneys were to be invested as from time to time sanctioned by law for the investment of trust moneys they were governed by the Trustee Investments Act 1961.

The proposed extensions would give power to the Trustees to:

1. invest in assets of any kind as if they were beneficial owners; and
2. delegate to investment managers; and
3. hold investments through nominees; and
4. borrow money for any purpose.

The proposals did not affect the beneficial interests under the will and they were supported by all the defendants.

Held

The proposals were approved.

Judge Paul Baker QC said that it was preferable to bring an application for an extension of investment powers under section 57 of the Trustee Act 1925 than under section 1 of the Variation of Trusts Act 1958 where the beneficial interests under a will or settlement were unaffected. Doubt had occurred as to the applicability of section 57 to the general enlargement of the power of investment because of the specific nature of the transactions which the section permitted. In his opinion there appeared to be no reason to adopt a restrictive view to the construction of the section: its manifest object was to enlarge the inherent administrative jurisdiction of the court – so far limited to cases of emergency – and there was a power 'either generally or in any particular instance' to effect a wide range of transactions, including investment. On the contrary, the terms of section 1 of the 1958 Act, although general, did not appear to enlarge the scope of powers that the court could authorise.

In circumstances in which the beneficial interests were not affected section 57 of the 1925 Act was more appropriate because:

1. The Trustees were the natural persons to make the applications;
2. The consent of every adult beneficiary was not essential; and
3. The court was not required to give consent on behalf of every category of beneficiary separately but rather it would consider their interests in income and in capital collectively, which was more realistic.

This meant that a less expensive application could be made without jeopardising the legitimate interests of the beneficiaries.

Beatty (deceased), Re [1990] 1 WLR 1503; [1990] 3 All ER 844 Chancery Division (Hoffmann J)

Testamentary power of appointment – scope of power

Facts

The testatrix had left an estate of £32 million. The testatrix had made a will in which she allocated her personnel chattels and cash to her trustees to whom she also gave the power to distribute these 'among such person or persons (whether individual or corporate) as they think fit', and that any assets not distributed within two years after her death were to become part of her residuary estate.

The residuary beneficiaries brought proceedings against the trustees questioning the distributions made and their power to do so.

Held

Hoffmann J stated that the trustees had a fiduciary power and upheld the defendants' argument that these powers were not invalidated by the rule that a testator could not delegate the making of his will. The trustees only had to consider the wishes expressed by the testatrix.

The judge applied the case of *Re Park* [1932] 1 Ch 580. The powers, being fiduciary, were not general powers, nor special powers, but were intermediate or hybrid powers. In *Re Park* the court had upheld the validity of such an appointment and its powers so long as it was not delegated to a donee.

The plaintiffs argued that such a delegation amounted to the making of a will for a testator who had failed to do so. That was rejected and interpreted instead as

> '... giving effect to the testator's will and not making a will for a testator...' at p1507.

Such a power would be valid by deed and there is no rule prohibiting the delegation of testamentary power which would cause this will to be invalid or to forbid the actions taken here by the trustees.

Caney v *Bond* (1843) 6 Beav 486 Court of Chancery (Lord Langdale MR)

Duty of personal representative to collect assets

Facts

In 1826 the testator loaned £500 to one Phillips, to invest in a mortgage security, and pending that Phillips gave the testator a promissory note. The testator died shortly afterwards and his executor allowed the £500 debt to remain outstanding on personal security. Phillips paid £100 to the executor in 1827 but in 1828 he died insolvent. It was sought to make the executor liable for the loss.

Held

As the loss was caused by the default of the executor he was liable to replace it.

Lord Langdale MR:

> 'At the death of the testator, part of his estate was outstanding on personal security. It was the duty of the executors, quite independently of any application being made to them by the persons interested in the estate, to take steps to get in this money. In the exercise of a fair discretion, they were not to commence legal proceedings unnecessarily, but they ought to have exerted themselves to get in the debt, and if necessary, to have commenced compulsory proceedings to obtain it.

The persons beneficially interested, not considering the money safe where it was, requested the defendant, Bond, to get it. Instead of complying with this request he refused to do so saying that the money was as safe as in the Bank of England; two years afterwards the money was lost by the insolvency of the debtor.

If, in any case, an executor is to be charged for wilful default, it is in a case of this sort, where the money not only is found on a security, not sanctioned by the Court, and which ought therefore to be got in, but where also the executor has been requested to call it in, and has refused on the ground that it is perfectly safe.'

Dowse* v *Gorton [1891] AC 190 House of Lords (Lords Herschell, MacNaghten and Hannen)

Personal representatives – authority to carry on business

Facts

The testator's business was carried on for about three years after his death by his executors, in accordance with a provision in his will empowering them to do so and with the assent of his creditors, in the interests of the creditors and the beneficiaries. The testator's business owed some large debts at his death and because of indebtedness the executors felt unable to continue any longer at the end of the three years. A receiver was appointed and afterwards one of the creditors issued an originating summons seeking a declaration that the assets of the business ought to be applied in payment of the debts due by the testator at his death in priority to any claim for an indemnity by the executors or those with whom they had dealt.

Held

The executors were entitled (in priority to claims by the testator's creditors) to be indemnified out of the testator's estate against the liabilities which they had properly incurred, and the indemnity was not limited to that portion of the assets which had come into existence or changed its form since the testator's death.

Lord Herschell:

> 'I think it is clear that where a business has been carried on under such an authority as was conferred upon the executors by the will of this testator, they would be entitled to a general indemnity out of the estate as against all persons claiming under the will. But I take it to be equally clear that they could not, by reason of such authority, maintain this right against the creditors of the testator. The executors would, no doubt be entitled to carry on a business of the testator for such reasonable time as was necessary to enable them to sell the business as a going concern, and would even, as against his creditors, be entitled to an indemnity in respect of liabilities properly incurred in so doing ...'

Lord MacNaghten:

> '... creditors of a deceased trader whose business has been continued by his executors, when they come for an administration decree must treat the continuance of the business either as proper or improper. If the business has been properly continued as between the executors and creditors, or if the creditors chose to treat it so, which comes to the same thing, the executors are entitled to be indemnified against all liabilities properly incurred in carrying it on. If it has been improperly continued and the creditors choose to treat the continuance as improper (which. of course, they are not bound to do), they may proceed in the proper way to make the executors accountable to the value of the assets used in carrying on the business, and they may also follow the assets and obtain a charge in the business in the hands of the executors for the value of the assets misapplied, with interest thereon; and they may enforce the charge if necessary, by means of a receiver and a sale. Then there can be no room for any claim to indemnify on

the part of the executors. The charge in favour of the trust estate must be satisfied first. The executors can only take what is left ...'

Harries and Others* v *The Church Commissioners for England and Another (1991) 135 SJ (LB) 180 Chancery Division (Sir Donald Nicholls V-C)

Trustees' powers of investment – relevant considerations

Facts

The Church Commissioners, a charity, were the trustees of the Church of England funds and responsible for its investment policy. One of the Commissioners, the Bishop of Oxford, sought certain declarations in relation to this investment policy. He argued that, in the implementation of their policy, undue importance was given by the Commissioners to financial considerations, and that they ought properly to bear in mind that the essential purpose for which they held the assets was the promotion of the Christian faith through the Church of England. Therefore, in his view, the Commissioners should take into account ethical considerations.

Held

Sir Donald Nicholls V-C held that where trustees held property as an investment to generate money, prima facie the purpose of the trust would be best served by the trustees seeking to obtain the maximum financial return, whether by way of income or capital growth which was consistent with commercial prudence. He allowed that there might be circumstances where trustees would be acting contrary to their duty if they disregarded non-financial criteria, for example by investing in companies which engaged in an activity which conflicted with the object of the charity or which might alienate the financial supporters of the charity. Nevertheless, he maintained that the trustees could not properly accommodate divergent views on moral questions if, by so doing, this would jeopardise the trust funds significantly. In his view the proper object of the trust funds in the present circumstances was the financial provision of the clergy. Moreover, the Commissioners already did not invest in companies whose main business was arms, gambling, alcohol, tobacco or newspapers since they were likely to be offensive to some members of the Church of England on moral grounds. They were entitled to do this since an adequate scope of alternative investments remained. However, where the non-financial ethical considerations would involve a risk or significant financial detriment to the trust funds then such investment decisions would constitute a breach of trust.

It was held that the declarations should be refused and it was ordered accordingly.

Ingall* v *Moran [1944] 1 KB 160 Court of Appeal (Scott, Luxmore and Goddard LJJ)

Powers of administrators – doctrine of relation back

Facts

The plaintiff's son was killed whilst riding his motor cycle in an accident caused by the negligence of the defendant. The son died intestate and the plaintiff issued a writ under the Law Reform (Miscellaneous Provisions) Act 1934 suing in a representative capacity as administrator of his son's estate. However, at the date of issue of the writ the plaintiff had not obtained letter of administration. The defendant claimed that the action was not properly constituted.

Held

The action was incompetent at the date the writ was issued the doctrine of relation back which applied to administrators could not be invoked so as to render the action properly constituted.

Luxmore LJ:

> 'The defendant has appealed to this court, and the only question arising in the appeal is whether the doctrine of relation back, which is well established in respect of an administrator's title to a deceased's estate, has any application to the status of a plaintiff who can only sue in a representative capacity in an action started before the grant of letters of administration. It is, I think, well established that an executor can institute an action before probate of the testator's will is granted, and that, so long as probate is granted before the hearing of the action, the action is well constituted, although it may in some cases be stayed until the plaintiff has obtained his grant. The reason is plain: the executor derives his legal title to sue from the testator's will. The grant of probate before the hearing is necessary only because it is the only method recognised by the rules of the court by which an executor can prove the fact that he is the executor. If any authority for this is required, it is to be found in the judgment of Lord Parker in *Chetty* v *Chetty* [1916] 1 AC 603. An administrator is, of course, in a different position, for his title to sue depends solely on the grant of administration. It is true that, when a grant of administration is made, the intestate's estate, including all choses in action, vests in the person to whom the grant is made and title thereto then relates back to the date of the intestate's death, but there is no doubt that both at common law and in equity, in order to maintain an action the plaintiff must have a cause of action vested in him at the date of the issue of the writ.'

Job* v *Job (1877) 6 Ch D 562 Chancery Division (Jessel MR)

Duty of personal representative to preserve assets

Facts

On the death of the testator, who was a watchmaker, his executor delivered part of his stock-in-trade, to the value of £160, to his son James Job, who was also a watchmaker and jeweller for the purpose of being sold in the ordinary course of trade. James Job became bankrupt and his trustee in bankruptcy took possession of all his stock-in-trade, including the goods of the testator, and sold them all as being within the order and disposition of a bankrupt.

Held

The executor was not liable for the loss as this had not been caused by his default, but, rather, by James Job mixing up the testator's goods with those of his own and therefore giving the trustee the right to sell them.

Jessel MR:

> '... the real question then is, what is the rule in equity? Now I refer to *Jones* v *Lewis* (1751) 2 Ves Sen 240 where a common decree was made against an administratix for an account. Part of the assets had been delivered by her to her solicitor, who was robbed, and it was held that she was not to be charged. Lord Hardwicke said:
>
> > "If a trustee is robbed, that robbery properly proved shall be a discharge, provided he keeps them (the goods) as he would keep his own. So it is as to an executor or administrator, who is not to be chargeable further than goods come to his hands; and for these not to be charged, unless guilty of a *devastavit;* and if robbed, and he could not avoid it, he is not to be charged, at least in this Court."
>
> That is an old case, and, as far as I know, it has been always followed.
>
> I will now take a modern authority. In *Williams on Executors*, the law is thus stated:
>
> > "Again, upon the supposition that goods come fully into the possession and hands of an executor or administrator, but are afterwards wrongfully taken from him, a question arises whether such goods shall be considered assets in his hands. There are some authorities for asserting that things taken out of the possession of the executor are assets in his hands, unless they were taken by the Queen's enemies. But it

> should seem, at least in a Court of Equity, that an executor or administrator stands in the condition of a gratuitous bailee; with respect to whom the law is that he is not to be charged, without some default in him. Therefore, if any goods of the testator are stolen from the possession of the executor, or from the possession of a third person, to whose custody they have been delivered by the executor, the latter shall not, in equity, be charged with these as assets."

Then, at p1807, the learned author refers to the passage I have read, and quotes a passage from Lord Ellenborough's judgment in *Crosse* v *Smith* (1806) 7 East 246 showing the rule at law to be that an executor was liable for the loss of assets once come into his hands. The rule there laid down is, however, as I have already intimated, not the rule now, even at law, for the Judicature Act 1873, provides by section 25, subsection 11, that where "there is any conflict or variance between the rules of equity and the rules of the common law with reference to the same matter, the rules of equity shall prevail". The rule then, at law as well as in equity, now is that an executor or administrator is in the position of a gratuitous bailee, who cannot be charged with the loss of his testator's assets without wilful default; and a further rule is that though he is liable in equity in case of wilful default, he cannot be charged with it unless an account is ordered against him on that footing; you cannot charge him with wilful default without making out a case; and therefore, under the old practice, unless wilfull default was charged in the bill, you could not so charge him in the accounts. I think, however, that under the new practice an order charging him with wilful default may be made at any time on a proper case being made.'

Owen* v *Delamere (1872) LR 15 Eq 134 Court of Chancery (Bacon V-C)

Note: nothing turns on the facts of this case so they are not cited here.

Bacon V-C:

'The plaintiff claims to be entitled as a simple contract creditor in respect of money lent and advanced, or paid and laid out, nominally on behalf of one person but really on behalf of the defendants – a simple case in which, if it be true, he can recover in an action at law, without the slightest difficulty. It is quite true that the testator did commit his estate to the care of his executors, with an authority to them to carry on business. What is the consequence of that? They carry on the business; they carry it on upon their own responsibility, and they have the testator's estate as a capital with which they can trade. How does that concern the creditors? The creditors have a right to be paid by the persons with whom they have contracted. They contracted, the plaintiff says, with Robert Tyrer, who represented the firm, who was either principal or agent with undisclosed principals. There is no difficulty in bringing an action in law; it is, as stated in the bill, as clear and plain a case in respect of a simple contract, as can be. The plaintiff says that the business was carried on, and that the testator's estate was employed in it. In the 4th paragraph it is stated:

> "In the course of such continuance and carrying on of the said business as aforesaid it has become largely indebted and (amongst others) the said business is indebted to the plaintiff in a sum of £386."

That can only be in respect of the contract which the plaintiff alleges in the bill. The sum can easily be recovered at law, and there is no reason in the world why a bill should be filed in this Court."

Although *Owen* v *Delamere* states that the personal representative is personally liable on contracts he makes in carrying on the business he is entitled to an indemnity. The nature of the indemnity depends on whether the business was carried on under authority (ie either with a view to proper realisation or in accordance with a direction in the will) or with the assent of the creditors.

Owers, Re [1941] Ch 389 Chancery Division (Simonds J)

Personal representatives – dealing with leaseholds – indemnity

Facts

The testator owned a large number of leaseholds at his death, and under the terms of the leases he had covenanted to pay the rent and perform obligations cast on the lessee and to keep the assignor of the lease indemnified in respect of these. The personal representatives entered into possession of the leaseholds on the testator's death incurring personal liability. They sought an indemnity from the estate to protect themselves.

Held

The indemnity should be given.

Simonds J:

> '... at the date of his death, the testator was possessed of a large number of leasehold properties. There is no question but that his executors entered into possession of them and became by virtue of the privity of estate thereby created, personally liable on the covenants contained in the leases. It is true that there are some limitations upon this personal liability of an executor, notably he may not be liable for the full rent reserved by the lease, but only for the letting value of the premises therein compromised, but he is under a personal liability and to protect him from personal liability the court will decree that a sufficient sum be retained for his protection. Where he is under no personal liability, but only under a liability as executor, the court will not decree that a fund is to be set aside for his protection. That is clear from the cases which have been cited, the last of which I think was *Re Nixon* [1904] 1 Ch 638, which I had occasion to review myself in the recent case of *Re Lewis* [1939] Ch 232. But this is a case where, apart from s26 of the Trustee Act, 1926, it would be proper to order that a fund should be set aside for the protection of the executors.
>
> It is said, however, that the section is a sufficient safeguard and that no fund need be set aside. I cannot take that view. The section is as follows [His Lordship read the section and continued]: It is clear to me that the section deals only with the liability of the executor as such and it is not intended to cover the cases where the executor has entered into possession of the testator's leasholds and thereby incurred in addition to his liability as executor, the personal liability of an assignee of the term ... Accordingly, since the section does not protect the executors, it is necessary to follow the old practice of the court and to decide that a sufficient indemnity be set aside for their protection.'

Oxley, Re [1914] 1 Ch 604 Court of Appeal (Buckley J)

Effect of creditors' assent to business being carried on

Facts

At his death in 1908 the testator, a boilermaker, owed a number of people money through his business. There was no authority in the will to carry on the business but the executors carried it on and by 1912 all but three of the creditors had been paid. However, shortly afterwards the executors were declared bankrupt and a receiver was appointed, who claimed the whole of the assets of the business. It was claimed by those who became creditors of the busines after the testator's death that those who were creditors of the business before the testator's death had assented to the carrying on of the business by the executors and accordingly that the executors could claim an indemnity over which they as creditors could claim subrogation. It was argued that the old creditors had assented to the carrying on of the business by not objecting to this.

Held

The claim must fail; assent could not be inferred from silence.

Buckley J:

> 'The second point upon which I want to say a word is this, and this is the main point of the case. The death was in August, 1908, the business was carried on until 1912, a period of four years, or something of that kind – I agree a substantial time. The proposition which has been argued before us may be expressed thus: if with knowledge on the part of the old creditors, that is to say the creditors at the testator's death, the business has been carried on and the old creditors have not interferred, that amounts to an assent on their part to the business being carried on by the executors for them or for the estate, with the result that the executors are entitled to be indemnified out of the estate, and consequently the creditors of the subsequent business are entitled to avail themselves of that indemnity.
>
> In my opinion there is no authority for that proposition; authority is against it. The assent referred to may be an assent in either one of three ways: (1) assent to carrying on the business in fact; (2) assent to carrying on the business for the old creditors as agents of the old creditors, or (3) assent to carrying on the business for the estate of which the old creditors are creditors and against which they have a right to claim.
>
> The most that can result from knowledge and absence of action of any kind is assent to carrying on the business in fact. The position is this: the old creditor is a person entitled to say: 'You must not carry on the business, you are doing it wrongfully as against me': by doing nothing he is simply abstaining from exercising a right of action which he would have. He would be entitled to insist that the business should be stopped and sold and that he should be paid. But it is a long step to say that by not intervening and insisting upon the business being stopped the old creditor assents to the executors carrying on the business for him as his agents so as to make him liable, or for the estate in the sense of acquiring further assets which will fall into the fund out of which he as creditor will be entitled to be paid. The argument that mere knowledge and absence of action one way or the other preclude the old creditor from saying that he stands upon his original rights is inconsistent with *Dowse* v *Gorton* [1891] AC 190.
>
> ... in order to introduce the principle of *Dowse* v *Gorton* it must I think be established that the old creditor has so acted, either by claiming (as he did in that case) the assets of the continued business or by affirmative acts by which he so adopts the action of the executors in carrying on the business, as to show that he has abandoned that which is prima facie his right, that which has been asserted by the plaintiffs in this case, to have the assets of their debtor administered in due course for payment of their debts, and that he has assented to another course, namely, that the fund to which he is entitled to look shall be risked in trade with the result that there may be loss or there may be further additions made for his benefit. It is necessary I think to show an active affirmative assent. Mere standing by with knowledge and doing nothing is not sufficient.
>
> For these reasons I think this appeal fails.'

Renshaw* v *Bassetlaw District Council [1991] EGCS 71 Court of Appeal (Fox and Leggatt LJJ)

Right of survivorship and joint tenancy.

Facts

Graham and Freda Renshaw, the appellant's parents, were granted a joint tenancy by the respondent council of the premises located at 33 Ramsden Avenue, Worksop. The appellant's claim arose subsequent to the death of Freda Renshaw on 6 July 1989.

Heald J in Worksop County Court dismissed the applicant's claim to succeed Freda as a secure tenant. This decision was the result of a 20 March 1989 transaction wherein Graham Renshaw terminated his part of the tenancy and on 1 May 1989 the council let the premises to Freda. The succession was barred after review of s88(1)(b) of the Housing Act 1985 which interpreted Freda Renshaw as a joint tenant who had become a sole tenant and thus a successor herself. The further succession to the appellant was not permitted.

Held

Although Graham Renshaw's notice of termination was effective, s88(1)(b) of the 1985 Act did not apply. The section states: 'The tenant is himself a successor if ... he was a joint tenant and had become the sole tenant ...'. First, Parliament was considering only a single tenancy under ss87 and 88 of the 1985 Act. Secondly, paragraph (b) refers to a tenancy agreement where the joint tenant becomes a sole tenant under its terms. Freda Renshaw could not have been both a joint tenant and a single tenant of the same premises at the same time.

10 Payment of Debts and Expenses

Atkinson, Re [1930] 1 Ch 47 (Clauson J)

Variation of statutory order – testator's right to deal with his/her own estate

Facts

A testator in his will directed the trustees to pay his funeral and testamentary expenses and debts out of the proceeds of sale and conversion of his personal estate.

Held

The effect of this direction was to make the personal estate applicable towards the discharge of the debts and expenses in priority to that part of the testator's real estate which was undisposed of by will as a result of a devisee predeceasing the testator.

Clauson J:

> '... here the will contains a clear direction to the trustees to convert the personal estate and out of the moneys produced by such conversion to pay his funeral and testamentary expenses and debts: until that provision is worked out there is no necessity to have recourse to Part II of the First Schedule to the Act ...'

Beaumont's Will Trusts, Re [1950] Ch 462 Chancery Division (Danckwerts J)

Incidence of pecuniary legacies – pre-1926 rules still applicable.

Facts

By her will the testatrix left a number of pecuniary legacies and then left her real and personal estate not otherwise disposed of upon trust for sale, after payment of debts and expenses, to four named persons. One of the four named persons predeceased the testatrix. One of the questions put before the Court was whether the statutory order for the payment of debts etc had been varied? Another was, how should the pecuniary legacies fund be set aside?

Held

The statutory order had been varied by the will; the pecuniary legacies fund was to be set aside and the debts paid before division of the estate into four equal parts. As to the setting aside of the pecuniary legacies fund the old rules still applied.

Danckwerts J:

> '... it seems to me that the old law applies unless something in the Administration of Estates Act 1925, demonstably eliminates or modifies the old law as to the extent of such burdens.
>
> On this point I am assisted by *In Re Thompson* [1936] Ch 676 in which Clauson J held that the old law, laid down in *In Re Boards* [1895] 1 Ch 499 still remained operative after the Administration of Estates Act, 1925, came into force, so as to cast the primary burden of legacies on the personal estate.
>
> It seems to me, therefore, that in the present case the pecuniary legacies and the specific legacies, and

> the duty on those legacies which is in the form, or has the effect, of an additional legacy, are all payable out of the whole estate before coming to what is divided into four equal parts and given to four named persons, so that the lapsed share is simply a lapsed share of the estate after those burdens have been cleared.'

Berrey's Will Trusts, Re [1959] 1 WLR 30 Chancery Division (Danckwerts J)

Variation of statutory order.

Facts

The testatrix made a homemade will by which she bequeathed two £500 legacies and provided: 'After all my debts, and funeral, and expenses are paid I give and bequeath all the residue of my estate in equal shares to …' four named persons. One of the named persons predeceased her and his share lapsed. The question arose whether the lapsed share was primarily liable or whether the statutory order had been varied.

Held

The statutory order had been varied and the residue was primarily liable for the payment of the expenses and debts.

Fegan, Re [1928] 1 Ch 45 Chancery Division (Tomlin J)

Administration of Estates Act 1925 s35 – debts charged on the deceased's property

Facts

By clause 2 of his will the testator devised and bequeathed certain freehold land and chattels to trustees to sell and out of the proceeds to pay his funeral and testamentary expenses and debts. By clause 8 of the will he left the proceeds of certain life insurance policies to his four daughters. Before his death the testator by a codicil revoked clause 8 and provided that each of his daughters was to receive a £1,000 legacy out of the proceeds of the life policies. The policies were worth about £6,000 at the testator's death but were subject to a mortgage for a substantial amount which if deducted would not have left sufficient to meet the legacies to the daughters. One of the questions was whether the mortgages must be paid out of the proceeds of the policies or whether a contrary intention had been expressed in clause 2 of the will to exclude the operation of s35(1).

Held

The fund in clause 2 was the primary fund for the payment of the mortgages on the policies, the testator had shown an intention to exonerate the policies from these mortgages in so far as the fund in clause 2 could satisfy them.

Tomlin J:

> 'Under clause 2 of the will there is a disposition under which the testator constitutes a specific fund consisting of freehold and leasehold property, chattels and some ready money as a fund for payment of his debts. He directs the trustee to "sell call in and convert the same into money and out of the moneys provided by such sale calling in and conversion and with and out of my ready money pay my funeral and testamentary expenses and debts."
>
> That fund is not one of the funds mentioned in s35, sub-s2. It is not a direction for payment of debts out of personal estate, or residuary real and personal estate, or residuary real estate. It is a direction for the payment of debts out of a fund to be constituted by the sale of specific property, consisting of freehold

> and leasehold property and chattels. That being so, the question is whether, apart from sub-s2, which does not apply in this particular case, there is a "contrary or other intention" expressed. It is difficult in the extreme to say that, if the testator has constituted a particular fund for payment of debts, he did not so intend, but meant that particular debt in question to be paid out of some other property. It seems to me that when once a testator directs payment of debts out of a specific fund, he has signified a contrary or other intention in respect of any debt which would othewise be payable out of another fund.
>
> Therefore I hold that a contrary intention has been expressed within the meaning of the section, and that the mortgages on the policies must primarily be borne by the fund created by clause 2.'

Gordon, Re [1940] Ch 769 Chancery Division (Bennett J)

The statutory order – property specifically appropriated and property charged

Facts

The testatrix made her will in 1939 by which she gave certain specific legacies and then gave her executors the sum of £50 in trust thereout to pay her debts and funeral and testamentary expenses and to pay any balance to the Rationalist Press Association Ltd. There was no residuary gift. The question arose whether the debts etc were primarily payable out of the £50 or out of the estate undisposed of by will.

Held

There was an intestacy as to the residue and as there was no direction in the will to vary the statutory order of application of assets, the debts etc were primarily payable out of property undisposed of.

Bennett J:

> 'In the present case it is clear that the testatrix has either bequeathed property for the payment of her debts or has bequeathed property charged with the payment of her debts. She has made no other disposition of her property. The facts of the case plainly fall within the reasoning of Maugham J with which, if I may respectfully say so, I entirely agree. Where a solvent testator has made by his will a disposition of property which falls either within para 3 of the Schedule or within para 4 and has made no other disposition of his property and has not otherwise indicated his intentions, there seems to me to be no grounds for a conclusion that such a testator has intended to vary or interfere with or alter the order in which the statute has said that assets are to be applied for the payment of debts and funeral and testamentary expenses.'

Harland-Peck, Re [1941] Ch 182 Court of Appeal (Scott and Luxmore LJJ)

Variation of statutory order – testaztor's right to deal with his/her own estate

Facts

By her will the testatrix provided: 'Subject to the payment of my funeral and testamentary expenses death duties ... and debts and the legacies bequeathed by this will ... I devise and bequeath all the rest and residue of my property ...' to X and Y. The testatrix died in 1939 but one of the residuary legatees had predeceased her.

Held

The order of administration under Part II of Sch 1 to the AEA 1925 did not apply, and the debts were payable out of the whole residuary estate and not out of the lapsed share in exoneration of the remaining share.

Luxmore J:

'... the direction in s34 subs 3, that the order is only to apply subject to the provision of the will means that the provisions of the will must be examined before it can be determined whether the order set out in Part II of the First Schedule is to apply either in its entirety or with or without variations, while para 8 of Part II of the Schedule provides that if the order there set out is applicable the prescribed order may be varied by the will. This may be either by express provision or by implication. It is therefore necessary first to consider whether the will contains provisions which prevent the application of Part II of the First Schedule. The will provides that "subject to the payment" of the various items specified the testatrix devises and bequeathes "all the rest and residue of any property of whatsoever kind or nature wheresoever situate whether real or personal" to the two named persons in equal shares. Since the primary liability of personal estate before real estate has been removed by s32 of the Act and realty and personalty are thereby placed on an equality, it follows that the provision referred to imposes a charge on the residuary personal and real estates in respect of the items specified in such a way that those items must be borne by those estates rateably as between the persons beneficially entitled thereto. The presence of that charge is inconsistent with the payment of the items specified out of the lapsed share of the residuary personal and real estates, since that share can only be ascertained after effect has been given to the charge imposed by the will. As already pointed out, the imposition of such a charge was held to be sufficient to effect a change in the order of administration applicable before the Act in question came into force, and we can see no valid reason why such a charge should not be sufficient to effect a change in the order of administration laid down in Part II of the First Schedule, and in the absence of any such reason we should have had no hesitation, apart from any binding decision to the contrary, in holding that the provision of para I of Part II of the First Schedule to the Act have no application to the administration of the testatrix's estate.'

John, Re [1923] Ch 370 Chancery Division (Farwell J)

Statutory order – property specifically devised or bequeathed

Facts

The testator devised certain property, which was subject to a mortgage to D, and another property, subject to certain legacies to J. The estate was insufficient to meet the pecuniary legacies, debts and expenses.

Held

'Value' for the purposes of para 6 means the value of the property to the testator. Thus the mortgages were deductable since the properties were only valued, less the mortgage debt. However, the legacies were not deductible from the value of the property charged with their payment as that property was worth its market value without any deductions to the testator.

Farwell J:

'... the testator has specifically devised certain properties to certain persons, and the question is how as between them the legacies and expenses are to be borne. Part II provides the various ways in which the property is to be applied for that purpose, and para 6 says property which is specificaly devised or bequeathed is to be applied rateably according to value. The testator had certain property which he devised subject to mortgage created in his lifetime. It is said with regard to the property so devised that the word "value" in para 6 means the value of the property as unincumbered property and not the value of the property in the hands of the testator. The testator had, in fact, in respect of these particular properties, only an equity of redemption, and that is the "value" which, in my judgment, must be taken for this purpose. The "value" cannot mean the actual price which the property would fetch in the open market free from incumbrance; it must mean the value to the testator, and since all he had was the equity of redemption, that is the value which must be taken.

Also, it seems too me that it is quite impossible to read the word "value" in para 6 as meaning the interest the beneficiary takes. It must mean the value of the property to the testatoor. Where the testator imposes on a legatee an obligation to make certain payments thereout as legacies, I cannot read "value" as meaning what the beneficiary is ultimately going to receive from the property. There will, therefore, be a declaration that there be deducted from the probate values the amount of the mortgage on the properties so charged, and that there be no deduction from the value of the properties devised to the defendant, J T John, in respect of the several legacies which under the will he is bound to pay.'

Kempthorne, Re [1930] 1 Ch 268 Court of Appeal (Lord Hanworth MR, Lawrence and Russell LJJ)

Variation of statutory order so as to make debts and expenses payable out of residue as a whole

Facts

The testator bequeathed

> 'all my leasehold property and all my personal estate and effects ... subject to and after the payment of my funeral and testamentary expenses and debts and the legacies bequeathed by this my will ...'

Held

The testator had shown an intention that Part II Sch 1 to the AEA 1925 should not apply to the lapsed shares of this residuary gift since the net amount of the residue available for distribution could not be ascertained until after the debts had been paid. The debts had to be paid out of the residuary gift and afterwards the lapsed share ascertained.

Kensington, Baron , Re [1902] 1 Ch 203 Chancery Division (Farwell J)

Two distinct gifts to same person – one generous, one beneficial – rights of election

Facts

The testator died in 1900 leaving a will made in 1898 by which he devised his freehold properties in London and Middlesex upon certain trusts for his mother and his freehold properties in Wales upon certain trusts for his brothers. He then bequeathed his leaseholds to be held upon trusts and left his residuary personal estate upon trust to pay his funeral and testamentary expenses and debts. At his death the testator had contracted to purchase an estate in Wales for £60,000 and had paid a £4,000 deposit. He also owned a leasehold house in Portland Place subject to a mortgage of £10,000 but which only realised £8,000. The question arose as to who should bear these deficits.

Held

The burden of paying the balance of the purchase price of the estate in Wales fell upon the devise of freehold in Wales, and the mortgage on the house in Portland Place fell upon the bequest of leaseholds.

Farwell J:

> '... the rule of law is well settled that where there are two distinct gifts to the same person, one being onerous and the other beneficial, the donee may disclaim the onerous gift and take the other. If however, the onerous and beneficial property are included in the same gift, prima facie the donee cannot disclaim the onerous and accept the beneficial property, but must take the whole or none. First of all, therefore, as a question of construction, I have to consider whether or not there is one gift of an aggregate whole.'

Lamb, Re [1929] 1 Ch 723 Chancery Division (Eve J)

Solvent estates – the statutory order – property undisposed of by will

Facts

A testator left his residuary estate to be divided equally between four persons including his brother, Thomas, who predeceased him. The question arose whether the debts, funeral and testamentary expenses of the testator's estate were primarily payable out of the lapsed share or otherwise.

Held

A share of residue which lapses because the person entitled to it predeceases the testator is 'property undisposed of by will' and therefore primarily liable for the debts and expenses.

Eve J:

> 'It was argued on behalf of the next-of-kin the "property of the deceased undisposed of by will" must be confined to property to dispose of which no attempt has been made by will, and ought not to be read as including a share of residue which has lapsed by reason of the legatee's death in the lifetime of the testator ... But the language is plain and unambiguous – a lapsed share of residue is properly described as property undisposed of by will ...'

Martin, Re [1955] Ch 698 Chancery Division (Danckwerts J)

Incidence of pecuniary legacies – pre-1926 rules not applied

Facts

By his will the testator bequeathed two pecuniary legacies and then left all his real estate to his daughter, Kathleen. There then followed a gift of the residue of the personal estate to trustees upon trust for sale with a direction to pay all debts and expenses thereout and divide the balance among named beneficiaries. The testator subsequently revoked the gift of real estate to his daughter Kathleen, but did not dispose of that property otherwise. Consequently, it was undisposed of at his death and fell within paragraph 1 of the statutory order. The question arose whether the pecuniary legacies fund should be retained out of the realty in para 1 before the residuary personalty in paragraph 2.

Held

The pecuniary legacies fund was to be retained out of the realty in paragraph 1.

Danckwerts J:

> '... the question remains whether the legacies are to be paid primarily out of the undisposed of real estate or whether, as indeed was the old law in operation before the Administration of Estates Act, 1925, came into force, the legacies are charged primarily on the personal estate.
>
> I have been referred to a large number of cases very properly by counsel in this case, to whose arguments I am very much indebted, but there is no case, except *Re Atkinson* [1930] 1 Ch 47, so far as it goes, which really applies, in my opinion, to the present case. This is a case which I have to consider to some extent without much guidance. I do not propose to go through all the cases, though I have considered them carefully in the course of counsel's argument, but they are all distinguishable in some respect or other (except as I shall mention presently).
>
> *Re Thompson* [1936] Ch 676 a decision of Clauson J, was not quite the same as the present, because in that case the testator, after bequeathing an annuity and certain legacies, devised and bequeathed all his real and personal estate not otherwise devised or bequeathed to certain persons, and he left personal estate, and real estate of considerably greater value. In that case there was no question of intestacy, but there was

merely a common fund comprised of the real and personal estate; and the question was as there was no direction in the will how the legacies were to be borne, whether the Administration of Estates Act 1925 threw the burden of the legacies rateably on the real property and the personal property, or whether the old law applied, which made the personal estate the primary fund to meet the legacies. Clauson J held that the law in force before the Administration of Estates Act 1925 as regards the primary fund for payment of legacies as between the personal and the real estate, had not been altered by s34(3) and para 2 and para 8(b) of Part 2 of Sch 1 to that Act, that the personal estate must be treated as primarily liable, and that recourse would not be made to the real estate until the personal estate had been exhausted ...

... there Clauson J was dealing with para 2 which directed the retention of funds for legacies out of a mixed fund, and he decided that there was nothing in the paragraph which made the personalty or realty primarily bear the burden in respect of that obligation, and therefore the old law applied, and he applied it accordingly. That paragraph is not one which applies to the present case; it is para 1 which applies.

I will mention in passing that I followed that in *Re Beaumont's Will Trusts* [1950] Ch 462 which was very different from the present case, because there was in that case a trust for sale, and there was not, as there is in the present case, an intestacy as regards a particular asset of the testator's estate, but merely an intestacy as regards a share of the fund given in the will. Therefore, as it seems to me, *Re Beaumont* has no application to the case which I have to decide now. There are no other cases which give me any real assistance at all.

What is the result, therefore, of the provision contained in para 1 of Part 2 of Sch 1 to the Administration of Estates Act 1925? That paragraph, just as in the case of s33(2) directs that the undisposed of property of the deceased is to be the fund for the debts, and so on, subject to the retention thereout of a fund sufficient to meet any pecuniary legacies. It has been argued that that merely requires the setting aside of a fund, and contains no provision for the payment of the legacies out of that fund. *Re Thompson* was called in aid to that extent to show that a mere direction to set aside did not settle the matter of payment, but I am unable too see what is the object of setting aside a fund unless that fund is to be used for the payment of the legacies for which it is to provide. Under para 2 the fund has to be set aside, and, indeed, there was no real dispute in *Re Thompson* that that fund was the fund which was to meet the legacies. The point in *Re Thompson* was whether the fund for that purpose had to be taken wholly out of the personal estate, or had to be taken rateably out of the real and personal estate of the deceased.

It seems to me that here I am dealing simply with one assets, the undisposed of real estate, and out of that undisposed of real estate a fund is to be raised to provide for the pecuniary legacies and if the fund is not to be raised for the payment of the pecuniary legacies, it is difficult to see what reason there is for setting aside the fund. Therefore, I am necessarily driven to the conclusion that according to the provisions contained in para 1 of Part 2 of Sch 1 to the Act, the proper fund to meet the legacies in the present case is the undisposed-of property.'

Meldrum, Re [1952] Ch 208 Chancery Division (Upjohn J)

Variation of statutory order – property specifically appropriated and property charged

Facts

A testator made a bequest in his will by which he gave to A

> 'the sum of £500 for her immediate expenses ... and all moneys standing to the credit of my current account at Lloyds Bank at Dartmouth ... and also my War and National Savings Certificates and the residue of my deposit account at Lloyds Bank Dartmouth after all legacies, debts, funeral and other expenses have been liquidated but excluding death duties and testamentary expenses'.

The testator then devised and bequeathed 'all the residue of my property to my trustees upon trust, after discharging death duties and testamentary expenses thereout, to pay the income' etc. The question arose whether the statutory order had been varied.

Held

The order had been varied because the testator had shown a clear intention that his debts funeral and other expenses, but not his death duties and testamentary expenses, should be paid out of the deposit account primarily. To this extent only there was a variation.

Upjohn J:

> '... I turn to the authorities to see whether there is anything in them which prevents me from giving effect to what, I think, are the intentions of the testator, which, in my judgment, clearly vary the order of application of assets laid down in the Administration of Estates Act 1925, sched 1 Part II. Counsel for the second defendant relied on the decision of Maugham J, in *Re Kempthorne* [1930] 1 Ch 268, which was overruled by the Court of Appeal, but only on a point of construction of that particular will. Referring to para 3 and para 4 of Sched 1 Part II, to the Act of 1925, Maugham J said:
>
> > "Then come two further paragraphs, which I think are somewhat difficult to understand, in relation to the subject-matter."
>
> After reading para 3 and para 4, Maugham J continued:
>
> > "Now in both of those cases it is to be noticed that the legislature is assuming that the testator by his will has specificaly appropriated in one case, or devised or bequeathed in the other, property for the payment of debts; or that he has charged with payment of debts specific property, or some property, under a general description, or devised or bequeathed property subject to a charge for payment of debts, and I cannot help concluding that those two paragraphs mean that the fact that the testator has done one of those things is not *per se* to constitute, to use the words of s34(3), a provision in the will which operates to alter the order of application which is specified in Part II of the Schedule."
>
> That statement of the law was acted on by Bennett J in *Re Gordon* [1940] Ch 769 and was treated by him as being binding notwithstanding that the decision of Maugham J was reversed on the particular facts of that case. As I understand Maugham J he is saying that, having regard to the presence of para 1 and para 2 in Sched. 1 Part II, an indication in the will that a particular piece of property is to be charged with payment of debts is not sufficient to enable one to assume that the testator is intending to alter the order of application of assets, because, if that were so, one could never give effect to these paragraphs even where there was a partial intestacy, bringing in para 1, or a gift of residue (as in this case), bringing in para 2. I think that Roxburgh J recognises that in *Re James* [1947] Ch 256. Nevertheless, it seems to me to remain a question purely of construction of each will whether or not the testator has varied the order of application of assets or not.'

Midgley, Re [1955] Ch 576 Chancery Division (Harman J)

Incidence of pecuniary legacies – pre-1926 rules not applied

Facts

By her will the testatrix gave a number of pecuniary legacies and then left her residuary estate on trust for sale to pay her debts etc and the balance to be divided among six named persons in equal shares. Less than year after making the will the testatrix executed a codicil thereto by which she revoked the one-sixth share given to a residuary legatee. It was conceded that the debts were payable out of the whole of the residue before division into six equal shares. This meant that the one-sixth share of residue revoked by the codicil fell into paragraph 1. The question arose whether the pecuniary legacy should be drawn from the one-sixth share in paragraph 1 only in the absence of any specific direction thereon in the will.

Held

The pecuniary legacies were payable primarily out of the property falling within paragraph 1.

Harman J:

'The question now arises: Out of what sum are legacies to be paid? Having regard to the form of the will, it is clear that the debts, funeral and testamentary expenses are to be paid out of the whole fund before the division of the shares, and that is conceded, but the trust for sale created by the will says nothing about legacies and they are not charged by the will on any specific portion of the estate.

I am to look, as it seems to me, to s34 of the Administration of Estates Act 1925. Section 34(3) deals with the method of administering the estate of a deceased person who is solvent. The section only purports to apply to the method of the discharge of the funeral, testamentary and administration expenses, debts and liabilities and there is nothing in the section about legacies. So far apparently the law about payment of legacies has not been altered, but in Para 2 of Sch 1, referred to in s34(3) as controlling the order of administration, I find:

> "Order of application of assets where the estate is solvent. 1. Property of the deceased undisposed of by will, subject to the retention thereout of a fund sufficient to meet any pecuniary legacies."

Therefore, one has first to retain out of the property undisposed of a fund sufficient to meet any pecuniary legacies, and one has to pay the debts, testamentary expenses and so forth out of the rest of the undisposed of property. What is one to do then with the fund that has been retained thereout? The answer, it seems to me, is that one must pay the pecuniary legacies because it has been retained to meet them. It is, if I may say so, a tortuous way of legislation, but that is what I should have thought it inevitably meant and so, indeed, Danckwerts J concluded recently in *Re Martin* [1955] Ch 698. It is quite true that in that case there was undisposed of real estate, and no trust for sale which applied to it. Any trust for sale would have failed because of the failure of the gift. Danckwerts J said:

> "It seems to me that here I am dealing simply with one asset, the undisposed of real estate, and out of that undisposed of real estate a fund is to be raised to provide for the pecuniary legacies and if the fund is not to be raised for the payment of the pecuniary legacies, it is difficult to see what reason there is for setting aside the fund. Therefore, I am necessarily driven to the conclusion that according to the provisions contained in para 1 of Part 2 of Sch 1 to the Act, the proper fund to meet the legacies in the present case is the undisposed of property."

That seems to me, if I may say so, to be right.

I am told, however, that that does not apply in a case where there is a trust for sale and I am referred to a former decision of the same judge, *Re Beaumont's Will Trusts* [1950] Ch 462. The end of the headnote reads as follows:

> "Held, that, in effect, no provision at all was made by s34(3) with regard to such things as legacies so that the law in force before 1926 applied to the legacies in question, and the pecuniary and specific legacies and the duty on them were all payable out of the whole estate before the division of the residuary estate into four equal parts."

The learned judge purports to follow *Re Thompson* [1936] Ch 676. The argument that prevailed in *Beaumont's case* was apparently that a trust for sale imposed by the will excluded the Act altogether, because it excluded s33 of the Act. I confess that I do not follow that argument. The decision of Roxburgh J in *Re Gillett's Will Trusts* [1950] Ch 102 was not apparently cited to the learned judge. In the latter case Roxburgh J (it is true on some concessions from counsel), held that para 1 of Part 2 of Sch 1 made the legacies payable out of the undisposed of property. That rule may not apply when there is no intestacy apparent at the death of the testator. I am not suggesting that anything I say covers that case, but where, as here, it is apparent that the testator is to some extent intestate at his death and where no contrary intention appears from the will, then, as it seems to me, the effect of para 1 of Part 2 of Sch 1 applies to make the pecuniary legacies payable out of the undisposed of property, and I so hold.'

Palmer (deceased) (A Debtor), Re [1994] 3 WLR 420 Court of Appeal (Balcombe, Evans and Roch LJJ)

Insolvent estate – joint tenancy – whether half-share passes by survivorship or severed by insolvency administration order

Facts

In 1989 the deceased, a debtor, and his wife became joint tenants of a house. After the deceased's death in November 1990 large claims against his estate caused his executor to present a petition for an insolvency administration order. This was made in August 1991. A trustee of the estate was appointed in October 1991. The trustee was granted a declaration pursuant to s283 of the Insolvency Act 1986 as modified by paragraph 12 of Part II of Schedule 1 to the Administration of Insolvent Estates of Deceased Persons Order 1986. The deceased's estate included a beneficial tenancy in common with his wife in the house prior to his death, thereby serving retrospectively the joint tenancy with his wife before the deceased's death. The widow appealed.

Held

Appeal allowed. The power conferred did not enable the Order to extend the ordinary meaning of 'estate of a deceased person' so as to include within it property which would not otherwise have formed part of that estate.

Evans LJ:

> 'The respondent's submission in the present case is that the insolvency administration order which was made on 17 August 1991 is deemed by paragraph 12 of Part II of Schedule 1 to the Order of 1986 to take effect for the purposes of the vesting of property in the trustee as if it had been made on 22 November 1990, the date of Mr Palmer's death. To this statutory fiction, it is submitted, must be added the common law fiction that the Order was made at the earliest moment of that day, and therefore whilst Mr Palmer was alive.
>
> At this point in my judgment, the operation of the fiction comes into conflict, not only with common sense, but with the true effect of the statutory provisions themselves. Section 421 of the Act of 1986 alone gives power to regulate the administration of the insolvent estates of deceased persons. The Act itself provides for the affairs of living persons who become bankrupt. Mr Palmer did not die a bankrupt, nor is a deceased person, whose estate becomes insolvent, necessarily insolvent when he dies. (Many examples are possible of contingent liabilities which may accrue even years after death.) Nothing in the Act or in the Order, in my judgment, empowers the court to make an insolvency administration order in respect of the estate of a person who is not deceased, nor can any rule of law be relied upon to produce the fictional result that a person was dead at a time when in fact he was still alive. On a true analysis, in my view, this would be inconsistent with the lack of jurisdiction findings in *In re Seaford (decd)* [1968] P 53. In any event, it would produce an unrealistic result which, in my judgment, it should not be permitted to do.
>
> The respondent cannot claim more, in my judgment, than that the insolvency administration took effect, on a true construction of the statutory provisions, at the moment of Mr Palmer's death. His interest in the joint tenancy of the property could only continue whilst he was alive. The order could not take effect when he died. It follows that the interest was not affected by the order. It never formed part of his estate.'

Comment

This was clearly an important decision in the interests of common sense and fairness.

Petty, Re [1929] 1 Ch 726 Chancery Division (Astbury J)

Variation of statutory order – testator's right to deal with his/her own estate

Facts
A testator devised and bequeathed his residuary real and personal estate to his trustees upon trust for sale and conversion and out of the proceeds to pay his funeral and testamentary expenses and debts and legacies and to divide the balance of residue into two parts, one which he gave to his wife. The share given to the wife lapsed as she predeceased the testator. The question arose whether the statutory order had been varied.

Held
The provisions of the will in this case clearly threw the payment of the debts and expenses on the residue and they were not primarily payable out of the lapsed share of residue.

Astbury J:

> '... I cannot believe that the statute intended to interfere with the testaor's right to deal with his own estate as he liked. Here it is plain that he created a mixed fund for the payment of funeral and testamentary expenses debts and legacies, and there was no undisposed of moiety of the balance of residue until those expenses and debts were ascertained and paid. In those circumstances the estate must be administered according to the testator's directions and the expenses and debts are not thrown primarily on the lapsed moiety.'

Taylor's Estate, Re [1969] 2 Ch 245 Durham Chancery Court (Salt QC Chancellor)

Incidence of pecuniary legacies – pre-1926 rules still applicable

Facts
By her will the testatrix bequeathed, inter alia, five pecuniary legacies and then devised and bequeathed the residuary estate to her executor on trust for sale to pay her debts and to divide the remainder equally amongst certain named nephews and nieces of the testatrix. One of the named nephews died before the testatrix and as there was no direction in the will as to the incidence of the pecuniary legacies the question arose whether they were payable (a) out of the residuary estate as a whole, (b) out of the lapsed and undisposed share of the residue, or (c) in some other way.

Held
The statutory order as to the payment of the debts had been altered; they were primarily payable out of the residue before ascertaining the undisposed of share, the pecuniary legacies fund would be set aside before this and it would be set aside in accordance with the old rules as there was nothing in the Administration of Estates Act to alter these.

Thompson, Re [1936] Ch 676 Chancery Division (Clauson J)

Incidence of pecuniary legacies – pre-1926 rules remain applicable

Facts
The testator left certain pecuniary legacies and an annuity in his will and then devised and bequeathed all his real and personal estate not otherwise disposed of to two hospitals. There was both real and personal estate falling witin the residuary gift but the personal estate was insufficient to meet the

pecuniary legacies in full. The question arose whether the pecuniary legacies could be paid out of the realty. As the residuary gift was in a form to which the rule in *Greville* v *Browne* applied the Court was asked (i) whether the realty was only liable in aid of the personalty, thus effectively concluding that the old rules stll applied or, (ii) whether the realty and personalty should be liable rateably, ie the old rules no longer applied.

Held

The realty was only to be used in aid of the personalty to meet the pecuniary legacies fund. There had been no change made in the rules on the incidence of pecuniary legacies by the 1925 legislation.

Clauson J:

> '... the law which operates under these circumstances is well settled, and I will take a statement of it from the headnote of *Re Boards* [1895] 1 Ch 499:
>
> > "When a testator bequeaths legacies and then bequeaths the residue of his real and personal estate, the legacies are charged upon the real estate or its proceeds, but they are payable primarily out of the personality, unless the testator directs that they are to be paid out of the mixed fund, in which case they are payable rateably out of realty and personalty."
>
> So it follows that the strict way to administer these assets is to apply the personal estate in paying legacies so far as it will go, and in so far as there is left something payable in respect of the legacies, that will be charged on the realty. The materiality of the matter is this, that in so far as legacies are made payable out of realty certain estate duties in respect of the realty have to be borne by so much of the proceeds of sale of the realty as is applied and appropriated for the legacies or annuity. That is the materiality of the matter. As far as regards the beneficial interests the matter is of no practical importance.
>
> It is suggested that, having regard to certain provisions, to which I will draw attention in a moment, of the Administration of Estate Act 1925, the rule stated in *Re Boards* is no longer law. It is suggested that by that Act a vast alteration has been made, which results in the law now being, so it is suggested, that, if a testator bequeaths legacies and then bequeaths the residue of his real and personal estate, the legacies are charged on the real estate or its proceeds and are not payable primarily out of personalty, but are payable out of personalty and realty *pro rata,* according to the proportions of personalty and realty. The suggestion that that is now the law is founded on this, that by the Administration of Estate Act 1924, s34(3) it is provided that where the estate of a deceased person is solvent his real and personal estate shall, subject to rules of court and the provisions thereinafter contained as to charges on property of the deceased, and to the provisions, if any, contained in his will, be applicable towards the discharge of the funeral, testamentary and administration expenses, debts and liabilities payable thereout, in the order mentioned in Sch 1 Part II to this Act: and Part II provides this. It provides in the first clause for the case of the deceased having died intestate or leaving property undisposed of by will. But it is the second clause with which I have to deal and I propose to make no further reference to the first clause. The schedule is headed "Order of application of assets where the estate is solvent", and Part II, clause 2, is in these terms:
>
> > "Property of the deceased not specifically devised or bequeathed but included (either by a specific or general description) in a residuary gift, subject to the retention out of such property of a fund sufficient to meet any pecuniary legacies, so far as not provided for as aforesaid."
>
> That means so far as not provided for by part of the estate in respect of which the testator died intestate.
>
> It is suggested that the effect of that provision is to alter the law and to provide that the fund which is to be retained out of the residuary realty and personalty in order to meet pecuniary legacies is to be retained in this way, that a proportionate part is to be retained out of realty and personalty *pro rata* the amount of the realty and personalty respectively. The provision does not say that. And the provision is not concerned with any such matter. The provision is concerned with the way in which funeral, testamentary and administration expenses, debts and liabilities are to be met. There is no indication that there is any intention to alter the law in regard to the rights of legatees as against those interested in the

residuary real estate, and I can see no foundation for the suggestion that the provision has in any way altered the law as laid down in *Re Boards*. It was suggested to me that a contrary view had been taken, if not in any decided case, by textbook writers. I have had the advantage of having my attention drawn to the statements in the textbooks, and I think it is only fair to the textbook writers to say that I cannot find anything in the textbooks which it is legitimate for me to refer, which suggests that the law has been altered in the manner in which I have spoken. It is true that my attention has been drawn to a statement in a book which cannot be treated as a textbook carrying any authority, as it is not edited by a member of the Bar, in which unquestionably there is a statement to that effect. But although I thought it only fair to look at the book in which that statement is made, I was not able to find on what it was founded, and counsel has not been able to suggest on what it was founded. I see no reason to believe that the law is different since the Act than it was before.'

Wilson, Re [1967] Ch 53 Chancery Division (Pennycuick J)

The statutory order – property included in a residuary gift

Facts

A testatrix made a will in 1962 and a codicil thereto by which she bequeathed a large number of pecuniary legacies amounting to £27,900 in all. The will concluded 'I devise and bequeath all my real estate and the residue of my personal estate to my said daughter ... absolutely.' The will contained no express directions as to the payment of debts and administration expenses and the estate was insufficient after paying all the outgoings in full to provide for the pecuniary legacies in full.

Held

Until 1925 all devises were, from their nature, specific, but this did not affect the subject-matter of a general or universal gift of real estate which fell within para 2 of Part II of Sch 1 to the AEA 1925. The language of para 2 clearly contemplated that there might be a real property which was not the subject of a specific gift but was included in the residuary gift and in this case a devise of all my residuary estate was such a residuary gift.

Pennycuick J:

'Apart from authority the natural view, it seems to me, is that where a testator makes a general or universal gift of his real estate, that is "all my property", the subject-matter of that gift falls under the second head (para 2 of Sched 1) that is, as being "property not specifically devised but included ... in a residuary gift". A gift in this form does not indicate any particlar item of property but covers all items of real property to which the testator may be entitled at his death. In ordinary language today lawyers would, I think, not inaptly describe such a gift as a residuary devise. They would certainly not describe it as a specific devise.

Mr Mummery, for Mrs Lambert, advanced certain arguments to the contrary. His first argument was that all devises are from their nature specific. It seems that this was indeed so, at any rate until 1925. See in particular *Hensman* v *Fryer* (1867) 3 Ch App 420 and *Lancefield* v *Iggulden* (1874) 10 Ch App 136.

On the other hand, as I have said, it is clear that Part II of the Schedule contemplates that real property may be capable of being comprised in a residuary gift. I do no think that in the context of the First Schedule to that Act one should put such a construction on the words "specifically devised" and "residuary gift" as would in effect deprive the class of residuary gifts of realty of any possible content at all.

Mr Mummery referred me to dicta in the two post-1925 cases in support of his argument on this point. In *In re Rowe* [1941] Ch 343 the relevant words of the will were: "I devise all my real estate and bequeath all the residue of my personal estate" to certain persons. Farwell J after deciding the question on a different ground, added:

> "Held (2) pecuniary legacies to be released out of all personal property even if insufficient to meet them, then pay debts etc. out of real estate, and pecuniary legacies to be paid out of fund rateably ... for according to the construction which I place upon this particular will the real estate is devised, not as part of the residue, but as a specific devise to the named persons, the residue which is given being the residue of the personal estate."

In *In Re Ridley* [1950] Ch 415, the relevant words were:

> "I give free of all death duties all my real estate which includes Manmead Covert and Maperton and my advowsons to the said GN absolutely ... I give the residue of my property including property over which I have a general power of appointment to the said GN ..."

Harman J pointed out [at 418, 419] that although by clause 7 the testatrix gives all her real estate, by clause 8 she gives the residue of her property, and that he describes as a "true residuary clause".

After referring to *Hensman* v *Fryer* and *Lancefield* v *Iggulden* he says [at 421]:

> "In my judgment, clause 6 of this will, although in a sense it contains a general devise of realty, is not a residuary gift. I cannot think that a clause placed as this one was, even though it might have a certain sweeping-up effect by virtue of section 24 of the Wills Act, really was in any sense a residuary gift within the meaning of the Act of 1925. I am supported in that view by a dictum of Farwell J in *In re Rowe* ..."

He then refers to that case. He concludes [at 422]:

> "If that be right, it is clear that the present case is a stronger one and, although I am not bound by that decision because it was not necessary for the conclusion at which he arrived, it is nonetheless a decision of that judge (Farwell J) and I should be very sorry to differ from it. I agree with the reasoning: I cannot think that clause 6 was what is meant in this schedule as being a residuary gift, and if necessary I should be prepared so to hold."

I must, of course, pay great respect to those two dicta, but it is important to observe that Harman J considered that it was clause 8 and not clause 6 which was the true residuary gift. On the best consideration I can give it I do not think it would be right for me to hold that for the purpose of paragraph 2 in Part II of the First Schedule there is no such thing as a residuary gift of realty and that all realty must be treated as specifically devised.

Mr Mummery's second point was that a devise is only residuary if there has been a previous devise, so that the residuary devise operates upon what remains after the previous devise has taken effect. That is grammatically a good point. On the other hand, the expression "residuary gift" is habitually used to denote a general or universal gift and, as I have said, it seems to me natural to treat the words "residuary gift" here.

The only alternative in the context of paragraph 2 is to treat a general or universal gift as a specific gift, and that I should have thought certainly it was not. This construction would produce an wholly illogical result, that is, as regards payment of debts; on the one hand a residuary devise following a specific devise, that would be a residuary gift for the purpose of paragraph 2; on the other hand, a general or universal devise would be a specific devise and would fall, not within paragraph 2, but paragraph 6. I cannot think that is right.'

Worthington, Re [1933] Ch 771 Court of Appeal (Lord Hanworth MR, Romer LJ)

Administration of Estates Act 1925 s33 – incidence of pecuniary legacies – insolvent estates

Facts

By her will the testatrix left a number of pecuniary legacies and then disposed of the residue of her estate to two named beneficiaries one of whom died before her. The question arose whether the legacies were payable out of the lapsed share first and if so, what property forming part of the lapsed share should be used to meet them. Bennett J at first instance, held that the legacies were payable out of the general estate before the shares of residue were ascertained. On appeal:

Held

The legacies were payable primarily out of the undisposed of share of residue and as regards realty and personalty compromised therein, it was to be used rateably to meet the pecuniary legacies.

Lord Hanworth MR:

> 'Having regard to those sections (ss 33(2)(7), 34(3) of and Schedule 1, Part II, para 1, AEA 1925) which I have read, is there any reason for the distinction made by Bennett J between debts and funeral expenses on the one hand and the pecuniary legacies on the other? The learned judge seems to have read the will as providing for the payment of the legacies first and to have thought that the residue was not to be ascertained until after they had been paid. But the provisions of the statute indicate that unless there is some provision in the will which negatives the prescribed order of administration, that order of administration must apply to both legacies and to debts.
>
> The learned judge seems to have thought that because of the specific reference to legacies in the will there was an indication of an intention that the statutory order should not apply to them. But, after all, if legacies are given by a will, there must be a specific reference to them, and I do not see how that be sufficient to alter the statutory order of administration.'

11 Distribution of the Estate

Akerman, Re [1891] 3 Ch 212 Chancery Division (Kekewich J)

Executor's power of set-off – scope of power

Facts

By his will the testator left each of his sons, Henry, William and James, a specific devise or bequest and then he devised and bequeathed the residue of his estate on trust for sale to pay his debts and expenses and to divide the balance in seven equal parts, with a one-seventh share given to each of his three above-named sons. Each of the three sons owed money to the testator at his death but these debts were statute barred. The question arose whether they were bound to bring into account what they owed the estate against either their specific gifts or their shares of the residue.

Held

The power of set-off did not apply to the specific gifts but it did apply to residuary gifts and it applied in the circumstances even though the debts were statute barred.

Kekewich J:

> '... on the other hand, a debt due to the estate of a testator is part of the residue. It has to be paid in whole or in part, in whole, if it can be recovered, in order that the residue may be constituted and there is, therefore, a clear distinction between a specific legacy and a residuary legacy so far as concerns a debt due from the legatee to the estate. No case has been cited to show and it seems to me to be contrary to principle to hold, that there can be a right of retainer in respect of the debts owing from a specific legatee to the estate of the testator.
>
> ... the principle is to be found laid down in *Cherry* v *Boultbee* (1839) 4 My & Cr 442 in the passage to which I have just referred, and also in *Courtenay* v *Williams* (1844) 3 Hare 539 and no doubt, if search were made, it would be found to have been laid down in many other cases. It is thus. A person who owes an estate money, that is to say, who is bound to increase the general mass of the estate by a contribution of his own, cannot claim contribution which completes it. Nothing in truth is retained by the representative of the estate; nothing is in strict language set-off; but the contributor is paid by holding in his own hand a part of the mass, which if the mass were completed, he would receive back. That is expanding what the Lord Chancellor calls in *Cherry* v *Boultbee* a conformity with what the Lord Chancellor, rather than a set-off and is in conformity with what the Lord Chancellor, Lord Lyndhurst, in *Courtenay* v *Williams* says,
>
> > "The defendants, the legatee's demand (the Court says) is in respect of the testator's assets, without which the executor is not liable; and it is very just and equitable for the executor to say, that the defendant, the legatee has so much of the assets already in his own hands, and consequently is satisfied pro tanto."
>
> Why should not that be applied to a case like this where the property is put together and the whole is given to the same person upon the same trusts, both for payment of debts and other deductions and for division among the same persons? The principle is the same. The contributor to the mass is in precisely the same position whether the mass is held by trustees or by an executor, and it would, to my mind, be introducing mere technicality into the principle ...
>
> ... therefore, I think that if there is a debt payable by a residuary legatee under such circumstances as

exist here, that debt must, for the purposes of computation, be included in the residue and – again for the purposes of computation, treated as part of the share going to the legatee debtor.'

Attenborough* v *Solomon [1913] AC 76 House of Lords (Viscount Haldane LC, Lords Atkinson and Shaw)

Assents to pure personality inferred from conduct

Facts

By his will the testator appointed his two sons A A and J D Solomon to be his executors and trustees and devised and bequeathed his residuary estate to them to hold on trust for sale and divide the same among all his children in equal shares. The testator died in March 1878 and within a year the executors paid all the debts and specific and pecuniary legacies and passed the residuary account, but they did not distribute the residuary estate. In 1892 A A Solomon pledged silver plate belonging to the residuary estate with Attenborough & Sons, a firm of pawnbrokers, to secure a personal loan. The pawnbrokers acted in good faith. A A Solomon died in 1907 and after his death the pledge of silver was discovered. The question arose whether the pawnbrokers had obtained a good title to the silver. If A A Solomon had pledged it to them as executor they were safe as the powers of executors to dispose of personalty are joint and several. But, if it was a pledge by him as a trustee, then their title was bad as trustee's power of disposal was joint.

Held

The proper inference to be drawn from the facts was that at the date of the pledge, the silver was held by A A Solomon as trustee. The passage of time and the passing of residuary accounts within one year of death supported this inference.

Viscount Haldane LC:

> '... the position of an executor is a peculiar one. He is appointed by the will, but then, by virtue of his office, by the operation of law and not under the bequest in the will, he takes a title to the personal property of the testator, which vests in him plenum dominium over the testator's chattels. He takes that, I say, by virtue of his office. The will becomes operative so far as its dispositions of personalty are concerned only if and when the executor assents to those dispositions. It is true that by virtue of his office he has a general power to sell or pledge for the purpose of paying debts and getting in the money value of the estate. He is executor and he remains executor for an indefinite time. Authorities were cited to us to the effect that an executor can sell at a period long after the death of the testator, and that where it is a question of conveyancing, as for instance in the case of the sale of leaseholds by the executor the purchaser is not entitled to make requisitions as to whether debts remain unpaid, because the executor's office remains intact and he may exercise his functions at any time. That is true as a general principle and I have no comment to make upon it except that it is qualified by another principle which is this. The office of executor remains with its powers attached, but the property which he (the executor) had originally in the chattels that devolved upon him, and over which these powers extended, does not necessarily remain. So soon as he has assented, and this he may do informally and the assent may be inferred from his conduct, the dispositions of the will become operative, and then the beneficiaries have vested in them the property in those chattels. The transfer is made not by the mere force of the assent of the executor, but by virtue of the dispositions of the will which have become operative because of this assent.
>
> Now, my Lords, in view of the residuary account passed as it was and in the form it was, in view of the evidence of Mr J D Solomon, and in view of the fourteen years which have passed since the testator died before the time when Mr A A Solomon made the pledge to the appellants in 1892, I am of the opinion that the true inference to be drawn from the facts is that the executors considered that they had

> done all that was due from them as executors by 1879, and were content when the residuary account was passed that the dispositions of the will should take effect. That is the inference I draw from the residuary account; and the inference is strengthened when I consider the lapse of time since then, and that in the interval nothing was done by them purporting to be an exercise of power as executors. My Lords, if this be so, this appeal must be disposed of on footing that in point of fact the executors assented at a very early date to the dispositions of the will taking effect. It follows that under these dispositions the residuary estate, including the chattels in question, became vested in the trustees as trustees ...'

Benjamin, Re [1902] 1 Ch 723 Chancery Division (Joyce J)

Distribution of estate – presumed death of named beneficiary.

Facts

The testator had 13 children and by his will made in 1891 he left his residuary estate in equal shares to such of his children who should be living at his death . One of the children, P D Benjamin, was last seen on 1 September 1892 at Aix-la-Chapelle departing on a train apparently for London. Nothing more was ever heard of him. The testator died on 25 June 1893 and the executors of the testator's will sought directions as to how P D Benjamin's share should be dealt with or disposed of by them. The executors sought an order giving them liberty to distribute the estate as if P D Benjamin had predeceased his father.

Held

The order sought would be granted.

Joyce J:

> 'I think in this case that Philip David Benjamin must be presumed to be dead. There is no reason why he should hesitate to come home now, although there might have been at first. The question is as to when he died. If he is to be presumed to be dead, I think the case of *Re Walker* (1871) LR 7 Ch App 120 distinctly applies, and the onus of proof is on the administrator. He has failed to adduce any evidence to show that P D Benjamin survived the testator. I myself consider it highly probable that he died on September 1, 1892, or at all events shortly after. I am clearly of the opinion that the onus is on those claiming under him to prove that he survived the testator. In my opinion, therefore, the trustees are at liberty to distribute. I am anxious, however, not to do anything which would prevent his representative from making any claim if evidence of his death at any other time should be subsequently forthcoming. I shall not, therefore, declare that he is dead ...'

Collin's Will Trusts, Re [1971] 1 WLR 37 Chancery Division (Brightman J)

Expenses of transfer – effect of exercise of power of selection.

Facts

The testator made a will under which he made several bequests of articles of furniture and personal effects to named beneficiaries as they should select. After the death of the testator his executors spent considerable sums in insuring and storing the furniture as it had been in rented accommodation before his death. The question arose whether the power of selection had any effect on this.

Held

The expenses of preservation incurred prior to the time of selection fall upon the residue.

Brightman J:

> '... since the death of the testator the executors have spent money on storing and insuring ... the furniture and effects left by the testator ... The question now arises whether the storage and insurance expenses in relation to those articles of furniture and personal effects, as may in due course of time be selected by the indicated beneficiaries ... ought to fall on the capital of the residue, or on the income of the residue, or on the particular beneficiary who makes the selection ... I start by directing my mind solely to such articles of furniture and personal effects as may in due course of time be selected by ... the indicated beneficiaries. In the normal case there can be no doubt that the title of the beneficiary stems, not directly from the will, but from the act of selection; just as in the case of a fund subject to a discretionary trust or power vested in the trustees or to a general power of appointment, the title of the beneficiary stems from the act of selection by the trustee or from the instrument of appointment. In those circumstances it seems to me that logically if the subject-matter of the power of selection had been income producing any income produced between the date of death and the date of selection would have belonged to the residue and not to the beneficiary in whose favour the selection was made; the income in such a case accrued prior to the moment of time at which the title of the beneficiary was created.
>
> I therefore reach the conclusion that in a case such as the present, where persons are given a power of selection so that the title of the beneficiary stems from the selection, had there been any profits ante-dating the time of selection, those profits would have belonged to the residue ...
>
> Accordingly, the expenses of preservation, such as storage and insurance, so far as incurred, prior to the time of selection fall upon the residue and not upon the person making the selection ...'

Commissioner of Stamp Duties (Queensland)* v *Livingston [1965] AC 694 Privy Council (Viscount Radcliffe, Lords Reid, Evershed, Pearce and Upjohn)

Vesting of subject matter of gift under a will – need for an assent

Facts

The testator died domiciled in New South Wales and by his will he left all his estate to his widow absolutely. The estate comprised both real and personal property situated in Queensland and in New South Wales. The widow died before the administration of the testator's estate had been completed; she left no will. The Commissioner of Stamp Duties for Queensland claimed that he was entitled to succession duty on the property in Queensland left to the widow in the will. The relevant statute charged succession duty on 'every devolution by law of any beneficial interest in property ... upon the death of any person ...'

Held

As the widow did not have a beneficial interest in the property in her husband's estate at her death, because it had not been assented to her, it followed that no succession duty was payable.

Viscount Radcliffe:

> 'When Mrs Coulson [the testator's widow] died she had the interest of a residuary estate in the testator's unadministered estate. The nature of that interest has been conclusively defined by decisions of long-established authority, and its definition no doubt depends upon the peculiar status which the law accorded to an executor for the purposes of carrying out his duties of administration. There were special rules which long prevailed about the devolution of freehold land and its liability for the debts of a deceased, but subject to the working of these rules whatever property came to the executor virtute officii came to him in full ownership, without distinction between legal and equitable interests. The whole property was his. He held it for the purpose of carrying out the functions and duties of administration, not for his own benefit; and these duties would be enforced upon him by the Court of Chancery, if application had to be made for

that purpose by a creditor or beneficiary interested in the estate. Certainly, therefore, he was in a fiduciary position with regard to the assets that came to him in the right of his office, and for certain purposes and in some aspects he was treated by the court as a trustee. "An executor" said Kay J in *Re Marsden* (1884) 26 Ch D 783 at 789 "is personally liable in equity for all breaches of the ordinary trusts which in Courts of Equity are considered to arise from his office. He is a trustee 'in a sense'."

It may not be possible to state exhaustively what those trusts are at any one moment. Essentially, they are trusts to preserve the assets, to deal properly with them, and to apply them in a due course of administration for the benefit of those interested according to that course, creditors, the death duty authorities, legatees of various sorts, and the residuary beneficiaries. They might just as well have been termed "duties in respect of the assets" as trusts. What equity did not do was to recognise or create for residuary legatees a beneficial interest in the assets in the executor's hands during the course of administration. Conceivably, this could have been done, in the sense that the assets, whatever they might be from time to time, could have been treated as a present, though fluctuating, trust fund held for the benefit of all those interested in the estate according to the measure of their respective interests. But it never was done. It would have been a clumsy and unsatisfactory device from a practical point of view; and, indeed, it would have been in plain conflict with the basic conception of equity that to impose the fetters of a trust upon property, with the resulting creation of equitable interests in that property, there had to be specific subjects identifiable as the trust fund. An unadministered estate was incapable of satisfying this requirement. The assets as a whole were in the hands of the executor, his property; and until administration was complete no one was in a position to say what items of property would need to be realised for the purposes of that administration or of what the residue, when ascertained, would consist or what its value would be. Even in modern economies, when the ready marketability of many forms of property can almost be assumed, valuation and realisation are very far from being interchangeable terms.

At the date of Mrs Coulson's death, therefore, there was no trust fund consisting of Mr Livingston's residuary estate in which she could be said to have any beneficial interest, because no trust had as yet come into existence to affect the assets of his estate. The relation of her estate to his was exactly the same as that of Mrs Tollmache's estate to that of her deceased husband's, as analysed in the well-known decision of *Sudeley* v *Attorney-General* [1897] AC 11.

Just as Mr Tollemache's rights in the mortgages of New Zealand land were the property of his executors for the purposes of the administration of his estate, and no one else had any property interest in them, so Mr Livingston's property in Queensland, real or personal, was vested in his executors in full right, and no beneficial property interest in any item of it belonged to Mrs Coulson at the date of her death. In their Lordships' opinion the decision of the *Sudeley* case is conclusive on this issue. It is sufficient to quote the words of Lord Herschell, which do no more than reflect the reasoning and views of all the members of the House who took part in the decision. "I do not think', he said (at p18), speaking of Mrs Tollemache's executors, 'that they have any estate, right, or interest, legal or equitable, in these New Zealand mortgages so as to make them an asset of her estate".'

Crowden and Another* v *Aldridge and Others (1992) The Times 30 November Chancery Division (Jonathan Sumption QC, sitting as a deputy High Court Judge)

Variation of will by residuary legatees – document of variation signed and variation communicated to executors – time at which variation became effective

Facts

The testator died on 3 August 1987, leaving an estate of about £90,000. By his will, which had been made some 21 years earlier, he left a legacy of £100 to a Mrs Violet Peppercorn and the residue was divided equally among all of his first cousins, living at the date of his death, of which there were 16 (the first to sixteenth defendants).

Mrs Peppercorn had been in the employ of the testator and his family for some 52 years in the capacity of housekeeper. She had lived in a small bungalow which had been provided for her and by the time of the testator's death, she was receiving £2.50 a week for her services and paying rent of £1.50 a week inclusive of rates for her bungalow.

At the funeral Mr Crowden, an executor, who had known the family for very many years, informed the 12 cousins who were present of the terms of the will. Mr Crowden was concerned that Mrs Peppercorn had received only a legacy of £100 and suggested that this amount should be improved as it seemed such a small reward for her services. Following this discussion the 12 cousins decided that Mrs Peppercorn should have £5,000, the testator's chattels and the freehold of the bungalow. They signed a memorandum which provided:

> 'I agree that the terms of the late Mr Farrington's last will be varied so as to give Mrs Violet Peppercorn all of Mr Farrington's personal chattels, together with the freehold bungalow at 27 Washingly Road, Folksworth, of which she is currently tenant (tax-free) and to give a tax-free legacy of £5,000 to Mr and Mrs Arthur Peppercorn. I am prepared to enter into a deed to formalise this gift.'

There were then spaces for signature, address and date. At the time one of the cousins, Mrs Gladwin, suggested that Mrs Peppercorn, who was then in the garden, should be invited in and told what they had done. However, Mr Crowden said that he would tell her later himself.

Later on in the afternoon, Mrs Gladwin went into the garden and told Mrs Peppercorn:

> 'You'll be all right, Violet; we have looked after you.'

Another cousin, Mrs Aldridge, came out and told her that the bungalow would be hers.

Finally, Mr Crowden spoke to Mrs Peppercorn, telling her that she would be entitled to retain the bungalow and the personal chattels and receive a legacy of £5,000.

The four remaining cousins signed their copies of the memorandum either on the day of the funeral or within a few days afterwards.

However, later in 1987 these feelings of generosity faded and four of the cousins, the first four defendants, who included Mrs Aldridge and Mrs Gladwin, had further thoughts.

Their argument in defence was that the memoranda were without legal effect, either because they recorded only a willingness to enter into a legally binding document in future or because they were simply evidence of an inchoate gift, revocable at any time before the transfer was actually made. Alternatively, if the memoranda were on their face legally effective documents, then in the circumstances of the funeral they had no intention of signing them to produce any legal effect.

Prima facie, the memoranda were intended to be immediately effective documents. They set out the following words at the commencement: 'I agree that the terms of the late Mr Farrington's will be varied ...'

That was the language of present agreement.

When the signatory said in the second sentence that he was 'prepared' to enter into a deed to formalise the gift, the question was whether or not he was postponing the legal effect of the document or reserving his final view or merely saying that he would be willing, if required so to do, to record in more formal terms the transaction that he was presently entering into.

Held

The judge discussed the various alternatives and the following possibilities if the memoranda did, on their face, have immediate legal effect:

a) the memoranda were contracts to dispose of the interests of the signatories in the estate to the extent of £5,000 and the house and chattels;
b) they recorded a gift by the signatories of part of their interest in the estate to Mr and Mrs Peppercorn; and

c) they were a direction to the executors, varying their obligations in the administration and distribution of the estate.

In his Lordship's judgment, the third analysis was correct.

The leading modern authority was *Commissioner of Stamp Duties* v *Livingston* [1965] AC 694. It followed from the words of Viscount Radcliffe (at p707) that at the time when the memoranda were signed none of the signatories had any beneficial interest in the estate, but they did have a right, enforceable in the Court of Equity, to compel the executors to do their duty.

There was no doubt that a will, or more precisely the obligations of executors in administering an estate pursuant to a will, might be varied by all the relevant legatees. Although the exact juridical analysis of such a transaction was obscure, in his Lordship's judgment it operated in the same way as a unanimous direction to trustees by all the relevant beneficiaries under a trust.

The memoranda took immediate legal effect as soon as all 16 were communicated to the executors, just as a declaration of a trust by the residual legatees in respect of their interest would have had taken effect at once. The effectiveness of the transaction did not depend on communication to Mr and Mrs Peppercorn.

It was for this reason as well that it was not revocable as an incorrect gift. Nor did it need to be effective as a contract or supported by consideration.

Further, the argument that the circumstances in which the memoranda was signed demonstrating that they were not intended to have legal effect – since they were like a domestic or social agreement which the law would assume to have been entered into without any intention to create legal relations – was irrelevant. Without a sustainable plea of non est factum, the question as to whether an instrument executed by a person was intended to produce a legal result had to depend on the impact which his or her outward words and acts would produce to an objective observer. Subjective intentions and misunderstandings could not determine the effect of a document or lack of it. Even if he had been persuaded that their state of mind was relevant, his Lordship would not have accepted that particular argument. The cousins must have appreciated that they had committed themselves there and then; otherwise it is unlikely that they would have suggested at their meeting that Mrs Peppercorn should immediately be told about it.

None of the sworn affidavits of the fifth to sixteenth defendants suggested they had had any difficulty in understanding the situation. In brief what had happened was quite plain and clear. The four defendants understood exactly what they were doing, but subsequently changed their minds.

Accordingly, it was held that there would be a declaration that the devolution of the estate of the testator had been varied.

Grandison, Re (1989) The Times 10 July High Court (Vinelott J)

Executor – discretion as to burial place

Facts

The testator had come to England from Jamaica in 1960 and lived in England until his death in 1989. His executor maintained that the testator had said that he wished to be buried in Jamaica and this evidence was supported by other members of the family. However, his only daughter, who was entitled to a half share in his estate and who had been on close terms with her father, objected and sought an interlocutory injunction to restrain the executor from removing the body from the jurisdiction.

Held

The application would be dismissed. Vinelott J said that the testator, despite his long residence in this country, should want to be buried in Jamaica did not cause him any surprise. Many men, when death was approaching, wished to return to the place of their birth or have their mortal remains taken there. The cases on domicile of origin and domicile of choice indicated the frequency with which those who lived apparently settled and firm lives abroad often harboured a desire to have their mortal remains conveyed to the place where they were born. Nor was his Lordship surprised that the testator did not discuss the matter with his daughter. It was natural that he should discuss it with his executor – for it was the latter who would have to make the necessary arrangements. But it might well have been too sombre a subject to discuss with a young and affectionate daughter. His Lordship did not find it necessary to decide when a near relative had a right to apply to the court to override or supplant an executor's decision, although he would be surprised to find that the court had no power in any circumstances. But it was plain that even if the performance of the executor's duty to bury the body was capable of being controlled at the suit of a relative, the executor still had a discretion and on ordinary principles the court would not interfere unless that discretion was exercised in a way that was dishonest, capricious or unreasonable. In his Lordship's judgment, on the facts of this case, the daughter did not come anywhere near establishing a ground for interference. She had allowed her own natural and strong feelings for her father to blind her to the perfectly proper desire of the executor, which was shared by the testator's brothers and sisters and many more remote relations, to have the testator buried in Jamaica.

King's Will Trusts, Re [1964] Ch 542 Chancery Division (Pennycuick J)

Administration of Estates Act 1925 s36(4) – written assent essential to vest legal estate in executor or beneficiary or trustee

Facts

The testatrix appointed X, Y and Z to be executors of her will and X and Y to be trustees thereof. On the testatrix's death only X and Y proved the will. In the course of administration of the deceased's estate the executors retained certain properties which were specifically devised on trust by the will. In 1951 Y died leaving X as sole trustee. In 1953 by a deed of appointment, X appointed A as a trustee to act jointly with himself. X died in 1958 and in 1959 A appointed B as a trustee jointly with himself. A died in 1962. B was left the sole surviving trustee and he took out a summons to determine (inter alia) whether the property was vested in him.

Held

Under s36(4) a written assent is essential to vest the legal estate in land in a trustee or beneficiary, even if the person holding the legal estate as personal representative is the same person as the trustee or beneficiary. Therefore, as the land had been held by X and Y as executors and had not been vested in them, as trustees, it followed that the land was now vested in their executors by representation under s7 of the Administration of Estates Act. A written assent was necessary to pass the title from the present executor to B.

Pennycuick J:

> '... it has been suggested that where the personal representative is also entitled in some other capacity, for example, as trustee of the will, as beneficiary or otherwise to the estate or interest, he may come to hold the estate or interest in that other capacity without any written assent. [Counsel] ... has mentioned but not stressed this contention, and in my judgment, the contention is not well founded ... It is well recognised by judicial decision that a personal representative may make a written assent in favour of himself in some other capacity: see *Re Yerburgh* [1928] WN 208 where Romer J said:
>
> > "At the moment when the event happened they ought to make a vesting assent under section 36, vesting the property in themselves as trustees."

> Such cases are of everyday occurrence in conveyancing practice. The first sentence of subsection (4) contemplates that for this purpose a person may by assent vest in himself in another capacity, and such vesting, of course, necessarily implies that he is divesting himself of the estate in his original capacity. It seems to me impossible to regard the same operation as lying outside the negative provisions contained in the second sentence of the subsection. To do so involves making a distinction between the operation of divesting and vesting the legal estate and that of passing the legal estate. I do not think that this highly artificial distinction is legitimate. On the contrary, the second sentence appears to me to be intended as an exact counterpart of the first.'

Leigh's Will Trusts, Re [1970] Ch 277 Chancery Division (Buckley J)

Transmissibility of chose in action vested in beneficiary.

Facts

By her will, a testatrix made a specific gift of 'all shares which I hold and any other interest or assets which I may have [in a named company]'. The testatrix never had any shares or any other interest in that company. However, at the date of her will and at her death she was the sole administratrix and sole beneficiary under her late husband's intestate estate which she never administered fully. The husband's estate comprises some shares and a debt due from the company. The question arose whether the shares and the debt could pass under the bequest in her will.

Held

The specific gift of the shares in the named company was effective. The testatrix did not have any beneficial interest in the property which she could pass, but did have a chose in action to ensure due administration and this could be transmitted or assigned by her to another who could then ensure due administration of the estate. In this case it passed to her executors.

Buckley J:

> '... what she could transmit was her own right to require the administrator of her husband's estate, whosoever he might be, to administer his estate in any manner she or her personal representatives might require consistent with the rights of any other persons having rights against the estate. This right she could transmit to her executor, coupled with a duty to exercise it in a particular manner. By her will, she has, in my judgment, clearly indicated that her executor should so exercise the right as to procure the 51 shares, and the company's indebtedness should to the largest possible extent become available to satisfy the specific bequest.'

McGeorge, Re [1963] Ch 544 Chancery Division (Cross J)

Law of Property Act 1925 s175 – effect of contingent residuary devises on intermediate income

Facts

By his will the testator devised land to his daughter on condition that the devise 'shall not take effect until after the death of my wife should she survive me'. However, the testator also directed that if the daughter should die before his wife, leaving issue, the issue would take by substitution on attaining the age of 21 years. The residuary estate was then bequeathed to the wife for life with remainder to the son and daughter in equal shares.

Held

The devise to the daugher or her issue was a future specific devise under s175 and carried the intermediate income. However, the income was to be accumulated until the death of the wife and paid to either the daughter or her issue when they became entitled to it.

Cross J: '

The devise ... is, it is said, a future specific devise within the meaning of the section (LPA 1925 s175); the testator has not made any express disposition of the income accruing from it between his death and the death of his widow, therefore that income is carried by the gift. At fist sight it is hard to see how Parliament could have enacted a section which produces such a result. If a testator gives property to A after the death of B, then whether or not he disposes of the income accruing during B's life he is at all events showing clearly tha A is not to have it ... Yet if the future gift to A is absolute and the intermediate income is carried with it by force of this section A can claim to have the property transferred to him at once, since no one else can be intersted in it. The section, that is to say, will have converted the gift in remainder into a gift in possession in defiance of the testator's wishes. The explanation for the section taking the form it does is, I think, probably as follows. It has long been established that a gift of residuary personalty to a legatee in being on a contingency or to an unborn person at birth, carries the intermediate income so far as the law will allow it to be accumulated, but that rule had been held for reasons depending on the old land law not to apply gifts of real property, and it was apparently never applied to specific dispositions of personalty. Section 175 of the Law of Property Act was plainly intended to extend the rule to residuary devises and to specific gifts whether of realty or of personalty. It is now, however, established at all events in courts of first instance, that the old rule does not apply to residuary bequests whether vested or contingent which are expressly deferred to a future date which must come sooner or later. See *Re Oliver* [1947] 2 All ER 162, *Re Gillett's Will Trusts* [1950] Ch 102 and *Re Geering* [1964] Ch 136. There is a good reason for this distinction. If a testator gives property to X contingently on his attaining the age of 30 it is reasonable to assume, in the absence of a direction to the contrary, that he would wish X if he attains 30 to have income produced by the property between his death and the happening of the contingency. If, on the other hand, he gives property to X for any sort of interest after the death of A, it is reasonable to assume that he does not wish X to have the income accruing to during A's lifetime, unless he directs that he is to have it. But this distinction between an immediate gift on a contingency and a gift which is expressly deferred was not drawn until after the Law of Property Act 1925 was passed. There were statements in textbooks and even in judgments to the effect that the rule applied to deferred as well as to contingent gifts of residuary personalty. (See Jarman, 7th Edn. (1930) p 1006).

The legislature, when it extended this rule to residuary devises and specific gifts, must, I think, have adopted this erroneous view of the law. I would have liked, if I could, to construe the reference to "future specific devises" and "executory interest" in the section in such a way as to make it consistent with the recent cases on the scope of the old rule applicable to residuary bequests. But to do that would be to rectify the Act, not to construe it, and I see no escape from the conclusion that whereas before 1926 a specific gift or a residuary devise which was not vested in possession did not prima facie carry intermediate income at all, now such a gift may carry intermediate income in circumstances in which a residuary bequest would not carry it.

It was argued in this case that the fact that the will contained a residuary gift constituted an express disposition of the income of the land in question which prevented the section from applying. I am afraid that I cannot accept this submission. I have little doubt that the testator expected the income of the land to form part of the income of residue during his widow's lifetime, but he has made no express disposition of it. I agree with what was said in this connection by Eve J in *Re Raine* [1929] 1 Ch 716.

As the devise is not vested indefeasibly in the daughter but is subject to defeasance during the mother's lifetime her intermediate income which the gift carried by virtue of section 175 ought prima facie to be accumulated to see who eventually becomes entitled to it ...'

Rooke, Re [1933] Ch 970 Chancery Division (Maugham J)

Expenses of transfer – who pays?

Facts

The testatrix made a specific devise and bequest of her house and its contents by her will. The executors incurred expense in the upkeep and preservation of the house and its contents and sought directions from the court before making an assent in relation thereto as to whether these expenses were to be borne by the specific devise and legatee or be the general estate of the testatrix.

Held

The expenses were to be borne by the specific devisee and legatee.

Maugham J:

> '... in *Re Pearce* [1909] 1 Ch 819 ... Eve J said:
>
> "Now it seems to me to be settled law that when an executor gives his assent to a specific legacy the assent relates back to the death of the testator, and the specific legatee is entitled to the profits accrued due from the time of the testator's death. That being so, it seems to me to be right and fair that the specific legatee should be charged with the costs of the upkeep, care, and preservation of the specific legacy from the time of the death until the executor's assent ...
> ... In my opinion it is difficult to explain on what principle the profits in such a case ought to be paid to the legatee, if he is not also to be made liable for the preservation and upkeep of the legacy. For those reasons I hold that, as from the date of the testatrix's death to the date of the assent, the costs of preservation and upkeep fall upon the legatee".'

West, Re [1909] 2 Ch 180 Chancery Division (Swinfen Eady J)

Effect of assent

Facts

The testatrix left a will and several codicils thereto. One of the codicils bequeathed some shares to the defendants and in due course of administration the executors transferred these shares to them. Several years later another codicil to the testatrix's will was found which revoked the bequest of the shares to the defendants and bequeathed them to the plaintiff. The question arose whether the plaintiff was entitled to the dividends which had been received on the shares by the defendants.

Held

The plaintiff was entitled to all the dividends between the date of the testatrix's death and his receipt of the shares.

Swinfen Eady J:

> 'The defendants do not dispute that the plaintiff is entitled to the shares bequeathed to him by the fifth codicil, which were erroneously but inadvertantly transferred to the wrong persons, but they contend that the plaintiff is not entitled to the dividends which in the meantime they have received and retained for thier own use.
>
> It is exceedingly difficult to see any principle upon which the defendants, whilst conceding that they are not entitled to retain the shares given to their brother by the fifth codicil, are yet entitled to retain for their own use the dividends on those shares which were not really bequeathed to them at all. It is said that where a legatee has been ordered to refund either in respect of a pecuniary legacy or in respect of a

share of residue, such refunding … is without interest; but it appears to me that the reasoning has no application to a case of this kind, where the legacy is of specific shares, because upon the assent of the executors those shares vest in the legatee, and the assent, when given, has relation to the time of the testatrix's death. In the case of a specific legacy it is well established that immediately after the executor's assent the legacy vests in the legatee, and he can maintain an action at law in respect of it. If the plaintiff has a legal right to the shares as from the testatrix's death, it seems to me that he also has a legal right to the interest or dividends …'